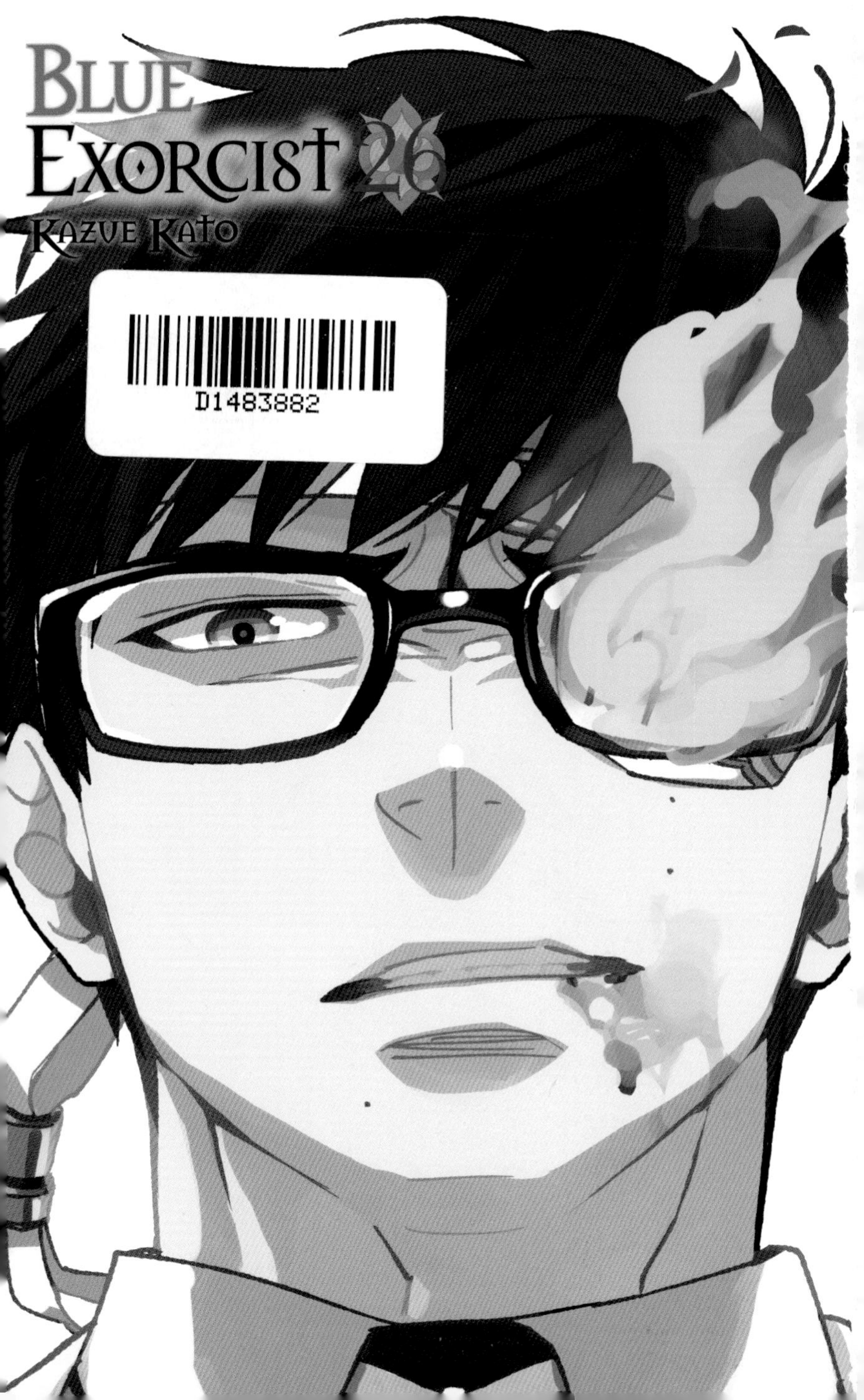
BLUE EXORCIST
26
KAZUE KATO

Blue Exorcist

Contents 26

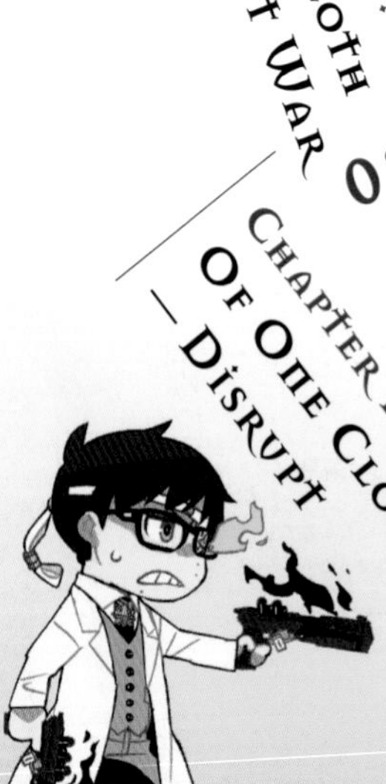

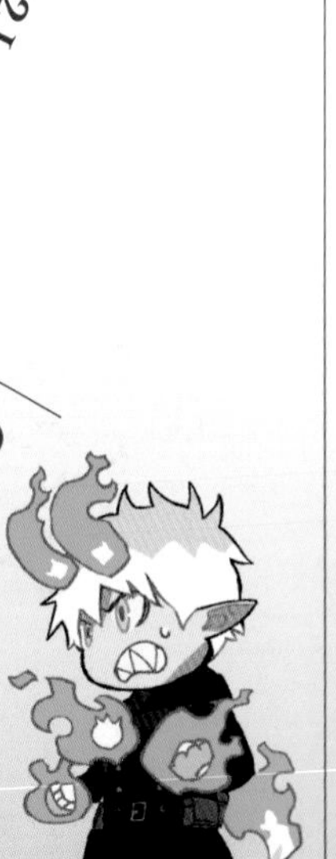

CAST OF CHARACTERS

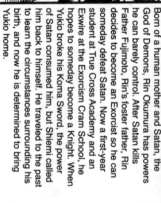

RIN OKUMURA

Born of a human mother and Satan, the God of Demons, Rin Okumura has powers he can barely control. After Satan kills Father Fujimoto, Rin's foster father, Rin decides to become an Exorcist so he can someday defeat Satan. Now a first-year student at True Cross Academy and an Exwire at the Exorcism Cram School, he hopes to someday become a Knight. When Yukio broke his Koma Sword, the power of Satan consumed him, but Shiemi called him back to himself. He traveled to the past to learn the circumstances surrounding his birth, and now he is determined to bring Yukio home.

SHIEMI MORIYAMA

Daughter of the owner of Futsumaya, an Exorcist supply shop. She possesses the ability to become a Tamer and can summon a baby Greenman named Nee. After quitting the Exorcism Cram School, personnel from the Grigori Agency take her to a garden called Ei inside Vatican headquarters.

RYUJI SUGURO

Heir to the venerable Buddhist sect known as Myodha in Kyoto. He wants to achieve the titles of Dragoon and Aria. He is Lightning's apprentice and they were conducting an investigation together.

KONEKOMARU MIWA

He was once a pupil of Suguro's father and is now Suguro's friend. He's an Exwire who hopes to become an Exorcist someday. He is small in size and has a quiet and composed personality.

IZUMO KAMIKI

An Exwire with the blood of shrine maidens. She has the ability to become a Tamer and can summon two white foxes. The Illuminati had taken her captive, but with help from Rin and the others, she escaped and settled her grudge against the insane professor Gedoin.

LEWIN LIGHT

An Arch Knight, he is Arthur's right-hand man as well as number two in the Order. An expert in Arias and summoning, he goes by the nickname Lightning. He is tracking down the connection between Draguiescu and the Illuminati.

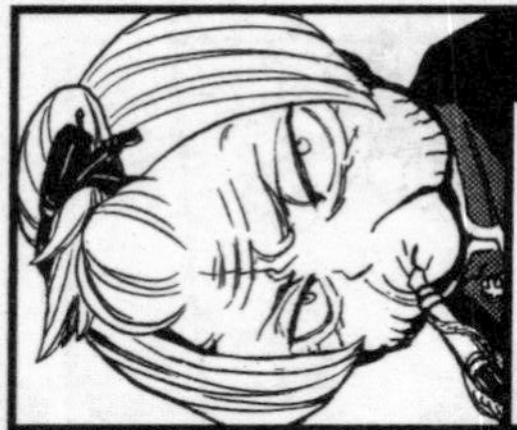

Lucy Yang

An Arch Knight from the China Branch.

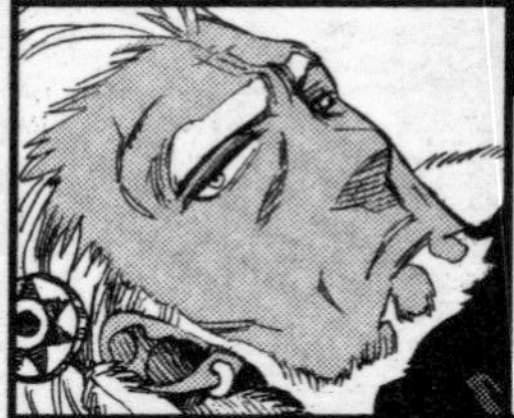

Osceola Redarm

An Arch Knight from the Mexico Branch.

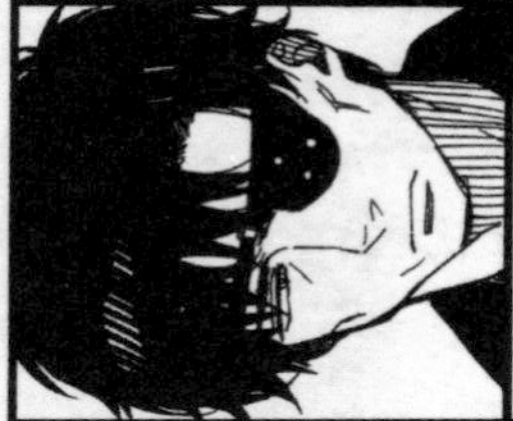

Igor Neuhaus

A Senior Exorcist First Class who holds the titles of Tamer, Doctor and Aria. Under orders from Mephisto, he was researching enhanced anti-demon compounds.

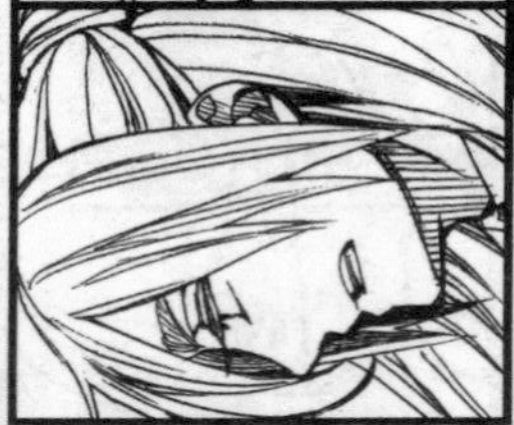

Arthur A. Angel

A Senior Exorcist First Class and the current Paladin. He's a survivor of Section 13 under suspicion of being the clone of a demon.

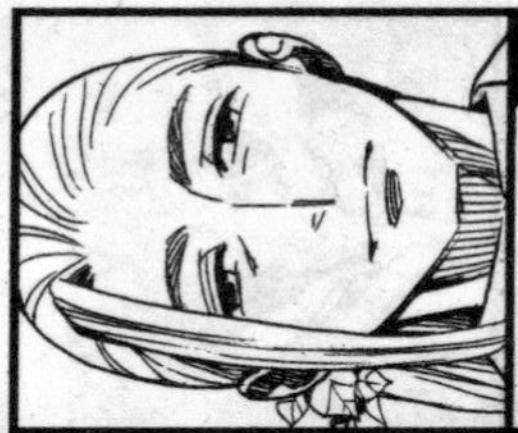

Jeremiah Uzai

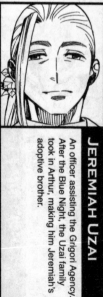

An officer assisting the Grigori Agency. After the Blue Night, the Uzai family took in Arthur, making him Jeremiah's adoptive brother.

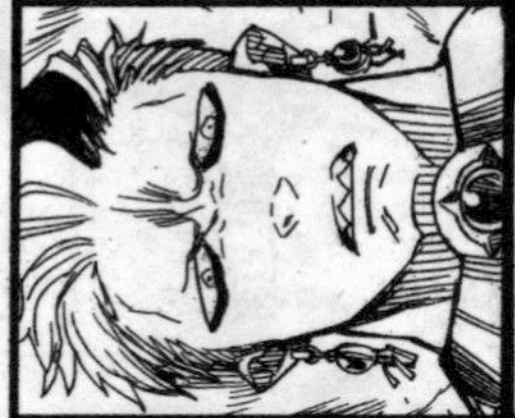

Vayu

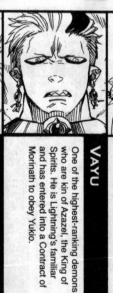

One of the highest-ranking demons, who are kin of Azazel, the King of Spirits. He is Lightning's familiar and has entered into a Contract of Morinath to obey Yukio.

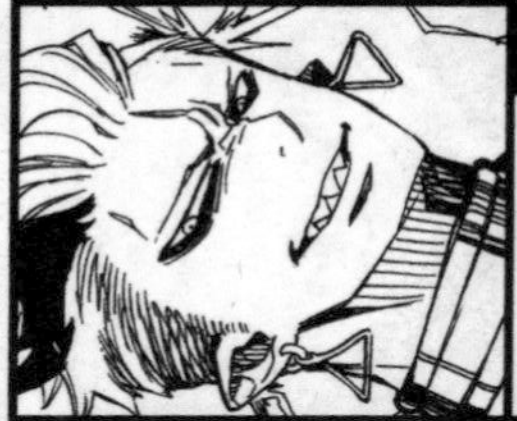

Indra

One of the highest-ranking demons, who are kin of Azazel, the King of Spirits. He is Lightning's familiar and has entered into a Contract of Morinath to obey Yukio.

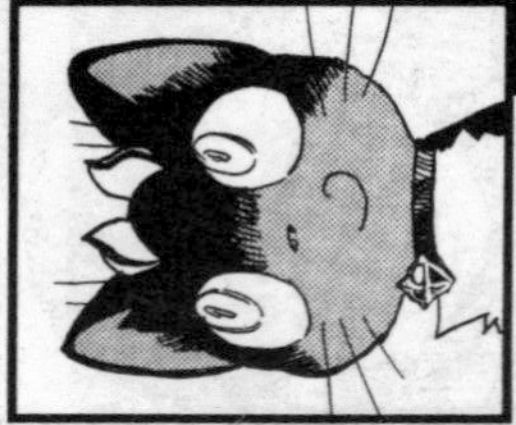

Kuro

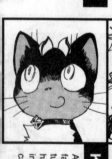

A Cat Sídhe who was once Shiro's familiar. After Shiro's death, he began turning back into a demon. Rin saved him, and now the two are practically inseparable. His favorite drink is the catnip wine Shiro used to make.

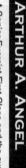

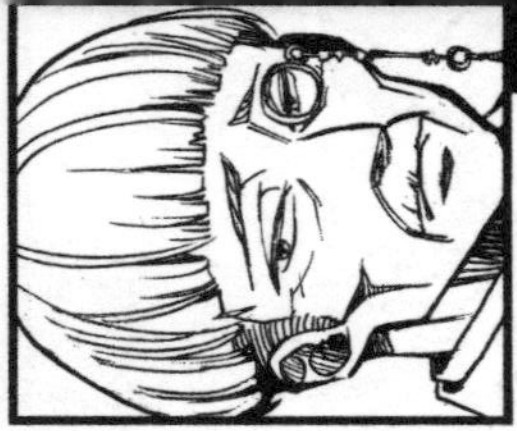

DRAC DRAGULESCU

An Arch Knight. As a researcher at Section 13, he was leading research into cloning for Satan and Lucifer. He continued his research later and has been in secret communication with the Illuminati.

THE ILLUMINATI

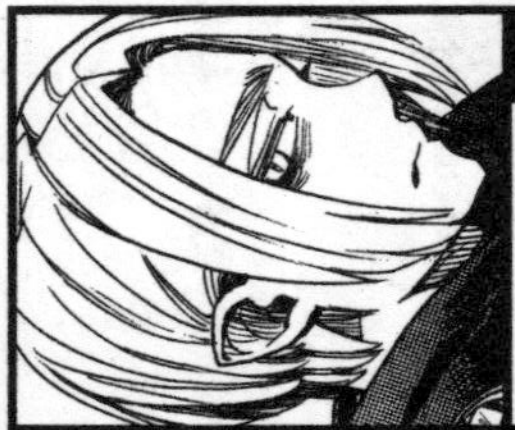

LUCIFER

Commander in chief of the Illuminati. Known as the King of Light, he is the highest power in Gehenna. He is plotting to bring Satan back and unite Assiah and Gehenna.

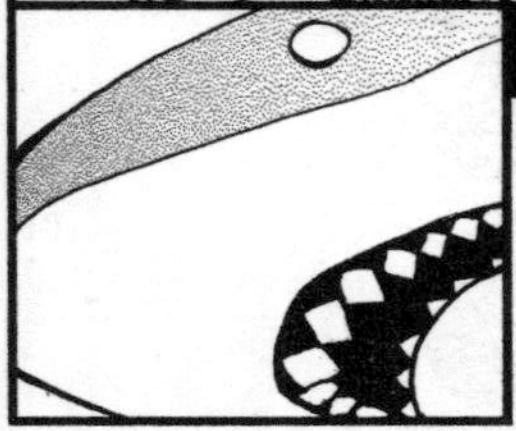

EGYN

One of the Baal and known as the King of Water. Assistant director of the airborne research laboratory on *Dominus Liminis*.

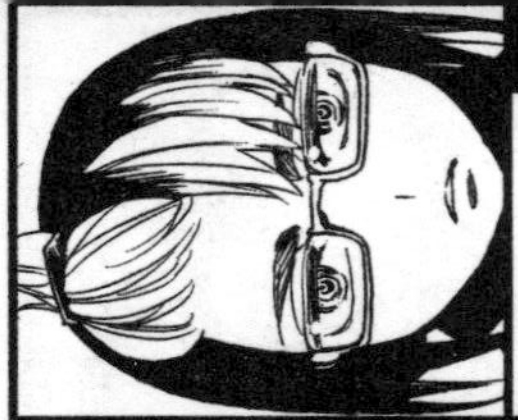

HOMARE TODO

Leader of Phosphorus, an organization of guards directly under Lucifer's command. She is Saburota Todo's daughter and Shima's superior officer, and holds a rank of Adeptus Minor or higher.

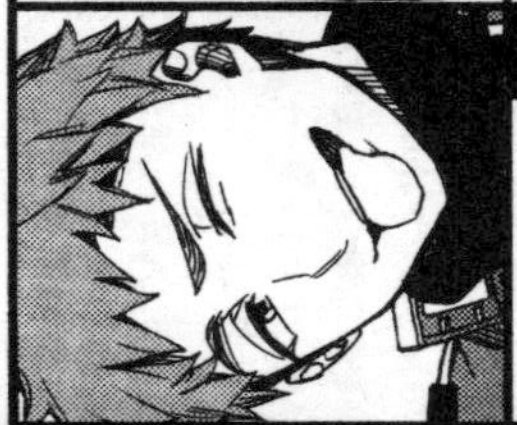

RENZO SHIMA

Once a pupil of Suguro's father and now Suguro's friend. Currently, he is a double agent providing information to both the Illuminati and the Knights of the True Cross.

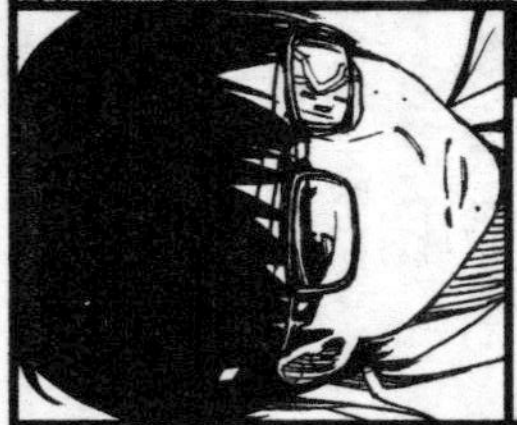

YUKIO OKUMURA

Rin's brother. He's a genius who is the youngest student ever to become an instructor at the Exorcism Cram School. He left the Knights of the True Cross and went over to the Illuminati, but now he has begun to rebel.

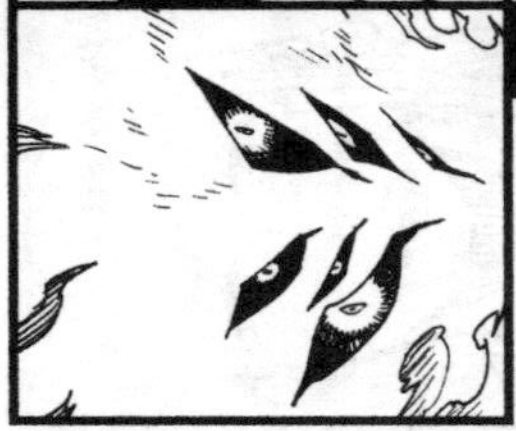

SATAN

Rin and Yukio's father. He is connected to and rules over almost all demons. He has inhabited Yukio's left eye to spy on Assiah.

⚜ THE STORY SO FAR ⚜

BOTH HUMAN AND DEMON BLOOD RUNS THROUGH RIN OKUMURA'S VEINS. IN AN ARGUMENT WITH HIS FOSTER FATHER, FATHER FUJIMOTO, RIN LEARNS THAT SATAN IS HIS TRUE FATHER. SATAN SUDDENLY APPEARS AND TRIES TO DRAG RIN DOWN TO GEHENNA BECAUSE RIN HAS INHERITED HIS POWER. FATHER FUJIMOTO FIGHTS TO DEFEND RIN, BUT DIES IN THE PROCESS. RIN DECIDES TO BECOME AN EXORCIST SO HE CAN SOMEDAY DEFEAT SATAN AND BEGINS STUDYING AT THE EXORCISM CRAM SCHOOL UNDER THE INSTRUCTION OF HIS TWIN BROTHER YUKIO, WHO IS ALREADY AN EXORCIST.

RIN AND THE OTHERS SUCCEED IN DEFEATING THE IMPURE KING, AWAKENED BY THE FORMER EXORCIST, TODO. MEANWHILE, YUKIO FIGHTS TODO, AND AS THE BATTLE RAGES, HE SENSES THE SAME FLAME IN HIS OWN EYES AS HIS BROTHER.

LATER, MYSTERIOUS EVENTS BEGIN OCCURRING AROUND THE GLOBE ORCHESTRATED BY A SECRET SOCIETY KNOWN AS THE ILLUMINATI. FINALLY, THE JAPANESE GOVERNMENT PUBLICLY RECOGNIZES THE EXISTENCE OF DEMONS.

IN ORDER TO LEARN ABOUT SATAN INHABITING HIS LEFT EYE AND THE SECRETS SURROUNDING HIS BIRTH, YUKIO TELLS RIN GOODBYE AND GOES TO JOIN THE ILLUMINATI. RIN REALIZES HE TOO MUST KNOW ABOUT HIS BIRTH IF HE EVER WANTS TO SEE YUKIO AGAIN, SO HE TRAVELS INTO THE PAST. FOR A TIME, HE THINKS HE SHOULD NEVER HAVE BEEN BORN. HOWEVER, HE LEARNS THAT SHIRO AND YURI RISKED THEIR LIVES TO SAVE AND RAISE HIM AND HIS BROTHER, SO HE DECIDES TO KEEP ON LIVING IN THEIR HONOR. IN THE SAME WAY THAT THEY REFUSED TO GIVE UP, RIN ALSO VOWS NEVER TO GIVE UP ON YUKIO.

YUKIO DEFIES THE ILLUMINATI AND BORROWS THE POWER OF LIGHTNING'S FAMILIARS VAYU AND INDRA IN AN ATTEMPT TO DESTROY THE *DOMINUS LIMINIS*. MEANWHILE, RIN USES A KAMIKAKUSHI KEY TO APPEAR BEFORE YUKIO!!

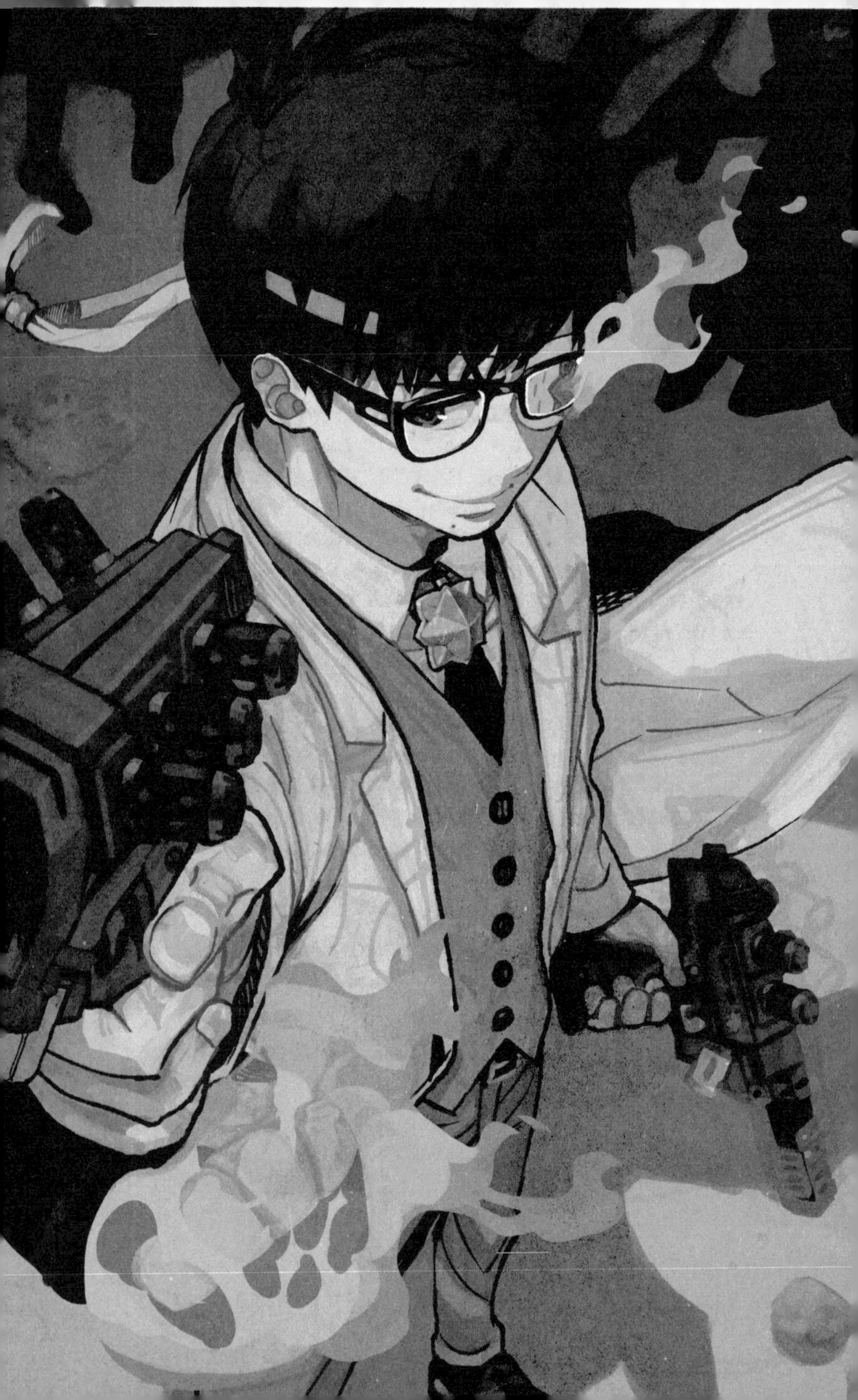

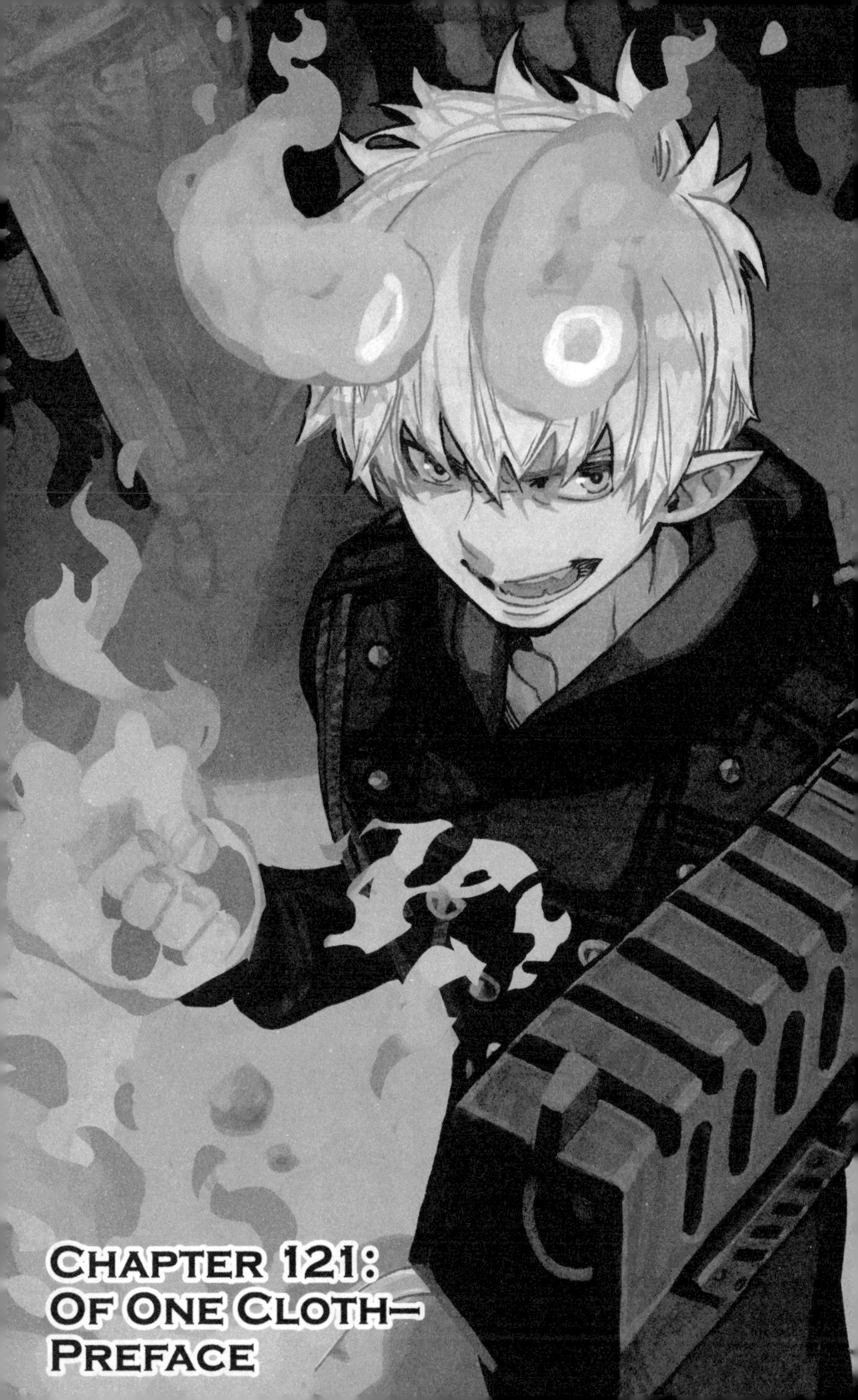

Chapter 121: Of One Cloth—Preface

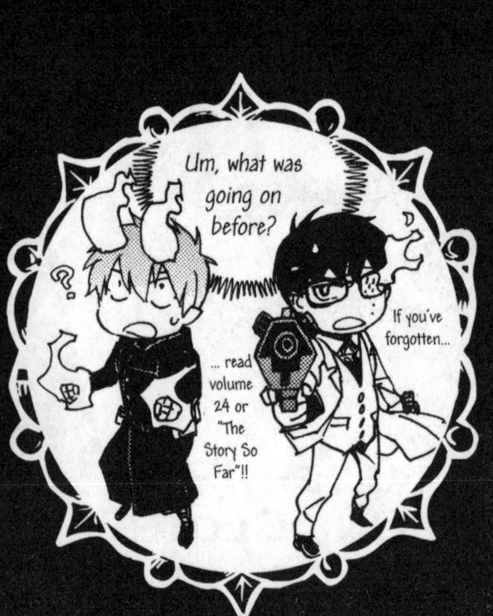
Um, what was going on before?
If you've forgotten...
... read volume 24 or "The Story So Far"!!

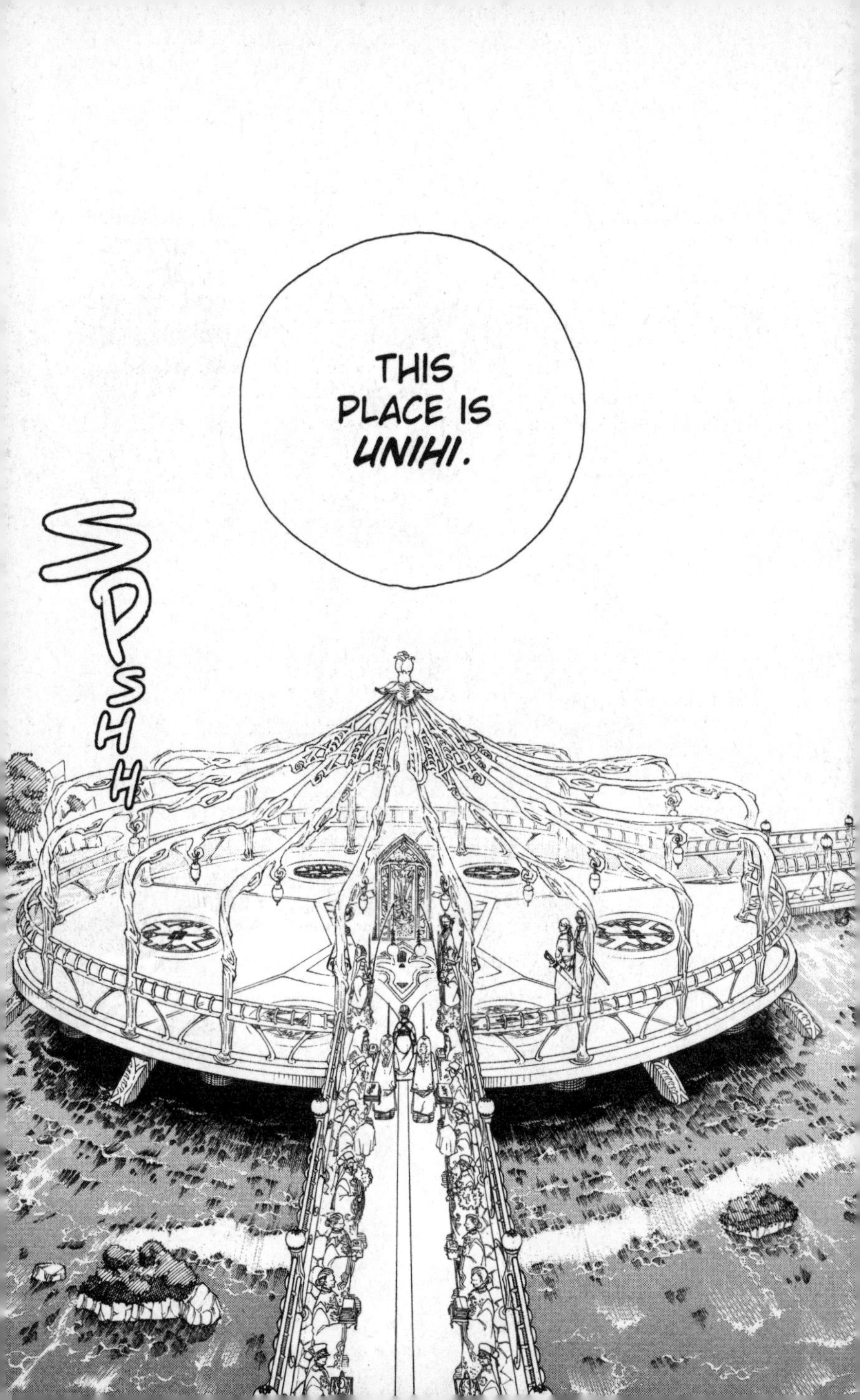
THIS PLACE IS UNIHI.
SPSHH

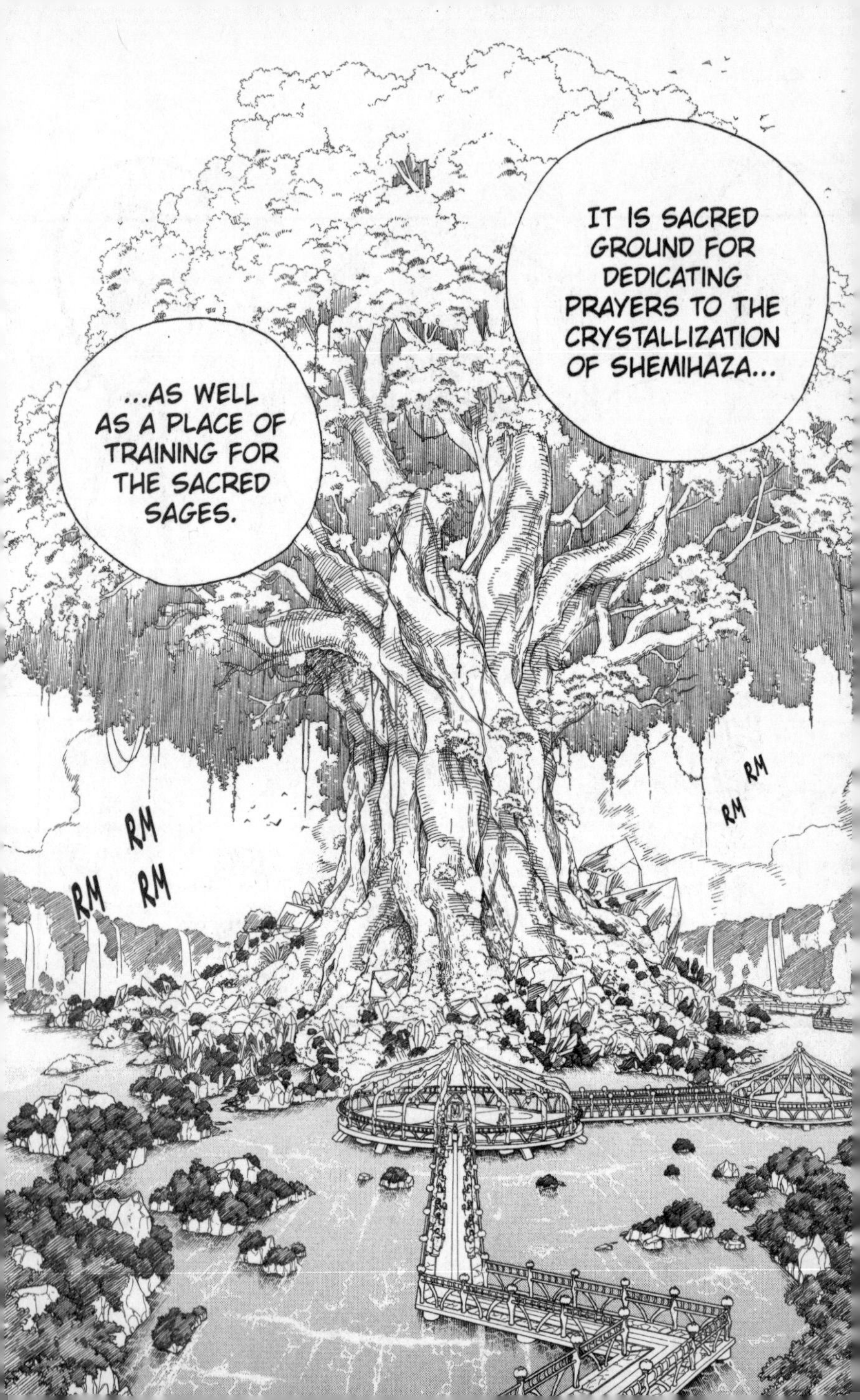
IT IS SACRED GROUND FOR DEDICATING PRAYERS TO THE CRYSTALLIZATION OF SHEMIHAZA...
...AS WELL AS A PLACE OF TRAINING FOR THE SACRED SAGES.
RM
RM
RM
RM
RM

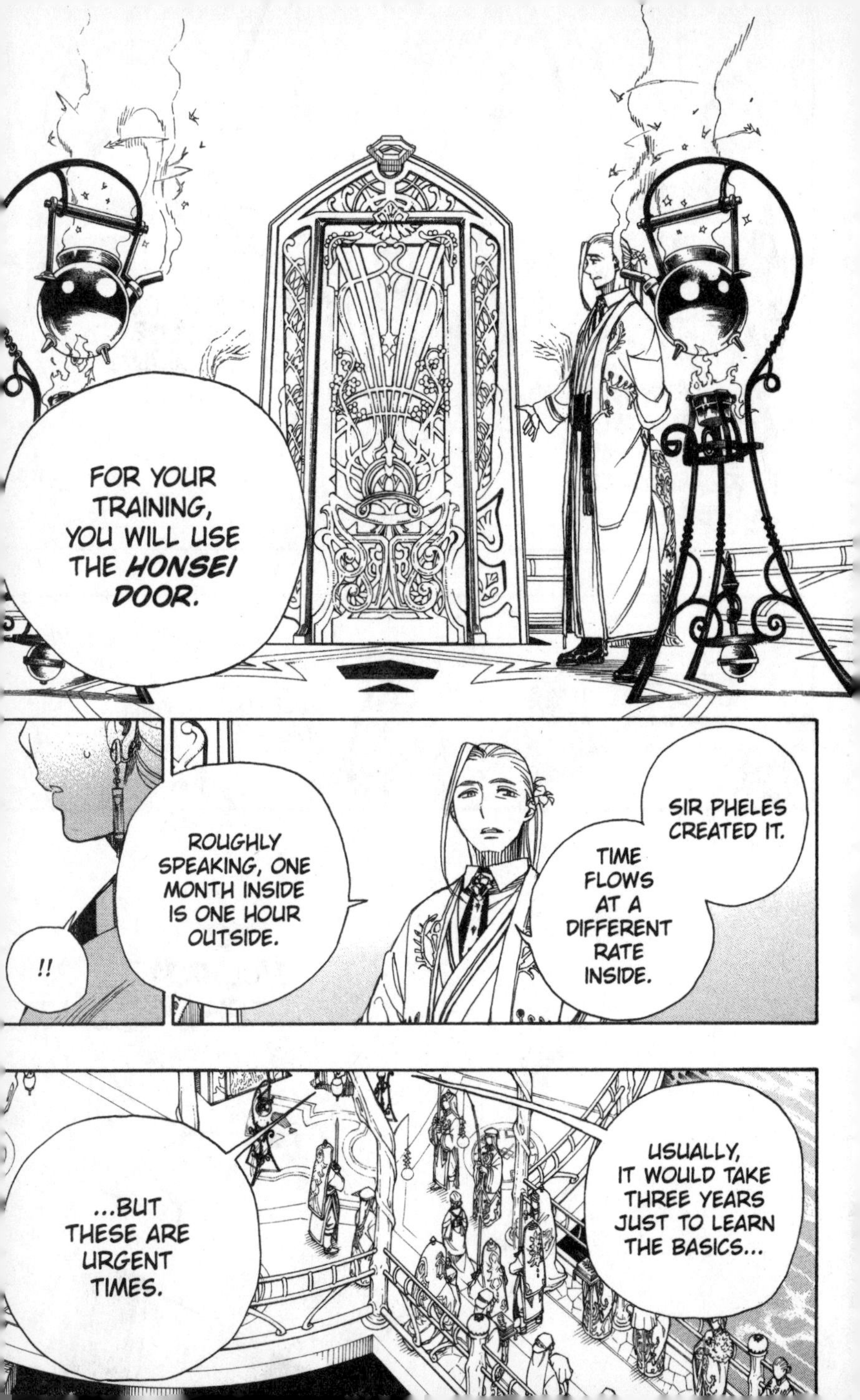

FOR YOUR TRAINING, YOU WILL USE THE ***HONSEI DOOR***.
SIR PHELES CREATED IT.
TIME FLOWS AT A DIFFERENT RATE INSIDE.
ROUGHLY SPEAKING, ONE MONTH INSIDE IS ONE HOUR OUTSIDE.
!!
USUALLY, IT WOULD TAKE THREE YEARS JUST TO LEARN THE BASICS...
...BUT THESE ARE URGENT TIMES.

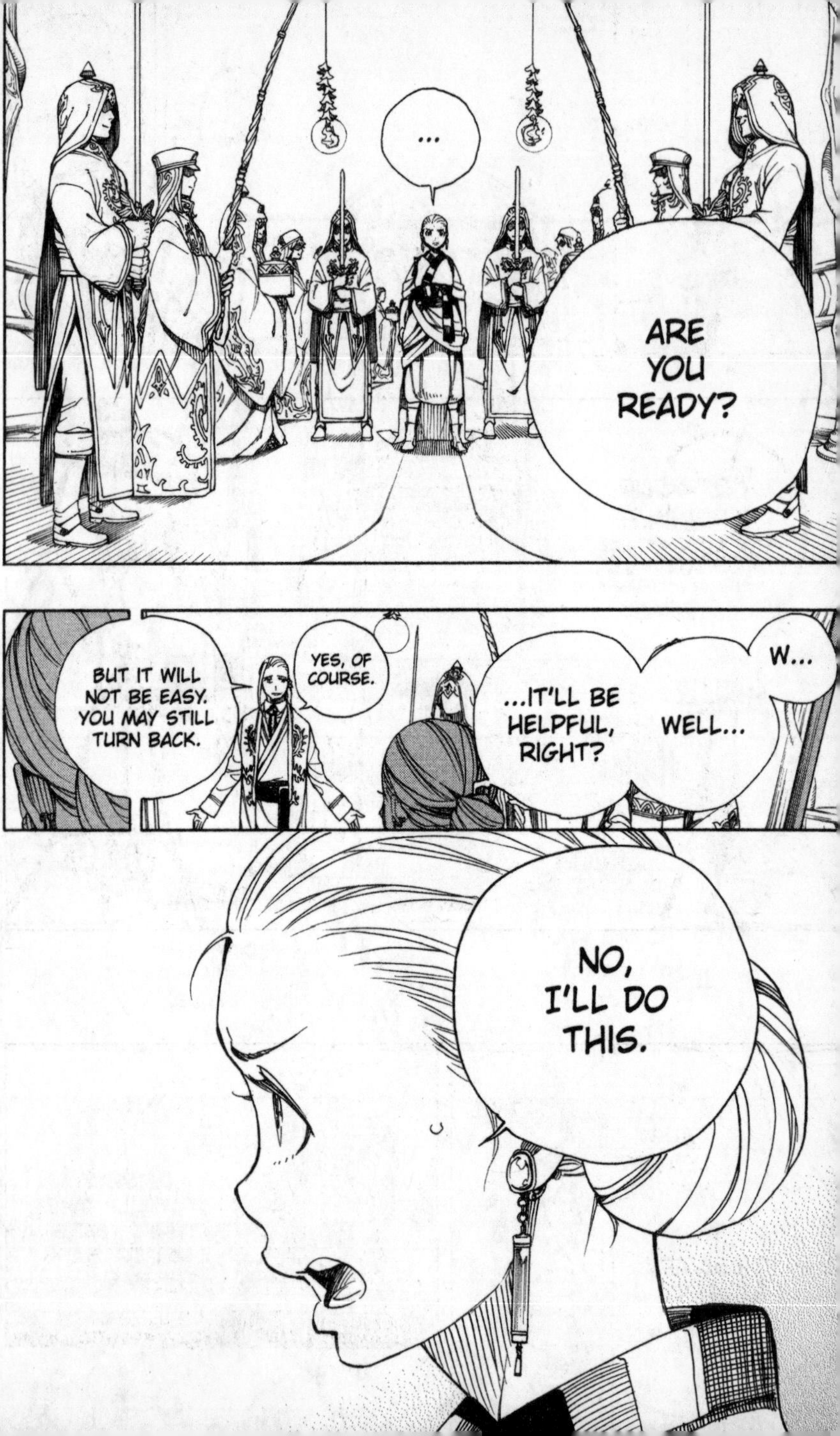
ARE YOU READY?
...
W...
WELL...
...IT'LL BE HELPFUL, RIGHT?
YES, OF COURSE.
BUT IT WILL NOT BE EASY. YOU MAY STILL TURN BACK.
NO, I'LL DO THIS.

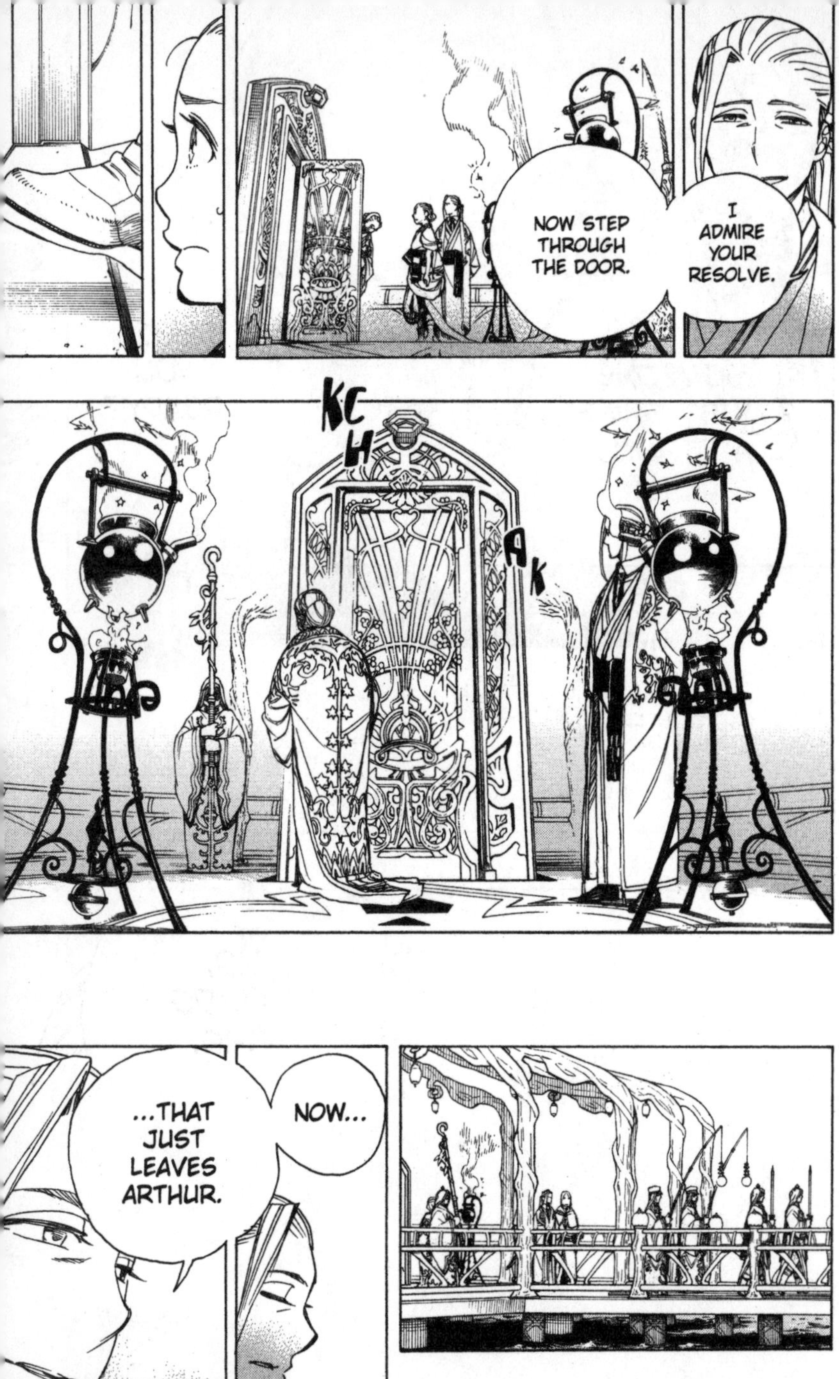
I ADMIRE YOUR RESOLVE.
NOW STEP THROUGH THE DOOR.
KCHAK
NOW...
...THAT JUST LEAVES ARTHUR.

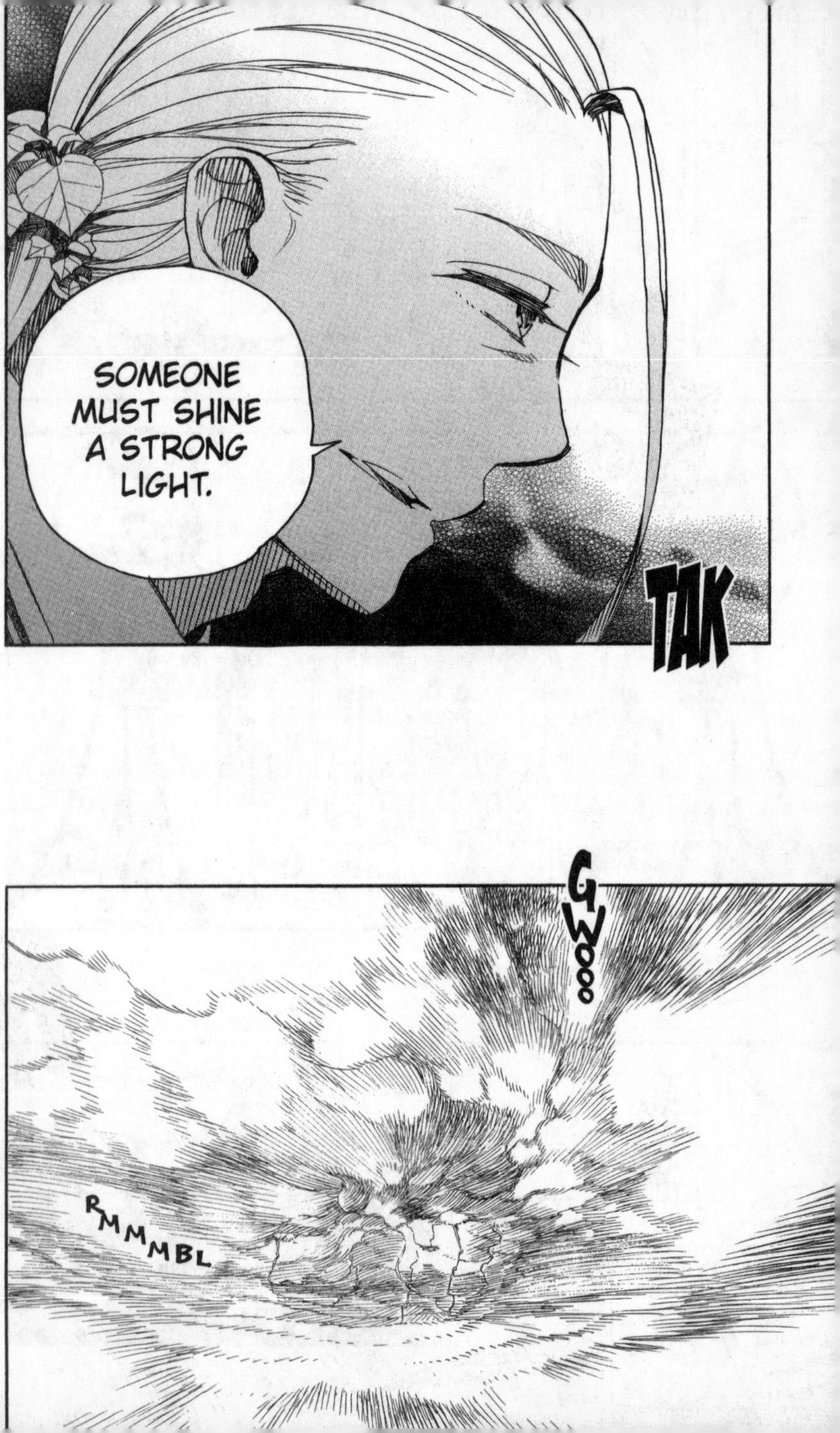
SOMEONE MUST SHINE A STRONG LIGHT.
TAK
GWOOO
RMMMBL

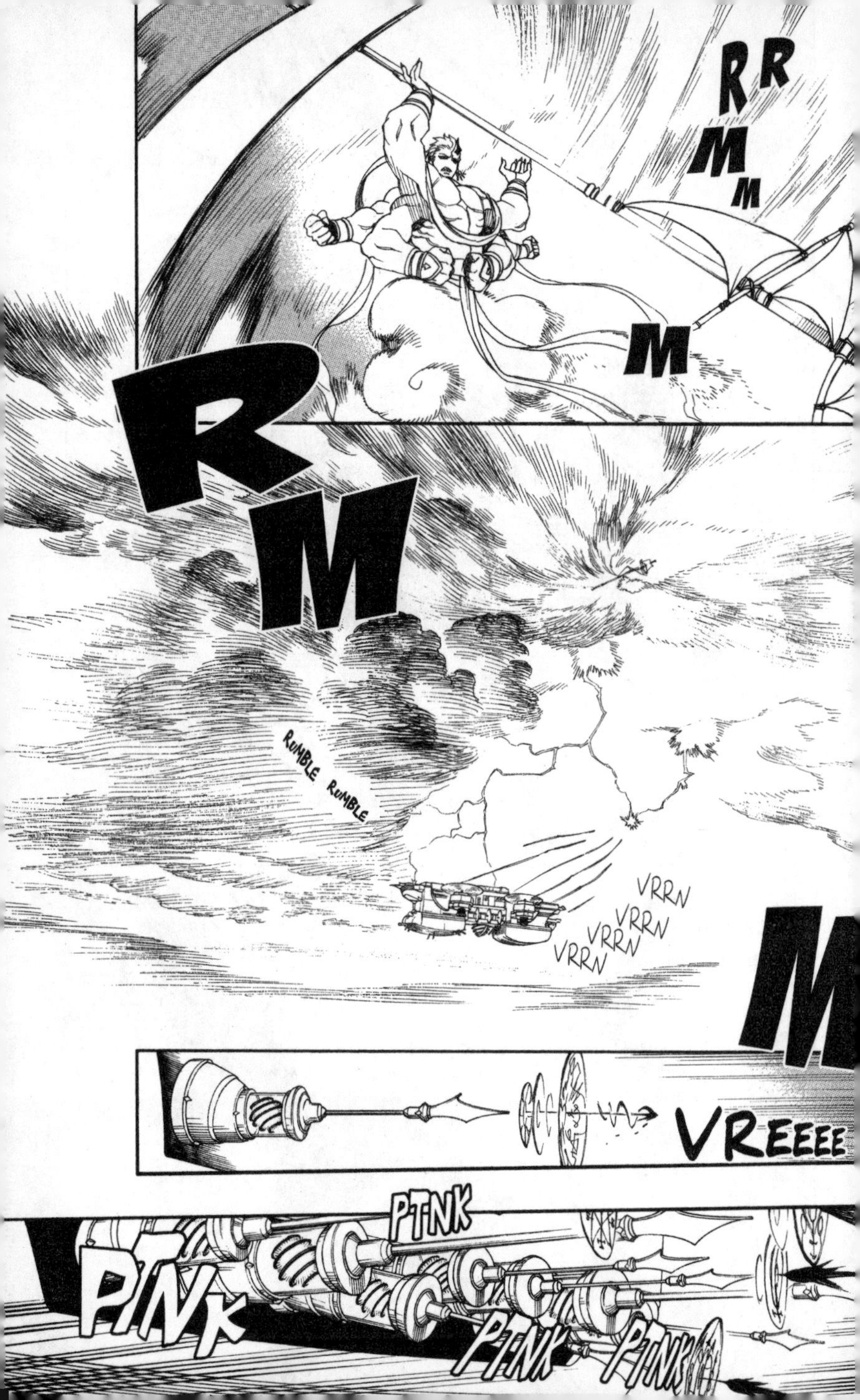
RRMMM
M
M
RM
RUMBLE RUMBLE
VRRN VRRN VRRN VRRN
VREEEE
PTNK
PTNK
PTNK
PTNK

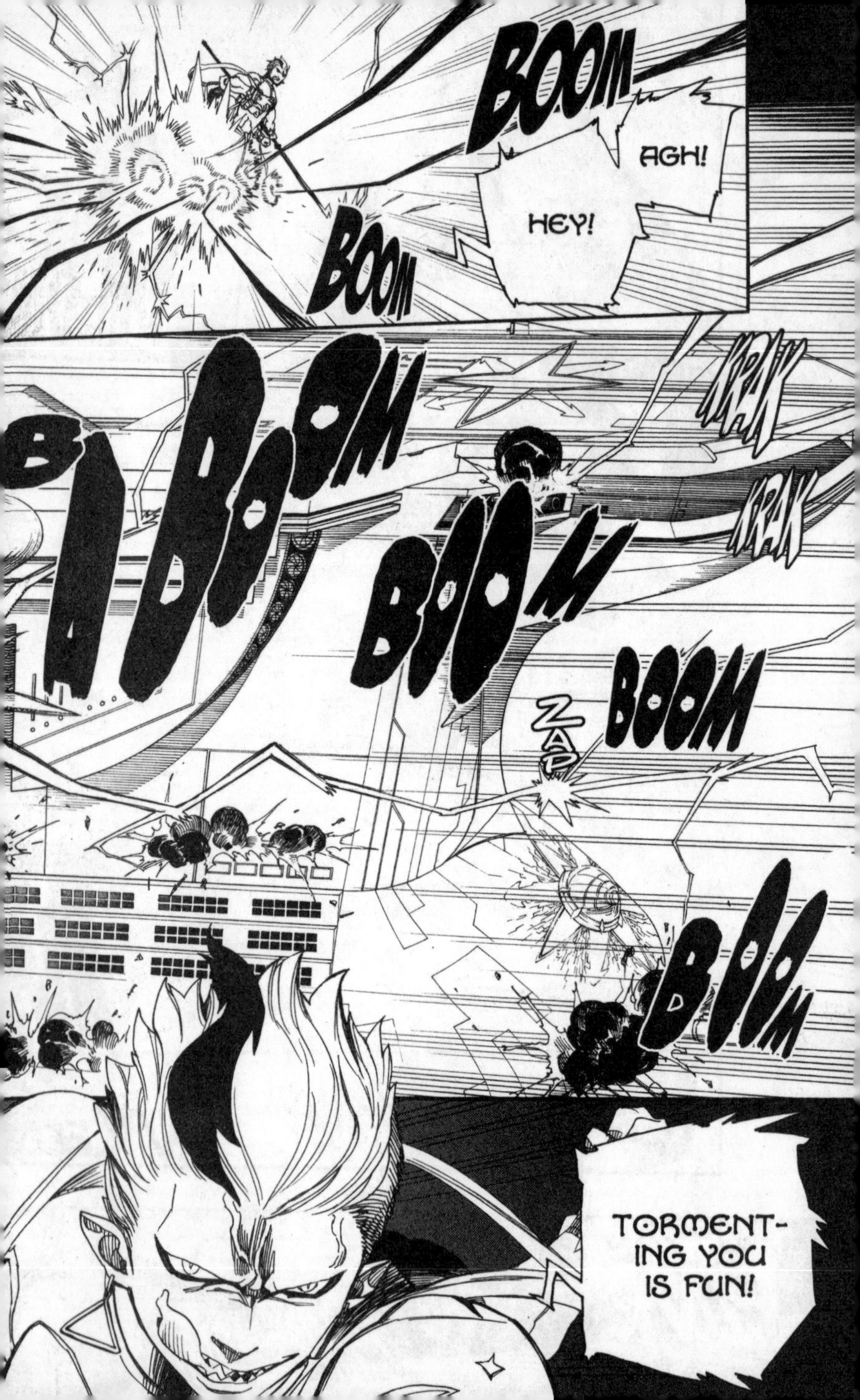
BOOM
AGH!
HEY!
BOOM
KRAK
KRAK
BOOM
BOOOM
BADOOOM
BOOM
ZAP
BOOM
TORMENT-
ING YOU
IS FUN!

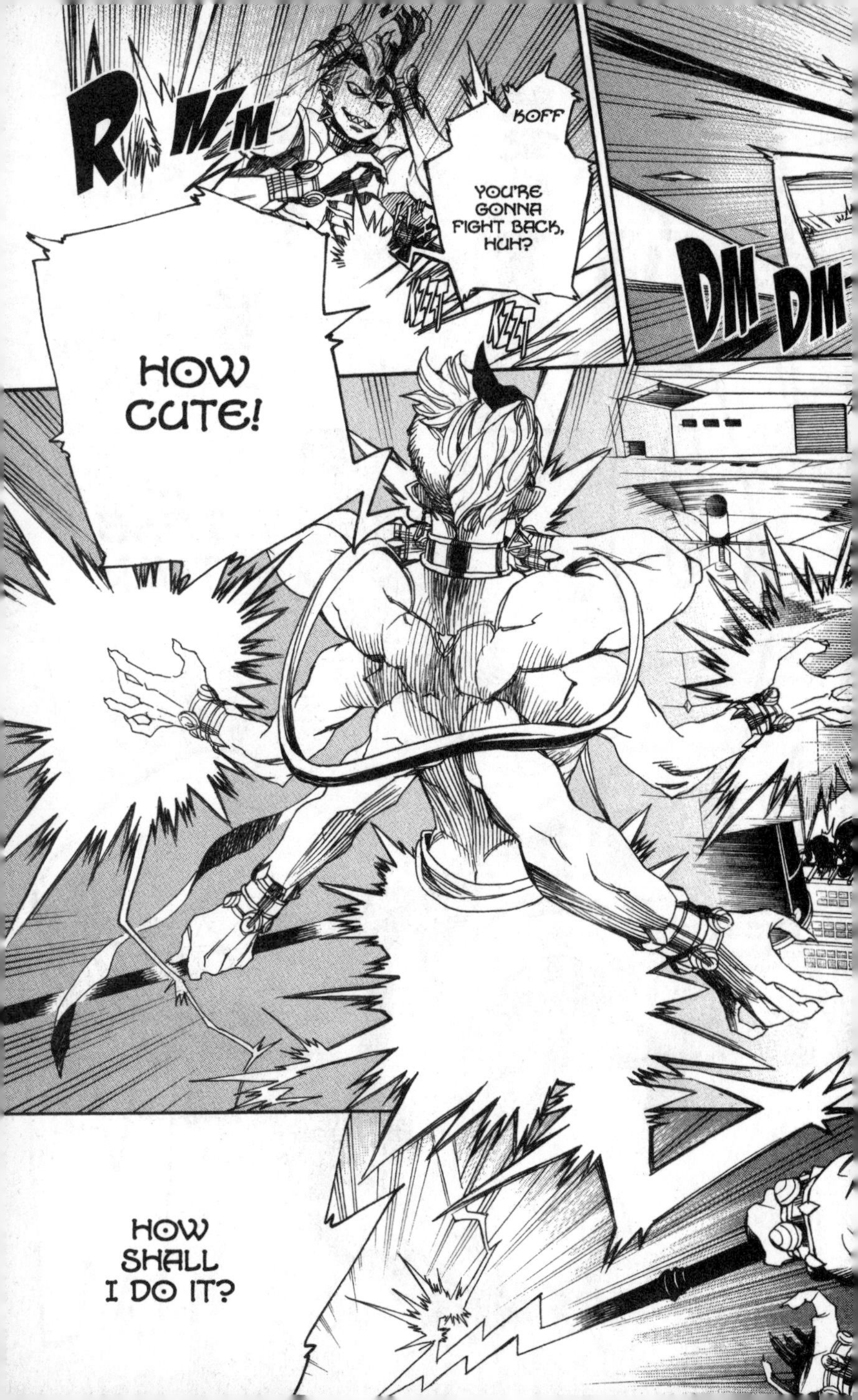
DM DM
KOFF
YOU'RE GONNA FIGHT BACK, HUH?
RMM
KZZT
KZZT
HOW CUTE!
HOW SHALL I DO IT?

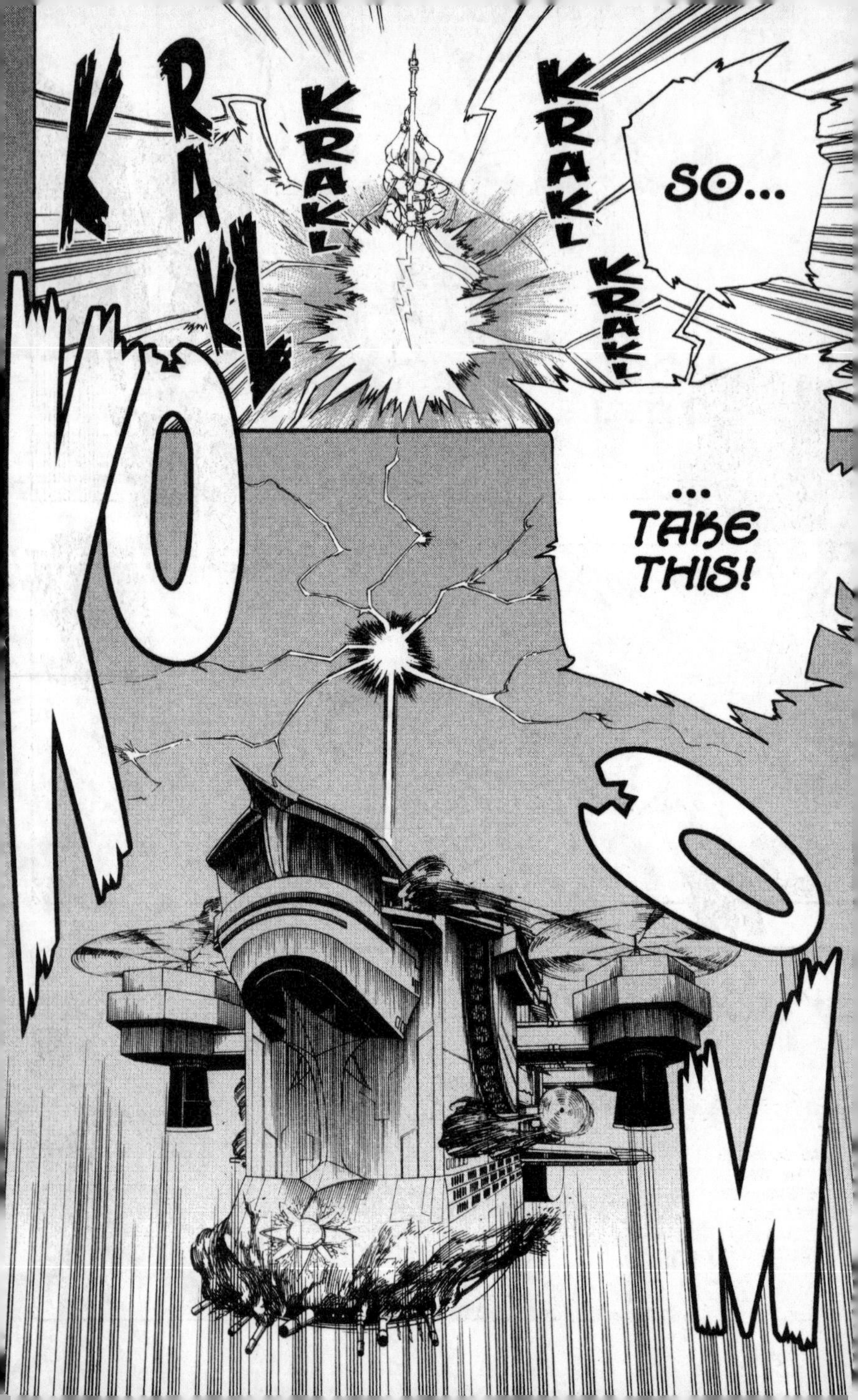
SO...
KRAKL KRAKL
KRAKL
KRAKL
...TAKE THIS!

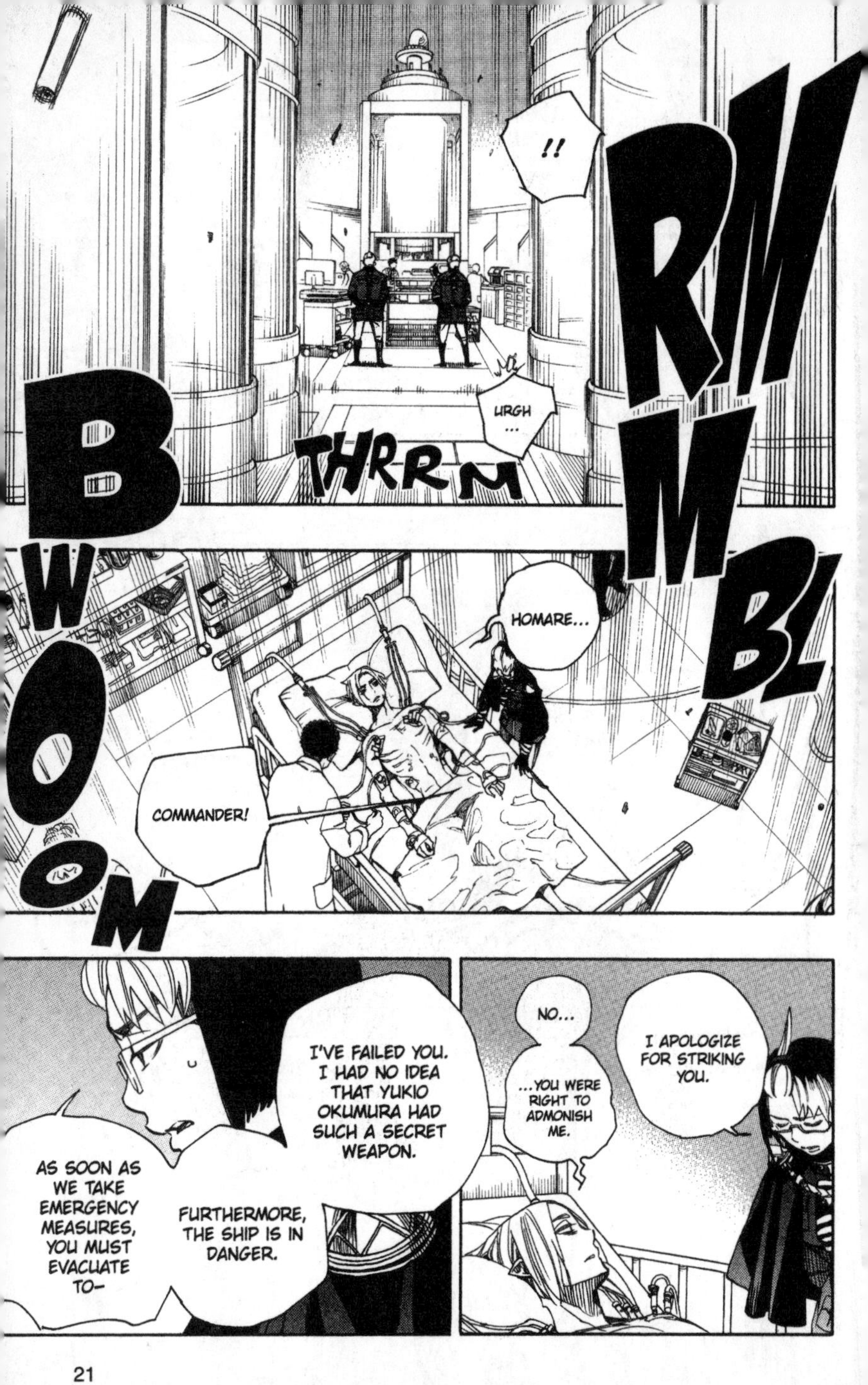
RMMBL
!!
URGH...
THRRM
BWOOOM
HOMARE...
COMMANDER!
I APOLOGIZE FOR STRIKING YOU.
NO...
...YOU WERE RIGHT TO ADMONISH ME.
I'VE FAILED YOU. I HAD NO IDEA THAT YUKIO OKUMURA HAD SUCH A SECRET WEAPON.
FURTHERMORE, THE SHIP IS IN DANGER.
AS SOON AS WE TAKE EMERGENCY MEASURES, YOU MUST EVACUATE TO–

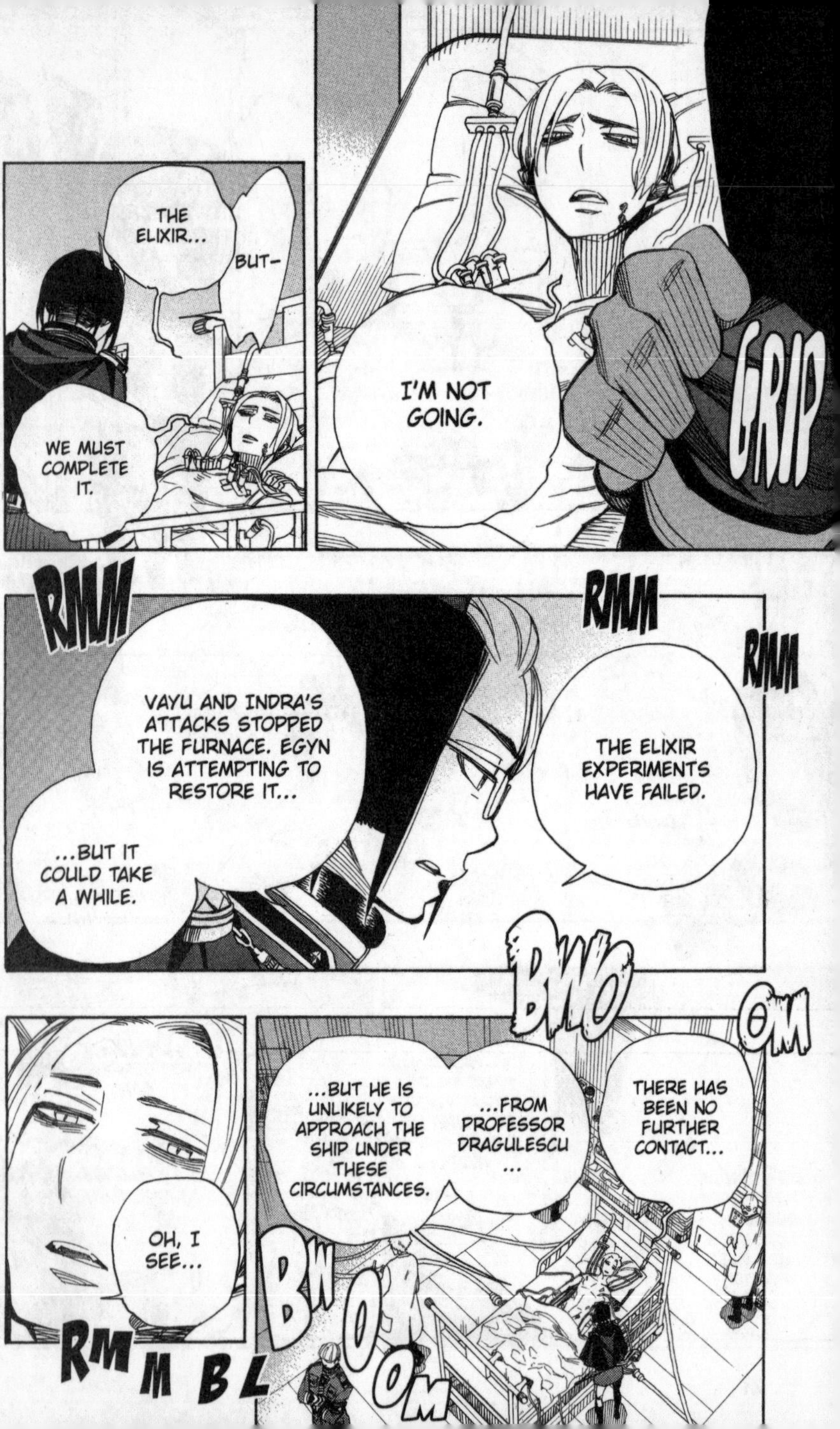
GRIP
I'M NOT GOING.
THE ELIXIR...
BUT-
WE MUST COMPLETE IT.
RMM
RMM
THE ELIXIR EXPERIMENTS HAVE FAILED.
VAYU AND INDRA'S ATTACKS STOPPED THE FURNACE. EGYN IS ATTEMPTING TO RESTORE IT...
...BUT IT COULD TAKE A WHILE.
RMM
BWOOM
THERE HAS BEEN NO FURTHER CONTACT...
...FROM PROFESSOR DRAGULESCU ...
...BUT HE IS UNLIKELY TO APPROACH THE SHIP UNDER THESE CIRCUMSTANCES.
BWOOOM
OH, I SEE...
RMMBL

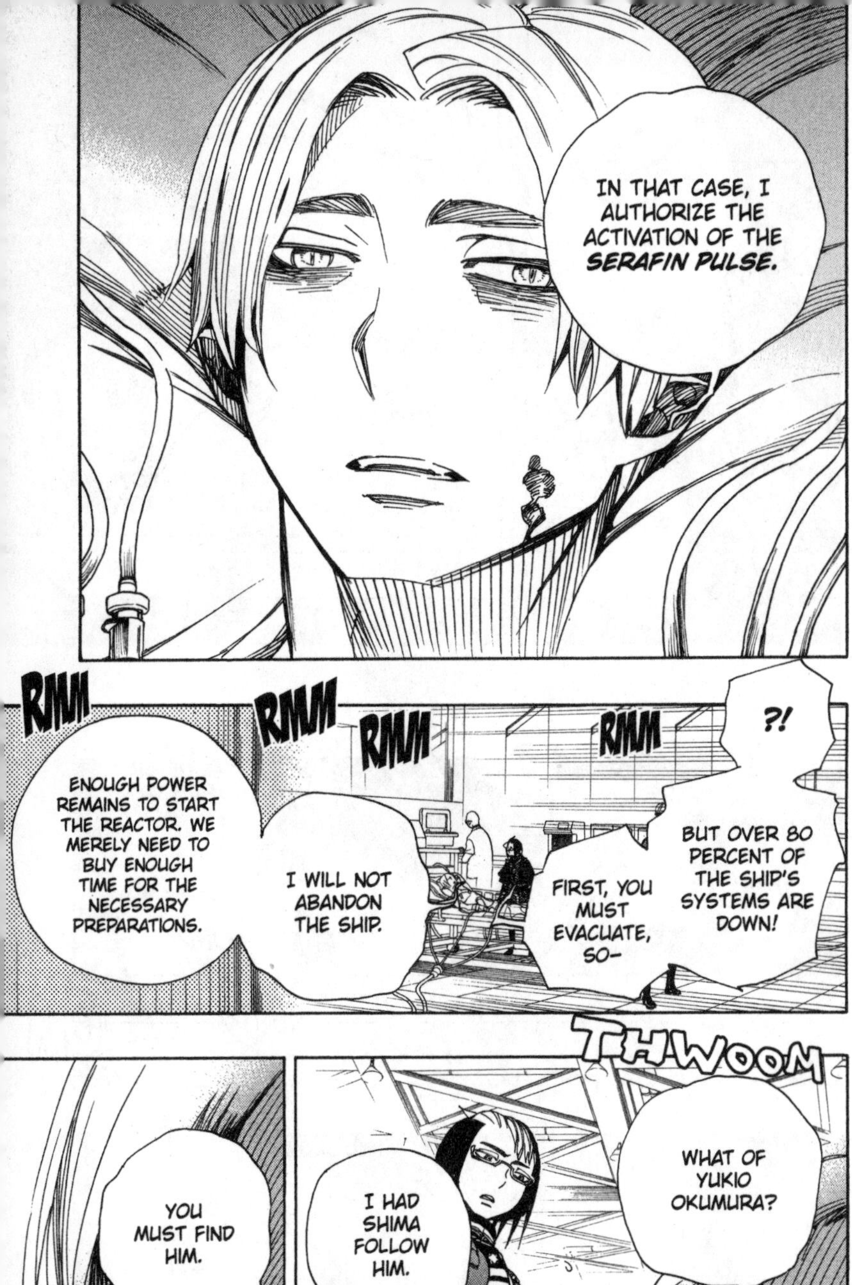
IN THAT CASE, I AUTHORIZE THE ACTIVATION OF THE *SERAFIN PULSE.*
RMM
RMM
RMM
RMM
?!
BUT OVER 80 PERCENT OF THE SHIP'S SYSTEMS ARE DOWN!
FIRST, YOU MUST EVACUATE, SO–
I WILL NOT ABANDON THE SHIP.
ENOUGH POWER REMAINS TO START THE REACTOR. WE MERELY NEED TO BUY ENOUGH TIME FOR THE NECESSARY PREPARATIONS.
THWOOM
WHAT OF YUKIO OKUMURA?
I HAD SHIMA FOLLOW HIM.
YOU MUST FIND HIM.

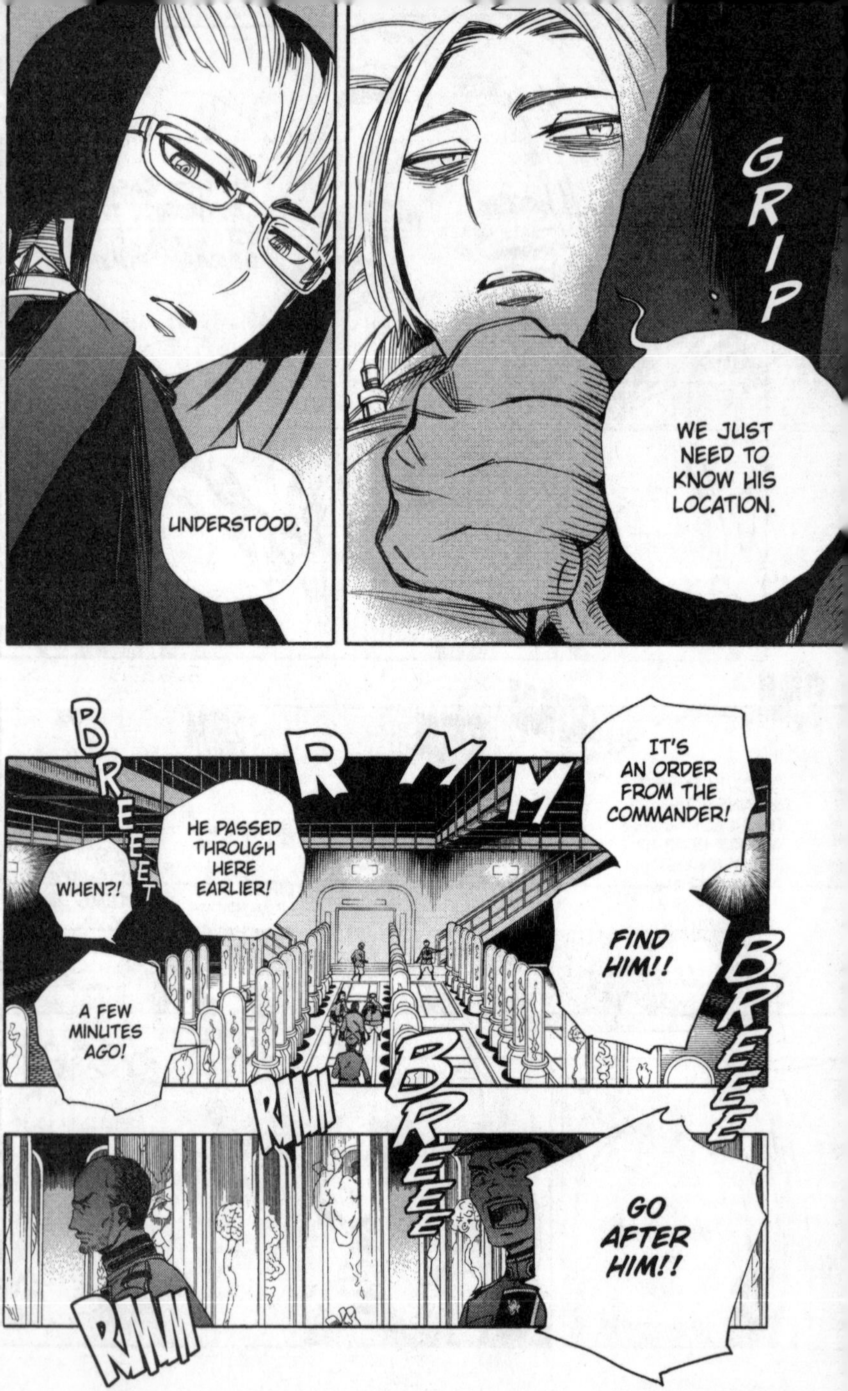
GRIP
WE JUST NEED TO KNOW HIS LOCATION.
UNDERSTOOD.
IT'S AN ORDER FROM THE COMMANDER!
RMM
FIND HIM!!
BREEEE
HE PASSED THROUGH HERE EARLIER!
BREEEET
WHEN?!
A FEW MINUTES AGO!
BREEE
RMM
GO AFTER HIM!!
RMM

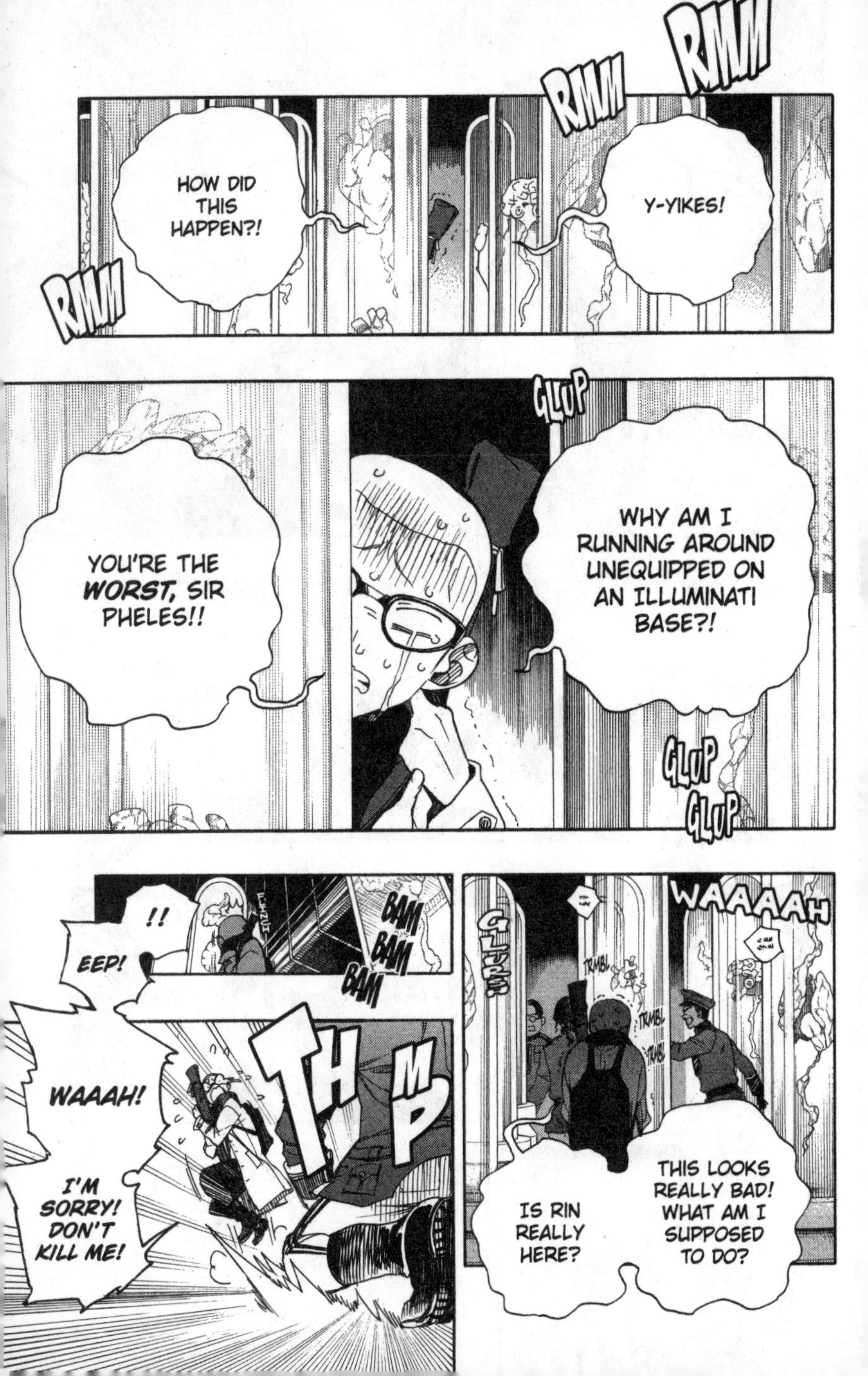
RMMM
RMMM
Y-YIKES!
HOW DID THIS HAPPEN?!
RMMM
GLUP
WHY AM I RUNNING AROUND UNEQUIPPED ON AN ILLUMINATI BASE?!
GLUP
GLUP
YOU'RE THE ***WORST,*** SIR PHELES!!
WAAAAH
TRMBL
TRMBL
TRMBL
GLURP
THIS LOOKS REALLY BAD! WHAT AM I SUPPOSED TO DO?
IS RIN REALLY HERE?
BAM
BAM
BAM
!!
EEP!
THMP
WAAAH!
I'M SORRY! DON'T KILL ME!

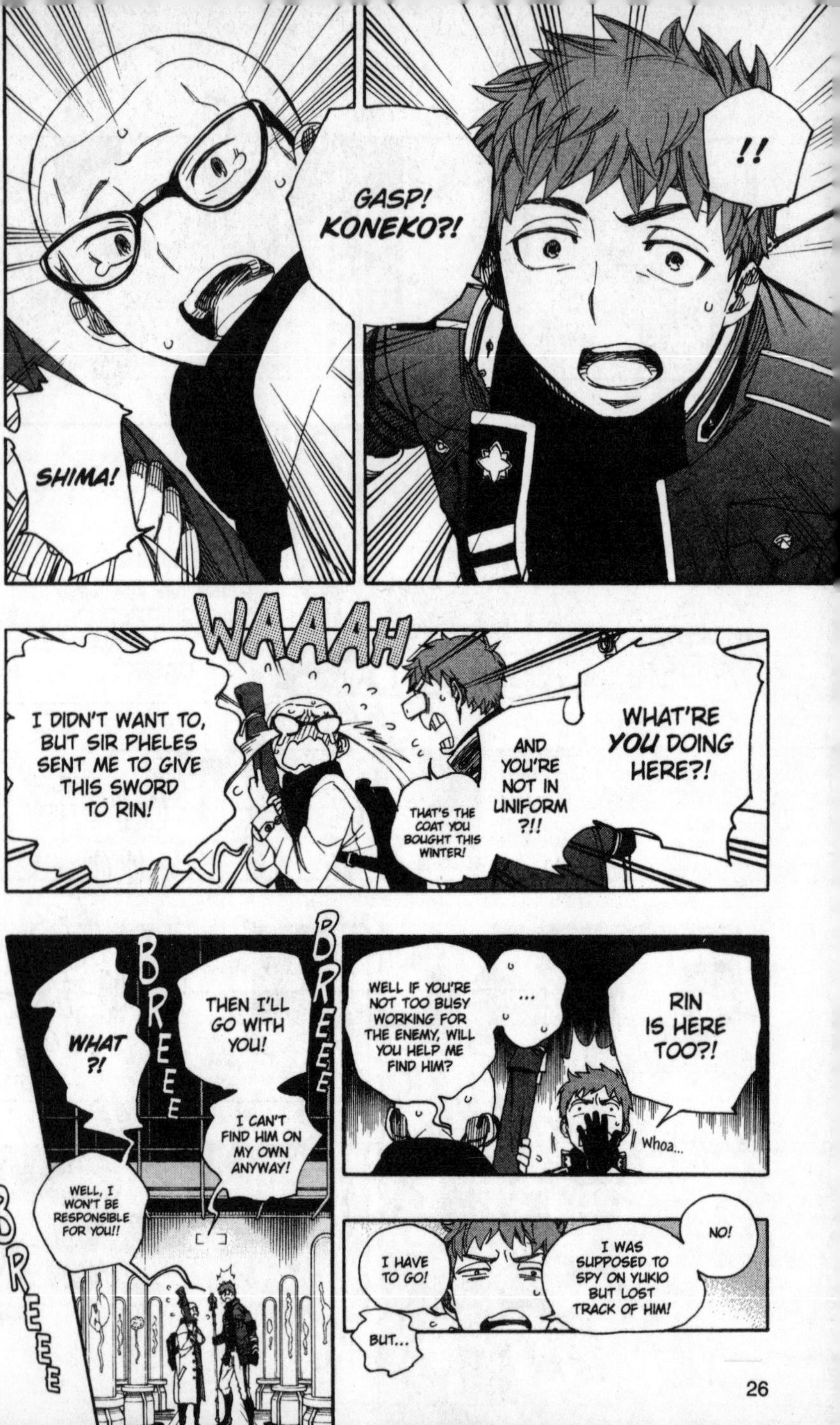
!!
GASP! KONEKO?!
SHIMA!
WHAT'RE YOU DOING HERE?!
AND YOU'RE NOT IN UNIFORM ?!!
THAT'S THE COAT YOU BOUGHT THIS WINTER!
WAAAAH
I DIDN'T WANT TO, BUT SIR PHELES SENT ME TO GIVE THIS SWORD TO RIN!
RIN IS HERE TOO?!
Whoa...
...
WELL IF YOU'RE NOT TOO BUSY WORKING FOR THE ENEMY, WILL YOU HELP ME FIND HIM?
NO!
I WAS SUPPOSED TO SPY ON YUKIO BUT LOST TRACK OF HIM!
I HAVE TO GO!
BUT...
BREEE
THEN I'LL GO WITH YOU!
I CAN'T FIND HIM ON MY OWN ANYWAY!
WHAT ?!
WELL, I WON'T BE RESPONSIBLE FOR YOU!!
BREEE

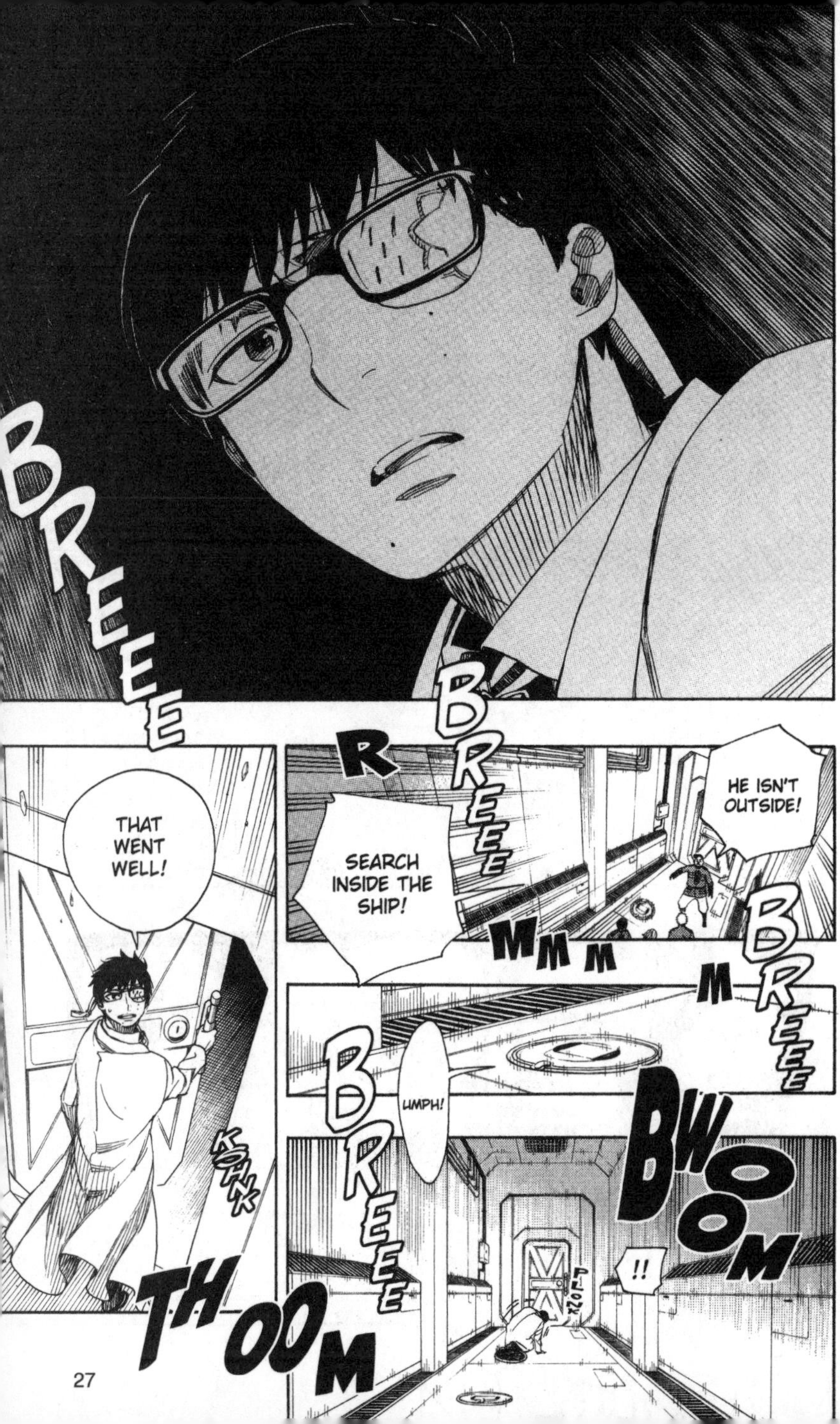
BREEE
HE ISN'T OUTSIDE!
SEARCH INSIDE THE SHIP!
R BREEE
MMMM BREEE
UMPH!
BREEE
!!
BWOOM
PLONK
THAT WENT WELL!
KOHNK
THOOM

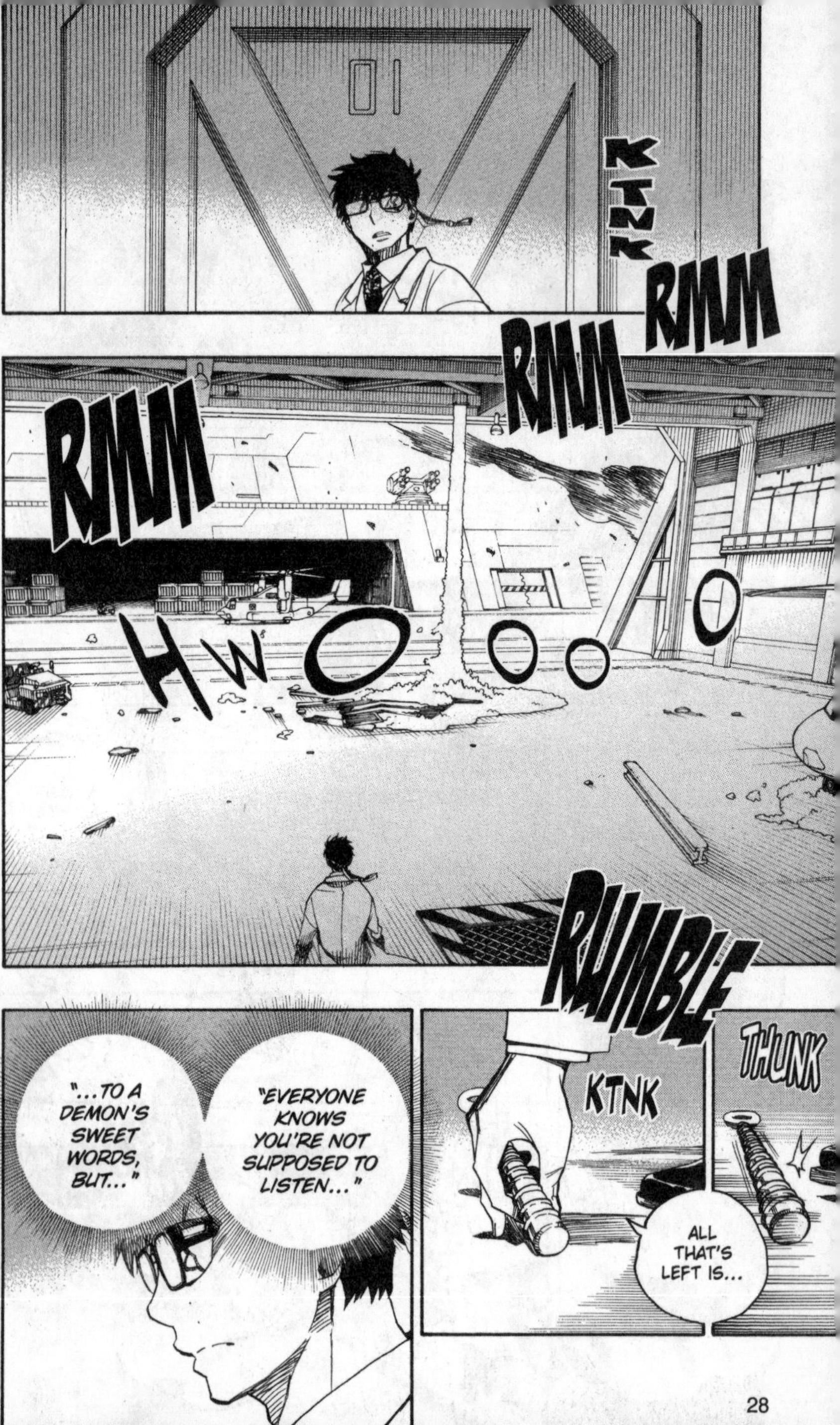
KTNK
RMMM
RMMM
RMMM
HWOOOO
RUMBLE
THUNK
KTNK
ALL THAT'S LEFT IS...
"EVERYONE KNOWS YOU'RE NOT SUPPOSED TO LISTEN..."
"...TO A DEMON'S SWEET WORDS, BUT..."

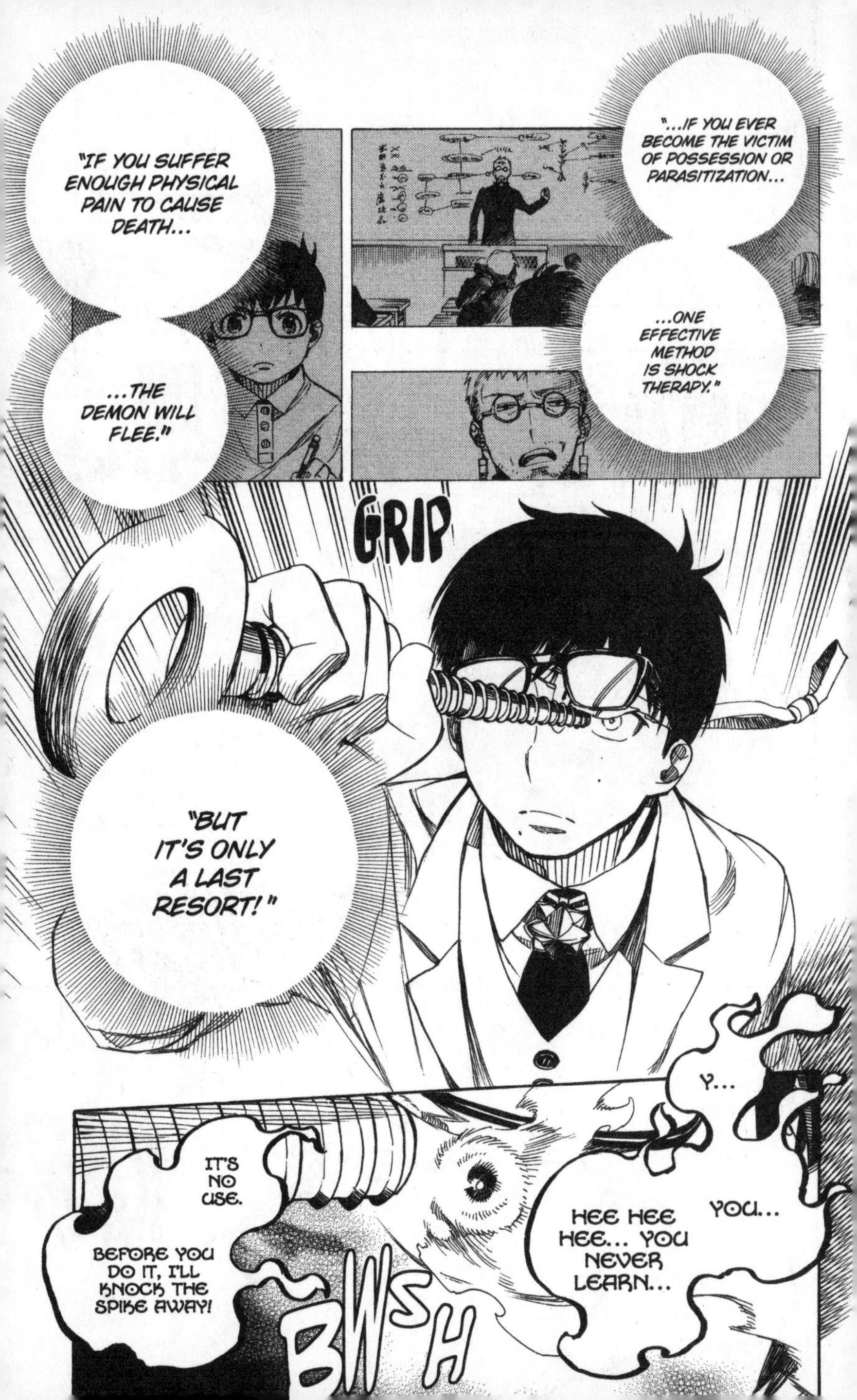
"...IF YOU EVER BECOME THE VICTIM OF POSSESSION OR PARASITIZATION...
...ONE EFFECTIVE METHOD IS SHOCK THERAPY."
"IF YOU SUFFER ENOUGH PHYSICAL PAIN TO CAUSE DEATH...
...THE DEMON WILL FLEE."
GRIP
"BUT IT'S ONLY A LAST RESORT!"
Y...
YOU...
HEE HEE HEE... YOU NEVER LEARN...
IT'S NO USE.
BEFORE YOU DO IT, I'LL KNOCK THE SPIKE AWAY!
BWSH

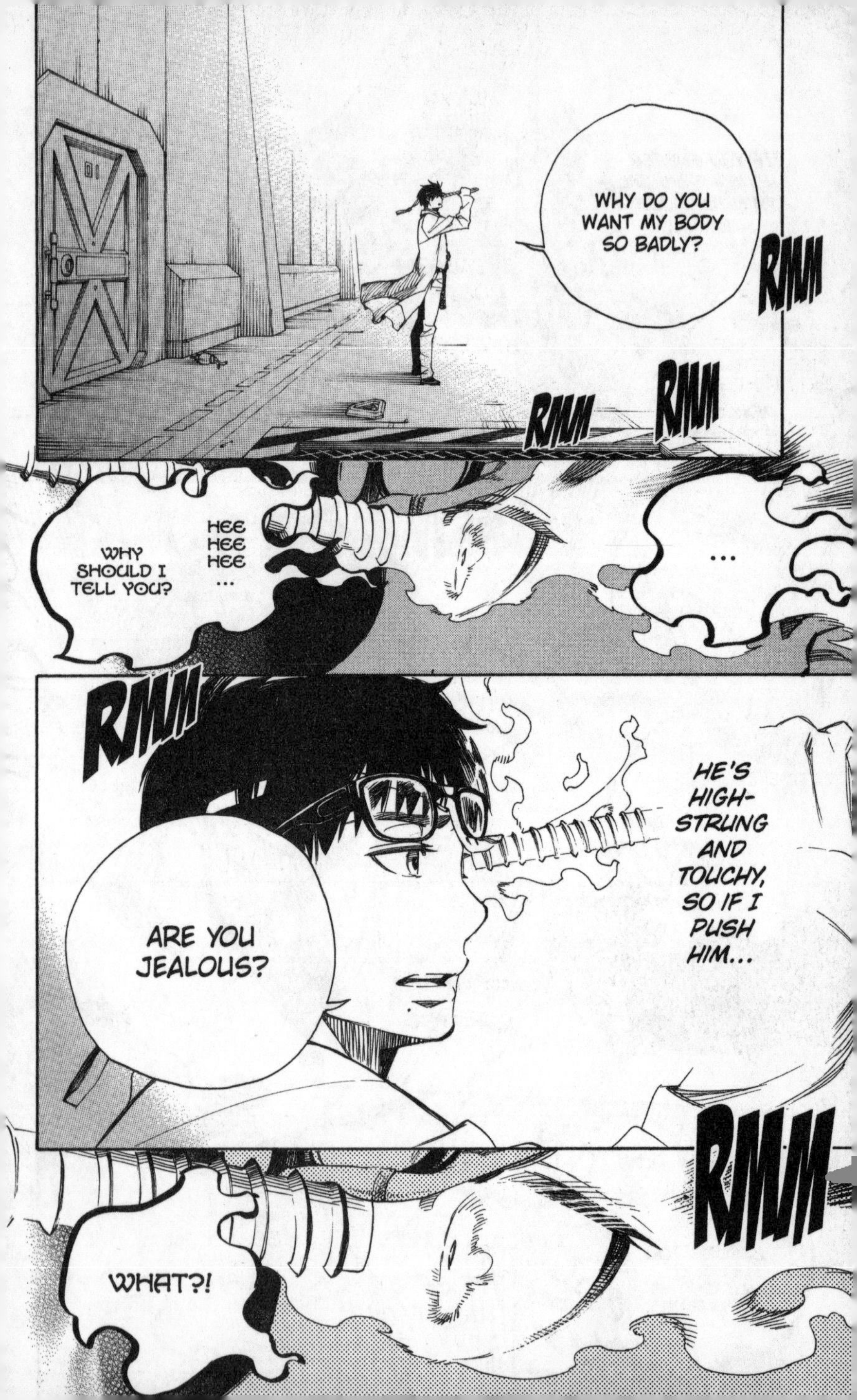
WHY DO YOU WANT MY BODY SO BADLY?
RMM
RMM
RMM
...
HEE HEE HEE ...
WHY SHOULD I TELL YOU?
HE'S HIGH-STRUNG AND TOUCHY, SO IF I PUSH HIM...
RMM
ARE YOU JEALOUS?
RMM
WHAT?!

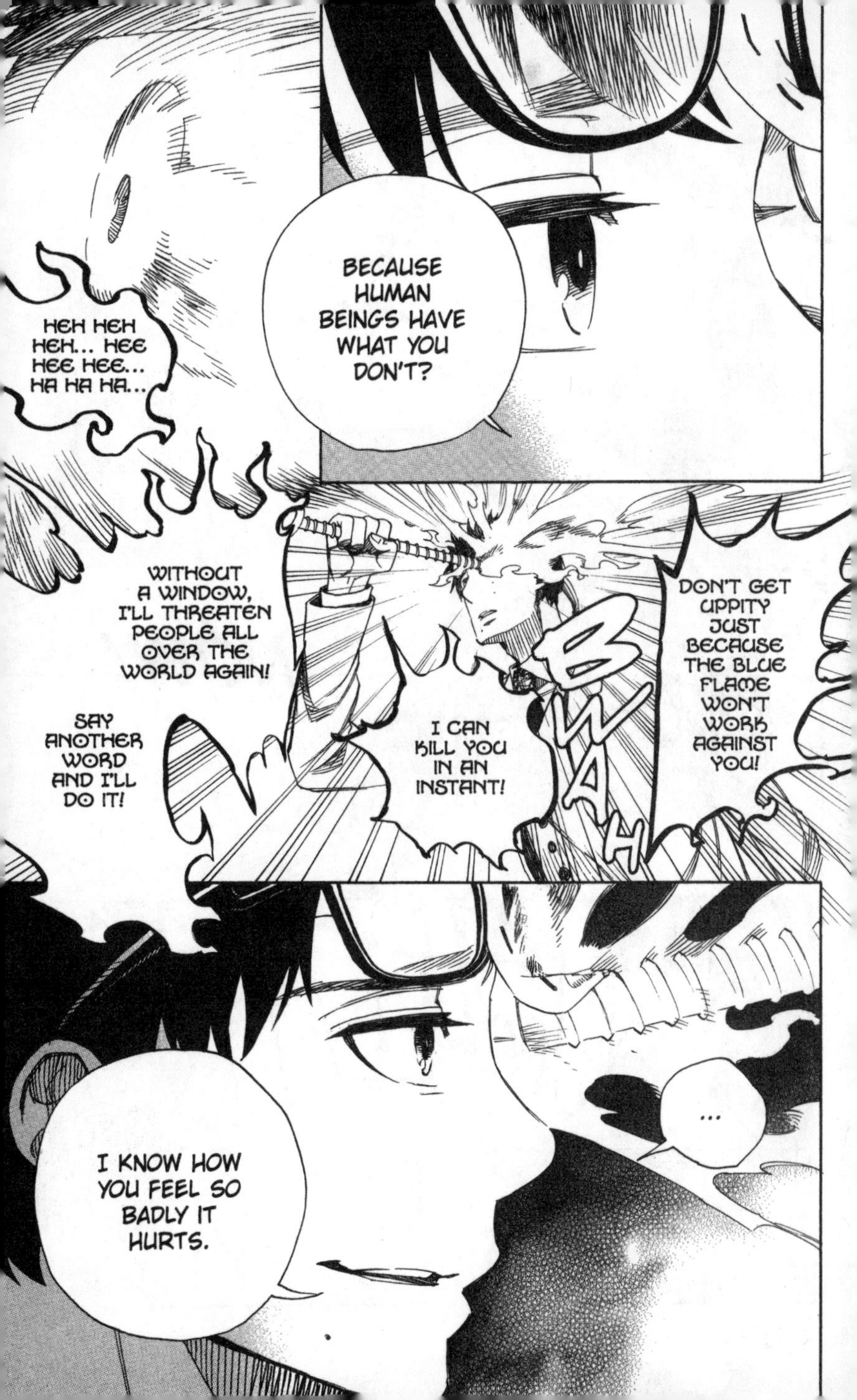

BECAUSE HUMAN BEINGS HAVE WHAT YOU DON'T?
HEH HEH HEH... HEE HEE HEE... HA HA HA...
DON'T GET UPPITY JUST BECAUSE THE BLUE FLAME WON'T WORK AGAINST YOU!
BWAH
I CAN KILL YOU IN AN INSTANT!
WITHOUT A WINDOW, I'LL THREATEN PEOPLE ALL OVER THE WORLD AGAIN!
SAY ANOTHER WORD AND I'LL DO IT!
...
I KNOW HOW YOU FEEL SO BADLY IT HURTS.

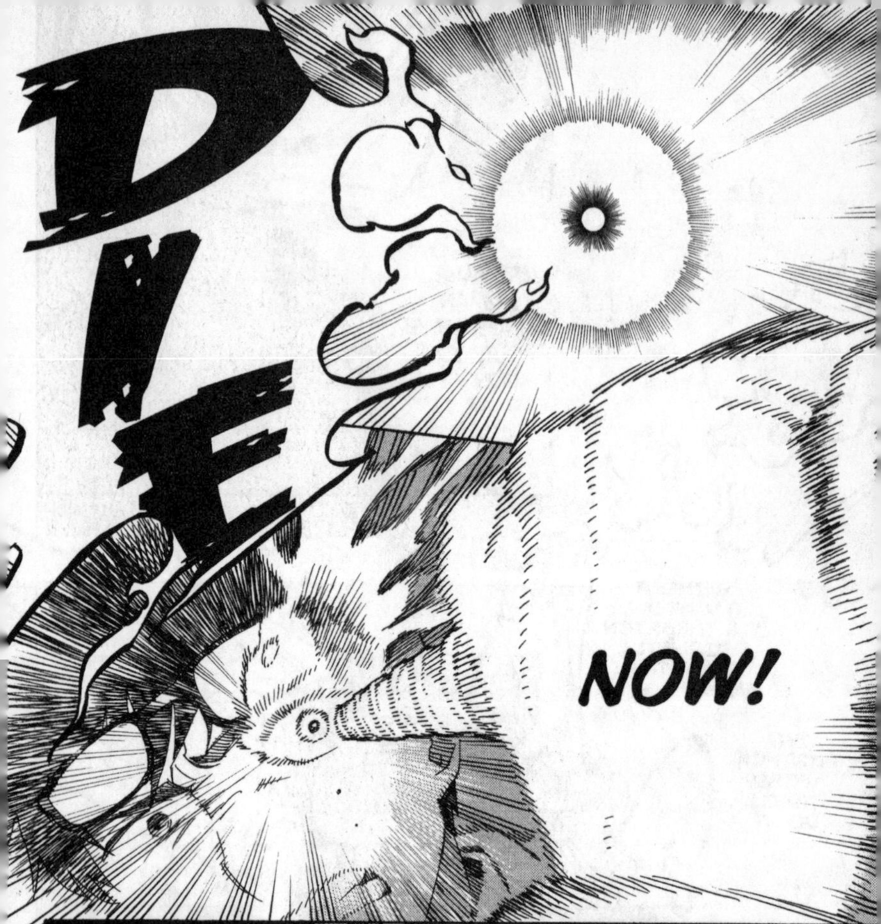
DIE
NOW!

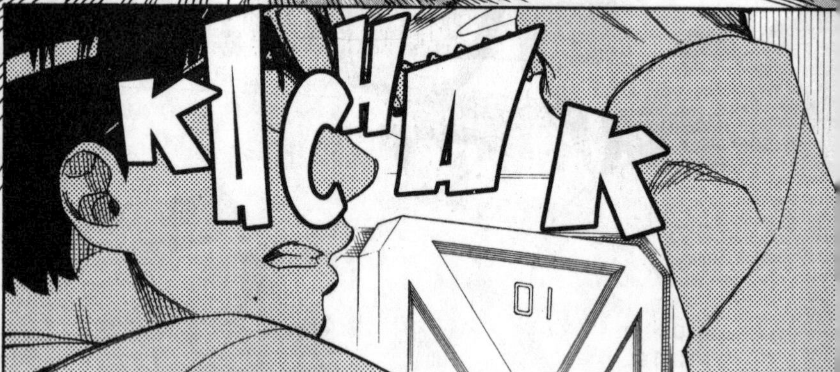
KACHAK
01

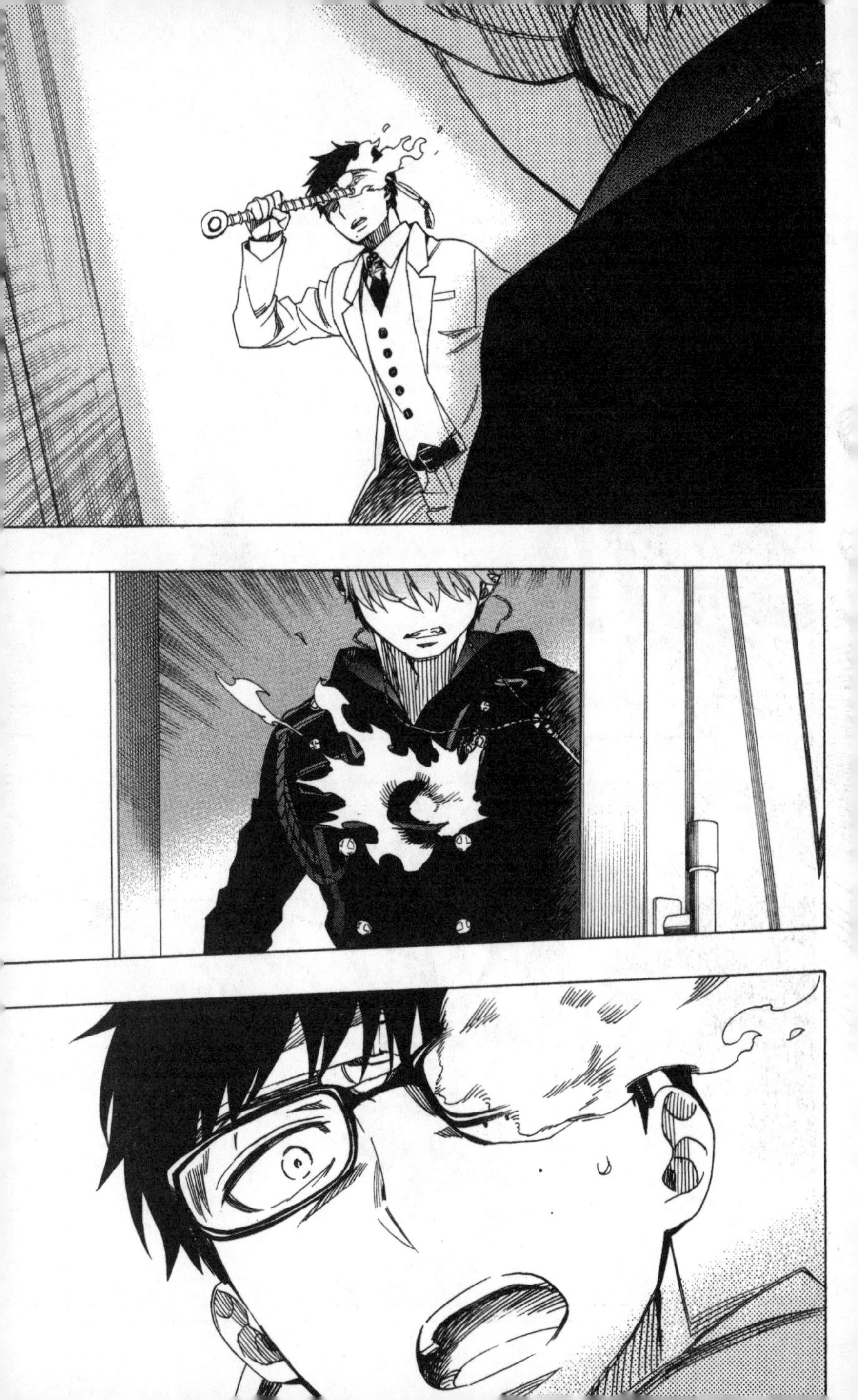

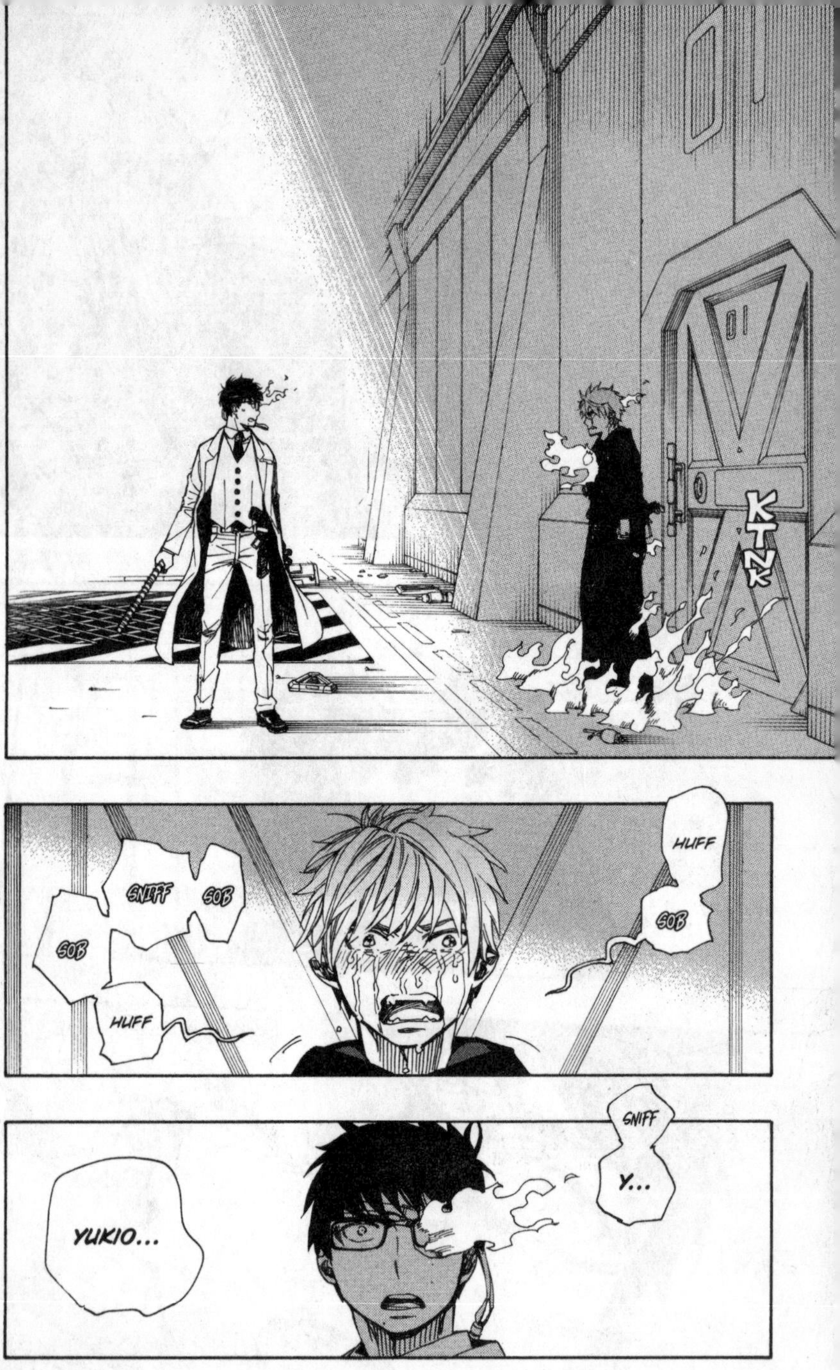
KTNK
HUFF
SOB
SNIFF
SOB
SOB
HUFF
SNIFF
Y...
YUKIO...

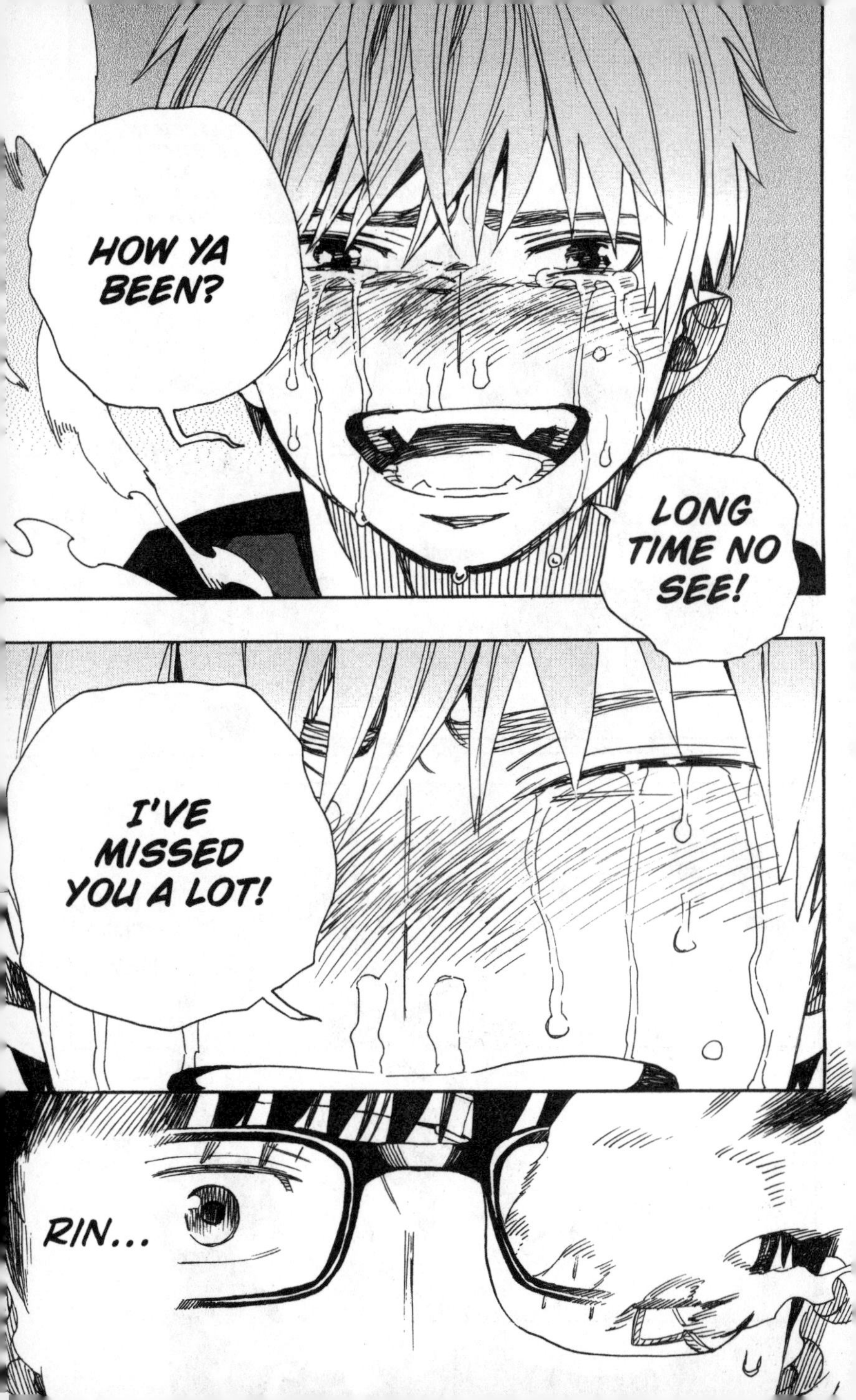
HOW YA BEEN?
LONG TIME NO SEE!
I'VE MISSED YOU A LOT!
RIN...

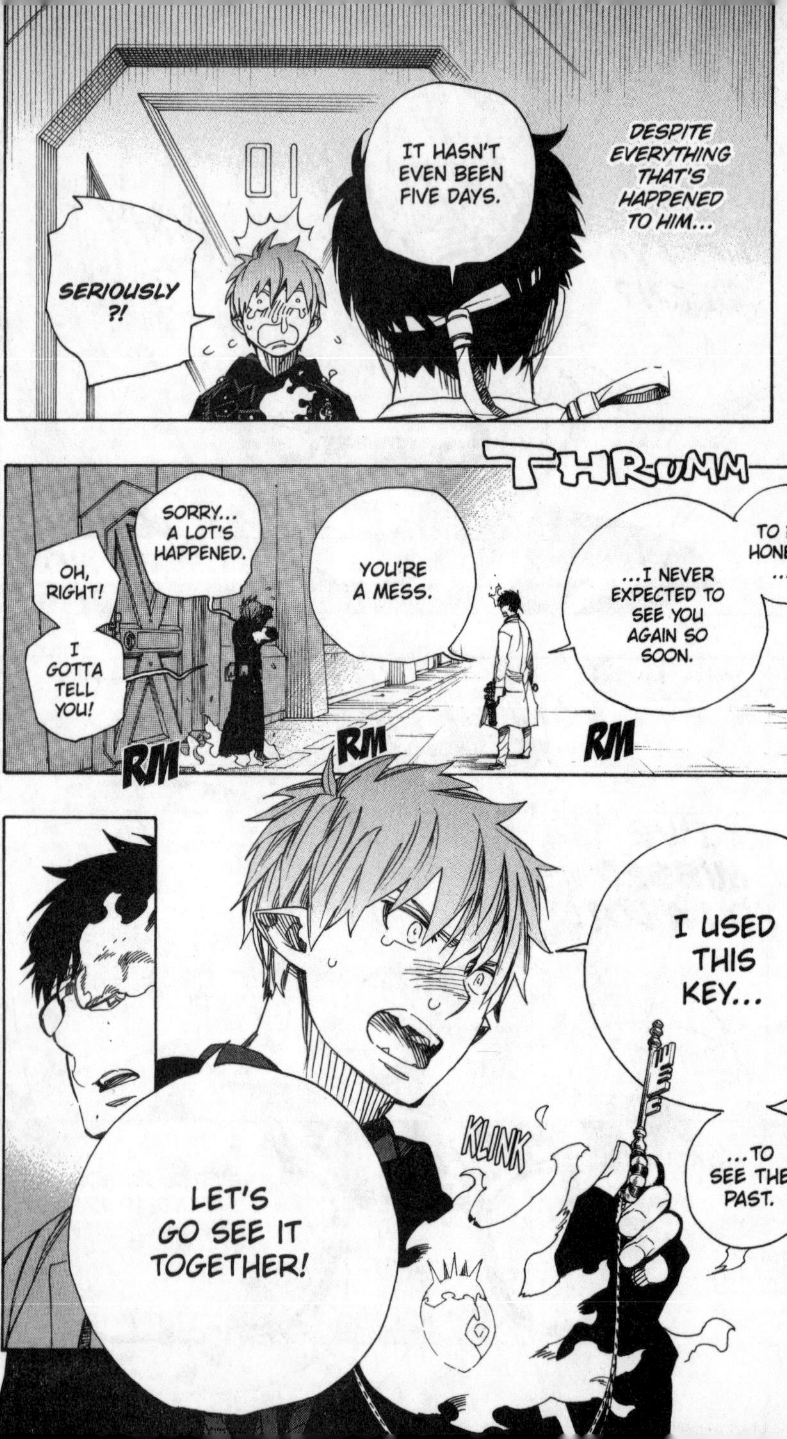
DESPITE EVERYTHING THAT'S HAPPENED TO HIM...
IT HASN'T EVEN BEEN FIVE DAYS.
SERIOUSLY ?!
THRUMM
TO BE HONEST ...
...I NEVER EXPECTED TO SEE YOU AGAIN SO SOON.
YOU'RE A MESS.
SORRY... A LOT'S HAPPENED.
OH, RIGHT!
I GOTTA TELL YOU!
RM
RM
RM
I USED THIS KEY...
...TO SEE THE PAST.
KLINK
LET'S GO SEE IT TOGETHER!

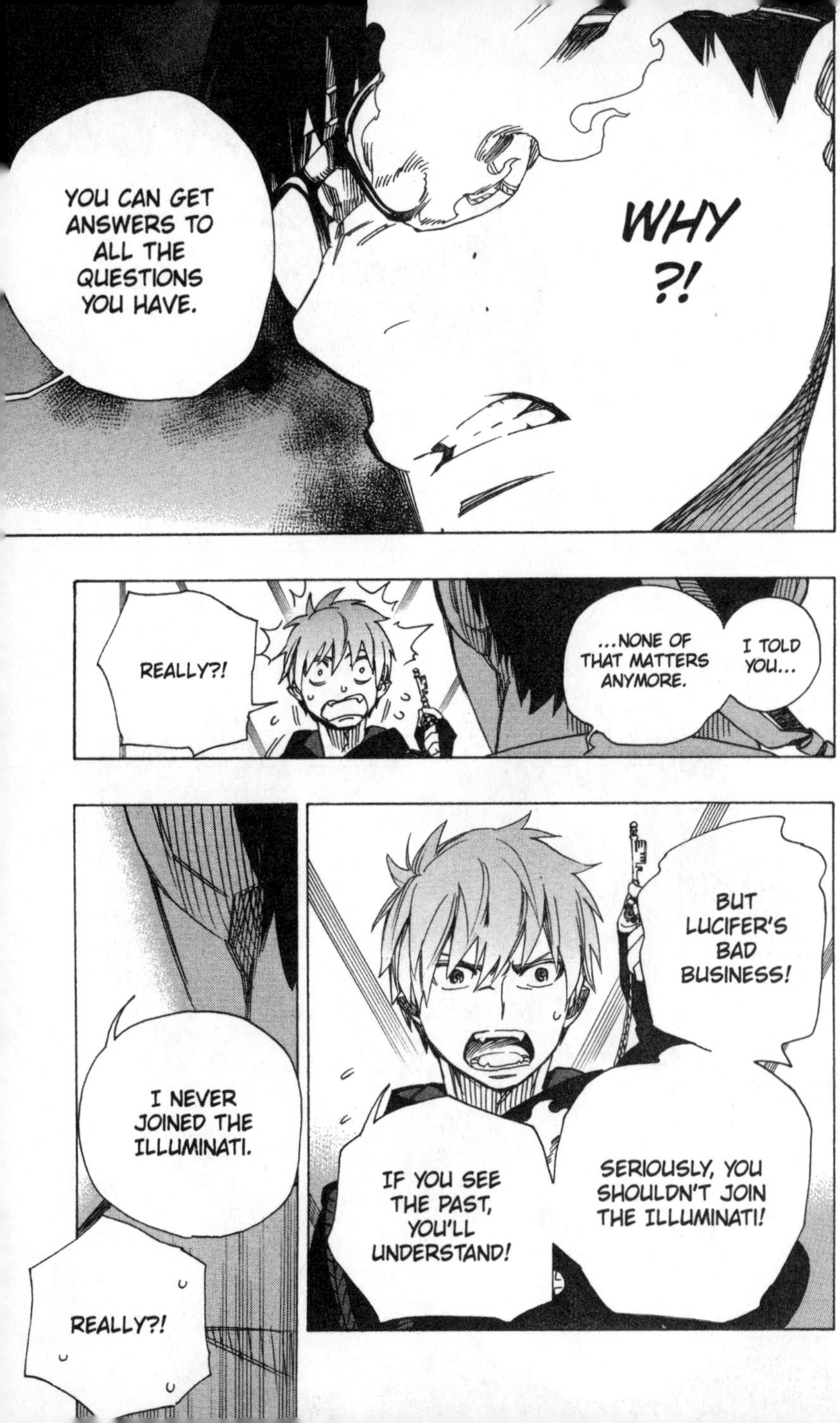
WHY ?!
YOU CAN GET ANSWERS TO ALL THE QUESTIONS YOU HAVE.
I TOLD YOU...
...NONE OF THAT MATTERS ANYMORE.
REALLY?!
BUT LUCIFER'S BAD BUSINESS!
SERIOUSLY, YOU SHOULDN'T JOIN THE ILLUMINATI!
IF YOU SEE THE PAST, YOU'LL UNDERSTAND!
I NEVER JOINED THE ILLUMINATI.
REALLY?!

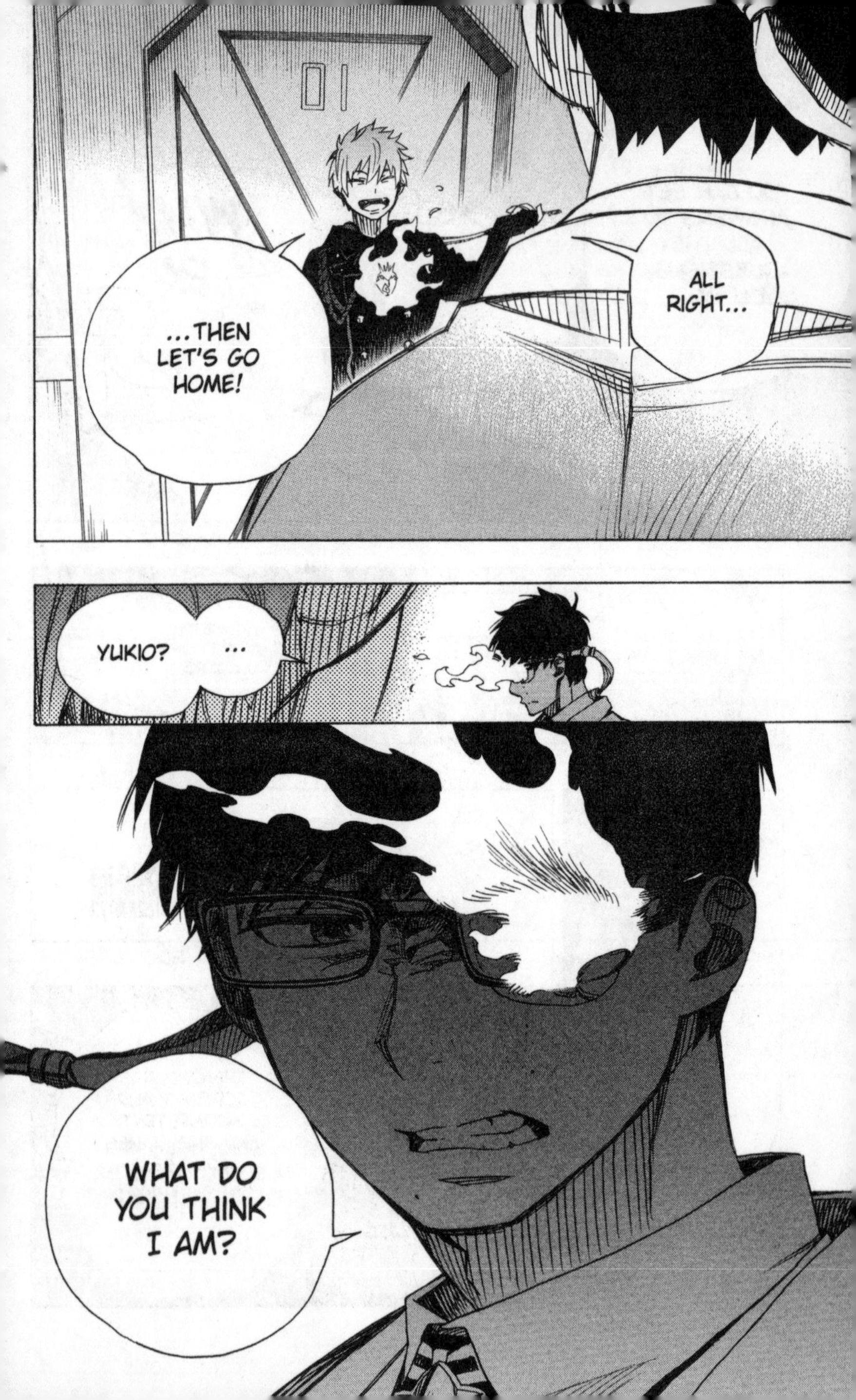
ALL RIGHT...
...THEN LET'S GO HOME!
...
YUKIO?
WHAT DO YOU THINK I AM?

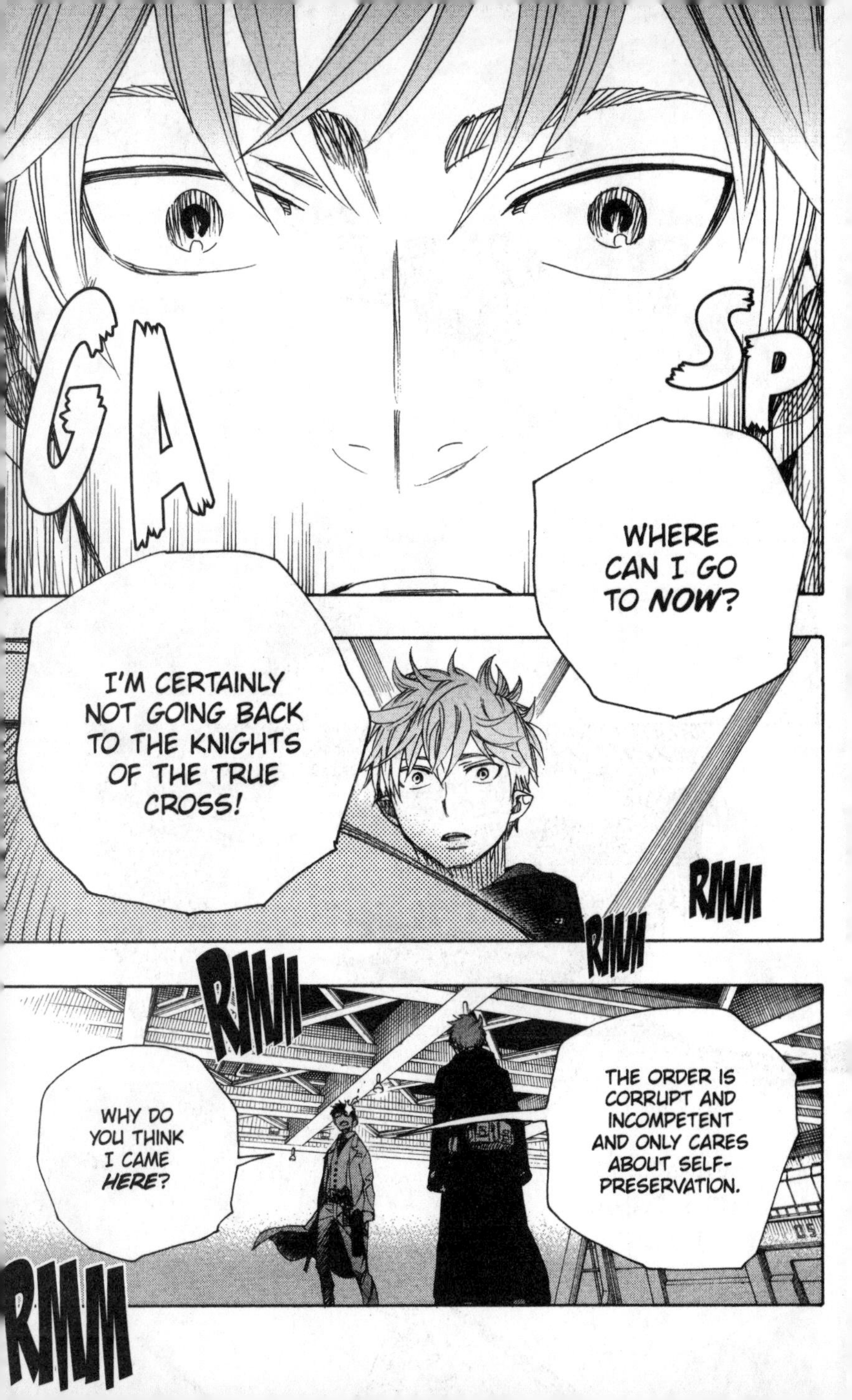
SP
GA
WHERE CAN I GO TO *NOW*?
I'M CERTAINLY NOT GOING BACK TO THE KNIGHTS OF THE TRUE CROSS!
RMM
RMM
RMM
THE ORDER IS CORRUPT AND INCOMPETENT AND ONLY CARES ABOUT SELF-PRESERVATION.
WHY DO YOU THINK I CAME *HERE*?
RMM

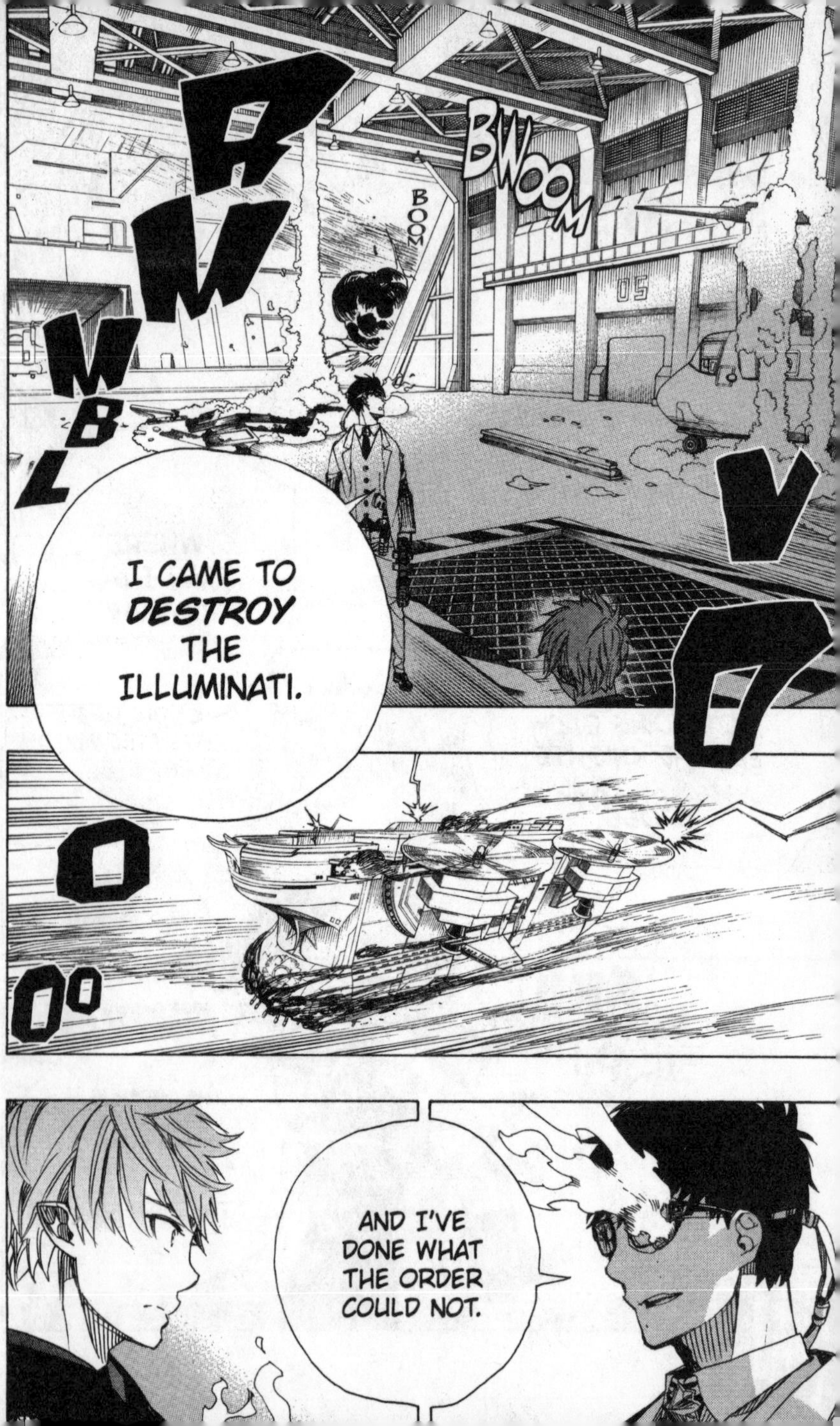
BWOOM
BOOM
I CAME TO *DESTROY* THE ILLUMINATI.
AND I'VE DONE WHAT THE ORDER COULD NOT.

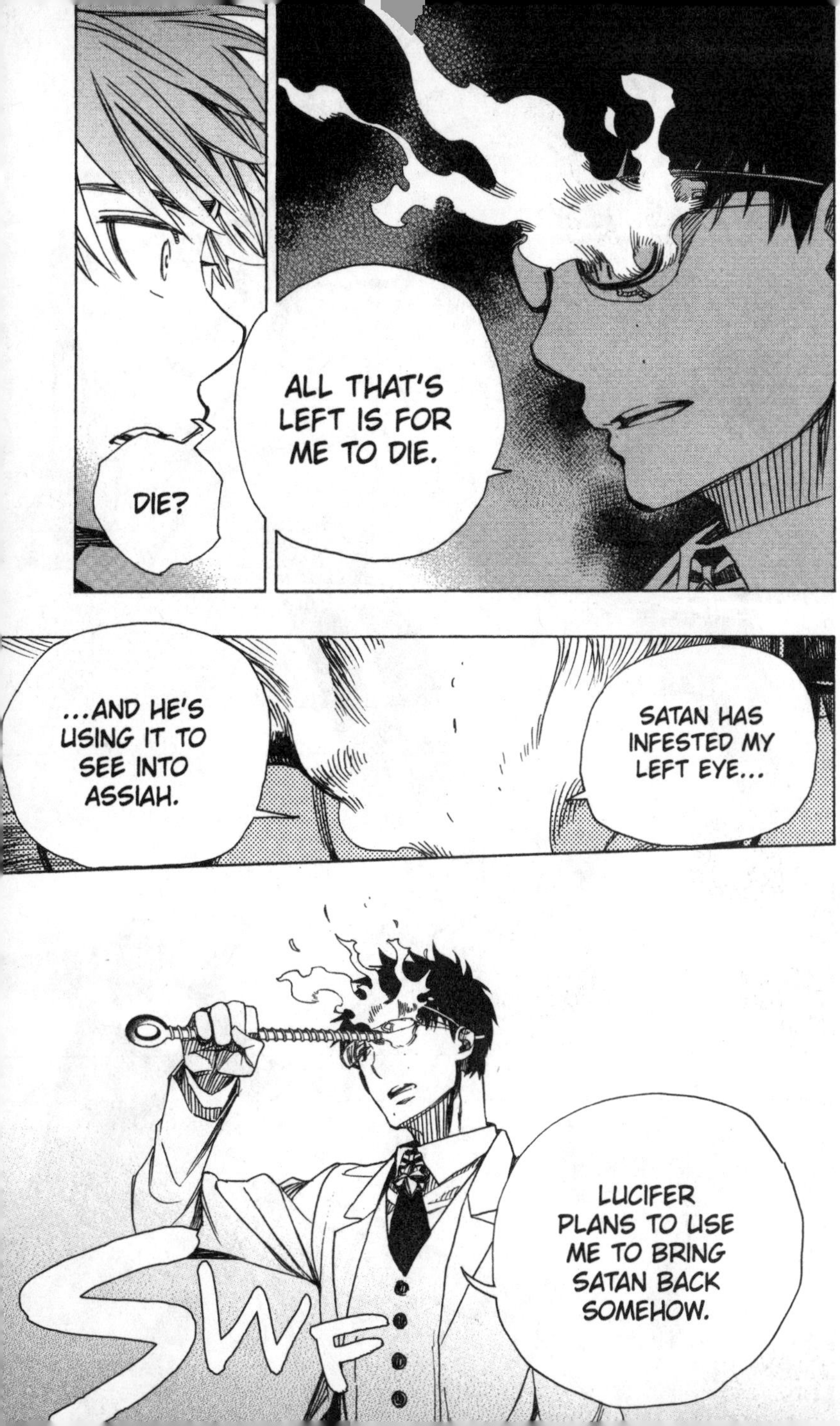
ALL THAT'S LEFT IS FOR ME TO DIE.
DIE?
SATAN HAS INFESTED MY LEFT EYE...
...AND HE'S USING IT TO SEE INTO ASSIAH.
LUCIFER PLANS TO USE ME TO BRING SATAN BACK SOMEHOW.
SWF

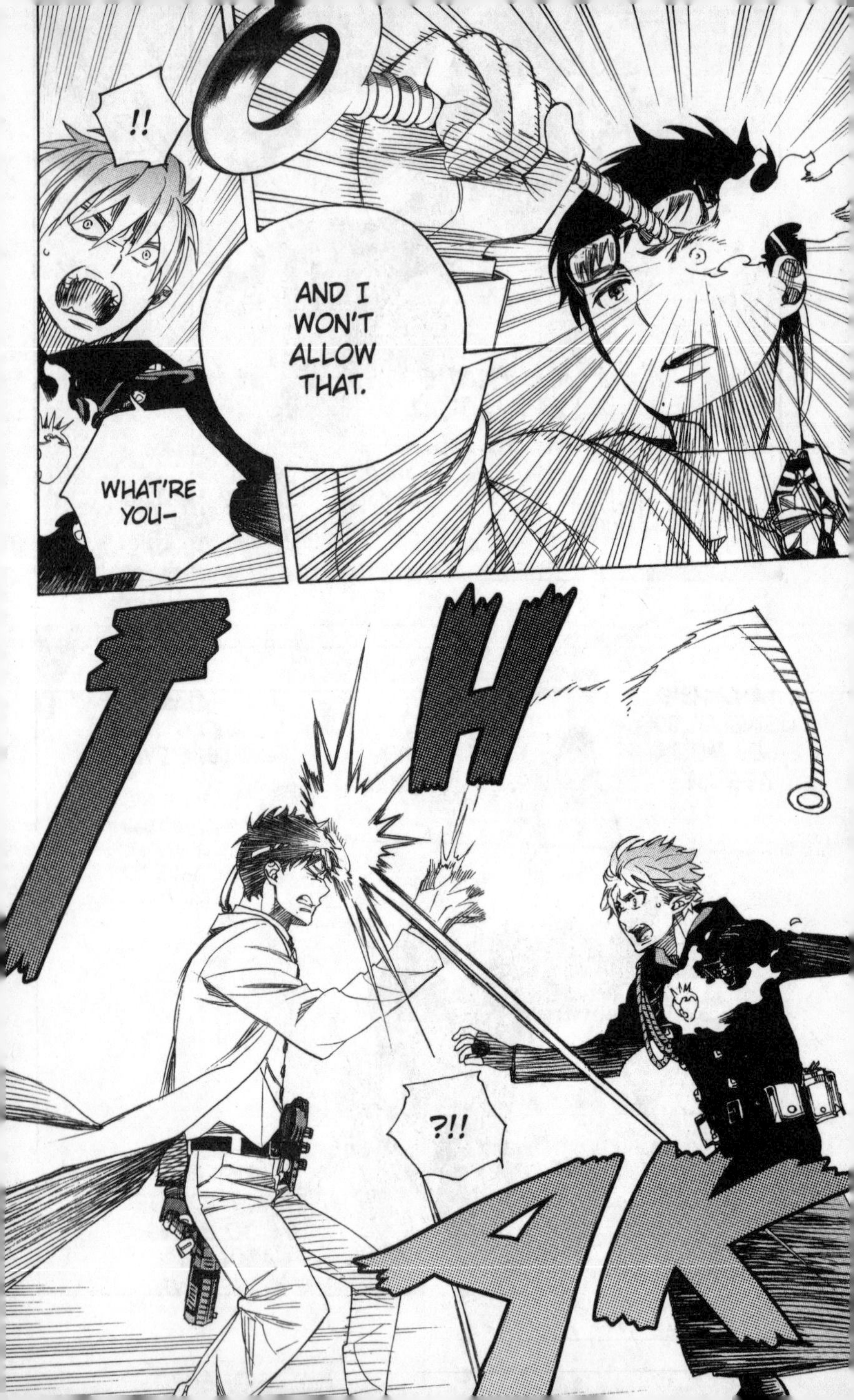
AND I WON'T ALLOW THAT.
!!
WHAT'RE YOU-
TH
?!!
AK

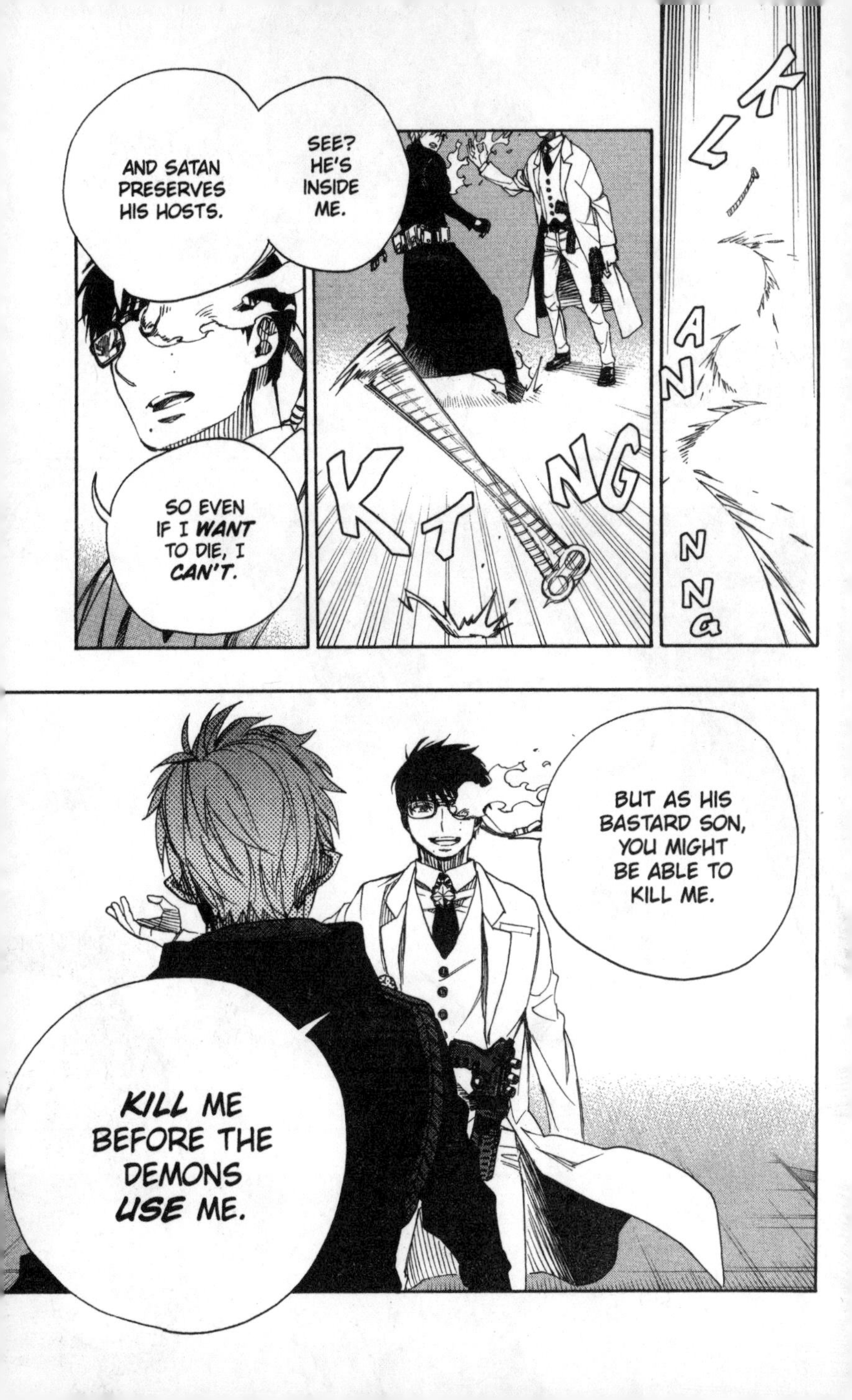
KLANNNG
SEE? HE'S INSIDE ME.
KTNG
AND SATAN PRESERVES HIS HOSTS.
SO EVEN IF I *WANT* TO DIE, I *CAN'T*.
BUT AS HIS BASTARD SON, YOU MIGHT BE ABLE TO KILL ME.
KILL ME BEFORE THE DEMONS *USE* ME.

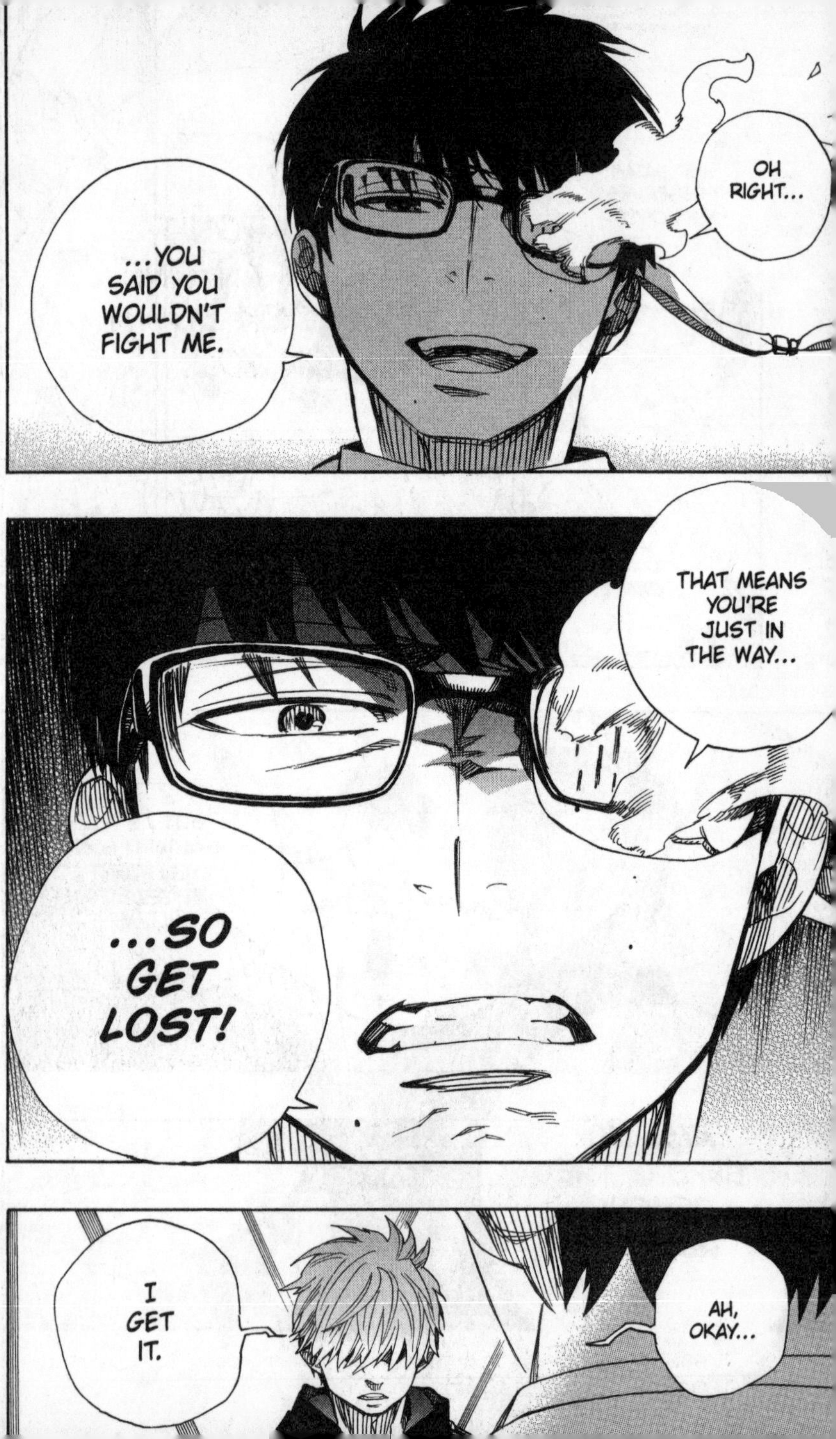
OH RIGHT...
...YOU SAID YOU WOULDN'T FIGHT ME.
THAT MEANS YOU'RE JUST IN THE WAY...
...SO GET LOST!
AH, OKAY...
I GET IT.

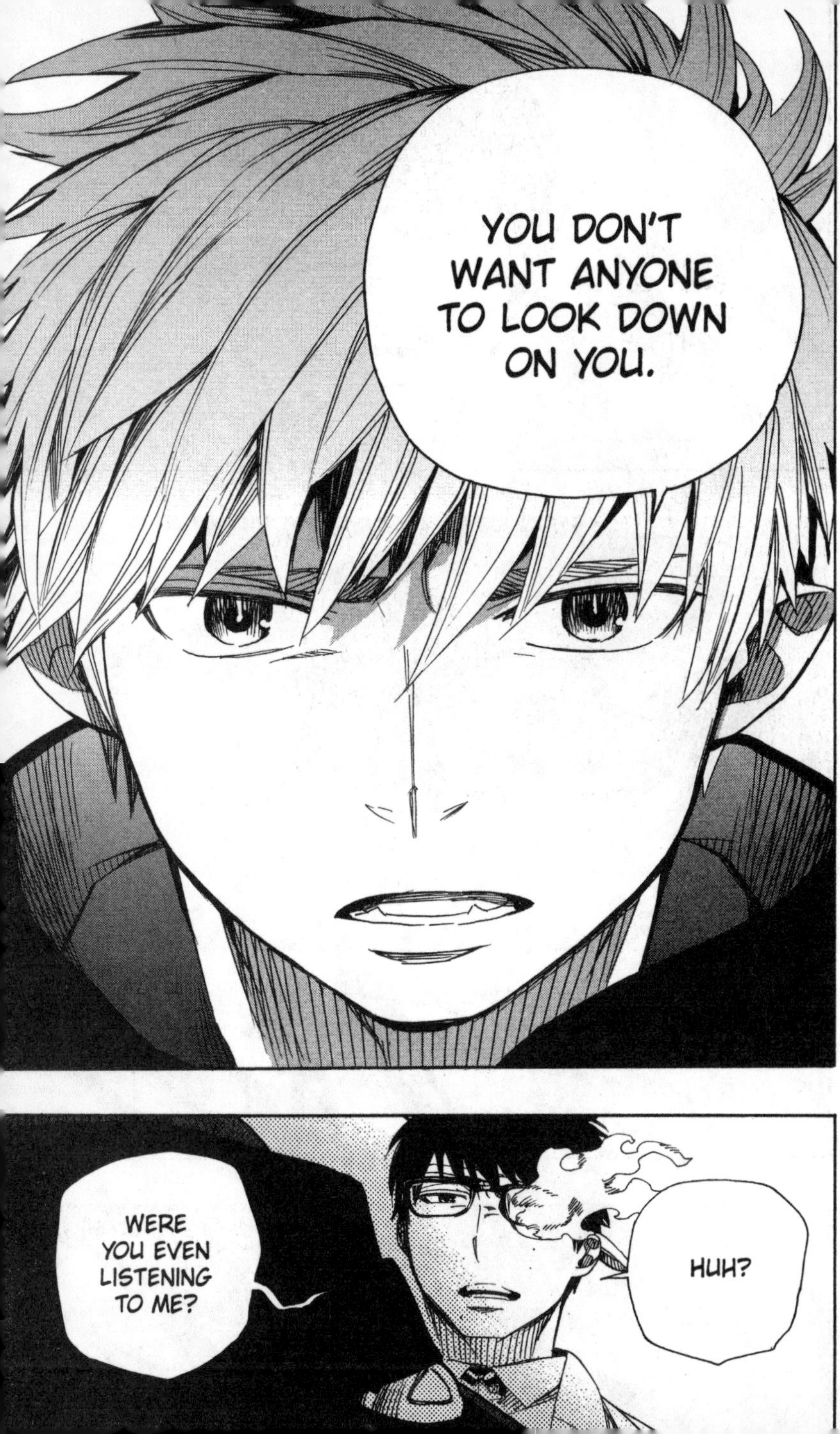
YOU DON'T WANT ANYONE TO LOOK DOWN ON YOU.
HUH?
WERE YOU EVEN LISTENING TO ME?

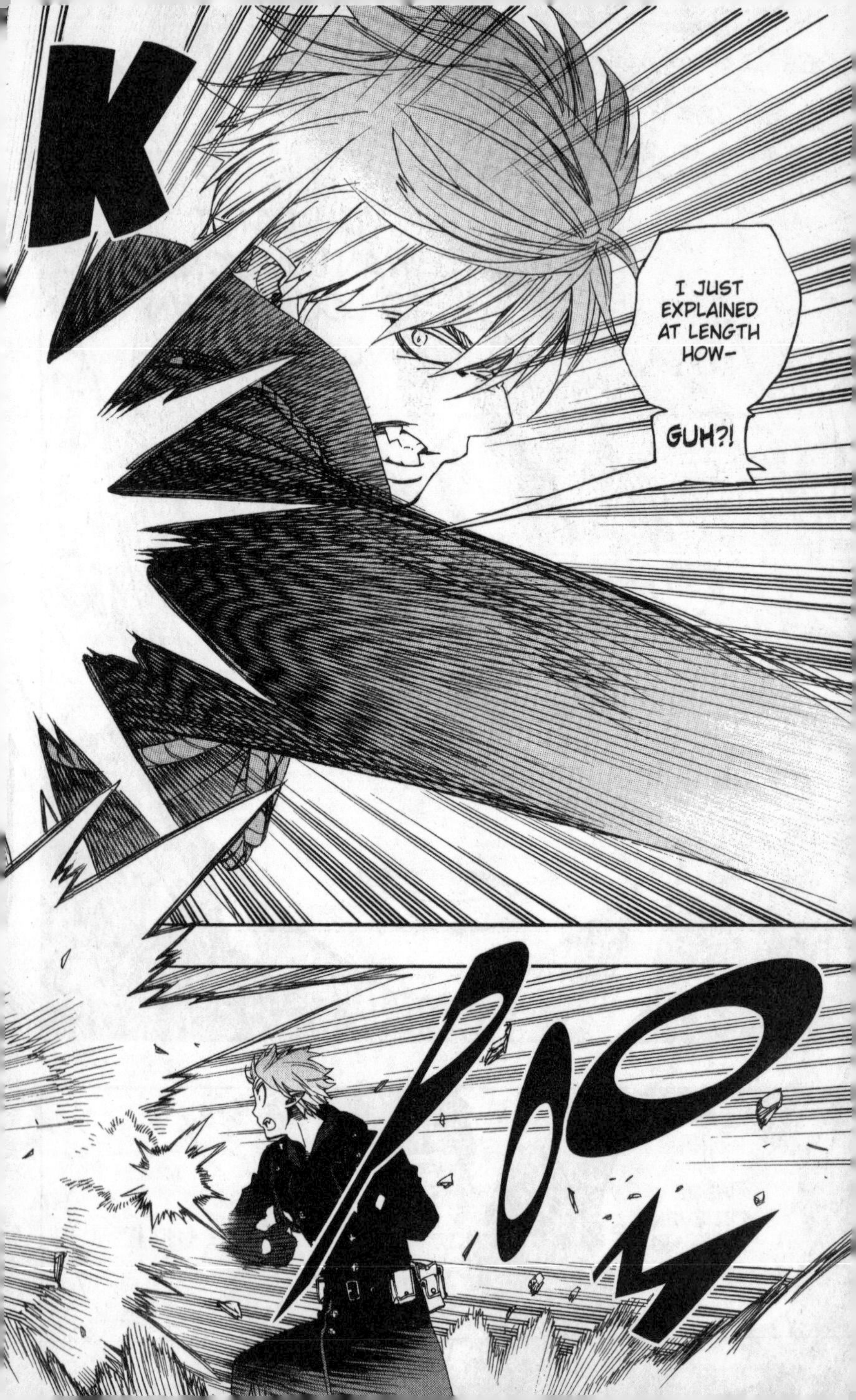
I JUST EXPLAINED AT LENGTH HOW-
GUH?!
K
BOOM

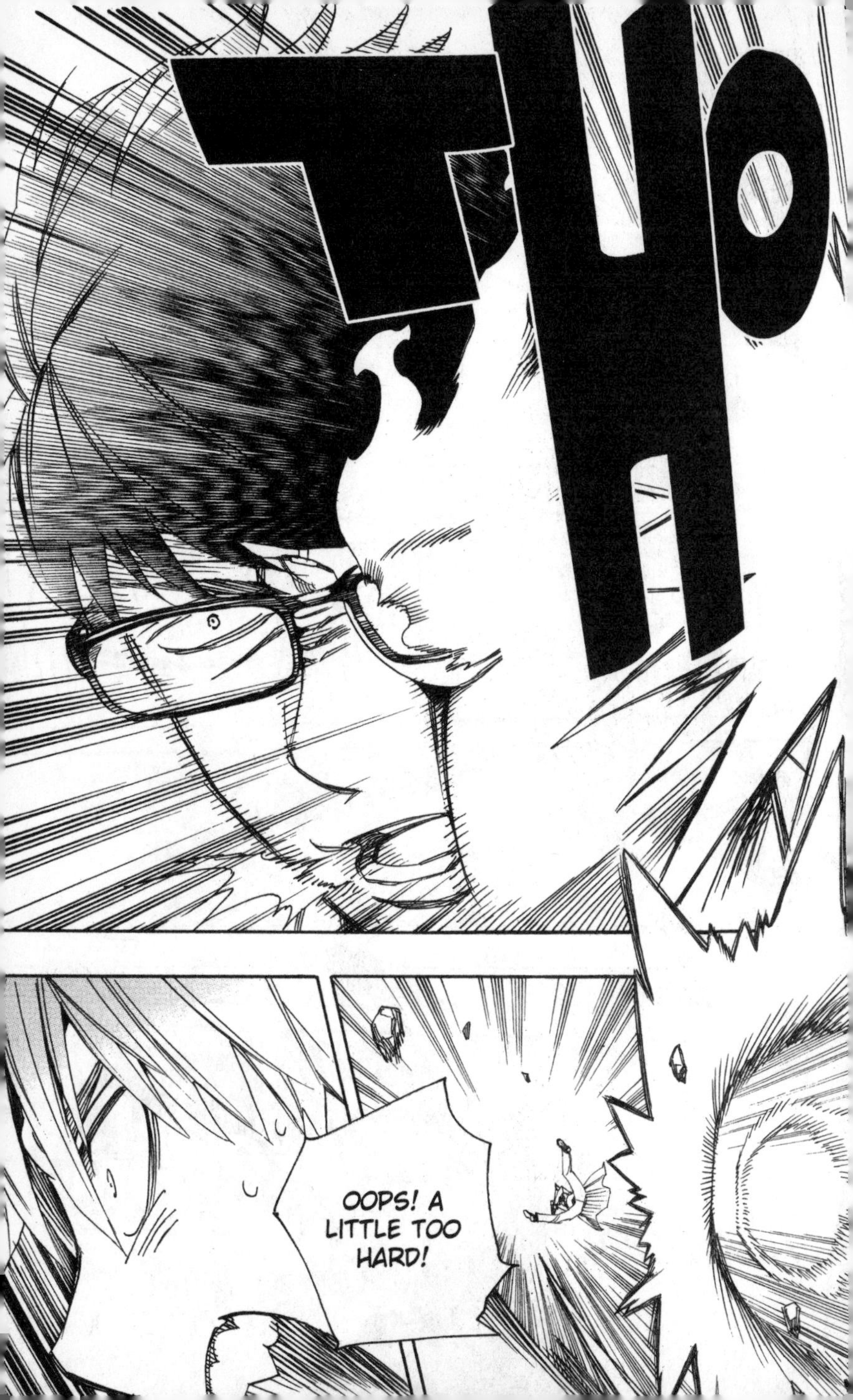
THOK
OOPS! A LITTLE TOO HARD!

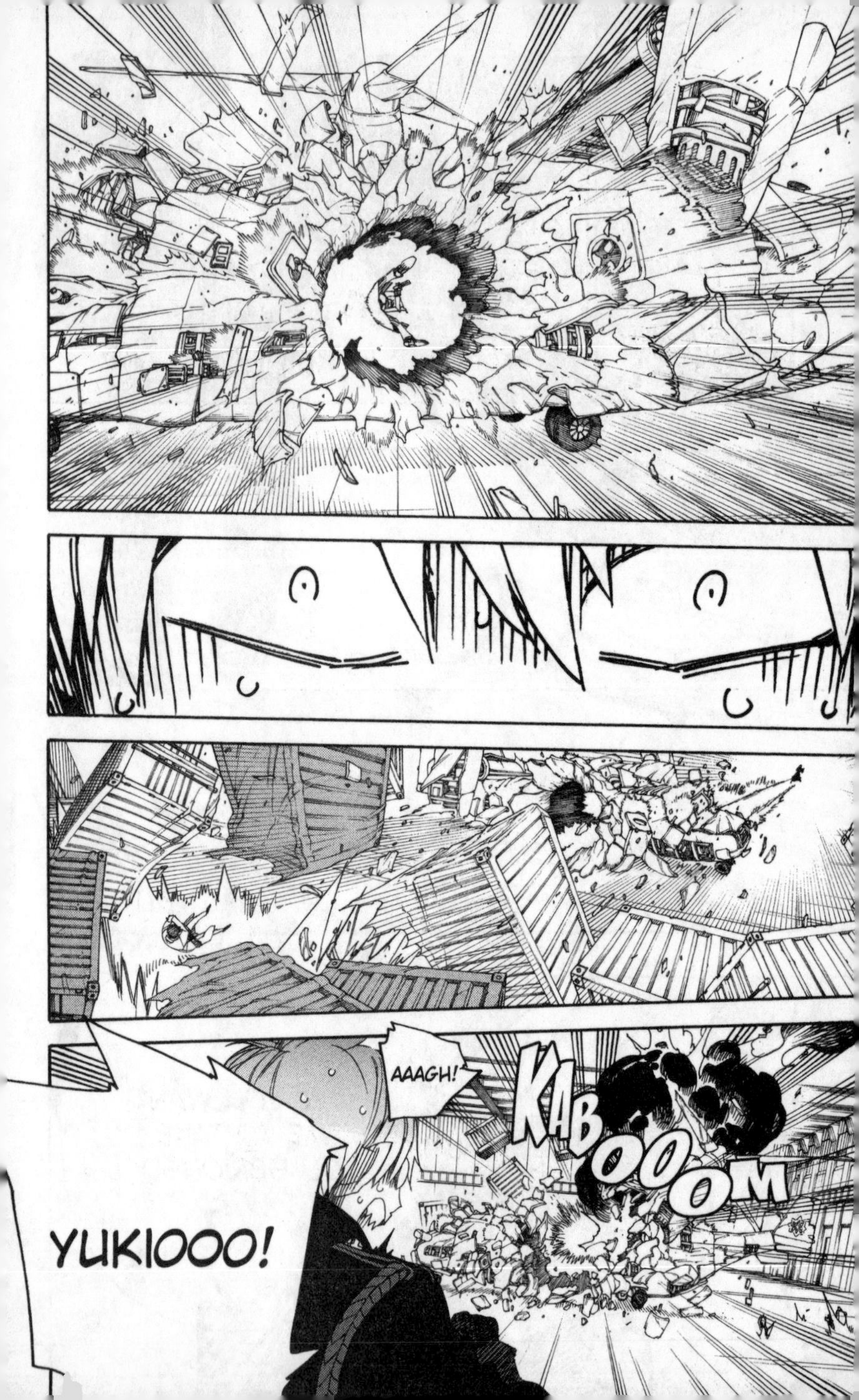

AAAGH!
KABOOOOM
YUKIOOO!

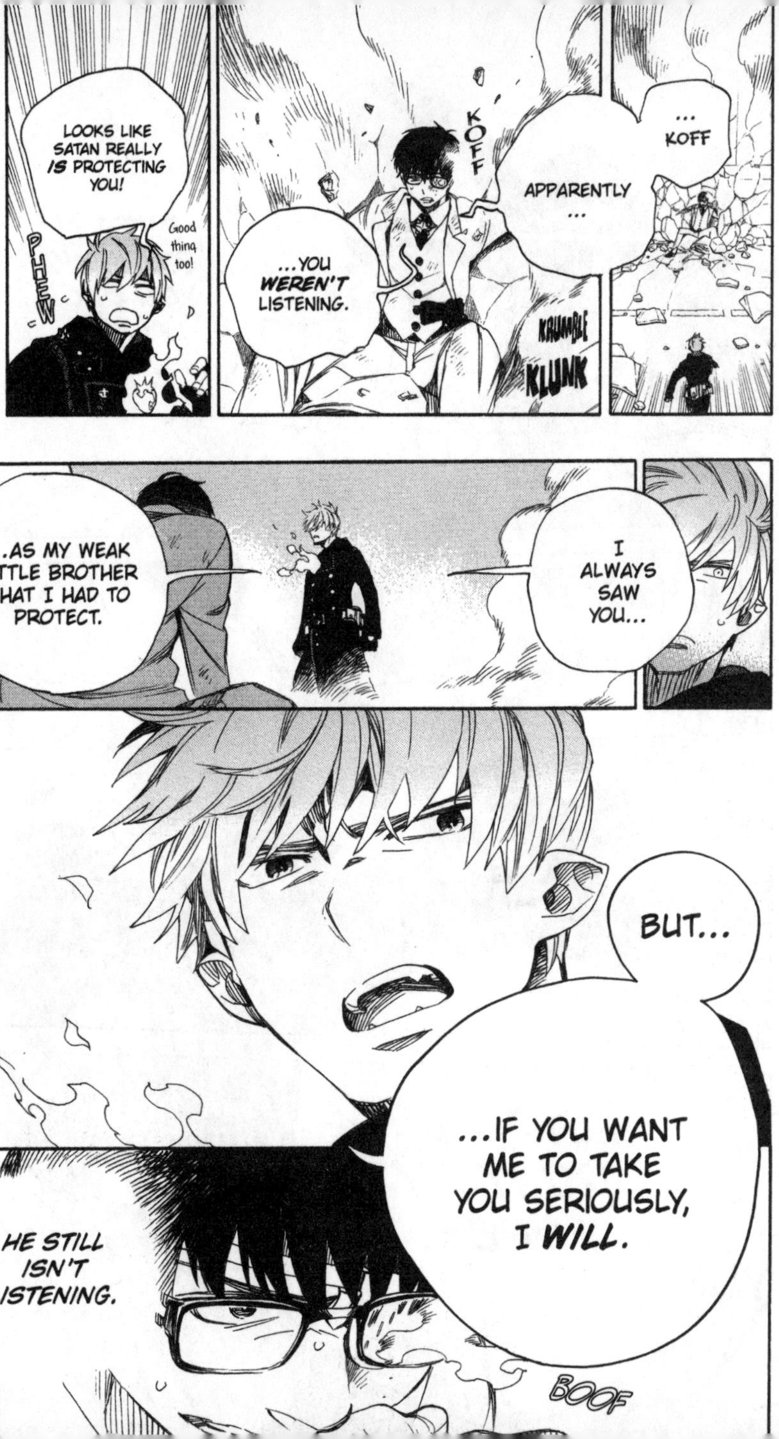
... KOFF
APPARENTLY ...
KOFF
...YOU WEREN'T LISTENING.
KRUMBLE
KLUNK
LOOKS LIKE SATAN REALLY IS PROTECTING YOU!
Good thing too!
PHEW
I ALWAYS SAW YOU...
...AS MY WEAK LITTLE BROTHER THAT I HAD TO PROTECT.
BUT...
...IF YOU WANT ME TO TAKE YOU SERIOUSLY, I WILL.
HE STILL ISN'T LISTENING.
BOOF

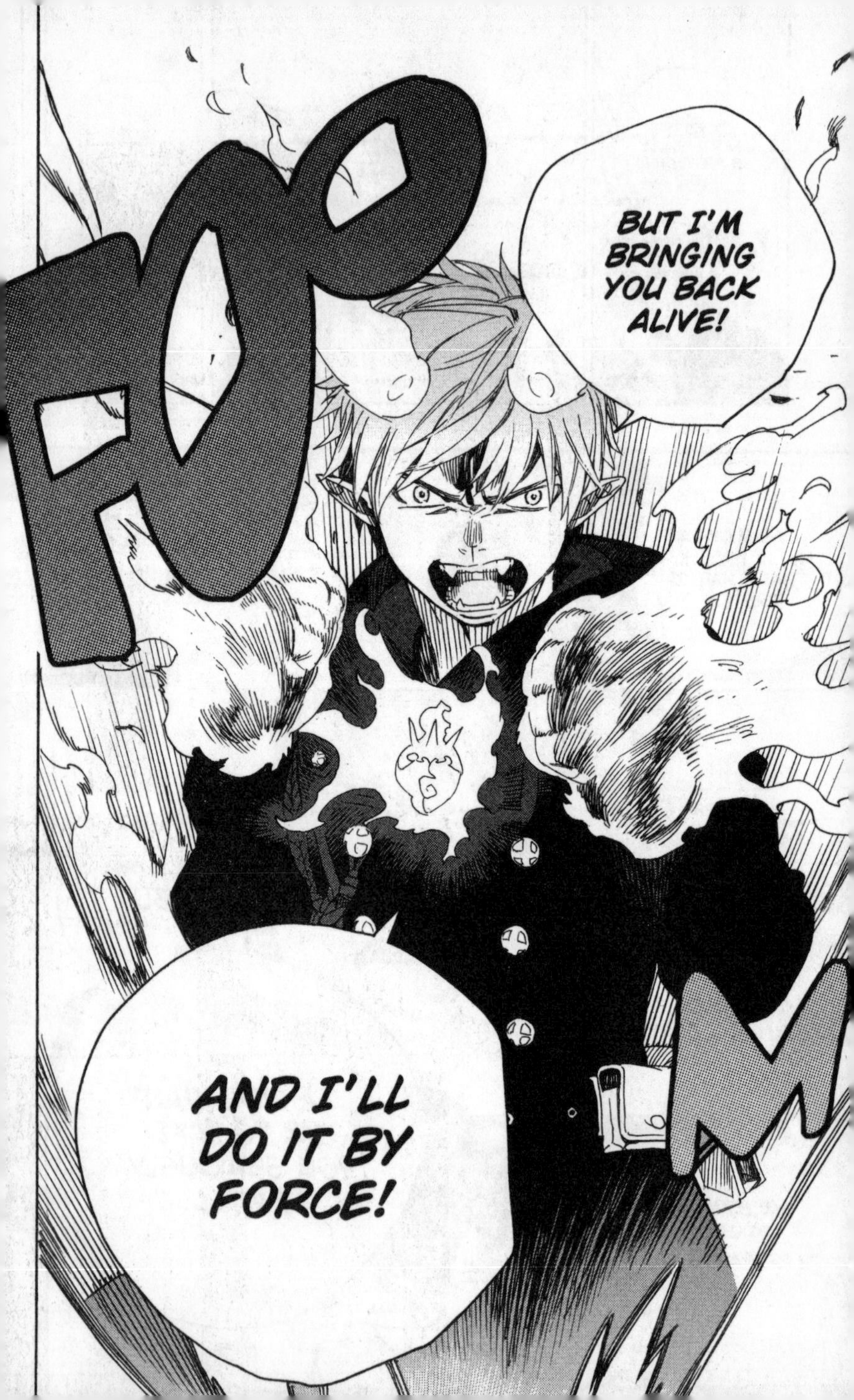
BUT I'M BRINGING YOU BACK ALIVE!
FOO
AND I'LL DO IT BY FORCE!
M

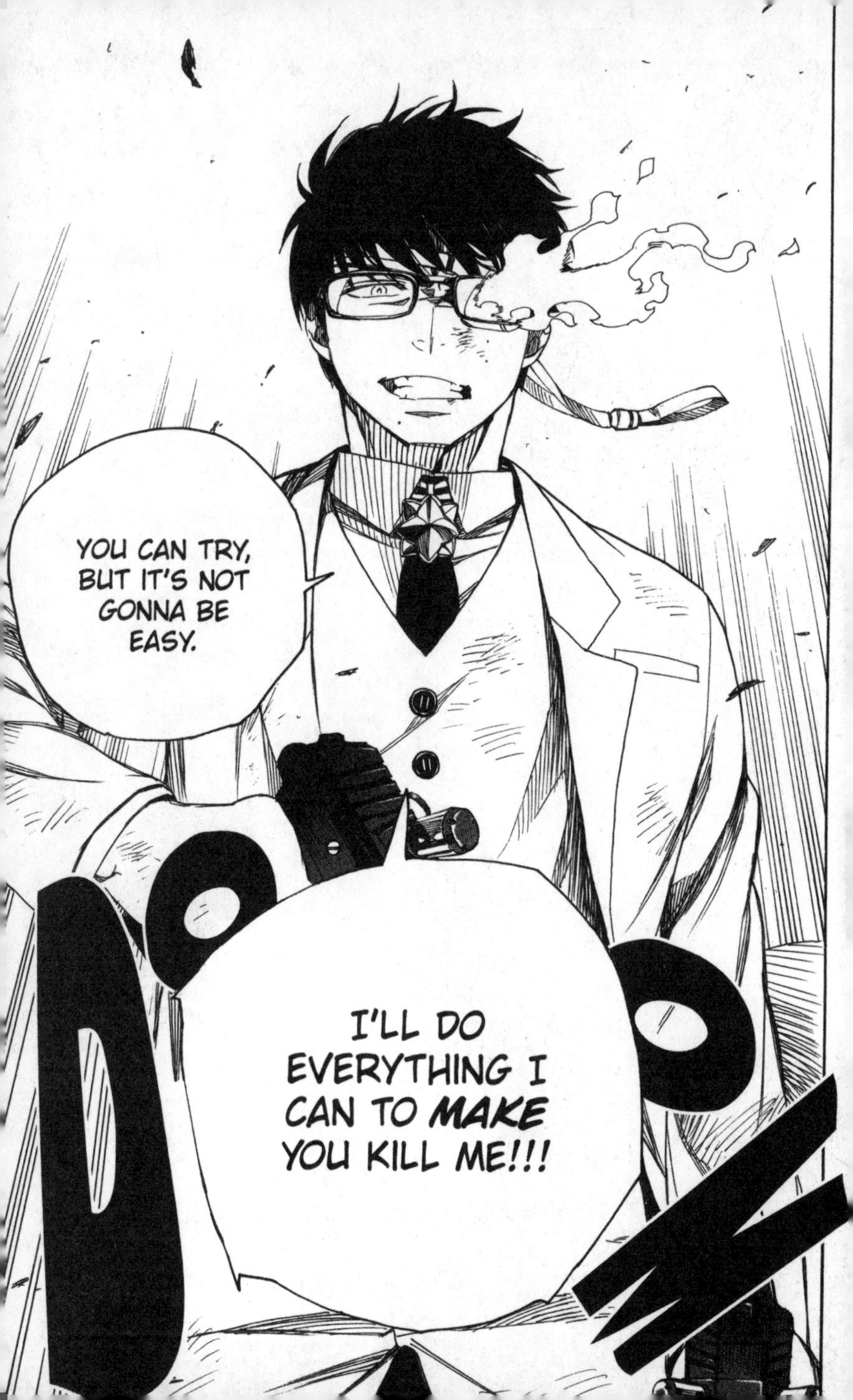
YOU CAN TRY, BUT IT'S NOT GONNA BE EASY.
I'LL DO EVERYTHING I CAN TO *MAKE* YOU KILL ME!!!

Blue Exorcist Chapter 121: Of One Cloth—Preface

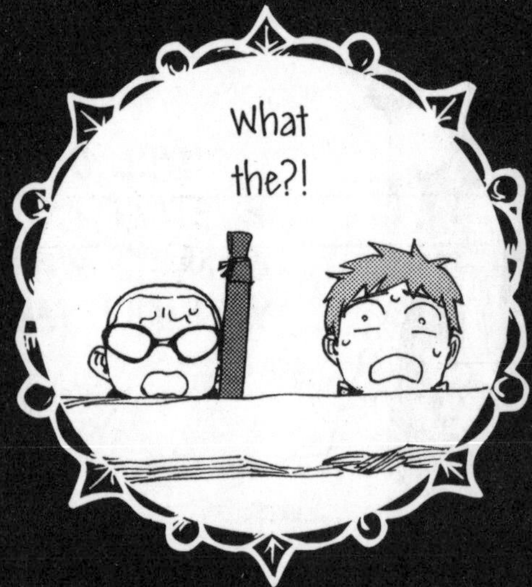
What the?!

Chapter 122: Of One Cloth—Starting a Fire

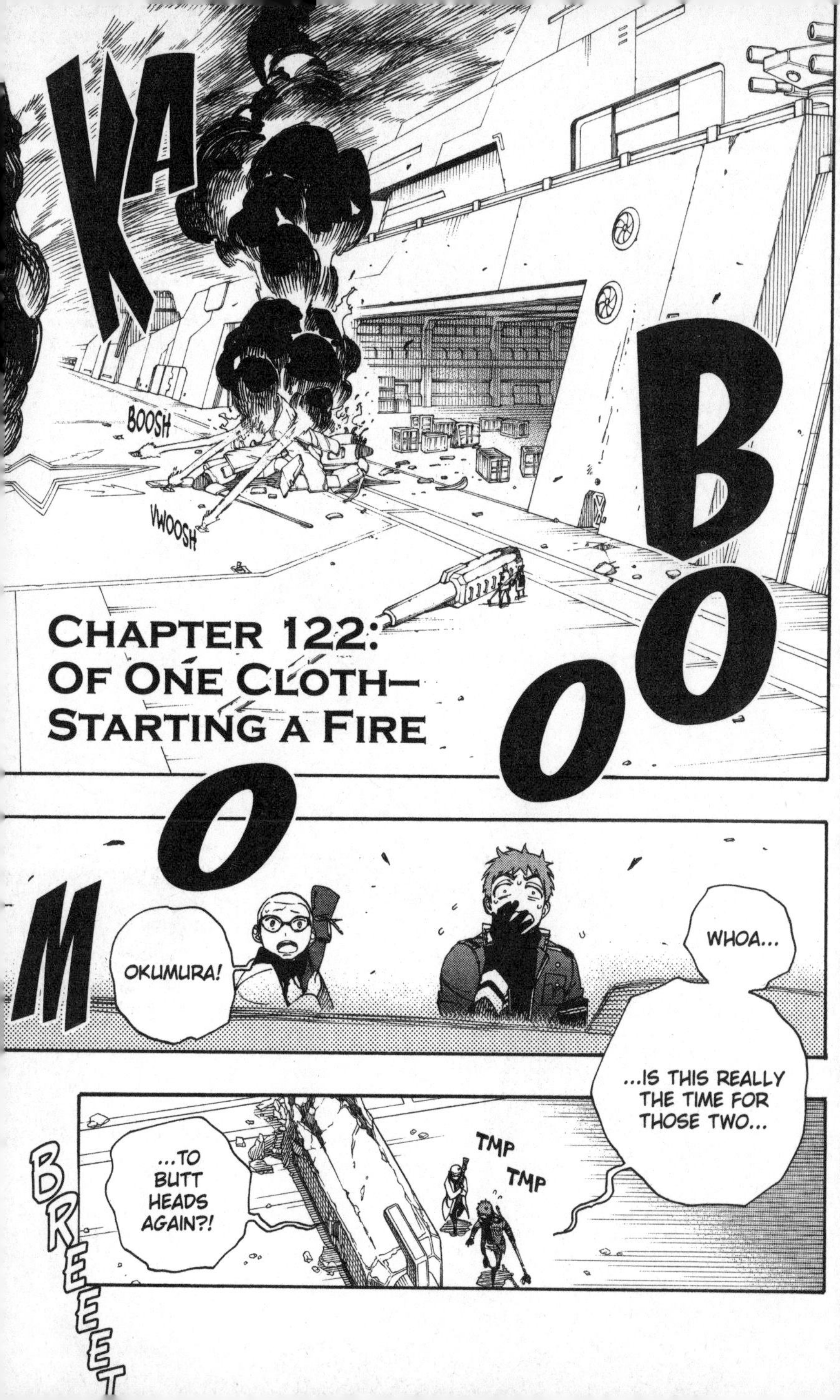
KABOOOOM
BOOSH
VWOOSH
WHOA...
OKUMURA!
...IS THIS REALLY THE TIME FOR THOSE TWO...
TMP
TMP
...TO BUTT HEADS AGAIN?!
BREEEET

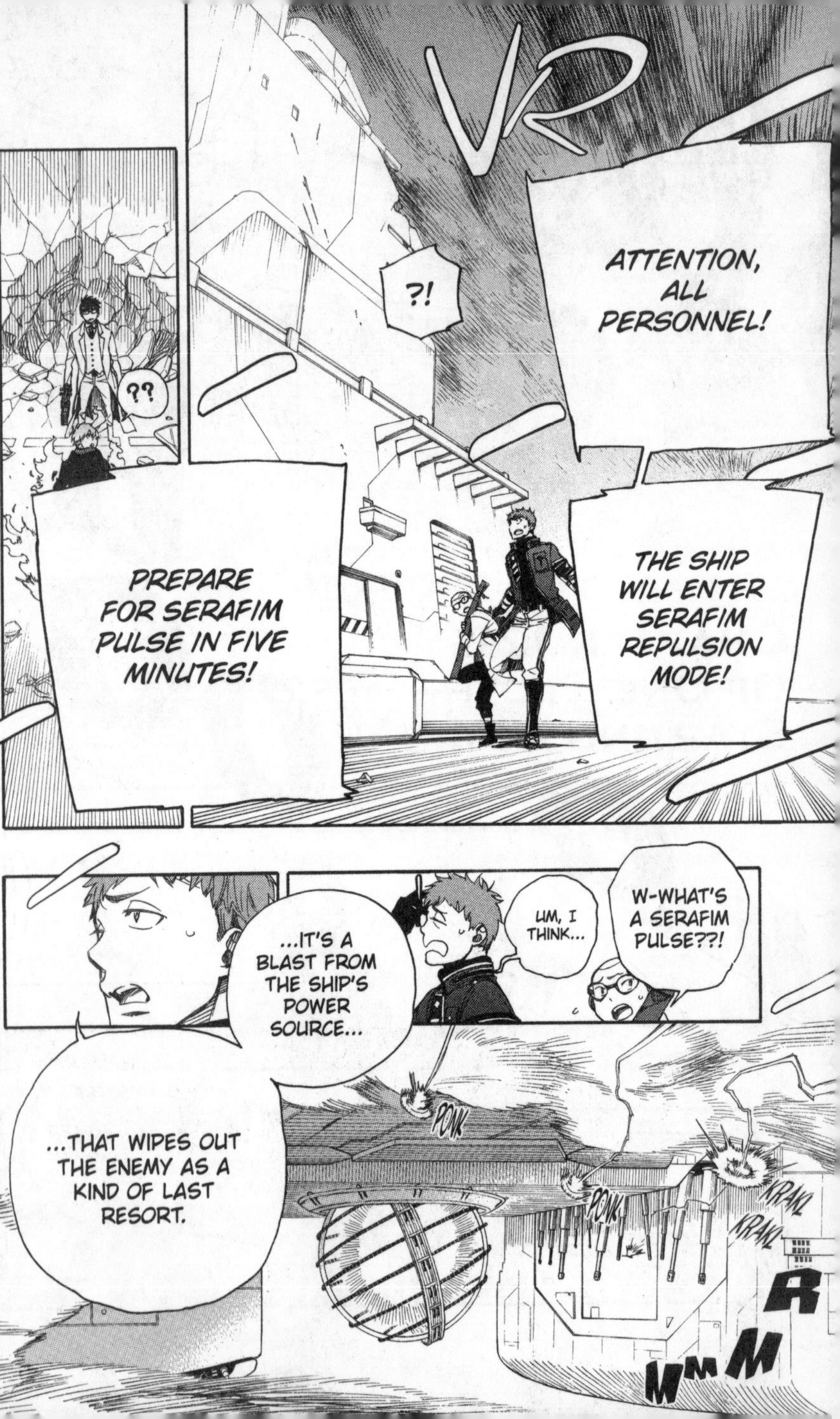

VR
ATTENTION, ALL PERSONNEL!
?!
THE SHIP WILL ENTER SERAFIM REPULSION MODE!
PREPARE FOR SERAFIM PULSE IN FIVE MINUTES!
??
W-WHAT'S A SERAFIM PULSE??!
UM, I THINK...
...IT'S A BLAST FROM THE SHIP'S POWER SOURCE...
...THAT WIPES OUT THE ENEMY AS A KIND OF LAST RESORT.
PONK
PONK
KRAKL
KRAKL
RMMM

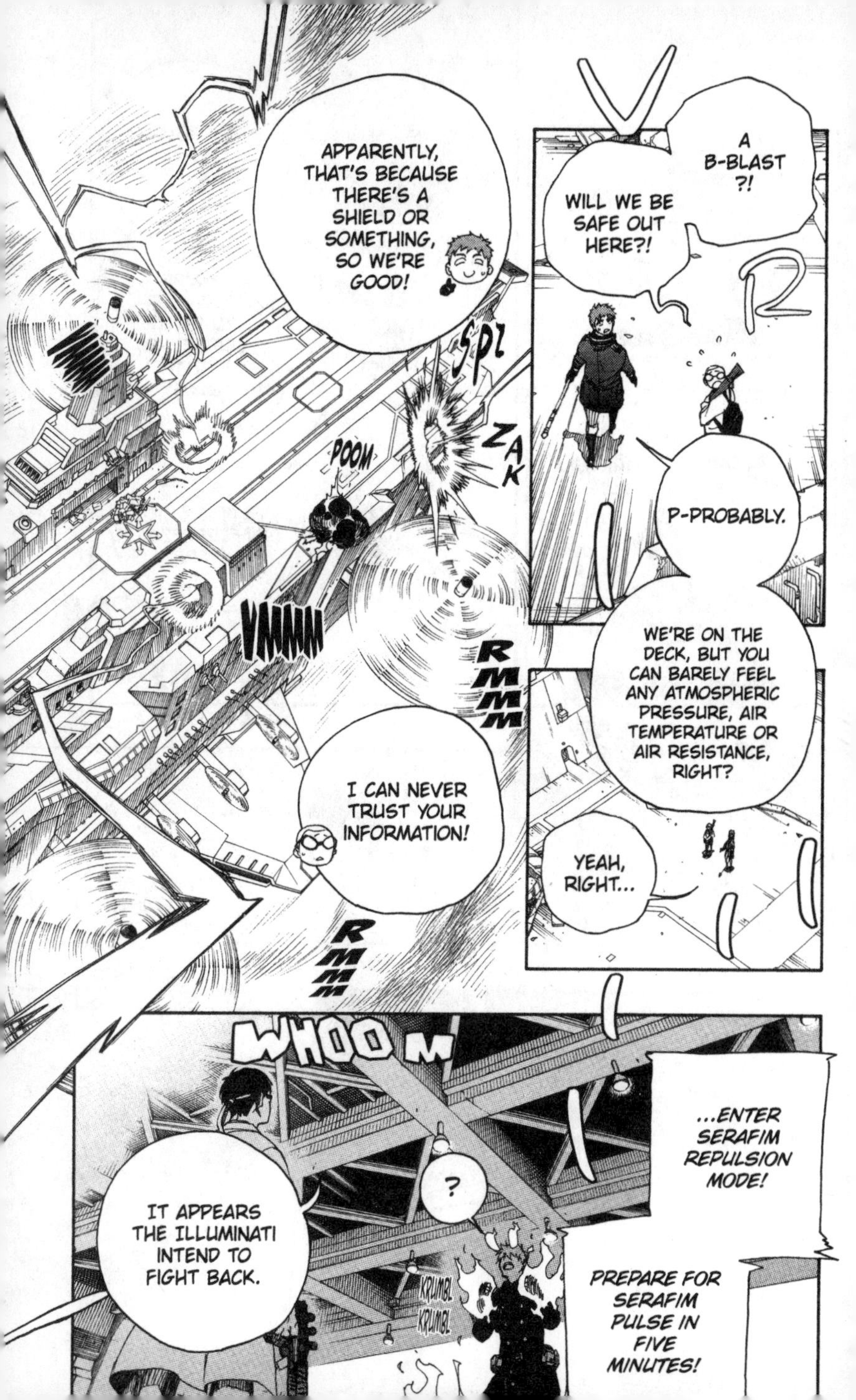
A B-BLAST ?!
WILL WE BE SAFE OUT HERE?!
P-PROBABLY.
WE'RE ON THE DECK, BUT YOU CAN BARELY FEEL ANY ATMOSPHERIC PRESSURE, AIR TEMPERATURE OR AIR RESISTANCE, RIGHT?
YEAH, RIGHT...
APPARENTLY, THAT'S BECAUSE THERE'S A SHIELD OR SOMETHING, SO WE'RE GOOD!
SPZ
ZAK
POOM
VMMM
RMMM
I CAN NEVER TRUST YOUR INFORMATION!
RMMM
WHOOM
...ENTER SERAFIM REPULSION MODE!
PREPARE FOR SERAFIM PULSE IN FIVE MINUTES!
?
KRUMBL KRUMBL
IT APPEARS THE ILLUMINATI INTEND TO FIGHT BACK.

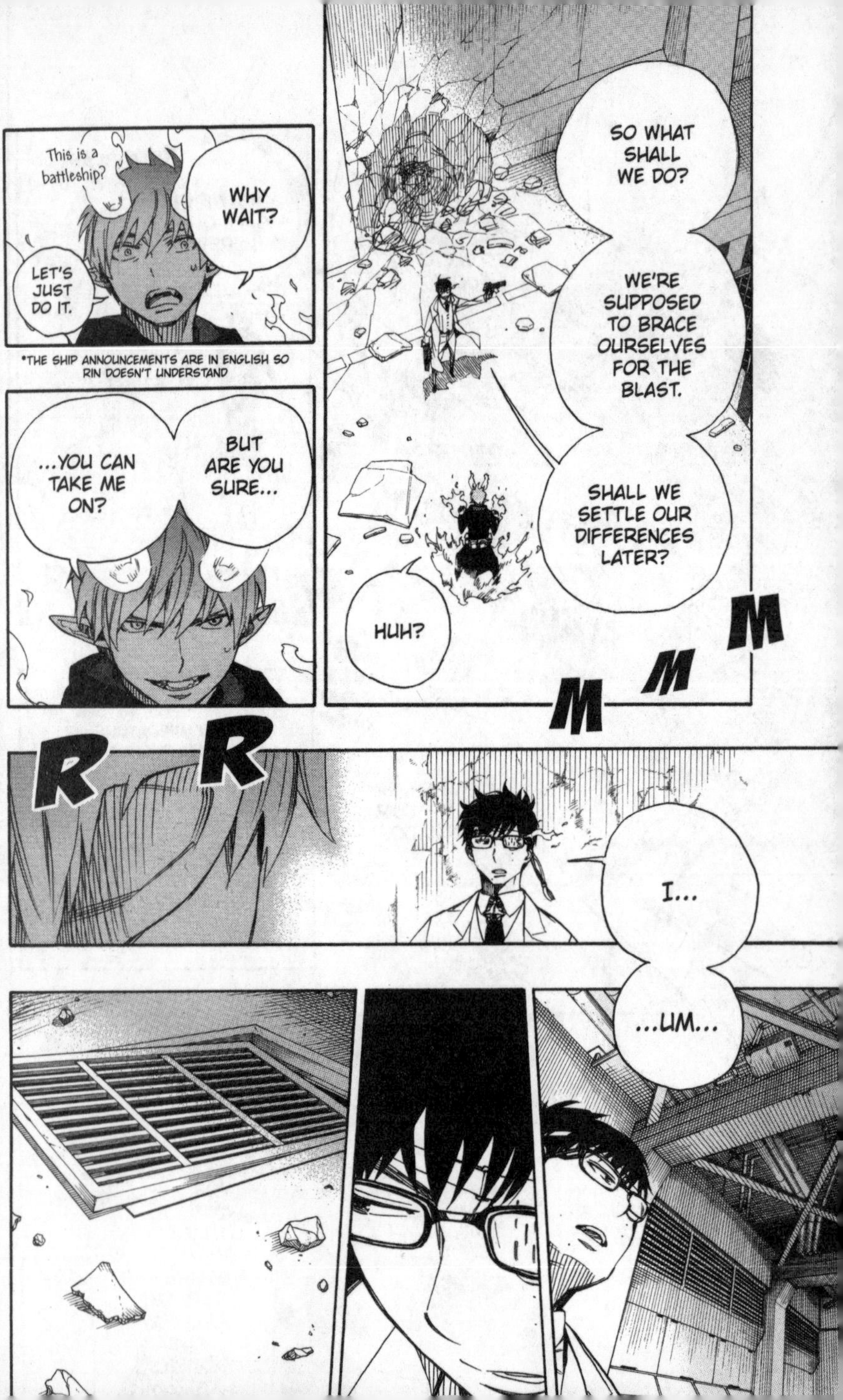
SO WHAT SHALL WE DO?
WE'RE SUPPOSED TO BRACE OURSELVES FOR THE BLAST.
SHALL WE SETTLE OUR DIFFERENCES LATER?
HUH?
This is a battleship?
WHY WAIT?
LET'S JUST DO IT.
*THE SHIP ANNOUNCEMENTS ARE IN ENGLISH SO RIN DOESN'T UNDERSTAND
BUT ARE YOU SURE...
...YOU CAN TAKE ME ON?
MMM
RR
I...
...UM...

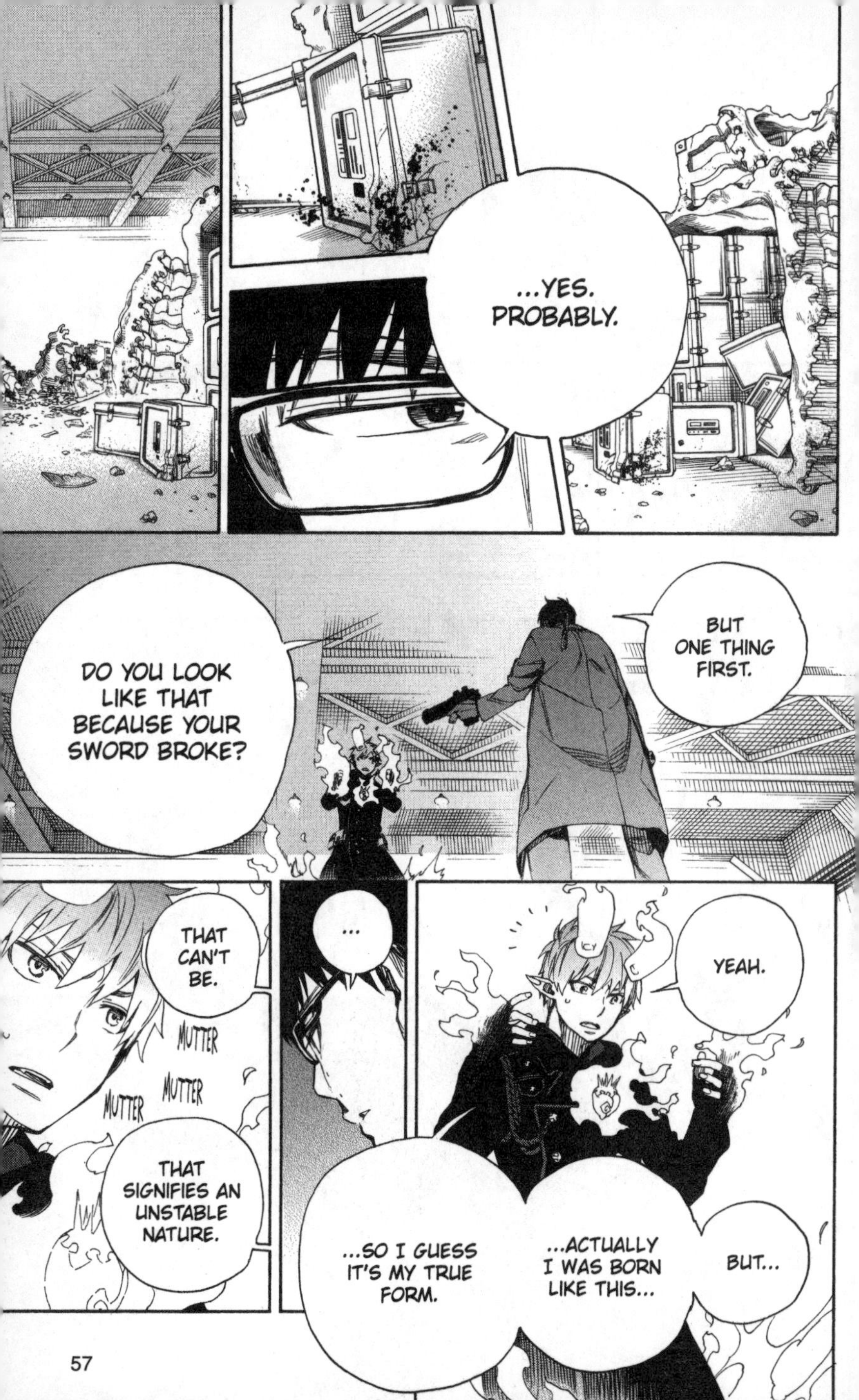
...YES. PROBABLY.
BUT ONE THING FIRST.
DO YOU LOOK LIKE THAT BECAUSE YOUR SWORD BROKE?
YEAH.
BUT...
...ACTUALLY I WAS BORN LIKE THIS...
...SO I GUESS IT'S MY TRUE FORM.
...
THAT CAN'T BE.
MUTTER
MUTTER
MUTTER
THAT SIGNIFIES AN UNSTABLE NATURE.

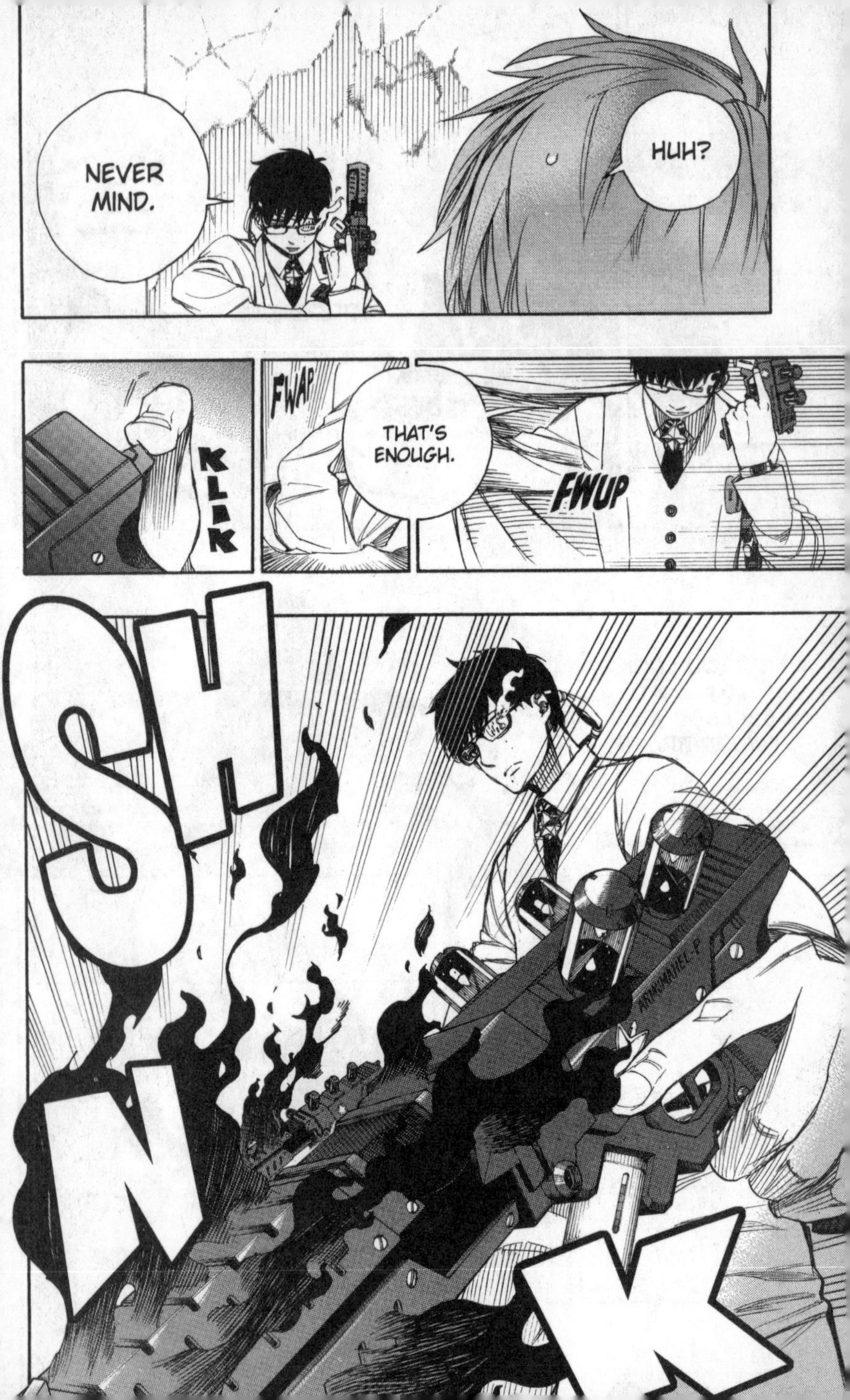
HUH?
NEVER MIND.
FWUP
FWAP
THAT'S ENOUGH.
KLIK
SHNK

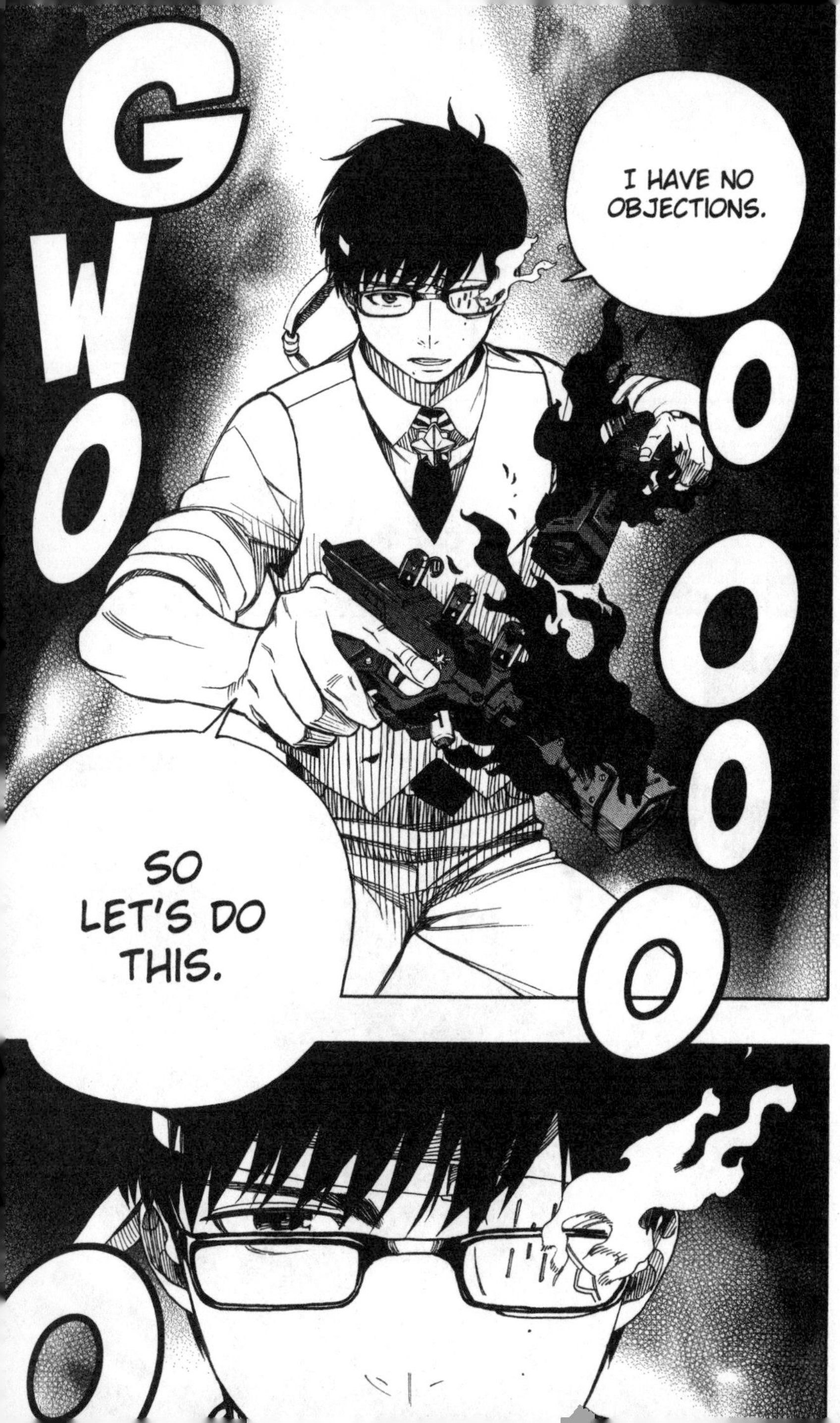
I HAVE NO OBJECTIONS.
GWOOOOOO
SO LET'S DO THIS.

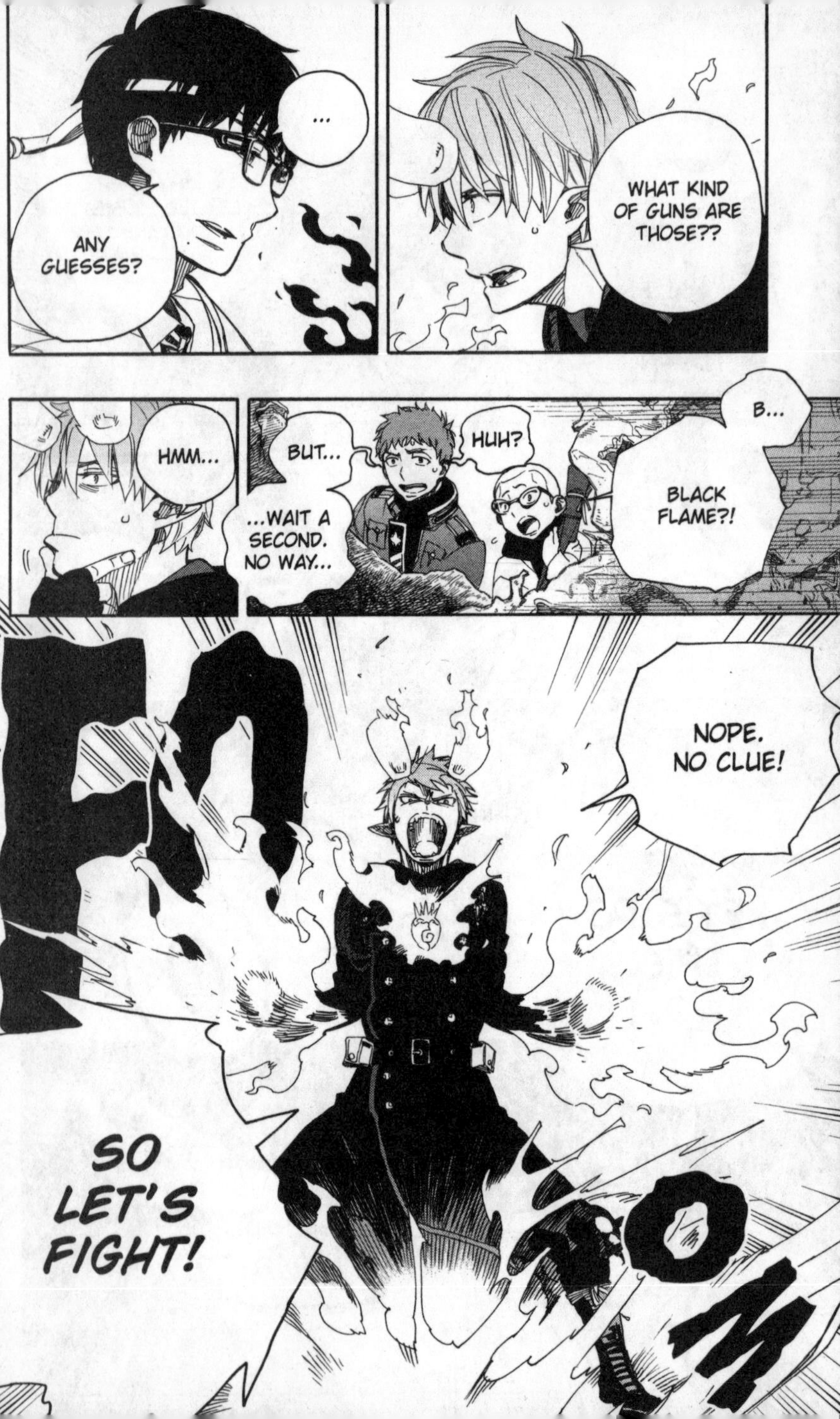
WHAT KIND OF GUNS ARE THOSE??
...
ANY GUESSES?
B...
BLACK FLAME?!
HUH?
BUT...
...WAIT A SECOND. NO WAY...
HMM...
NOPE. NO CLUE!
SO LET'S FIGHT!

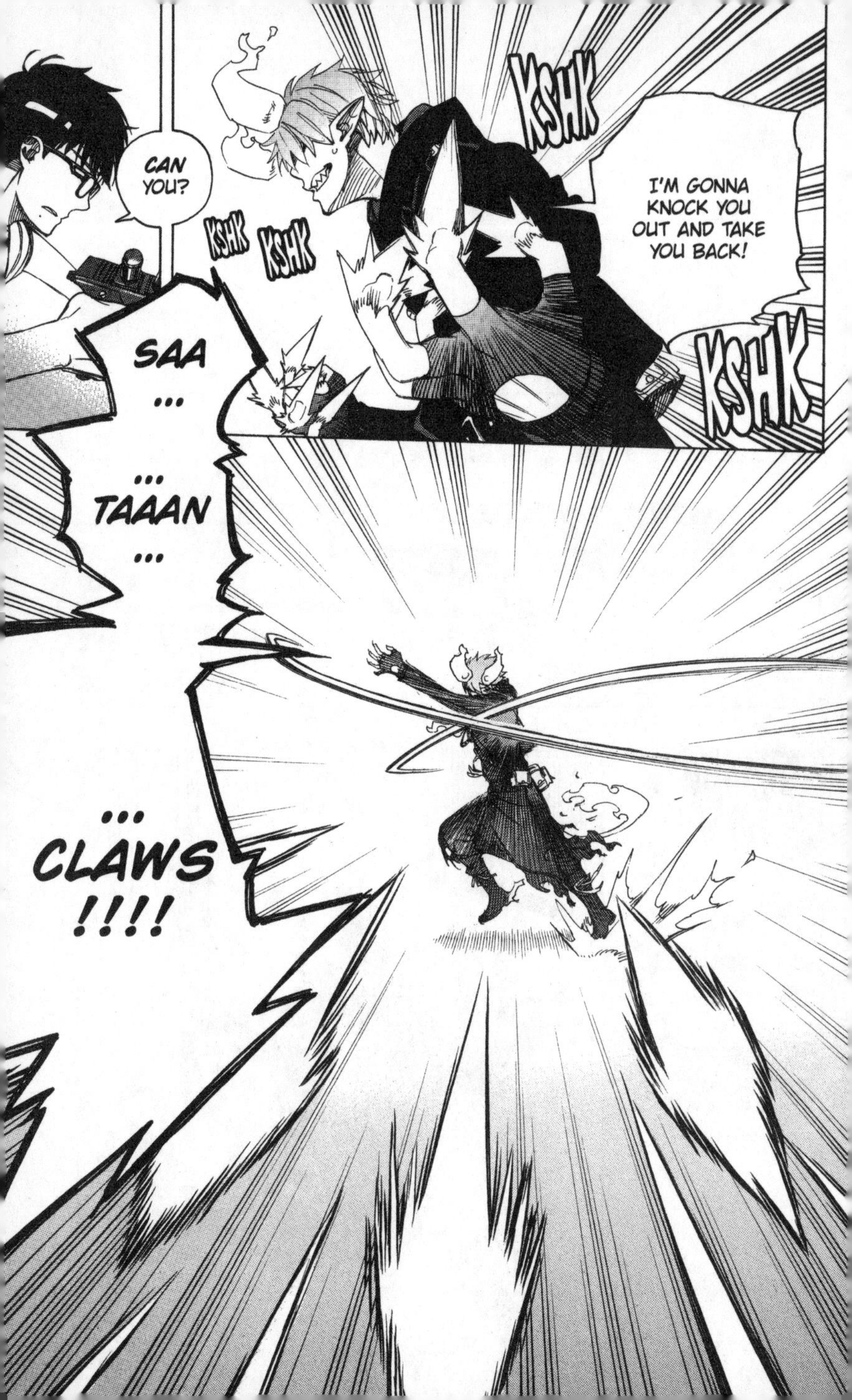
KSHK
I'M GONNA KNOCK YOU OUT AND TAKE YOU BACK!
KSHK
KSHK
KSHK
CAN YOU?
SAA ...
... TAAAN ...
... CLAWS !!!!

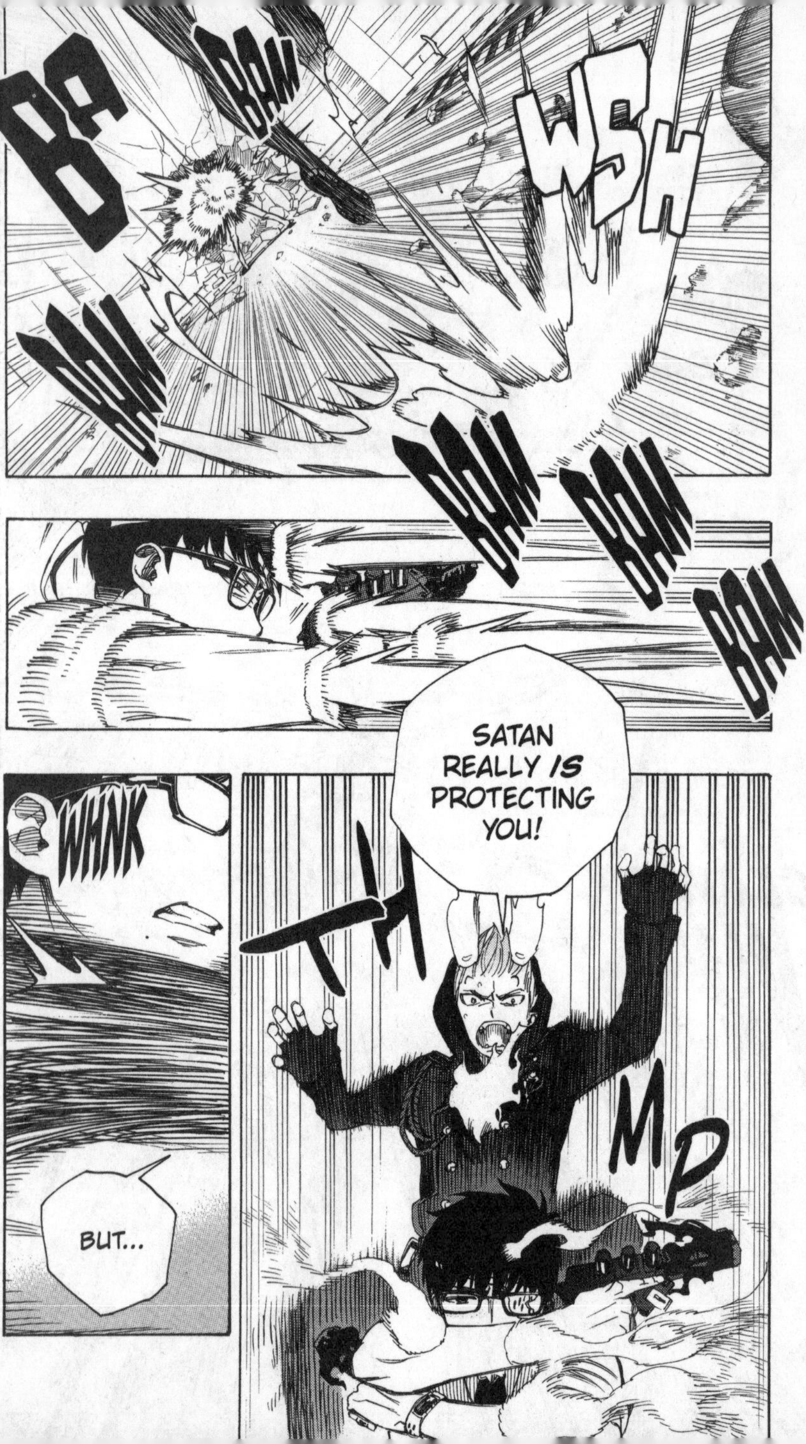
WSH
BA BAM
BAM
BAM
BAM
BAM
BAM
SATAN REALLY *IS* PROTECTING YOU!
THMP
WHNK
BUT...

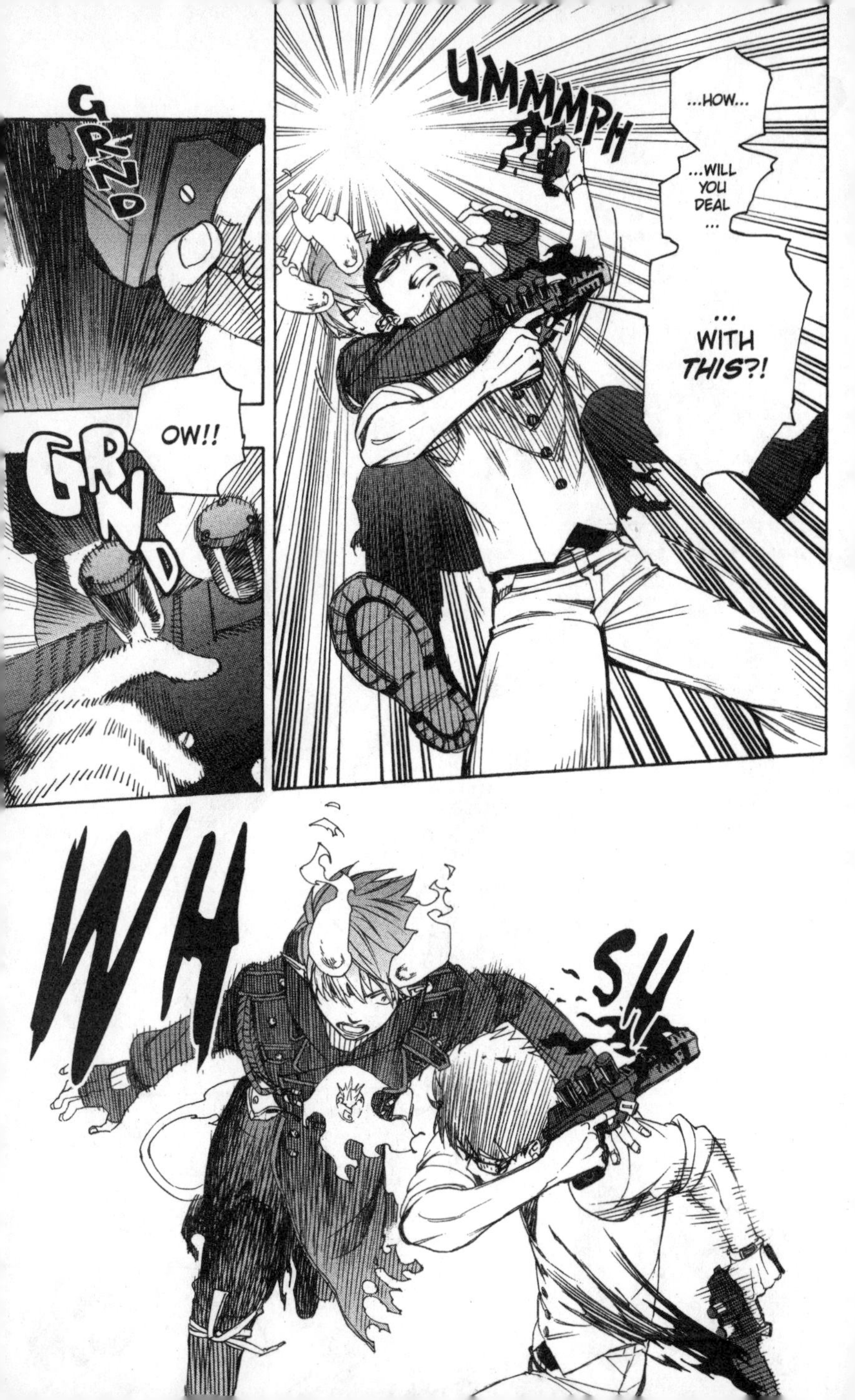
UMMMPH
...HOW...
...WILL YOU DEAL ...
... WITH THIS?!
GRND
OW!!
GRND
WH SH

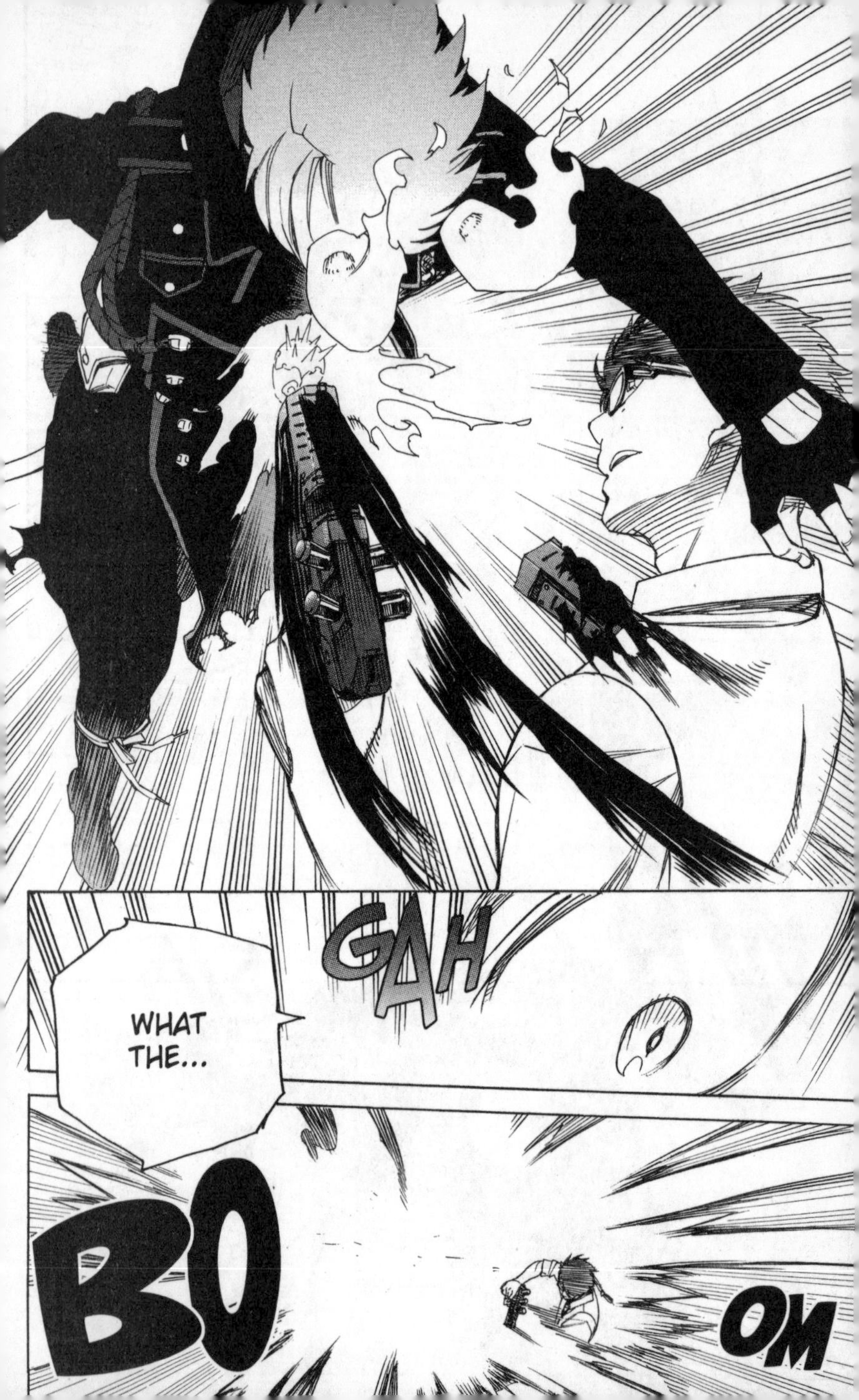
GAH
WHAT THE...
BOOM

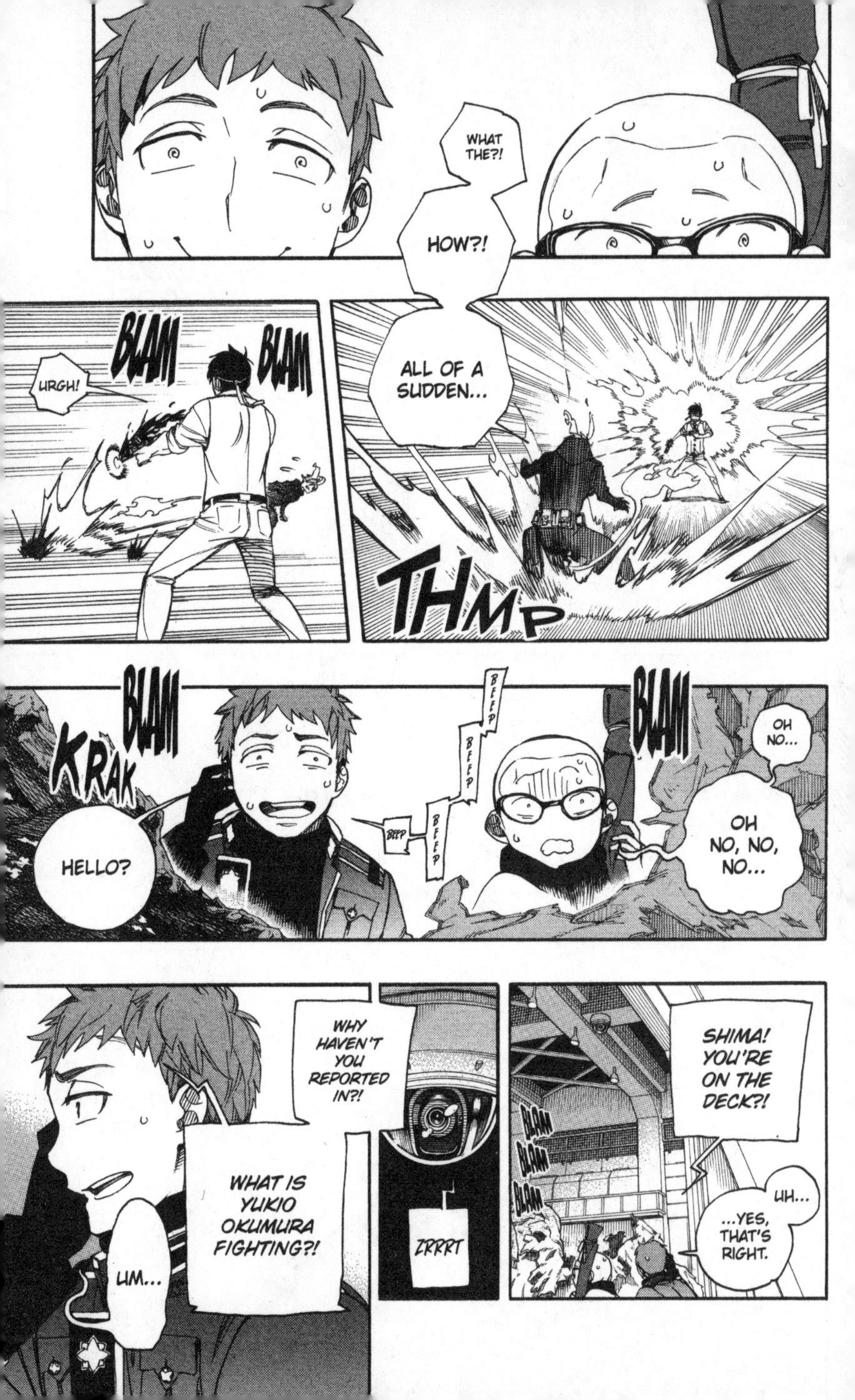
WHAT THE?!
HOW?!
ALL OF A SUDDEN...
THMP
BLAM
BLAM
URGH!
OH NO...
OH NO, NO, NO...
BLAM
BEEP
BEEP
BEEP
BEEP
BLAM
KRAK
HELLO?
SHIMA! YOU'RE ON THE DECK?!
BLAM
BLAM
BLAM
UH...
...YES, THAT'S RIGHT.
WHY HAVEN'T YOU REPORTED IN?!
ZRRRT
WHAT IS YUKIO OKUMURA FIGHTING?!
UM...

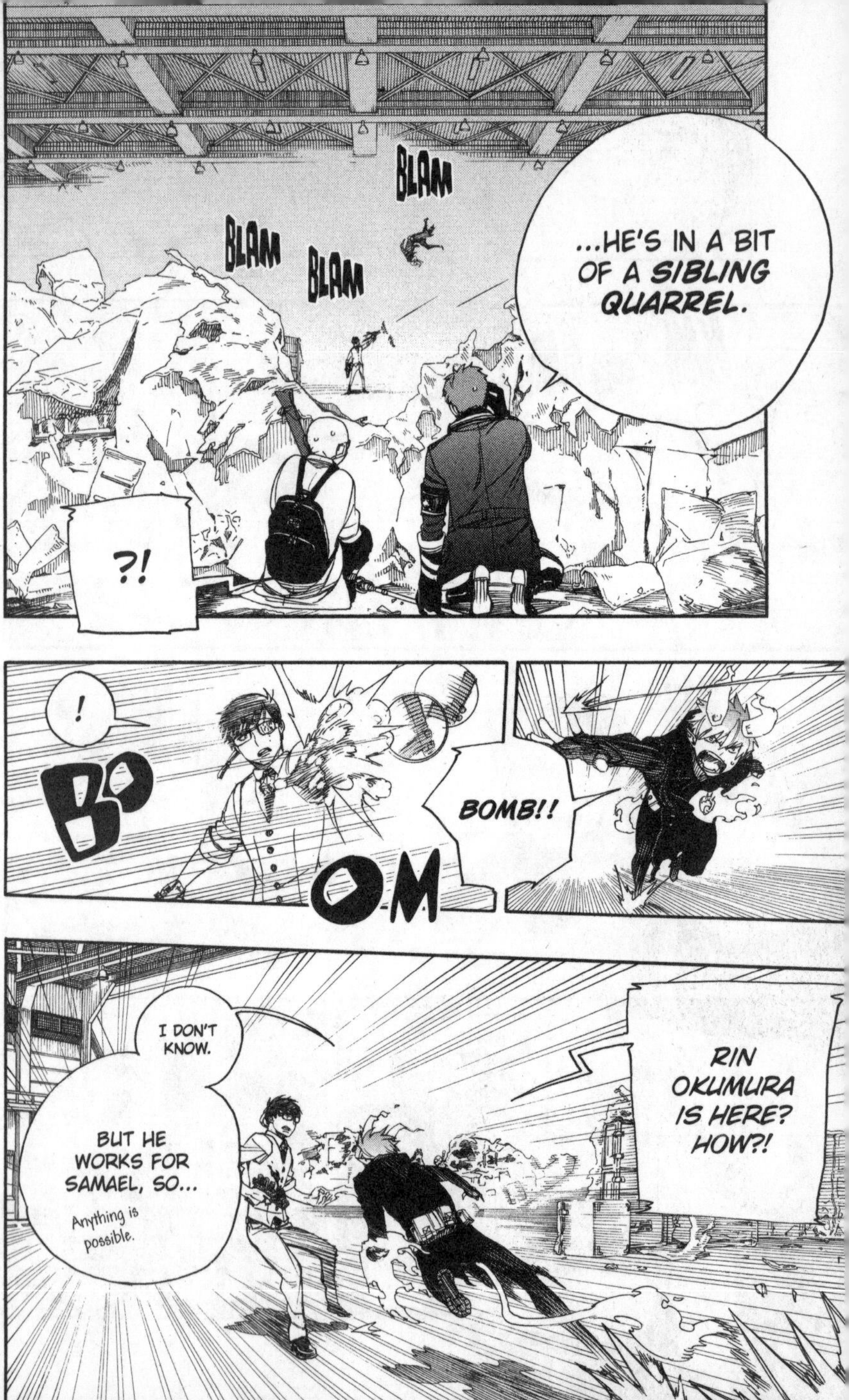
...HE'S IN A BIT OF A SIBLING QUARREL.
BLAM
BLAM
BLAM
?!
BOMB!!
!
BOOM
RIN OKUMURA IS HERE? HOW?!
I DON'T KNOW.
BUT HE WORKS FOR SAMAEL, SO...
Anything is possible.

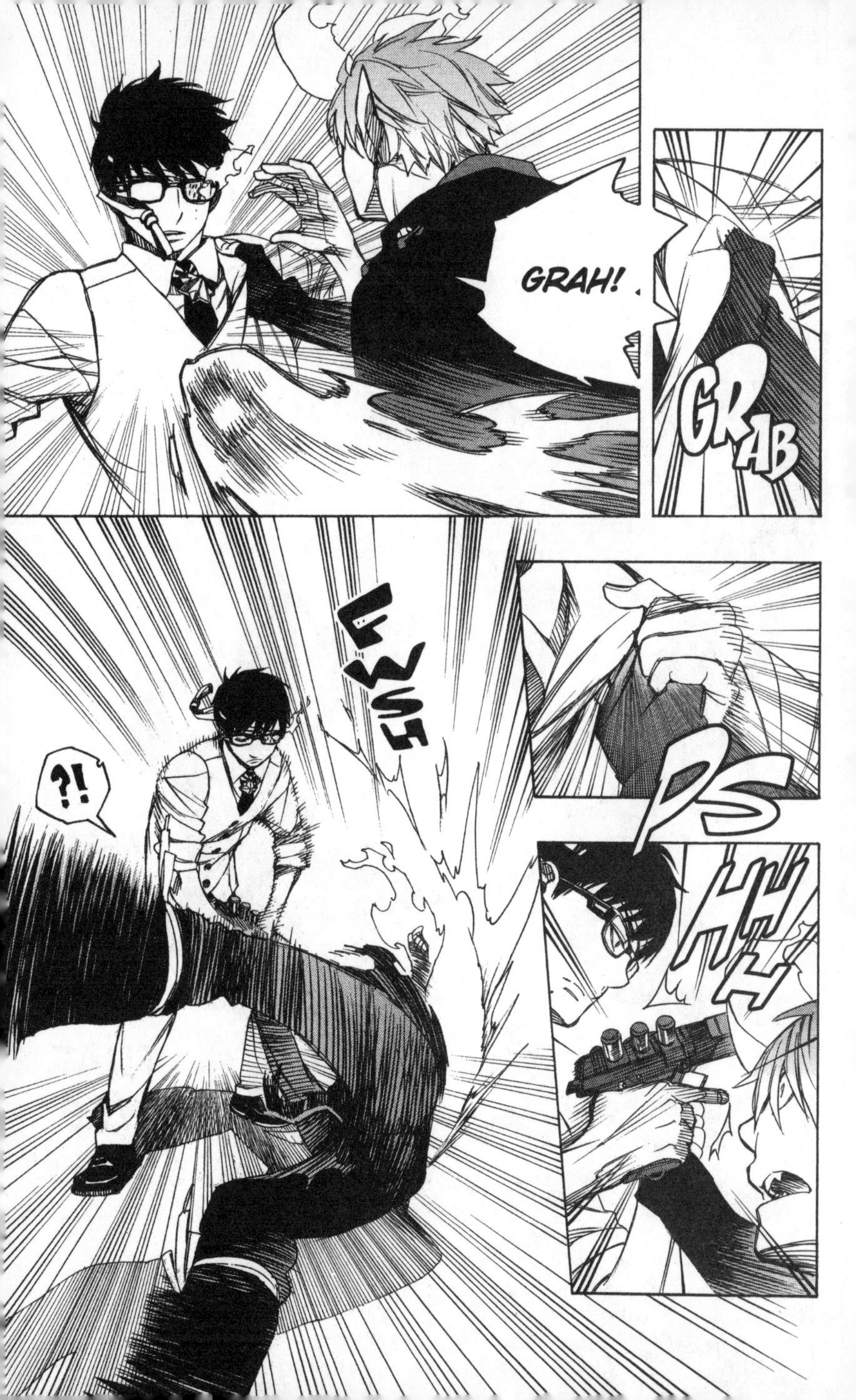
GRAB
GRAH!
PS
HHH
FWSH
?!

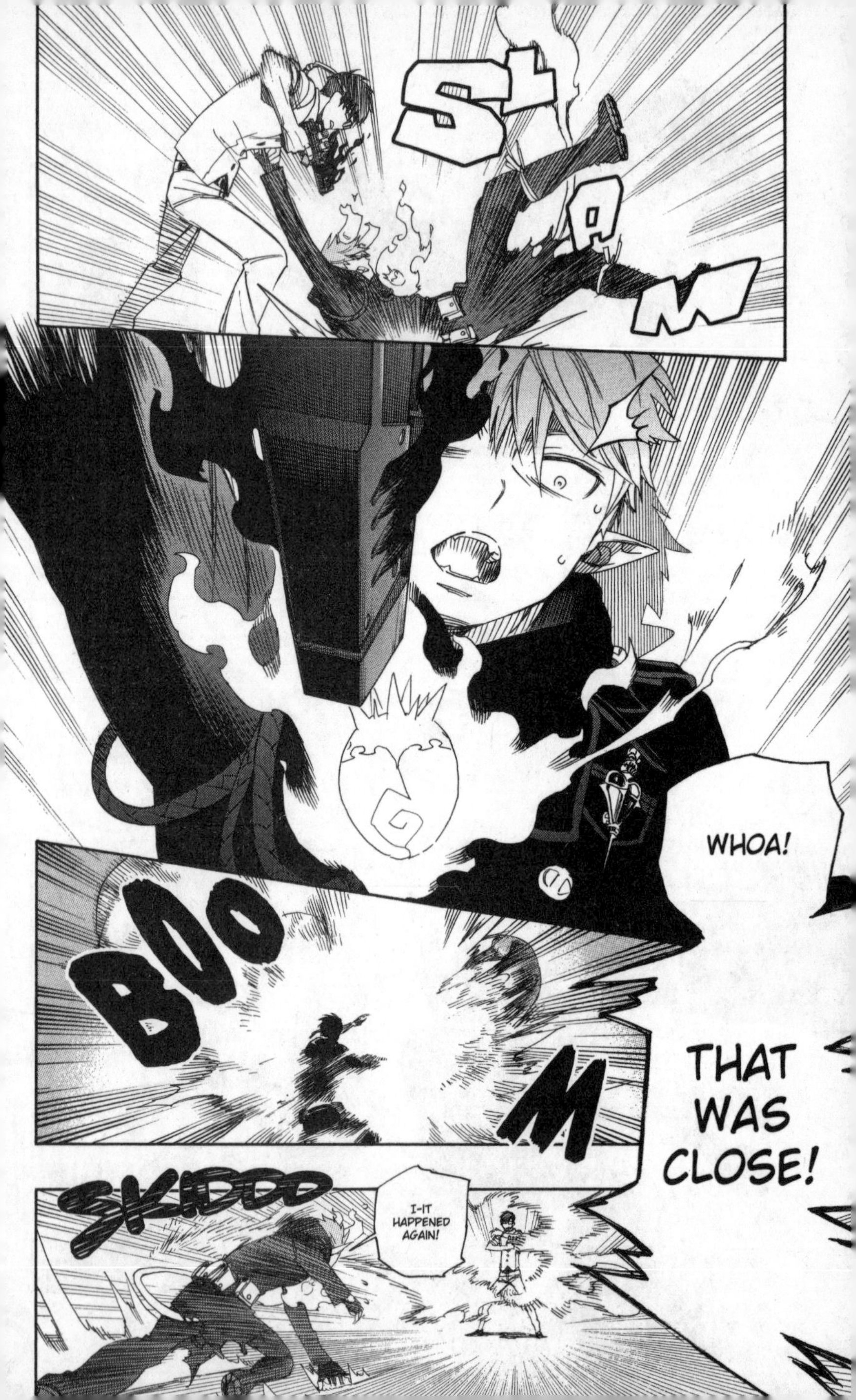
SLAM
WHOA!
BOOM
THAT WAS CLOSE!
SKIDDD
I-IT HAPPENED AGAIN!

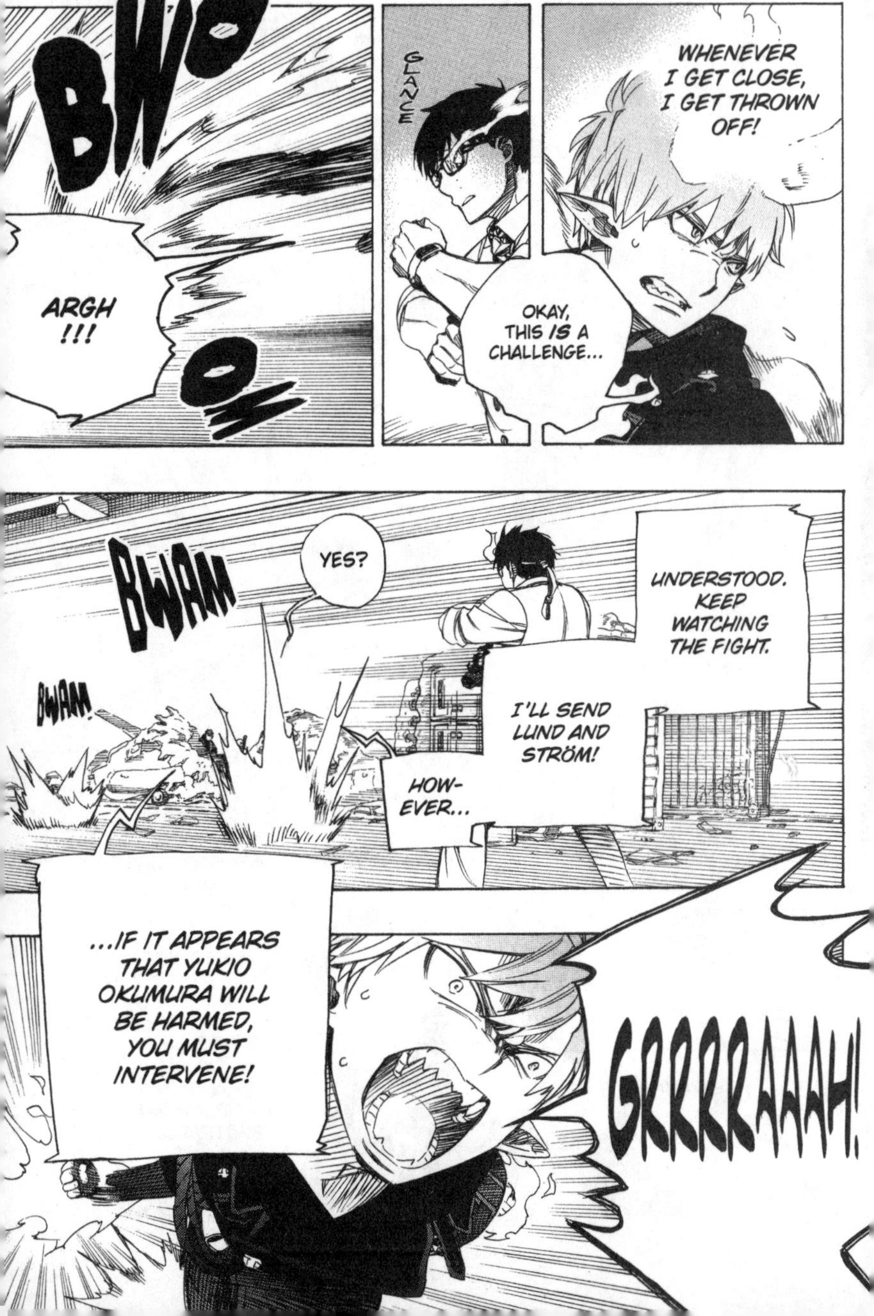
WHENEVER I GET CLOSE, I GET THROWN OFF!
OKAY, THIS IS A CHALLENGE...
GLANCE
BWOOM
ARGH!!!
UNDERSTOOD. KEEP WATCHING THE FIGHT.
I'LL SEND LUND AND STRÖM!
HOW-EVER...
YES?
BWAM
BWAM!
...IF IT APPEARS THAT YUKIO OKUMURA WILL BE HARMED, YOU MUST INTERVENE!
GRRRAAAH!

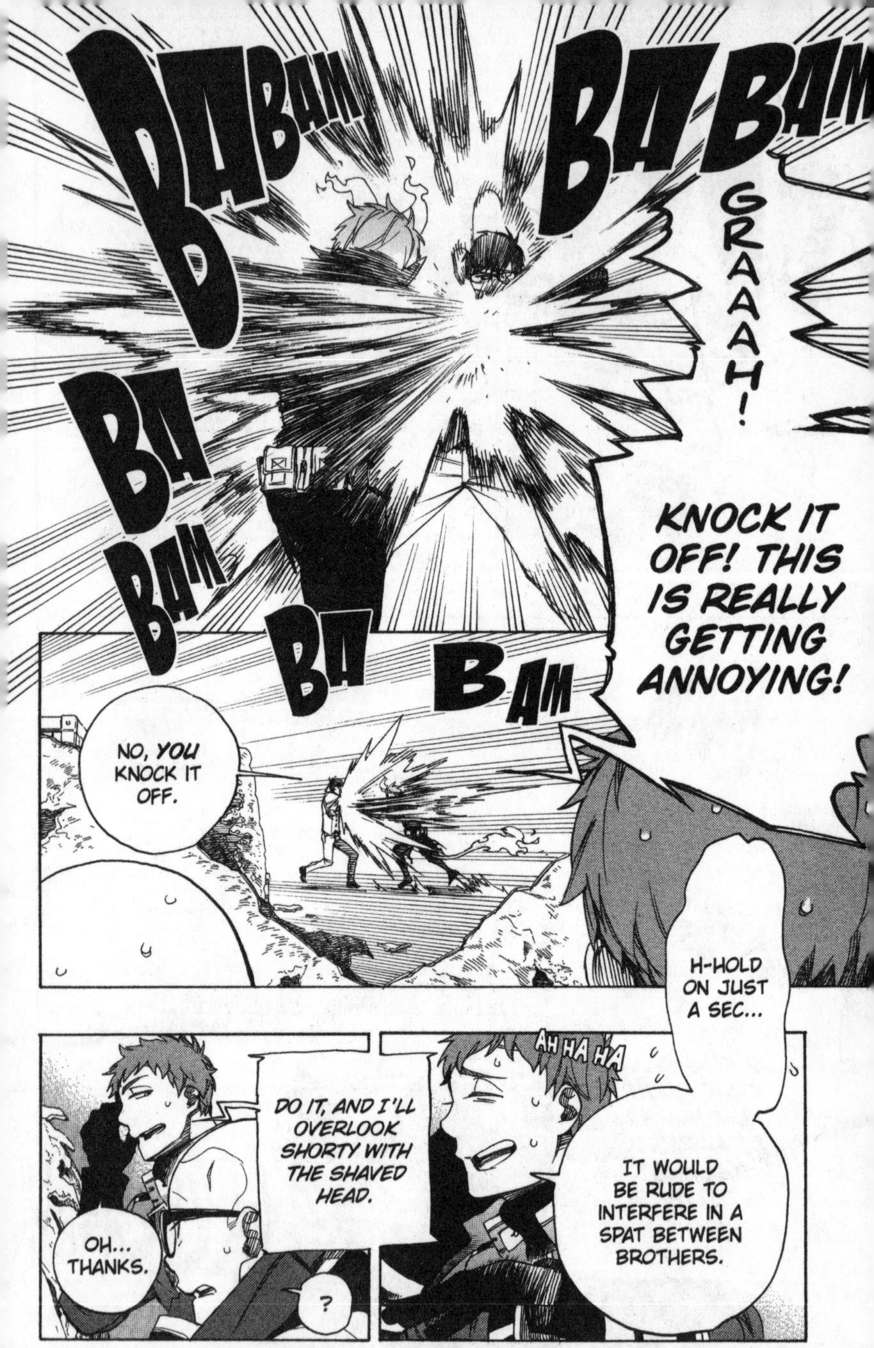
BABAM
GRAAAH!
BABAM
KNOCK IT OFF! THIS IS REALLY GETTING ANNOYING!
BABAM
BABAM
H-HOLD ON JUST A SEC...
NO, YOU KNOCK IT OFF.
AH HA HA
IT WOULD BE RUDE TO INTERFERE IN A SPAT BETWEEN BROTHERS.
DO IT, AND I'LL OVERLOOK SHORTY WITH THE SHAVED HEAD.
OH... THANKS.
?

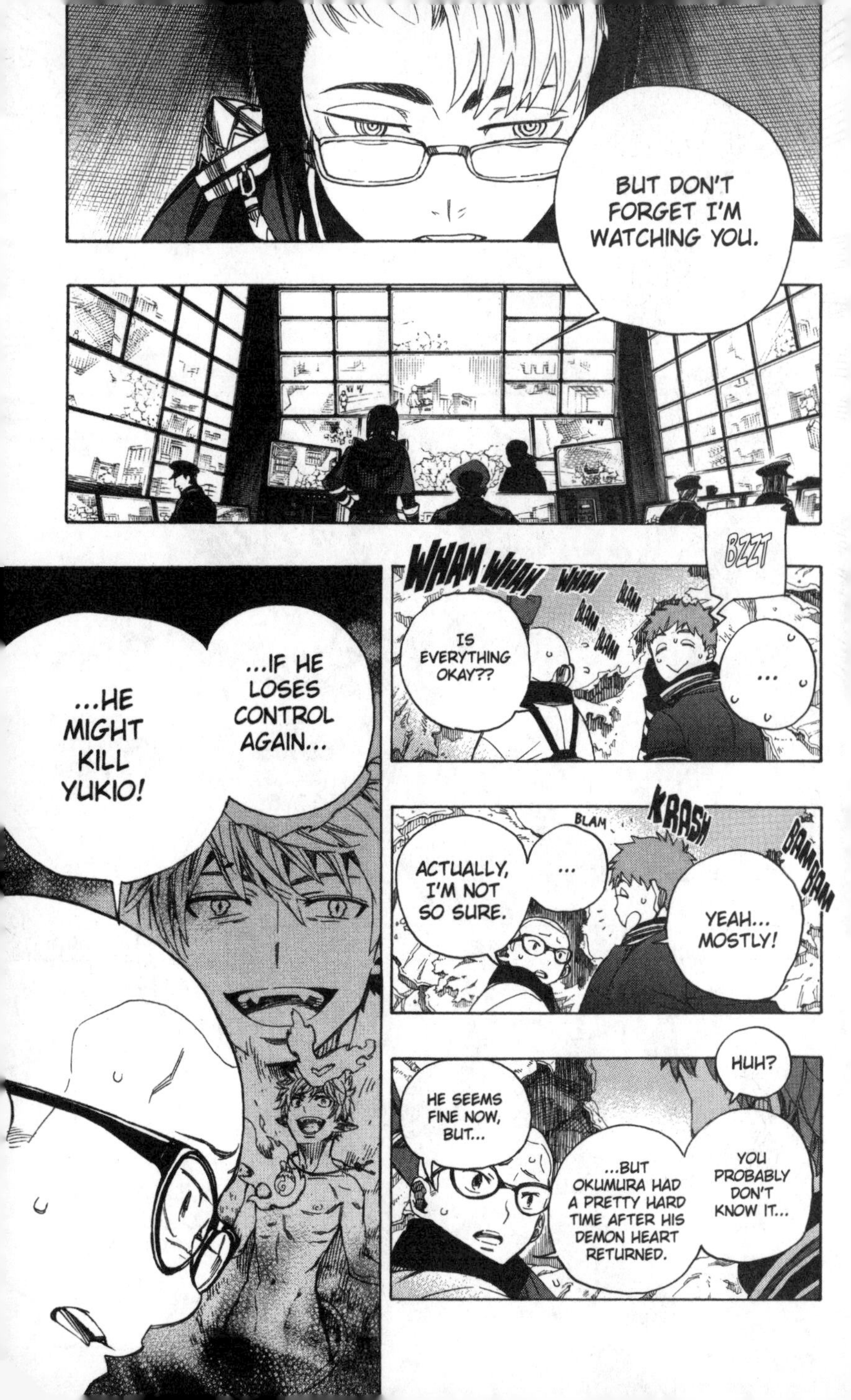
BUT DON'T FORGET I'M WATCHING YOU.
BZZT
WHAM WHAM WHAM
BLAM BLAM BLAM BLAM
IS EVERYTHING OKAY??
...
KRASH
BAM BAM
BLAM
YEAH... MOSTLY!
...
ACTUALLY, I'M NOT SO SURE.
HUH?
HE SEEMS FINE NOW, BUT...
YOU PROBABLY DON'T KNOW IT...
...BUT OKUMURA HAD A PRETTY HARD TIME AFTER HIS DEMON HEART RETURNED.
...IF HE LOSES CONTROL AGAIN...
...HE MIGHT KILL YUKIO!

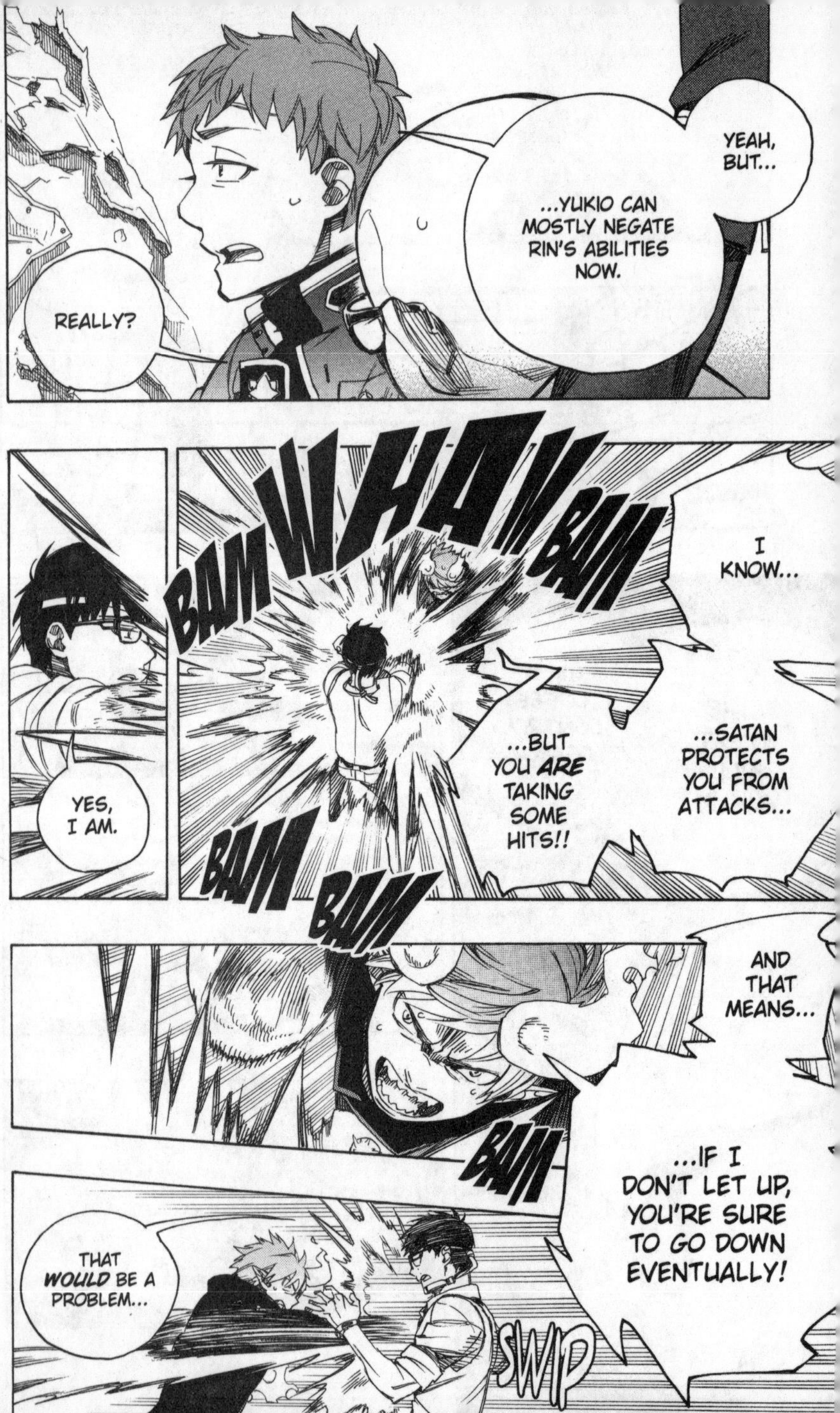
YEAH, BUT...
...YUKIO CAN MOSTLY NEGATE RIN'S ABILITIES NOW.
REALLY?
BAM WHAM BAM
I KNOW...
...SATAN PROTECTS YOU FROM ATTACKS...
...BUT YOU *ARE* TAKING SOME HITS!!
BAM
BAM
YES, I AM.
AND THAT MEANS...
BAM
...IF I DON'T LET UP, YOU'RE SURE TO GO DOWN EVENTUALLY!
THAT *WOULD* BE A PROBLEM...
SWIP

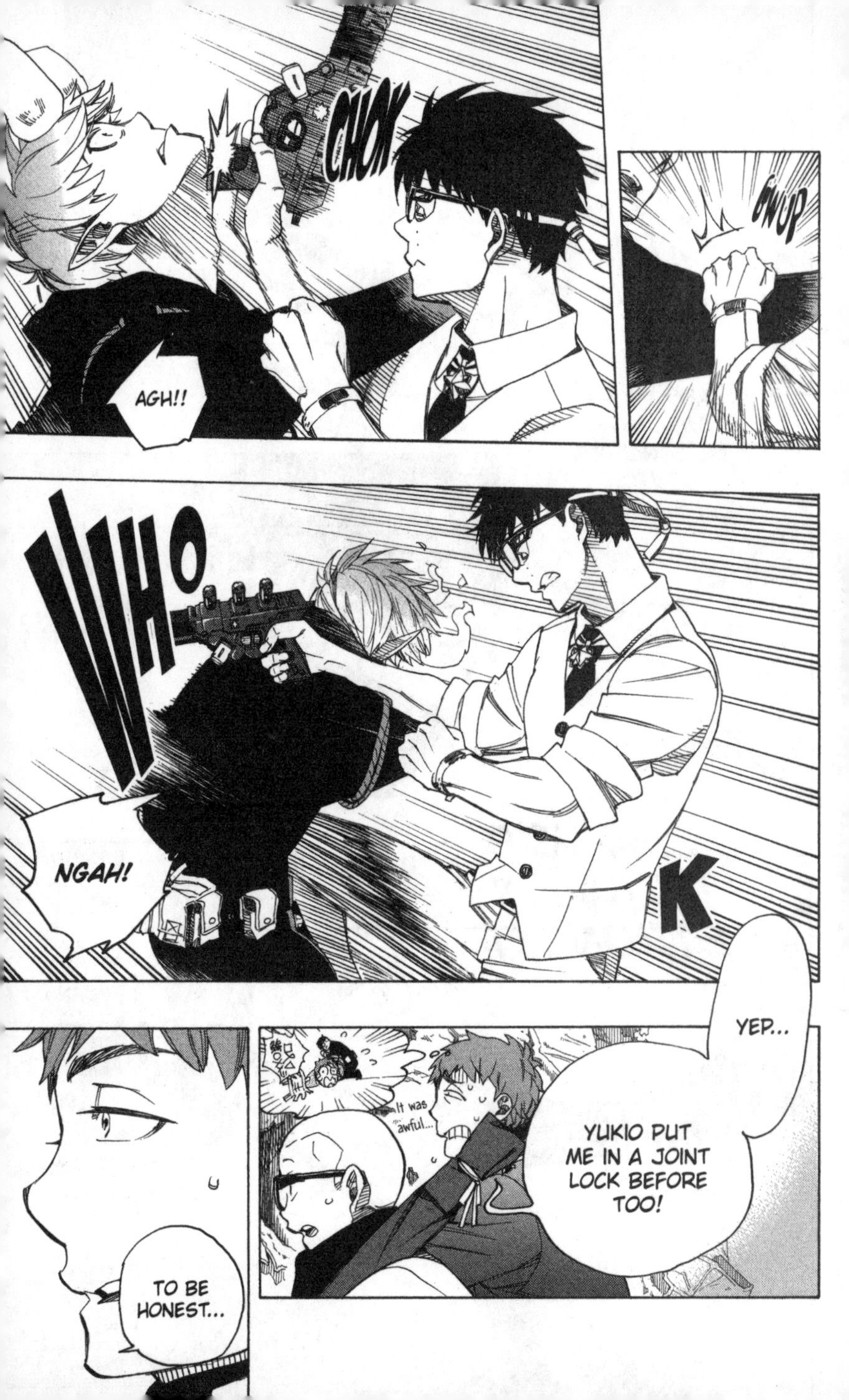
GWUP
CHOK
AGH!!
WHO
K
NGAH!
YEP...
YUKIO PUT ME IN A JOINT LOCK BEFORE TOO!
It was awful...
TO BE HONEST...

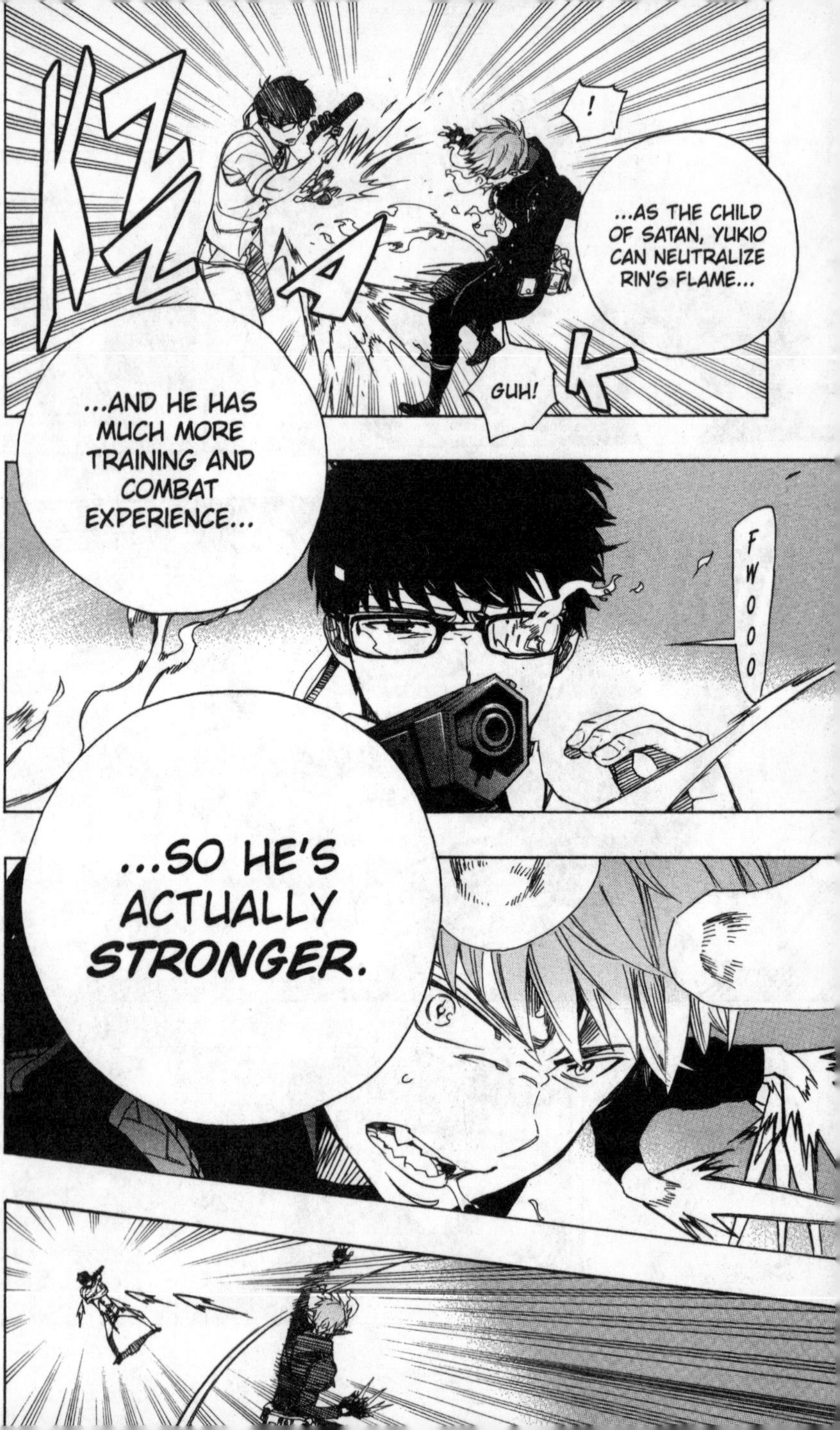
!
...AS THE CHILD OF SATAN, YUKIO CAN NEUTRALIZE RIN'S FLAME...
KZZAK
GUH!
...AND HE HAS MUCH MORE TRAINING AND COMBAT EXPERIENCE...
FWOOO
...SO HE'S ACTUALLY STRONGER.

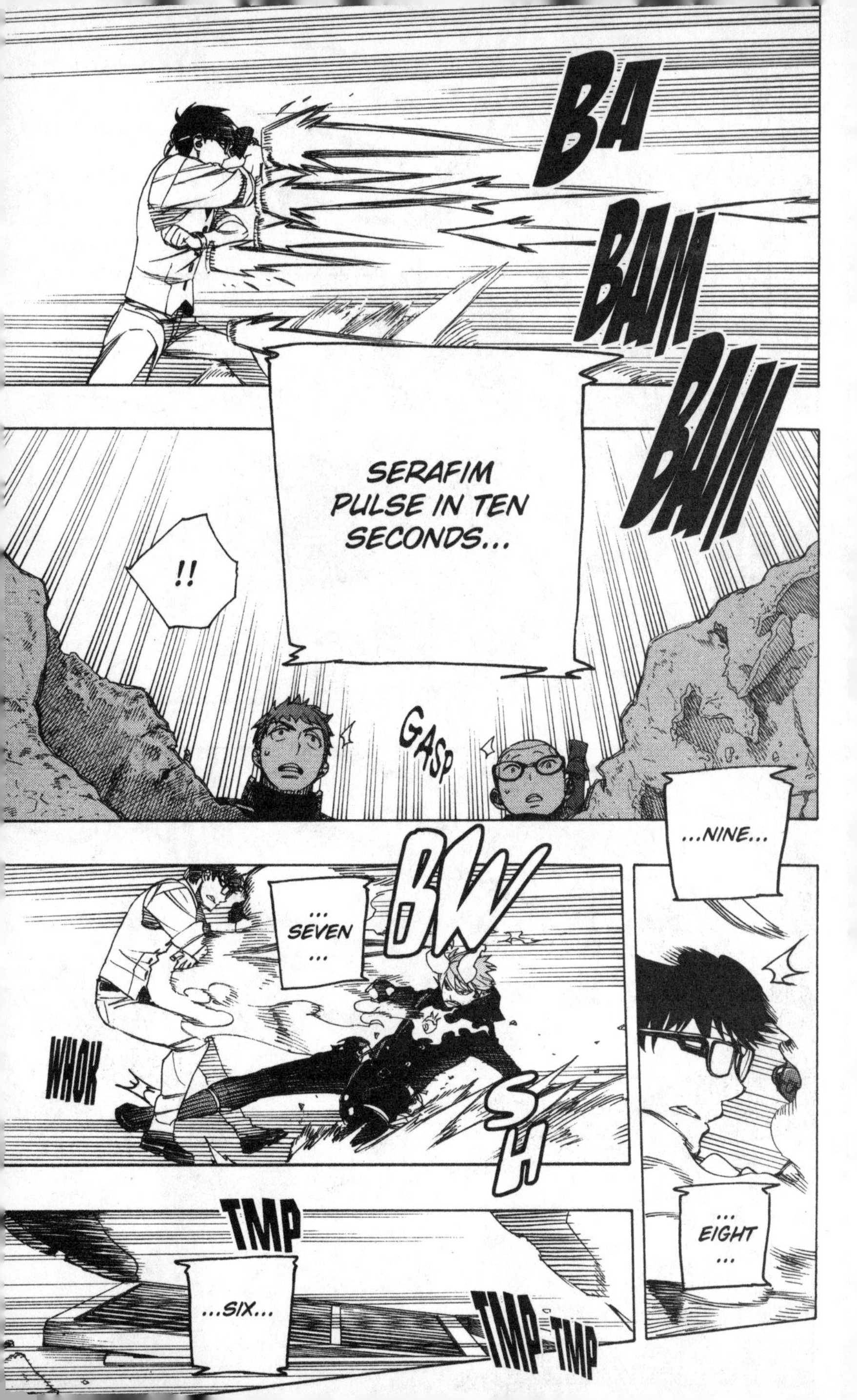
BA
BAM
BAM
BAM
SERAFIM PULSE IN TEN SECONDS...
GASP
!!
...NINE...
...EIGHT...
BW
...SEVEN...
SH
WHOK
TMP TMP
...SIX...
TMP

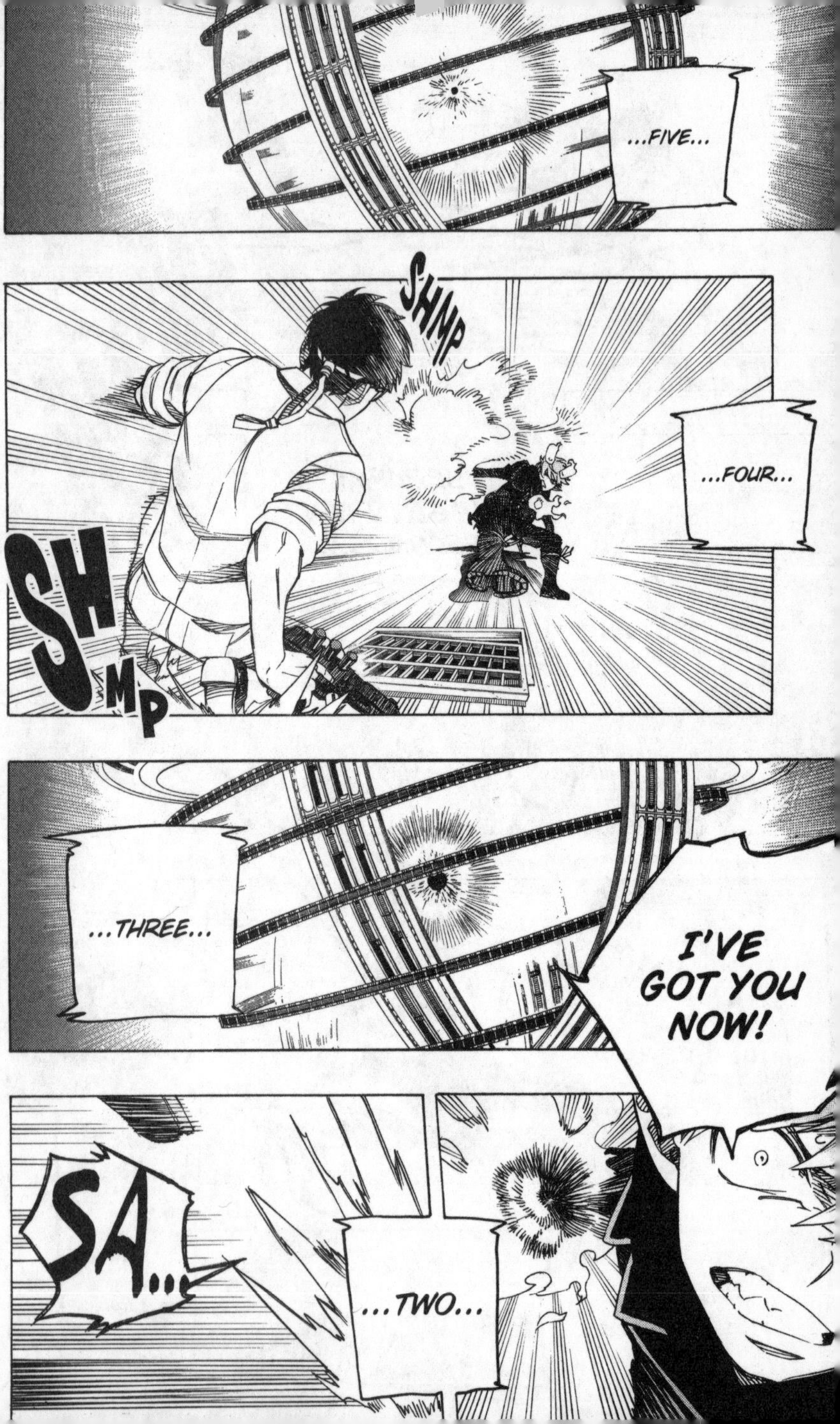
...FIVE...
SHMP
...FOUR...
SHMP
...THREE...
I'VE GOT YOU NOW!
...TWO...
SA...

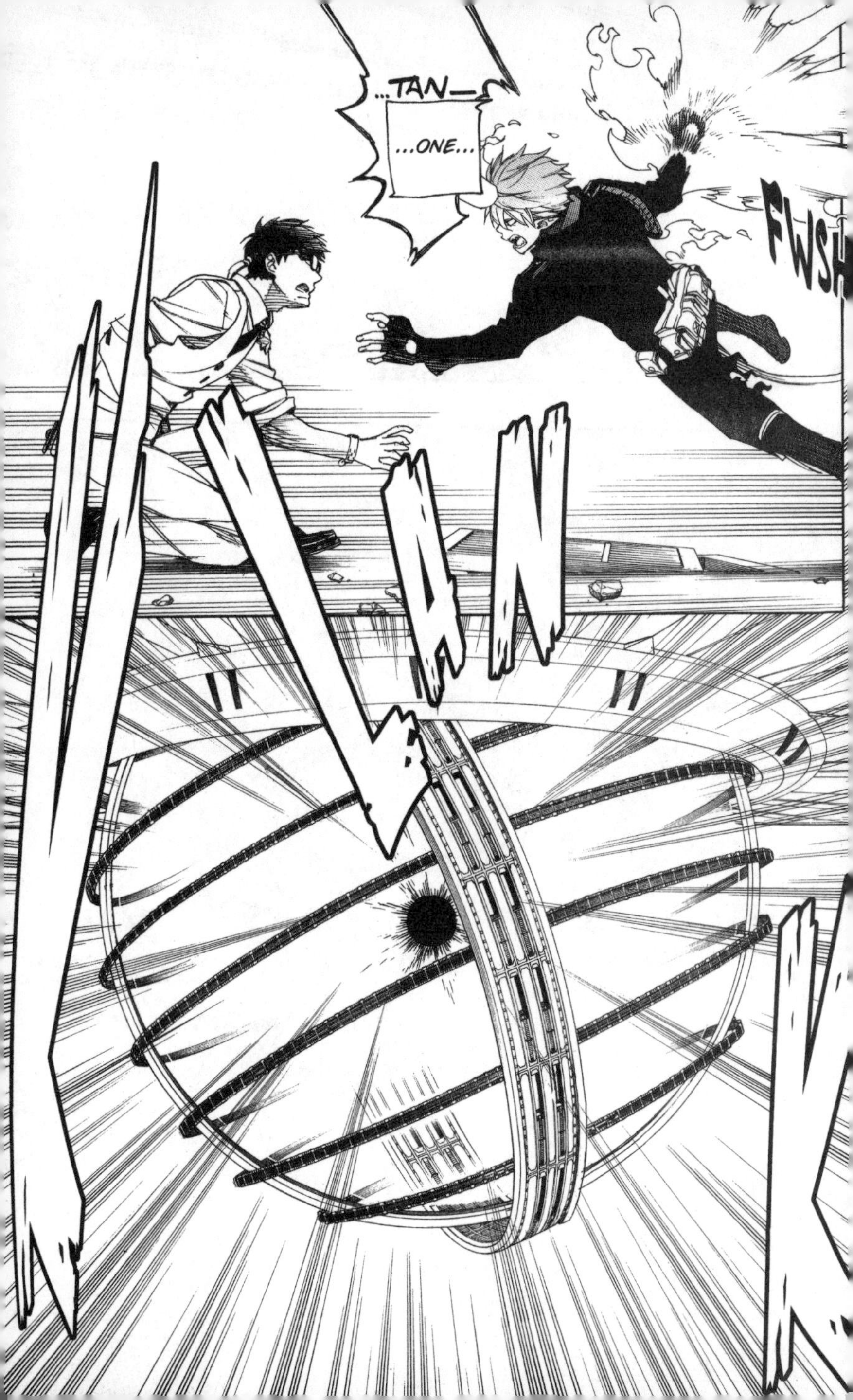
...TAN—
...ONE...
FWSH

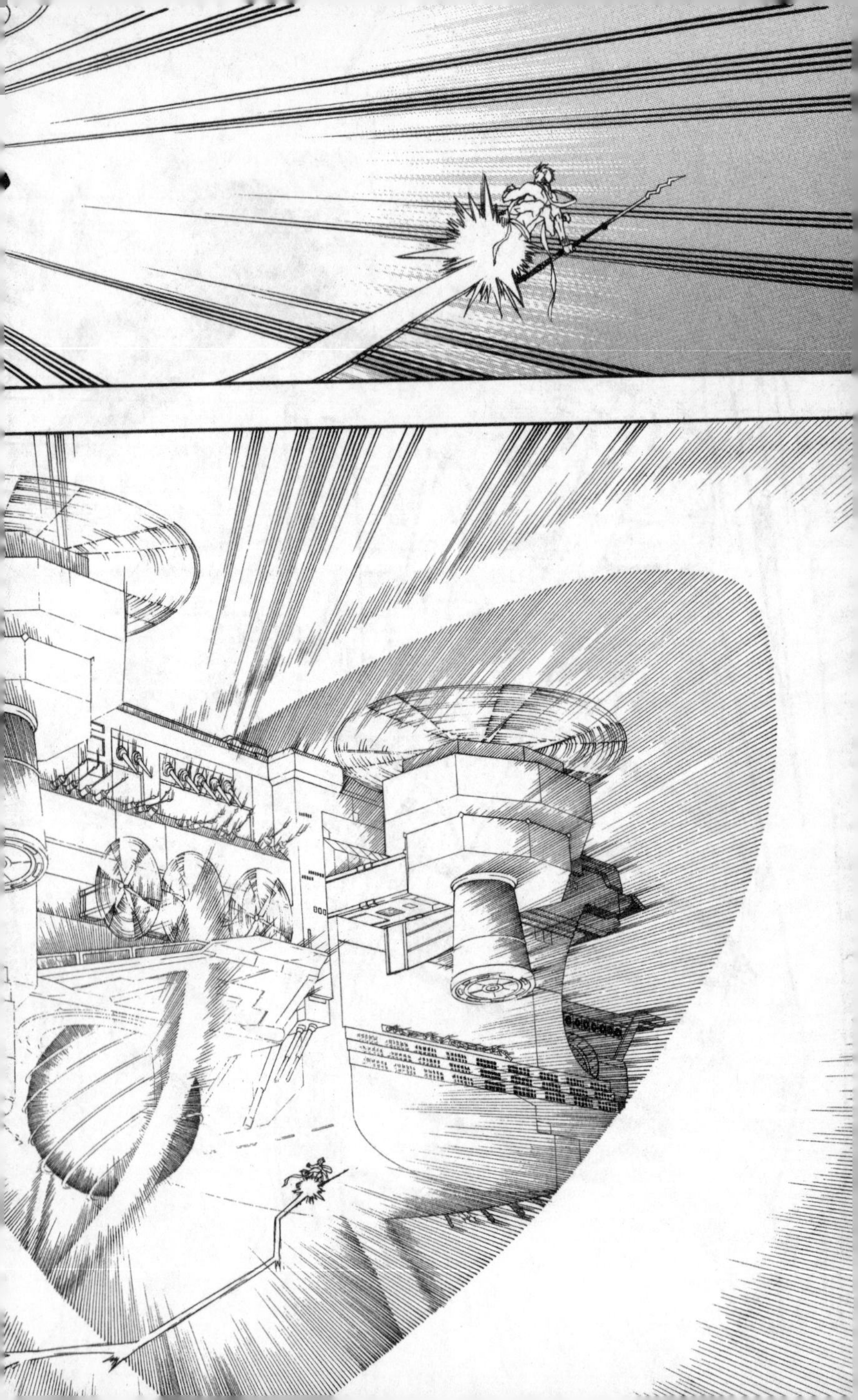

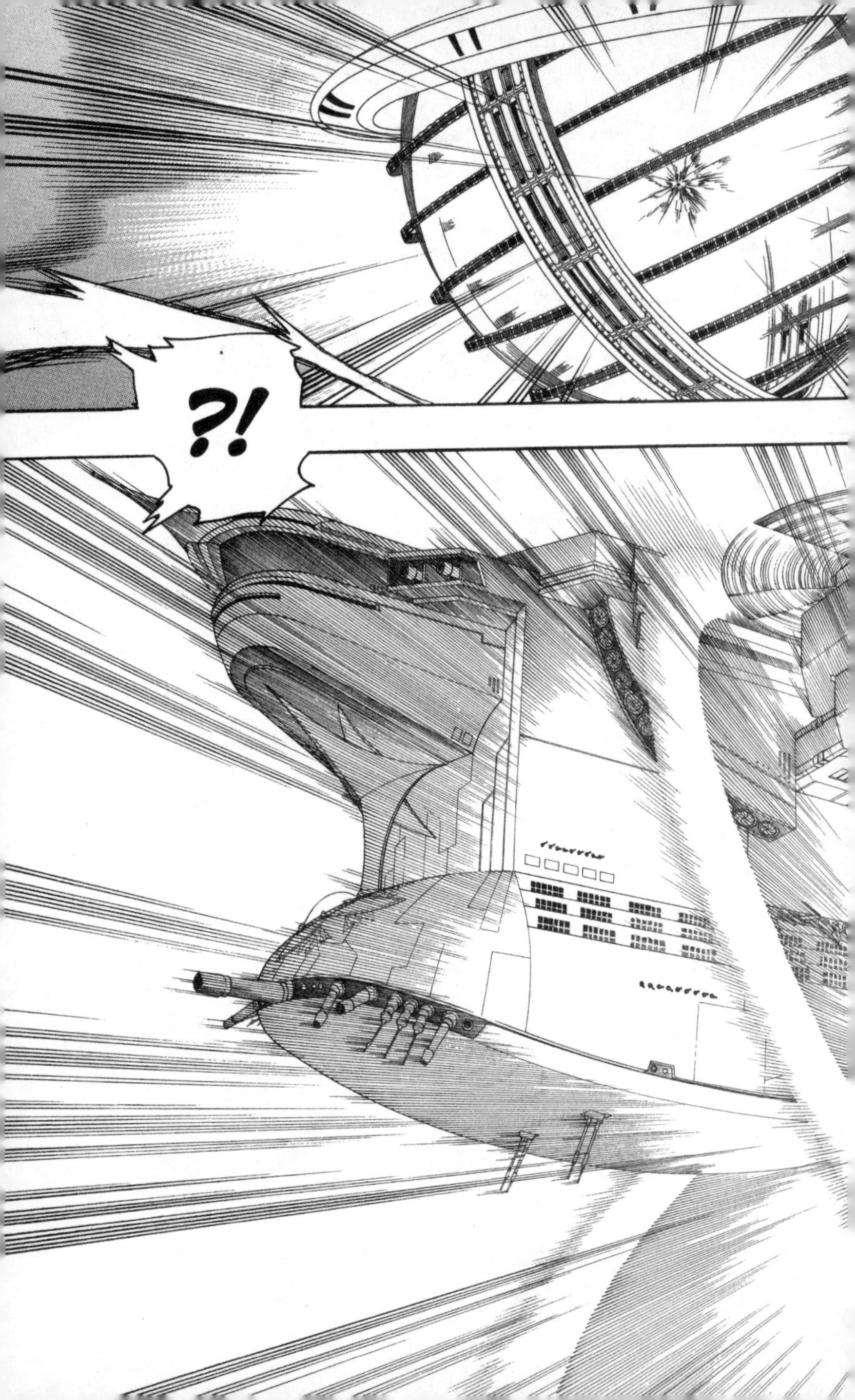
?!

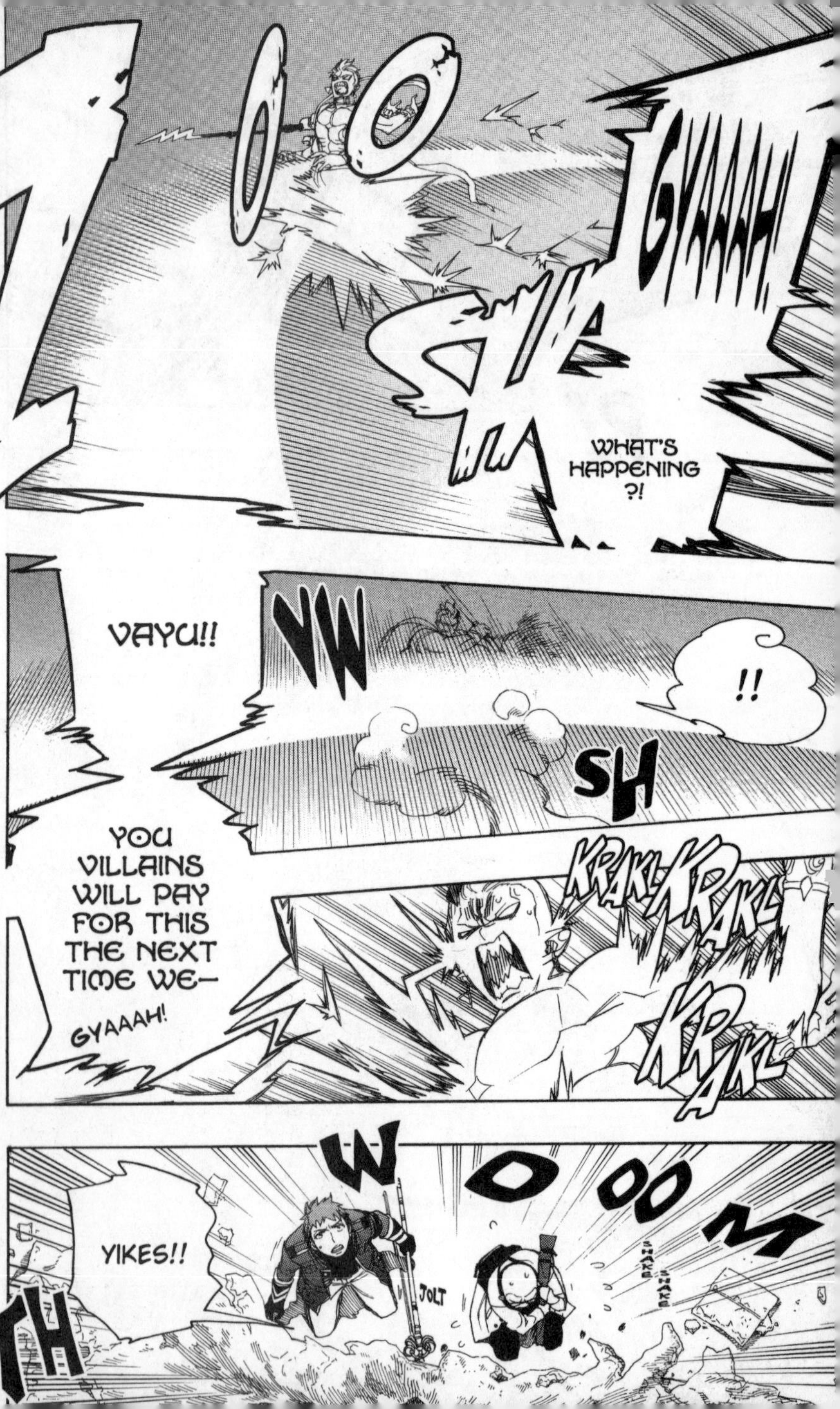
GYAAAH!
SHA
WHAT'S HAPPENING ?!
VW
!!
SH
KRAKL KRAKL
KRAKL
VAYU!!
YOU VILLAINS WILL PAY FOR THIS THE NEXT TIME WE—
GYAAAH!
WOOOM
SHAKE SHAKE
JOLT
YIKES!!
TH

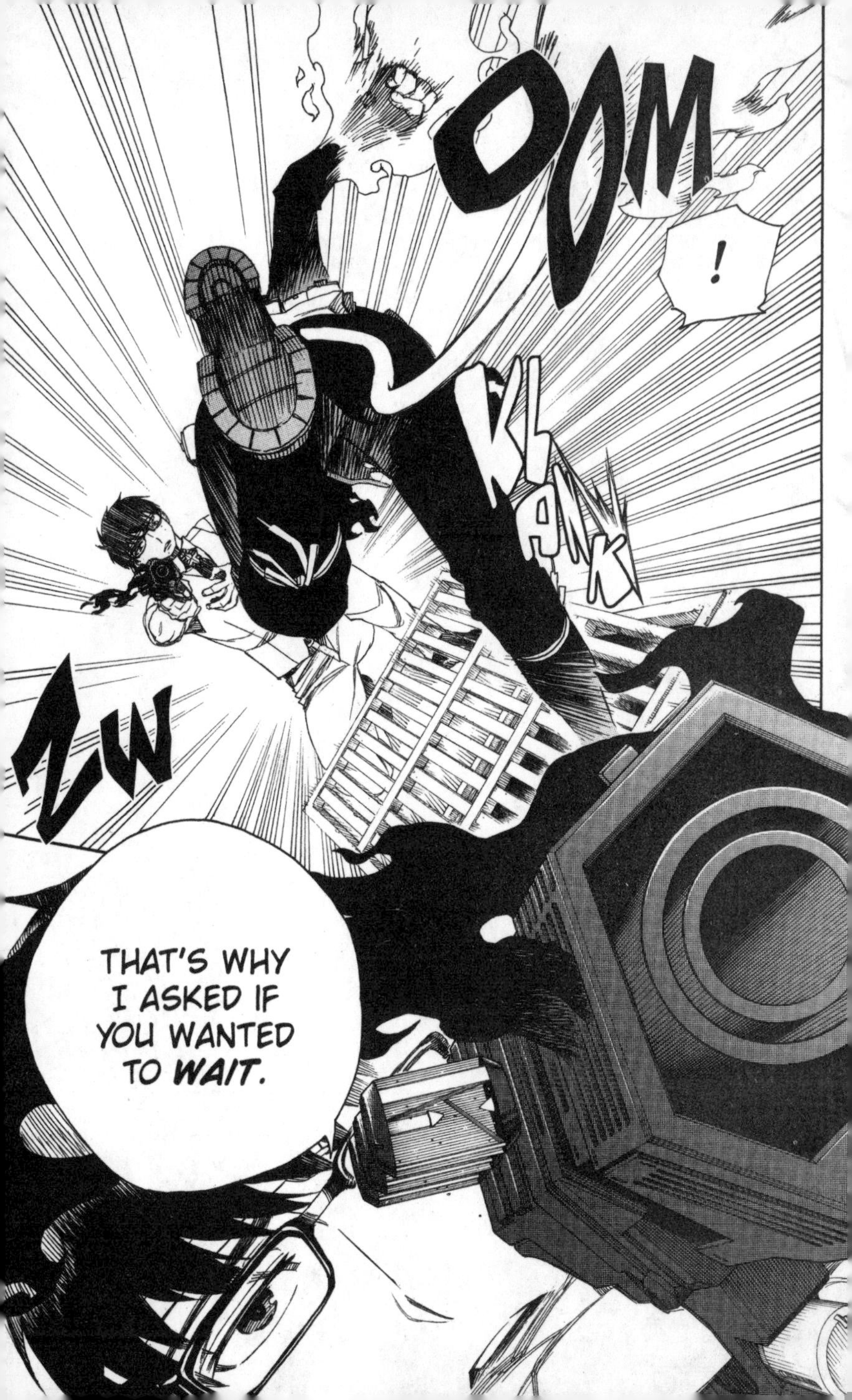
DOOM
!
KLANK
ZW
THAT'S WHY I ASKED IF YOU WANTED TO *WAIT*.

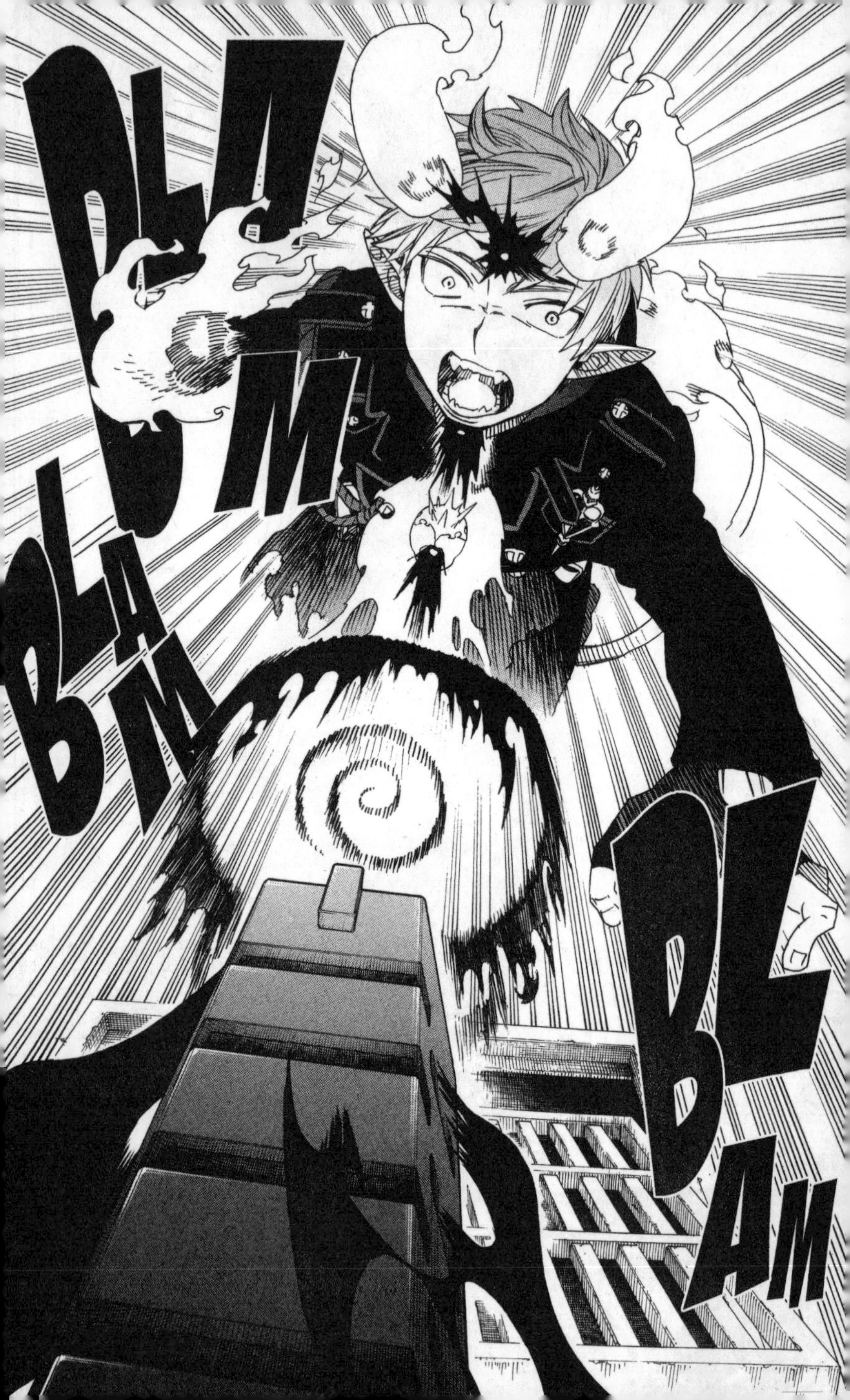
BLAM
BLAM
BLAM

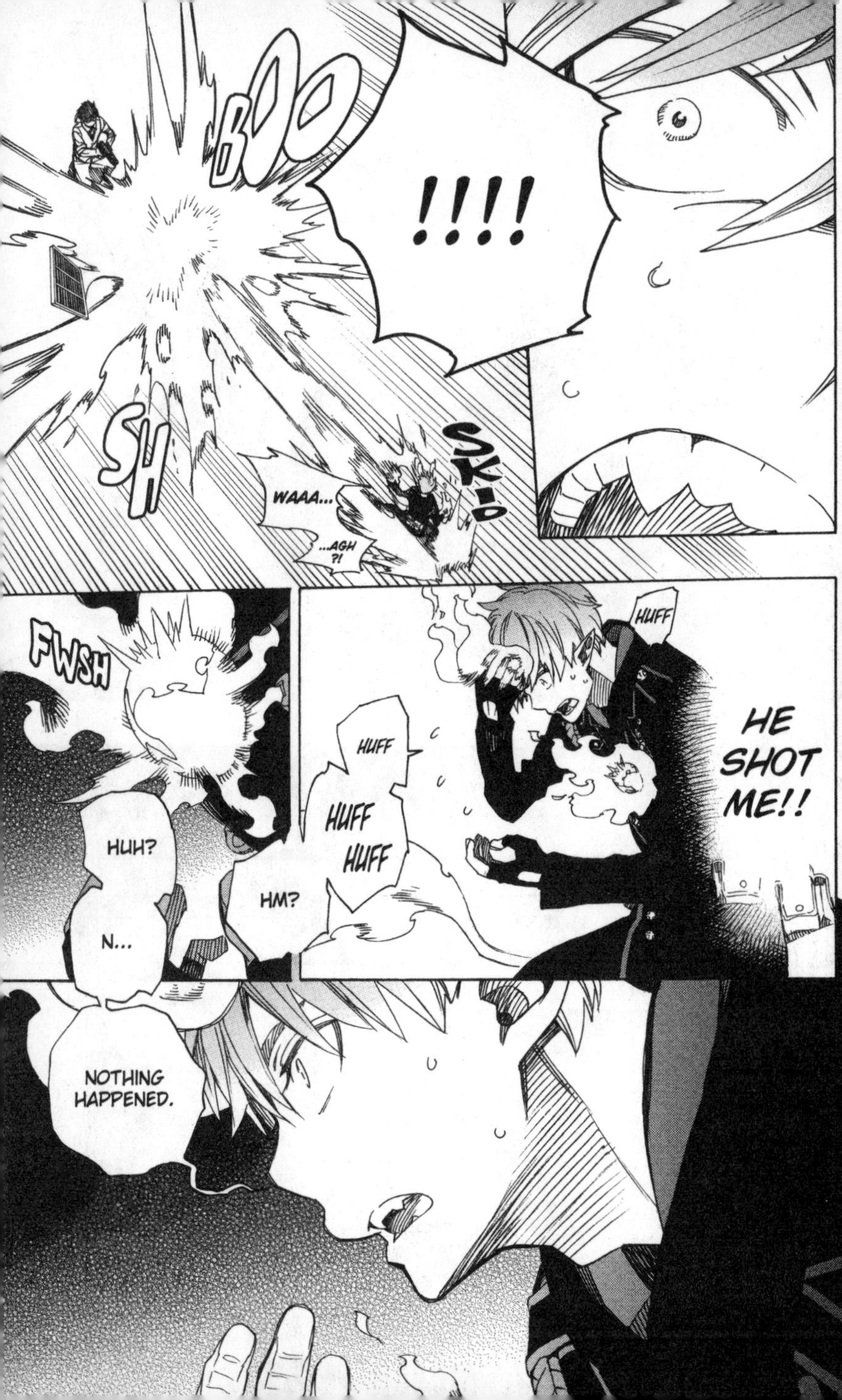
!!!!
BOO
SH
SKID
WAAA...
...AGH ?!
HUFF
HE SHOT ME!!
HUFF
HUFF
HUFF
FWSH
HUH?
HM?
N...
NOTHING HAPPENED.

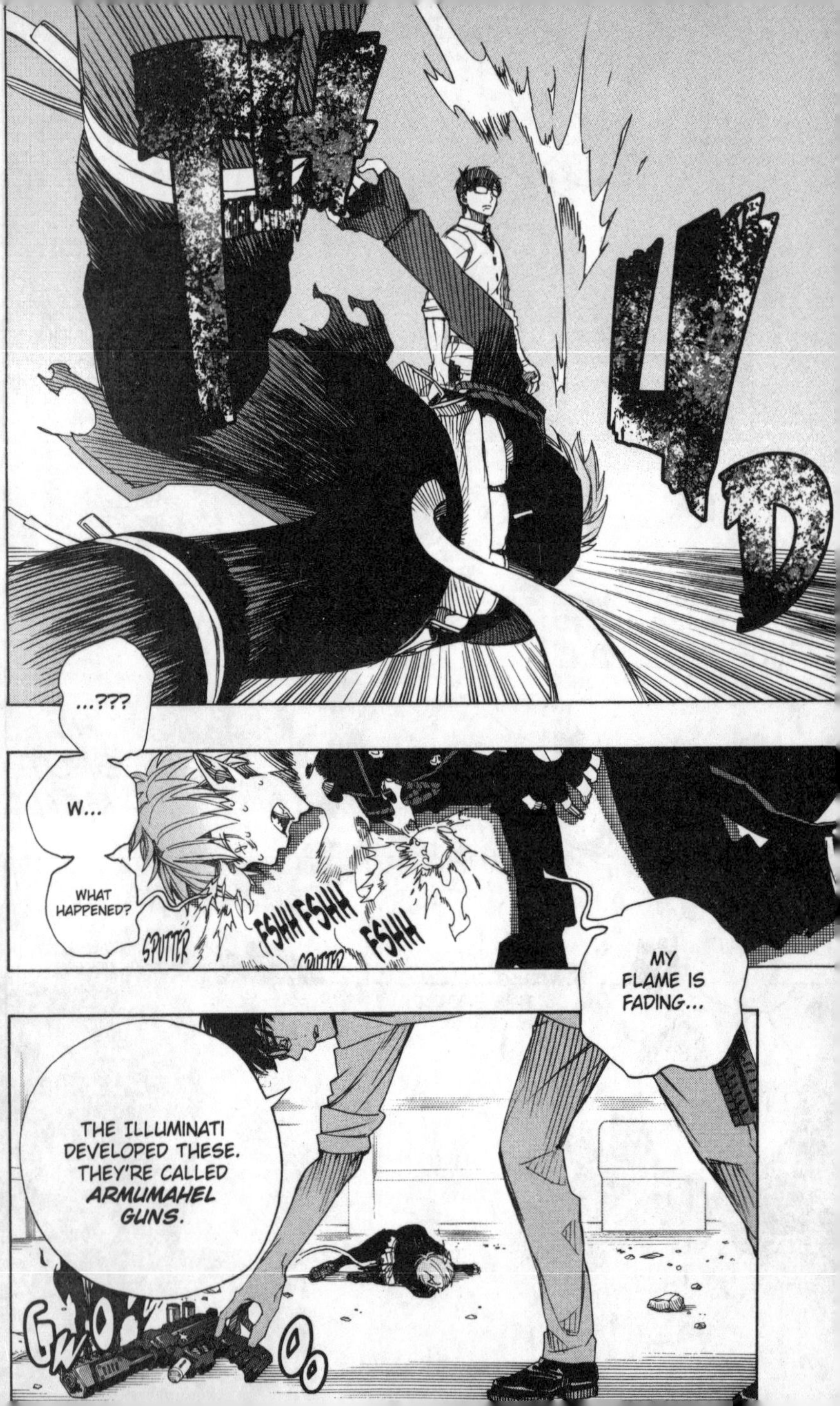
THUD
...???
W...
WHAT HAPPENED?
FSHH FSHH
FSHH
SPUTTER
SPUTTER
MY FLAME IS FADING...
THE ILLUMINATI DEVELOPED THESE. THEY'RE CALLED ***ARMUMAHEL GUNS***.
GWOOO

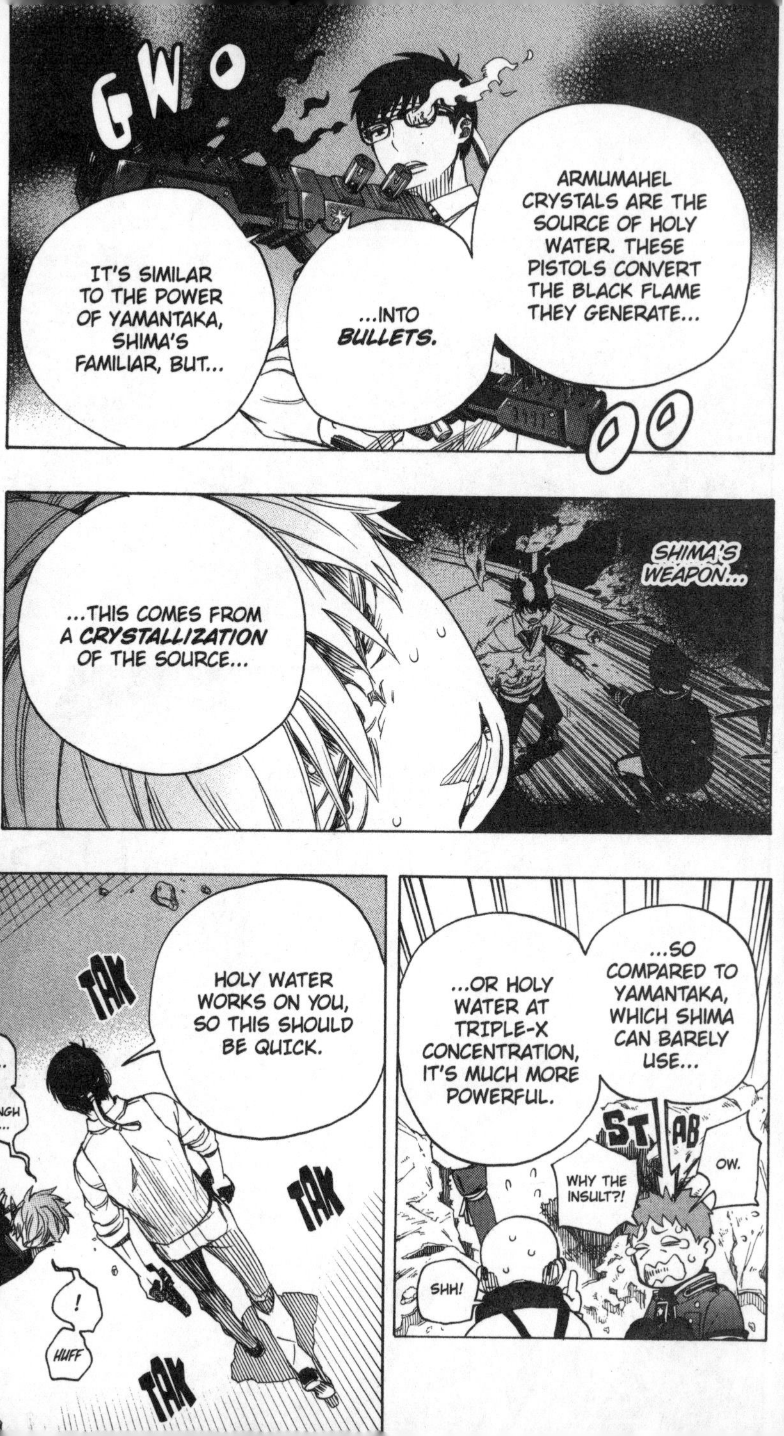
GWO
ARMUMAHEL CRYSTALS ARE THE SOURCE OF HOLY WATER. THESE PISTOLS CONVERT THE BLACK FLAME THEY GENERATE...
...INTO ***BULLETS.***
IT'S SIMILAR TO THE POWER OF YAMANTAKA, SHIMA'S FAMILIAR, BUT...
OO
SHIMA'S WEAPON...
...THIS COMES FROM A ***CRYSTALLIZATION*** OF THE SOURCE...
...SO COMPARED TO YAMANTAKA, WHICH SHIMA CAN BARELY USE...
...OR HOLY WATER AT TRIPLE-X CONCENTRATION, IT'S MUCH MORE POWERFUL.
STAB
OW.
WHY THE INSULT?!
SHH!
HOLY WATER WORKS ON YOU, SO THIS SHOULD BE QUICK.
TAK
TAK
... UNGH ...
!
HUFF
TAK

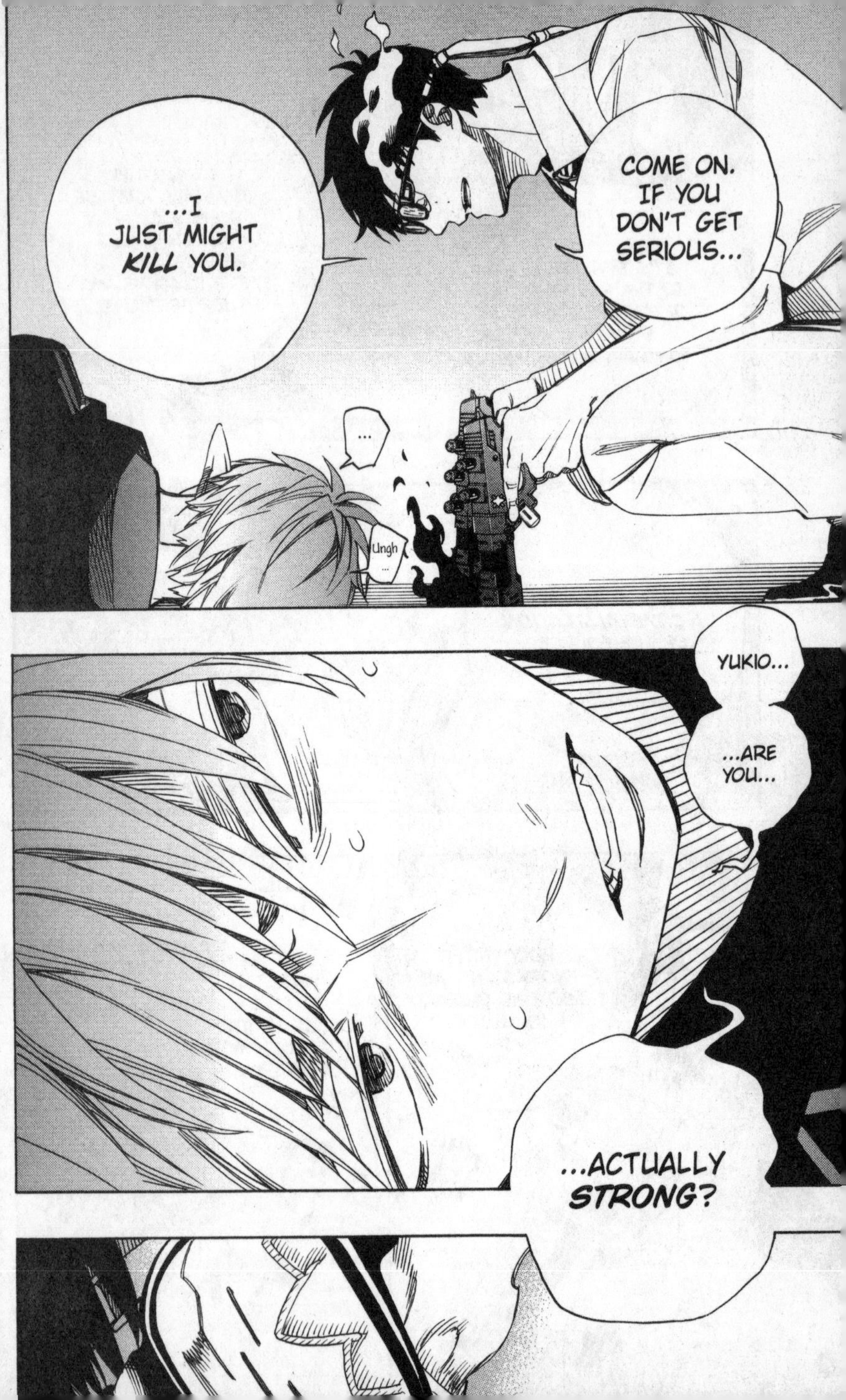
COME ON. IF YOU DON'T GET SERIOUS...
...I JUST MIGHT KILL YOU.
...
Ungh...
YUKIO...
...ARE YOU...
...ACTUALLY STRONG?

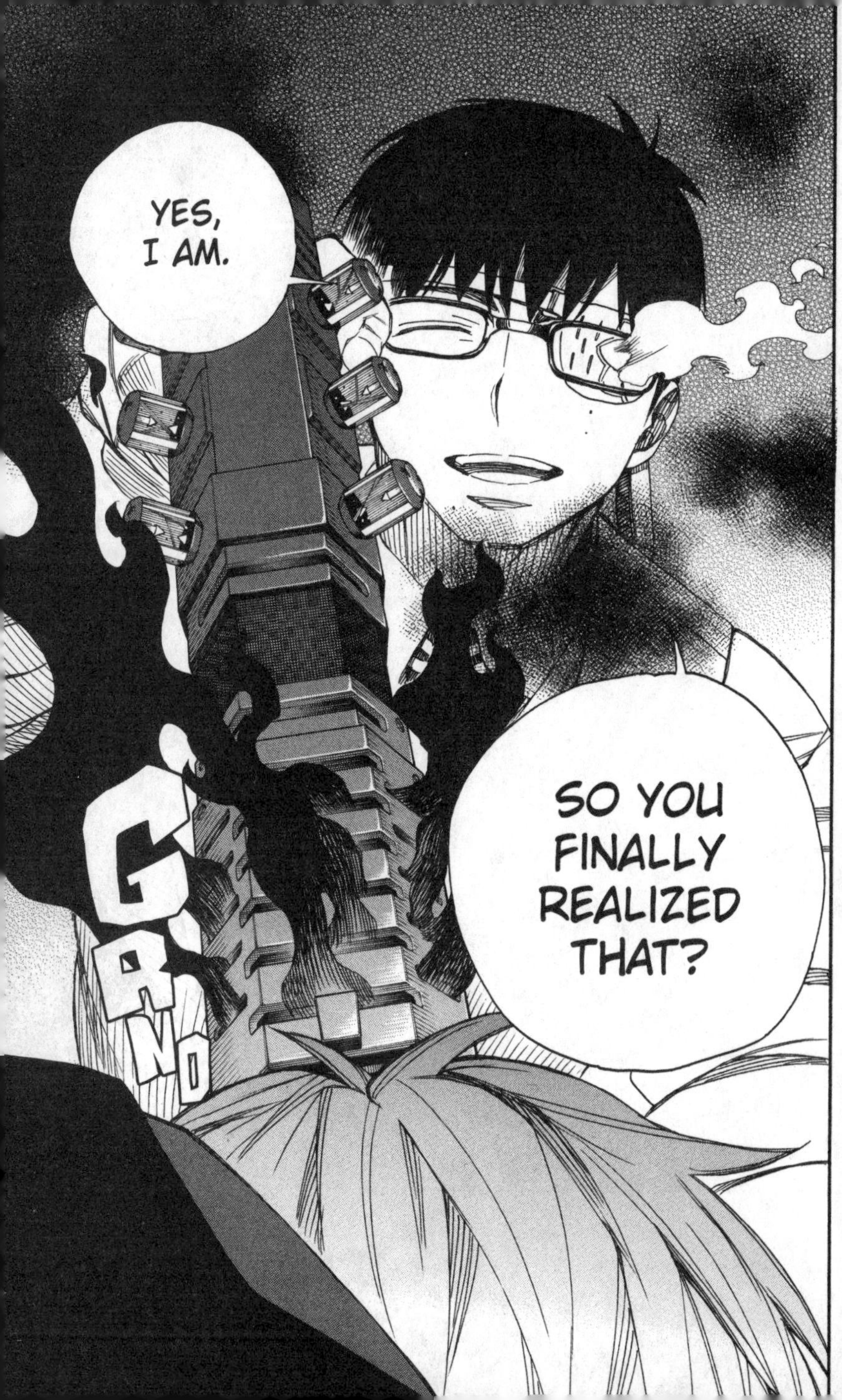
YES, I AM.
GRND
SO YOU FINALLY REALIZED THAT?

Blue Exorcist Chapter 122: Of One Cloth—Starting a Fire

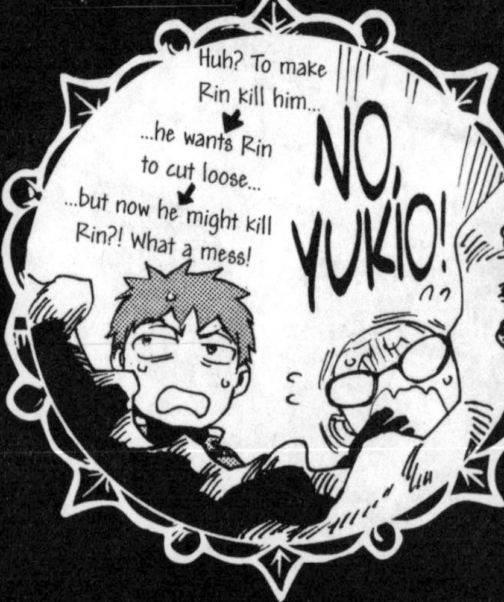
NO, YUKIO!
Huh? To make Rin kill him...
...he wants Rin to cut loose...
...but now he might kill Rin?! What a mess!

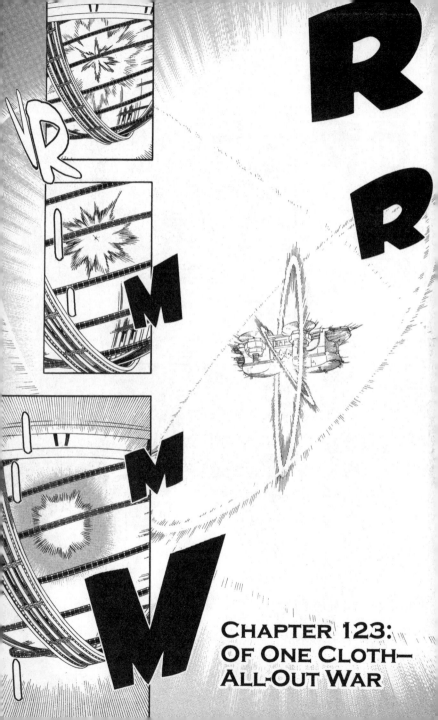

CHAPTER 123:
OF ONE CLOTH—
ALL-OUT WAR

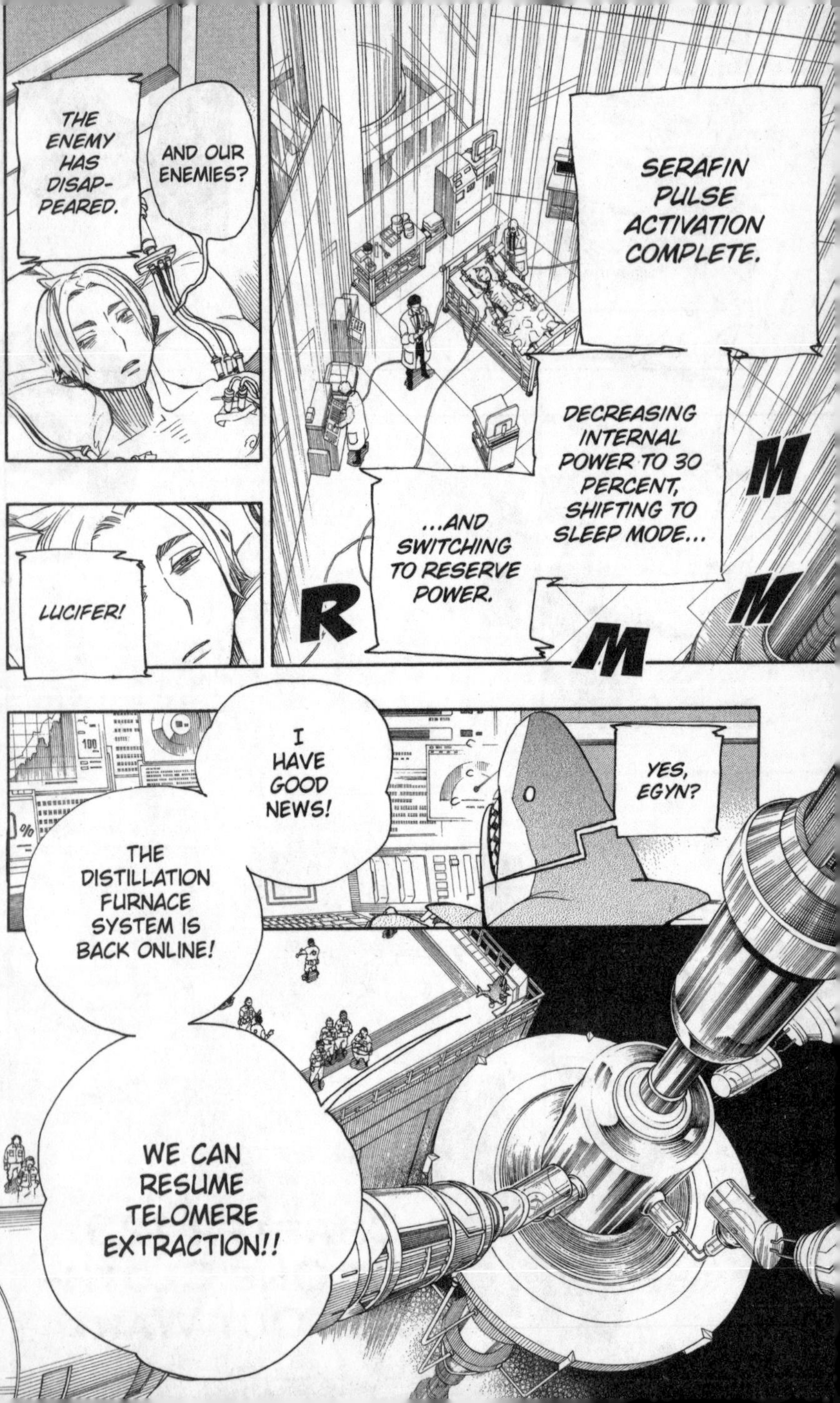
SERAFIN PULSE ACTIVATION COMPLETE.
DECREASING INTERNAL POWER TO 30 PERCENT, SHIFTING TO SLEEP MODE...
...AND SWITCHING TO RESERVE POWER.
M
M
M
R
AND OUR ENEMIES?
THE ENEMY HAS DISAP-PEARED.
LUCIFER!
YES, EGYN?
I HAVE GOOD NEWS!
THE DISTILLATION FURNACE SYSTEM IS BACK ONLINE!
WE CAN RESUME TELOMERE EXTRACTION!!

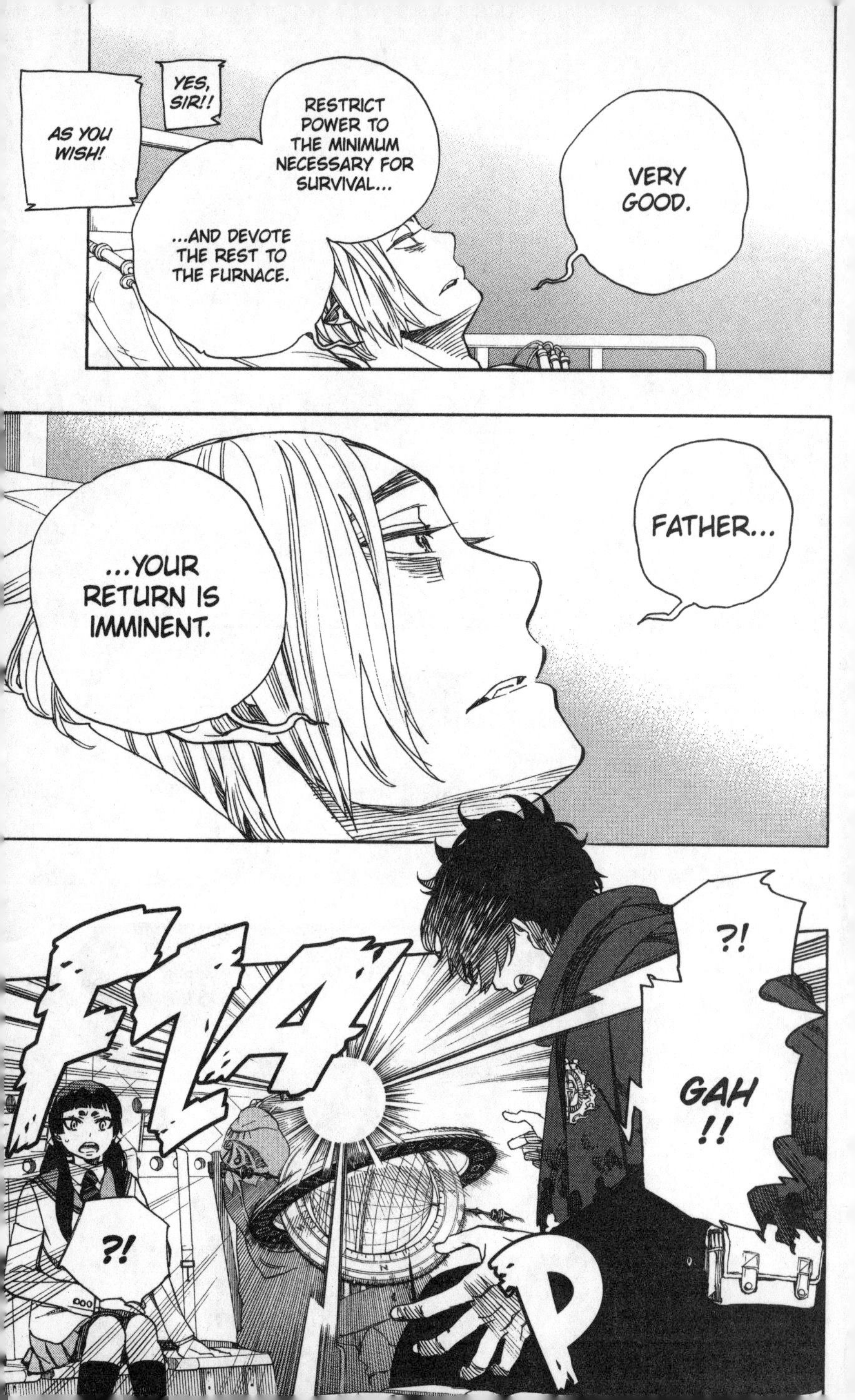
VERY GOOD.
RESTRICT POWER TO THE MINIMUM NECESSARY FOR SURVIVAL...
...AND DEVOTE THE REST TO THE FURNACE.
YES, SIR!!
AS YOU WISH!
FATHER...
...YOUR RETURN IS IMMINENT.
?!
GAH !!
FWAP
?!

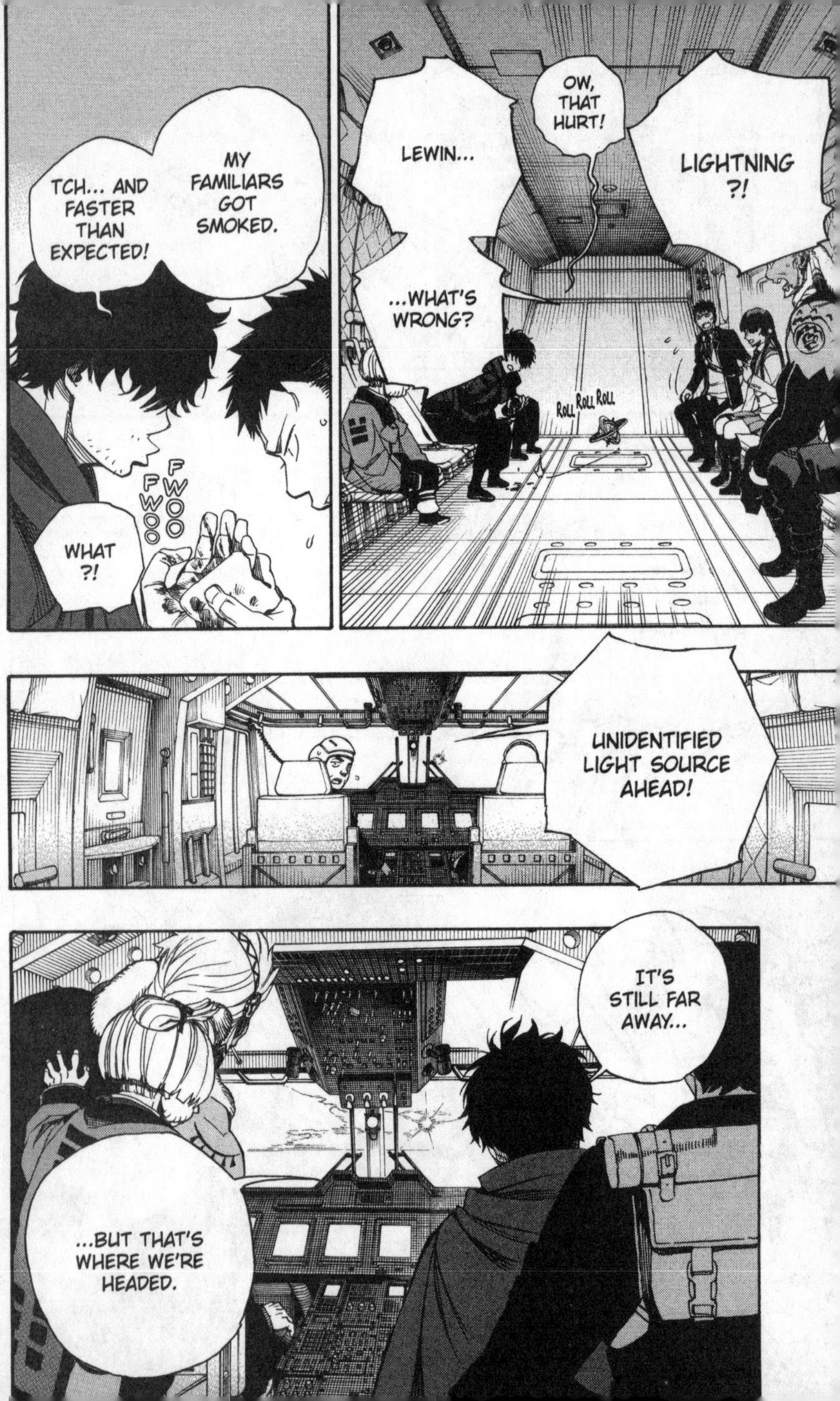
LIGHTNING ?!
OW, THAT HURT!
LEWIN...
ROLL ROLL ROLL
...WHAT'S WRONG?
MY FAMILIARS GOT SMOKED.
TCH... AND FASTER THAN EXPECTED!
FWOO FWOO
WHAT ?!
UNIDENTIFIED LIGHT SOURCE AHEAD!
IT'S STILL FAR AWAY...
...BUT THAT'S WHERE WE'RE HEADED.

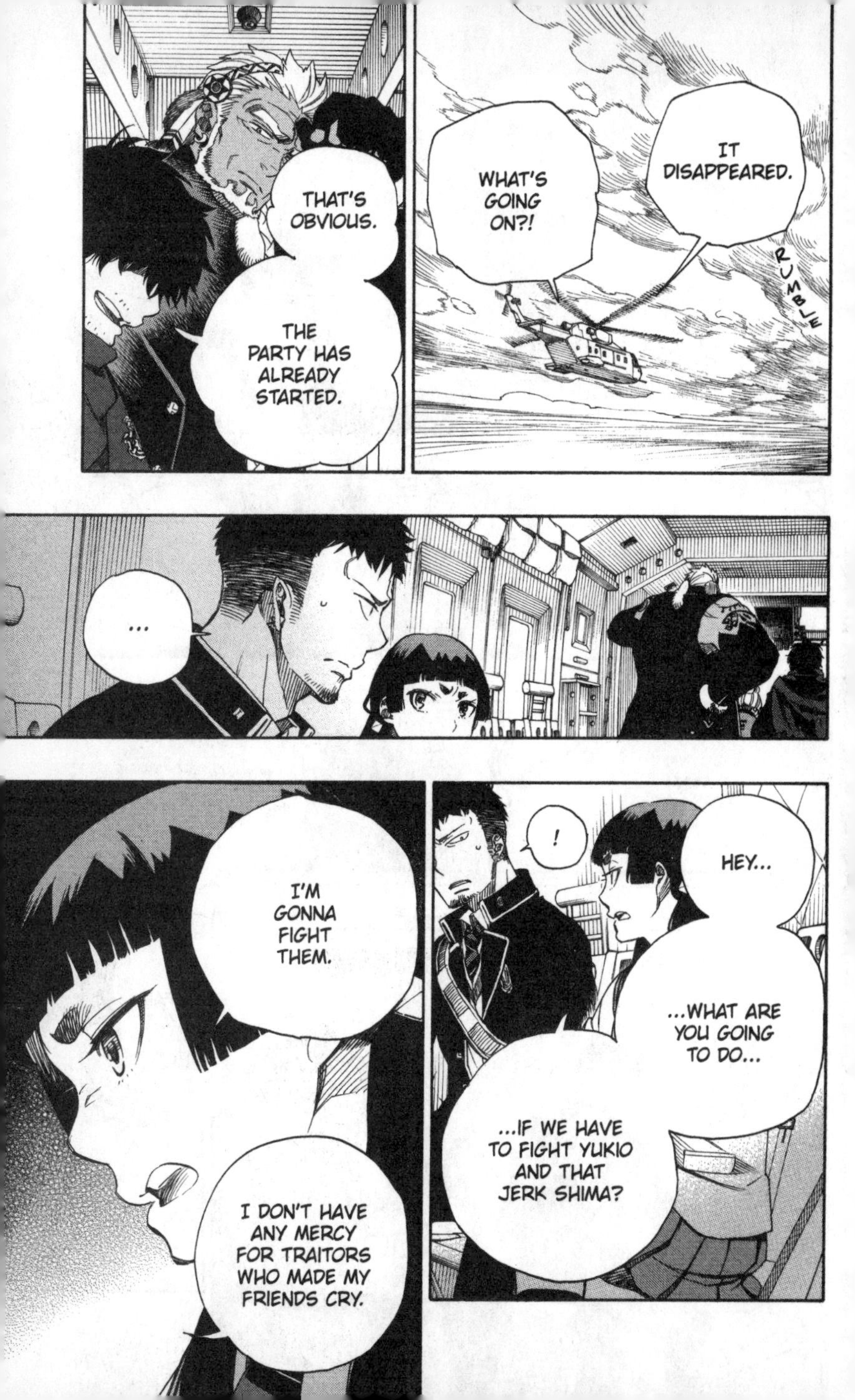
IT DISAPPEARED.
WHAT'S GOING ON?!
RUMBLE
THAT'S OBVIOUS.
THE PARTY HAS ALREADY STARTED.
...
HEY...
!
...WHAT ARE YOU GOING TO DO...
...IF WE HAVE TO FIGHT YUKIO AND THAT JERK SHIMA?
I'M GONNA FIGHT THEM.
I DON'T HAVE ANY MERCY FOR TRAITORS WHO MADE MY FRIENDS CRY.

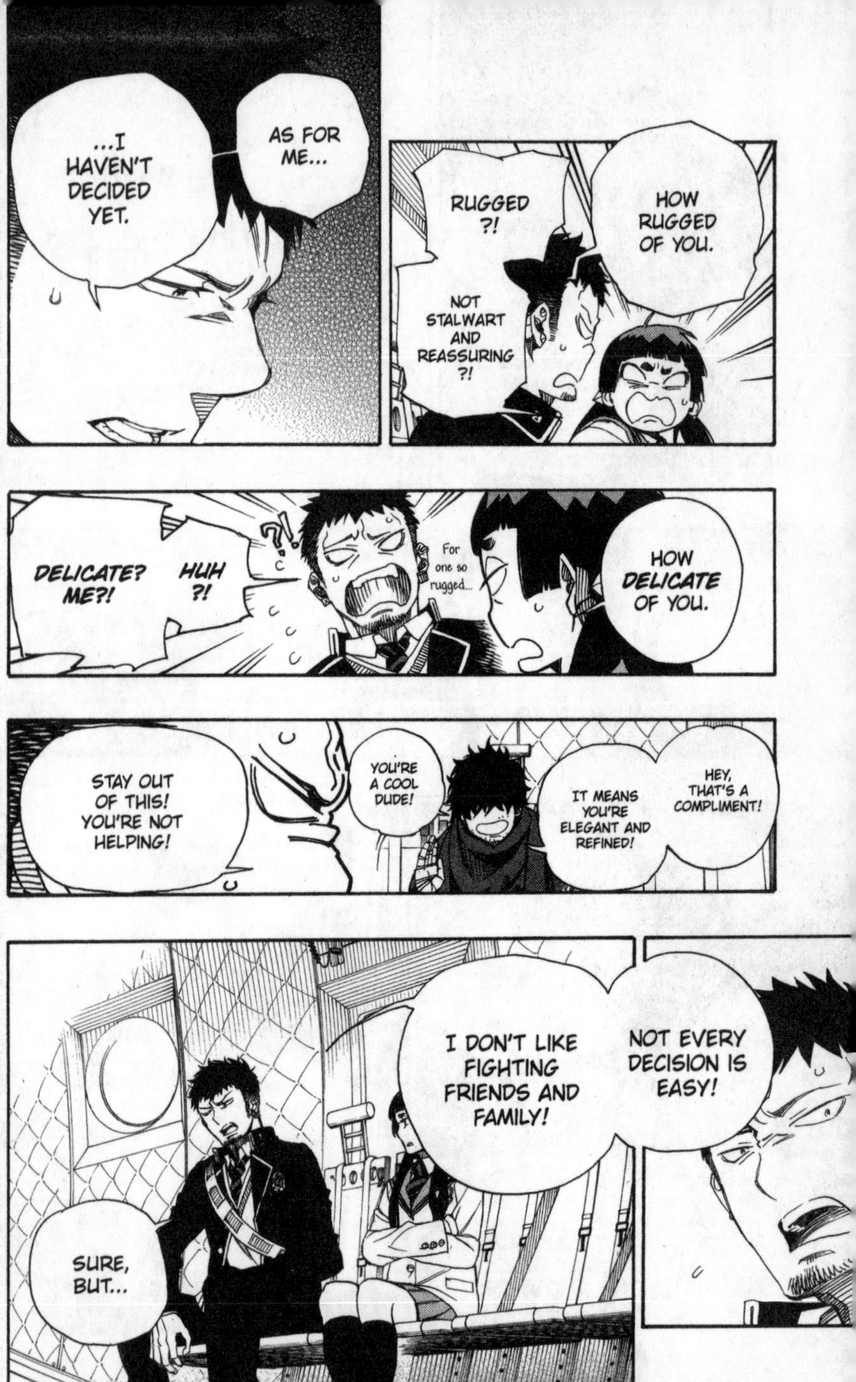
HOW RUGGED OF YOU.
RUGGED?!
NOT STALWART AND REASSURING?!
AS FOR ME...
...I HAVEN'T DECIDED YET.
HOW DELICATE OF YOU.
For one so rugged...
HUH?!
DELICATE? ME?!
HEY, THAT'S A COMPLIMENT!
IT MEANS YOU'RE ELEGANT AND REFINED!
YOU'RE A COOL DUDE!
STAY OUT OF THIS! YOU'RE NOT HELPING!
NOT EVERY DECISION IS EASY!
I DON'T LIKE FIGHTING FRIENDS AND FAMILY!
SURE, BUT...

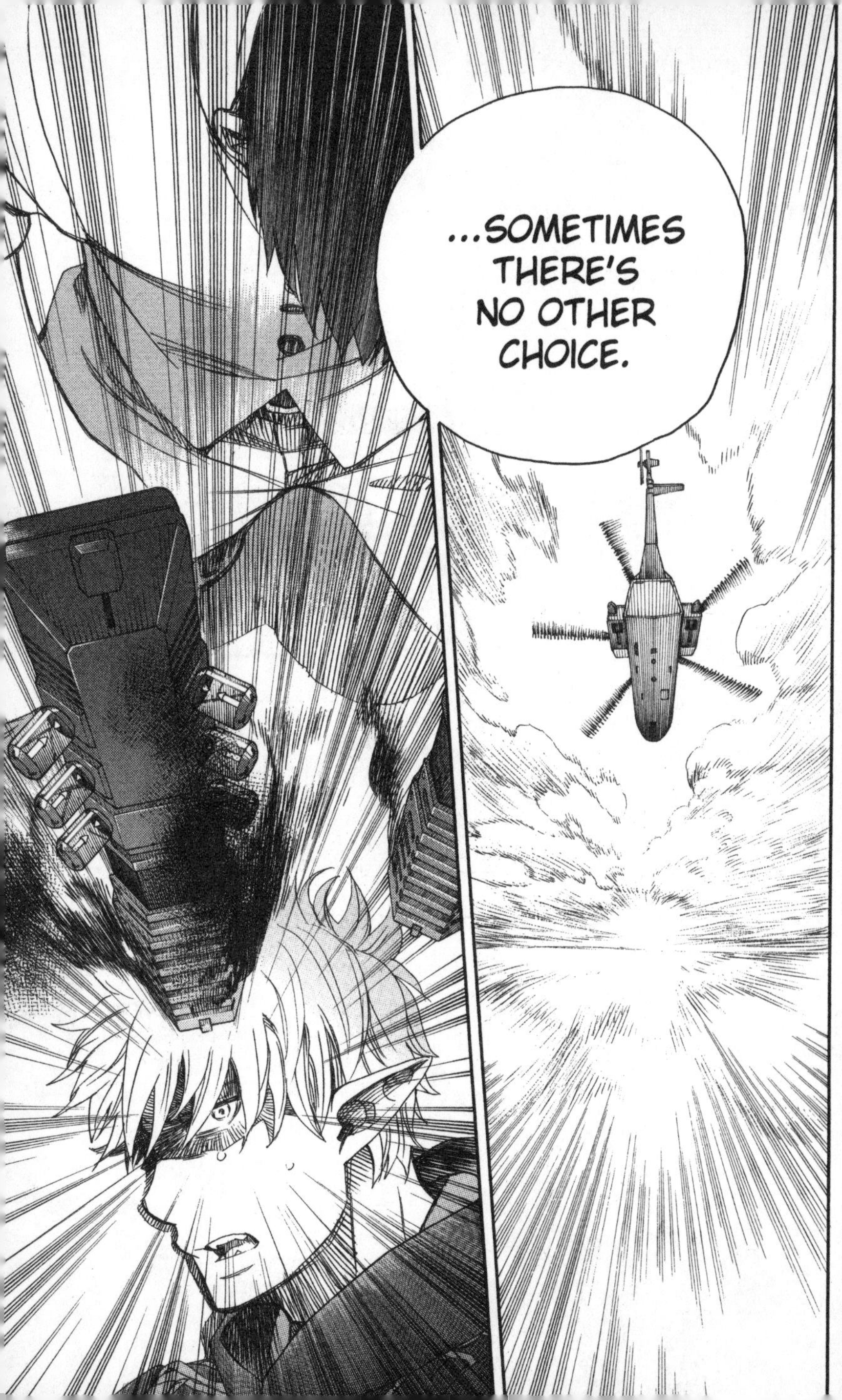
...SOMETIMES THERE'S NO OTHER CHOICE.

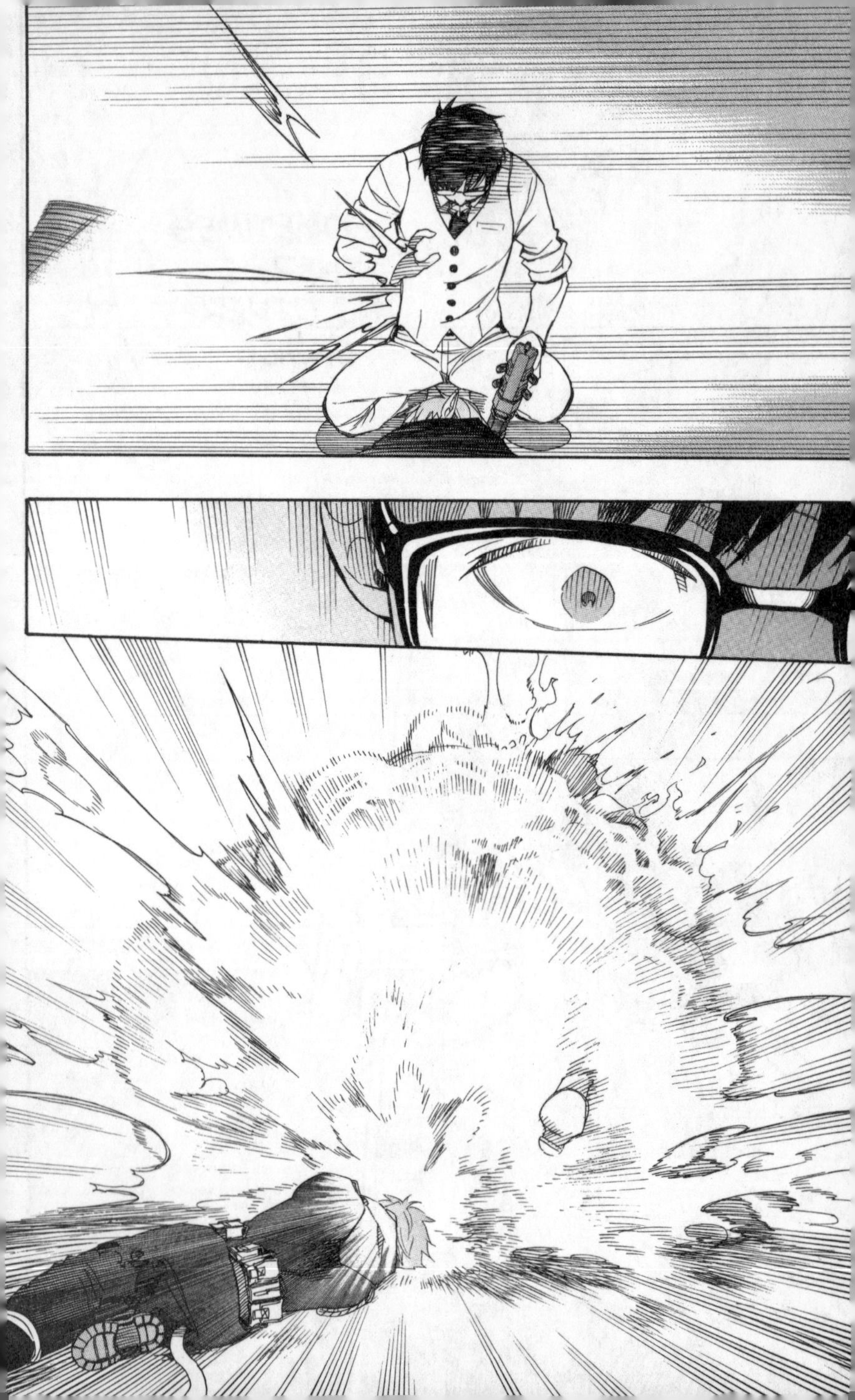

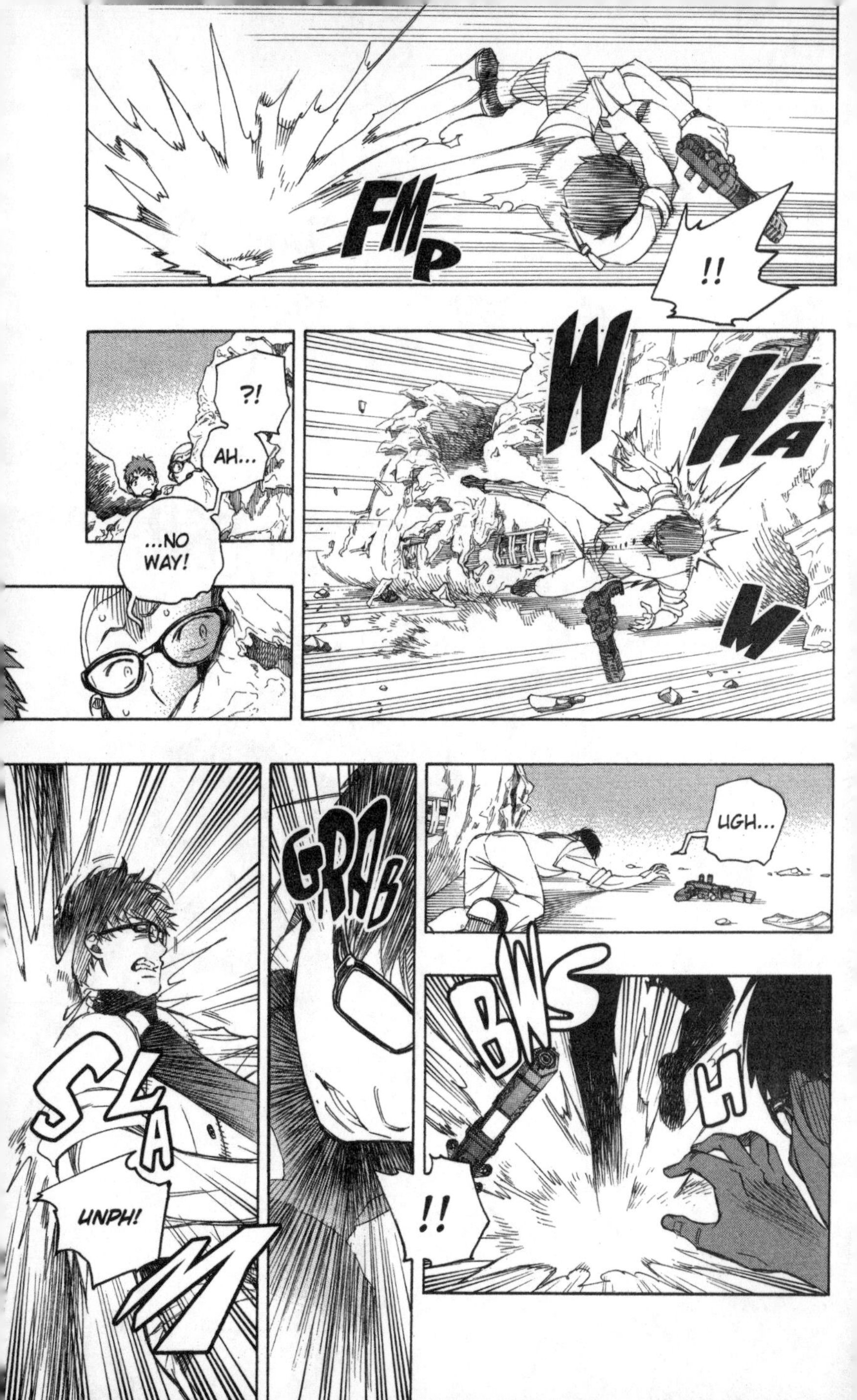
FMP
!!
WHAM
?!
AH...
...NO WAY!
UGH...
BWSH
!!
GRAB
SLAM
UNPH!

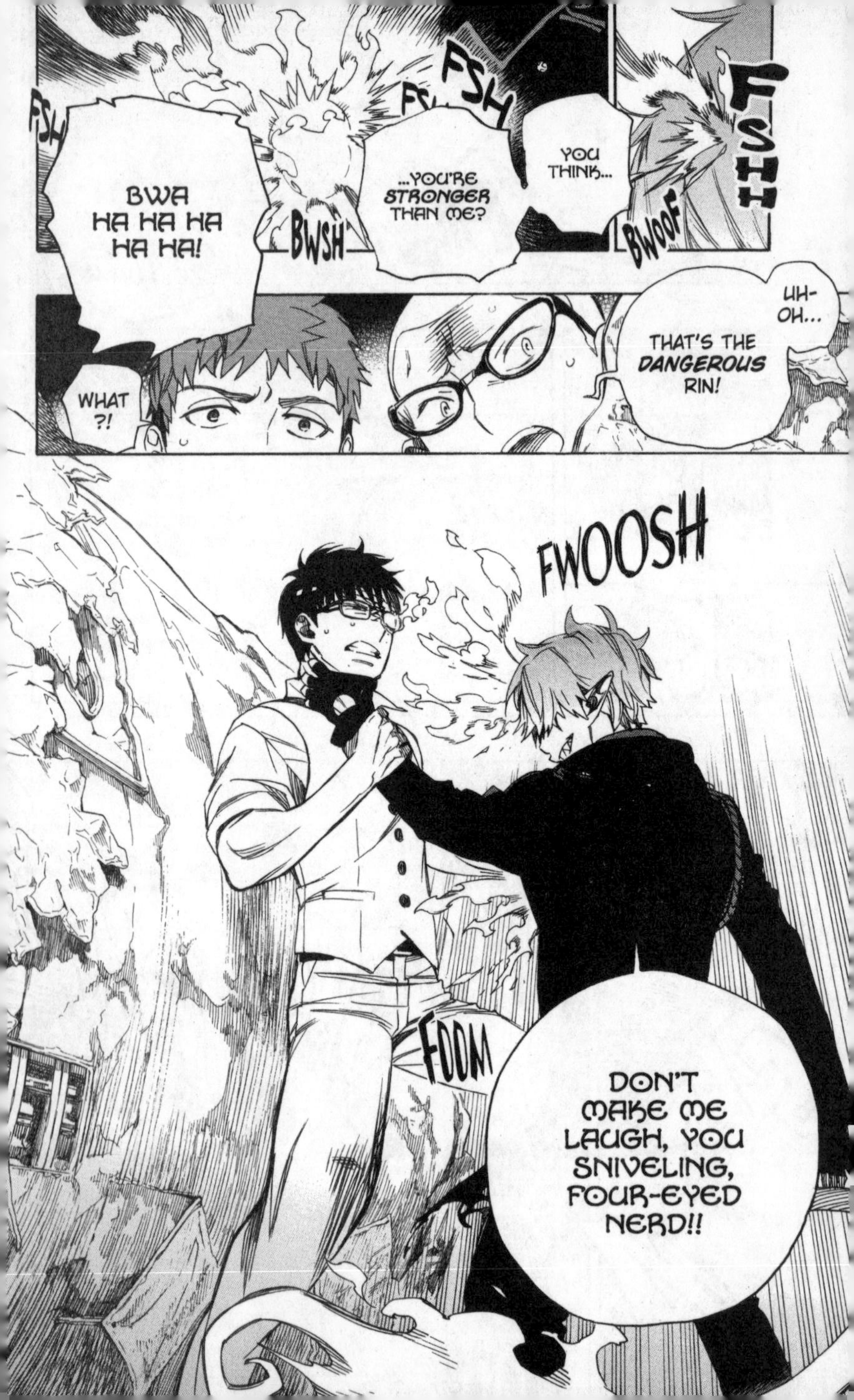
FSHH
BWOOF
YOU THINK...
FSH
...YOU'RE STRONGER THAN ME?
BWSH
FSH
BWA HA HA HA HA HA!
UH-OH...
THAT'S THE DANGEROUS RIN!
WHAT ?!
FWOOSH
FOOM
DON'T MAKE ME LAUGH, YOU SNIVELING, FOUR-EYED NERD!!

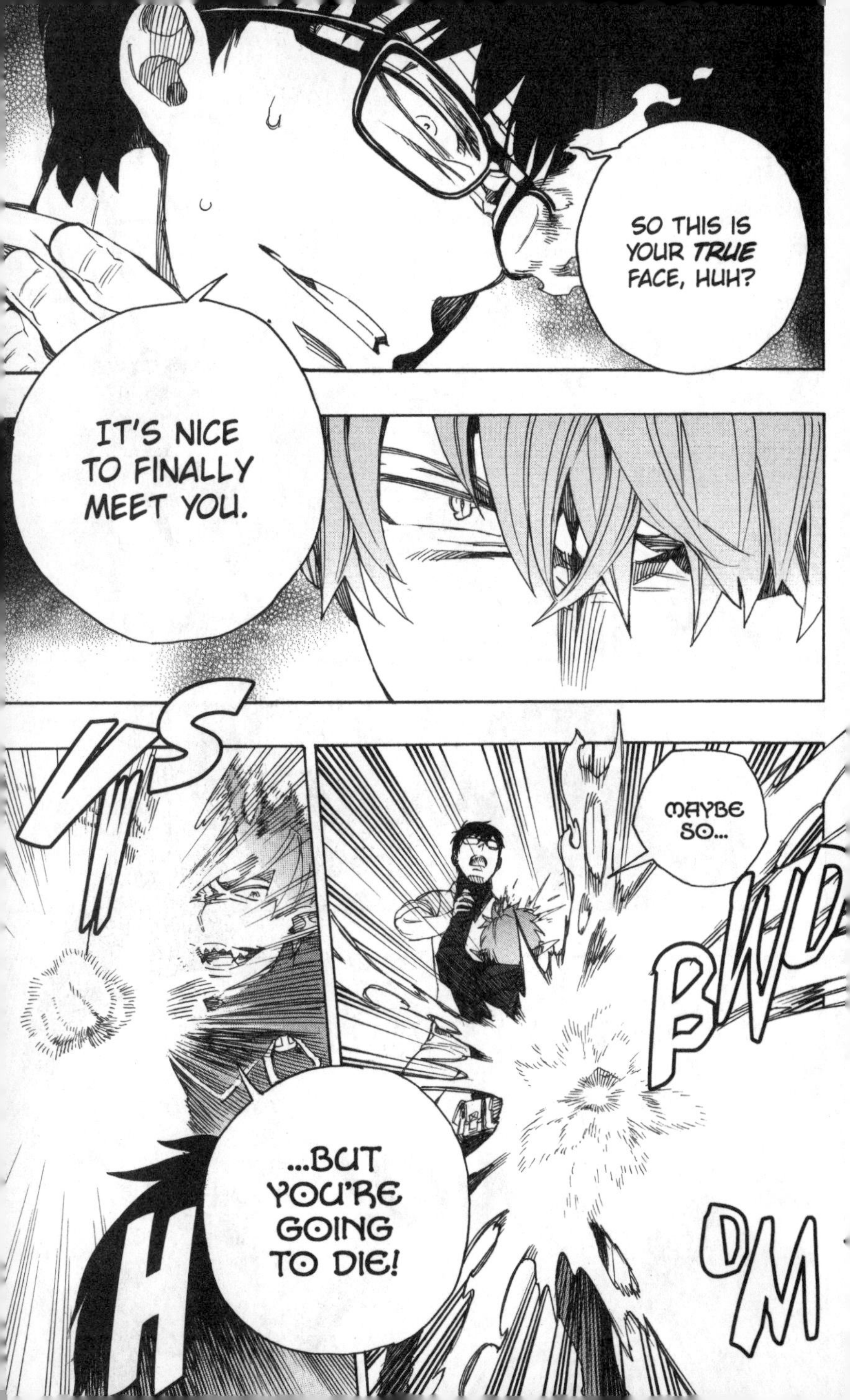
SO THIS IS YOUR TRUE FACE, HUH?
IT'S NICE TO FINALLY MEET YOU.
MAYBE SO...
...BUT YOU'RE GOING TO DIE!

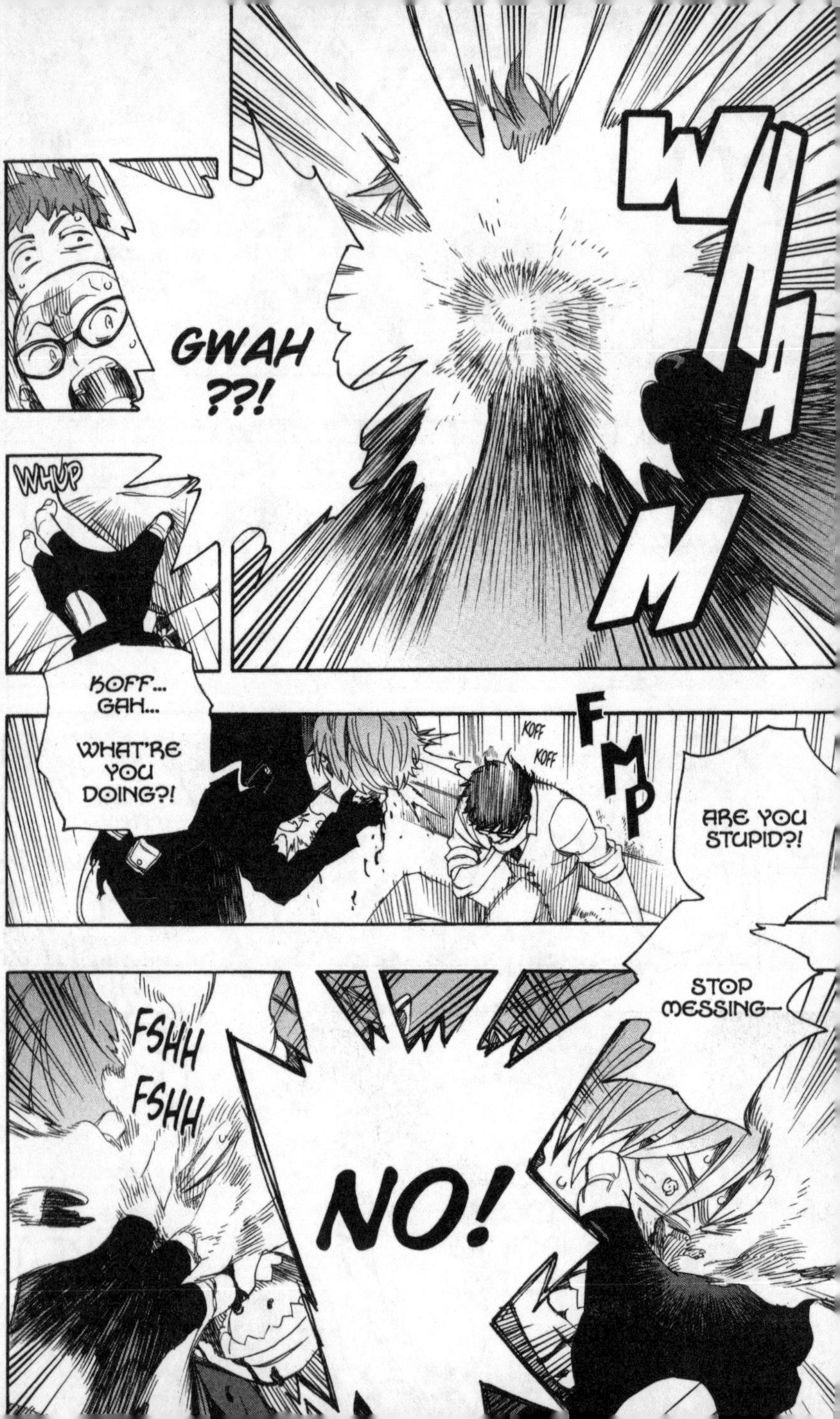
WHAMM
GWAH ??!
WHUP
KOFF... GAH...
WHAT'RE YOU DOING?!
FMP
KOFF
KOFF
ARE YOU STUPID?!
STOP MESSING—
NO!
FSHH
FSHH

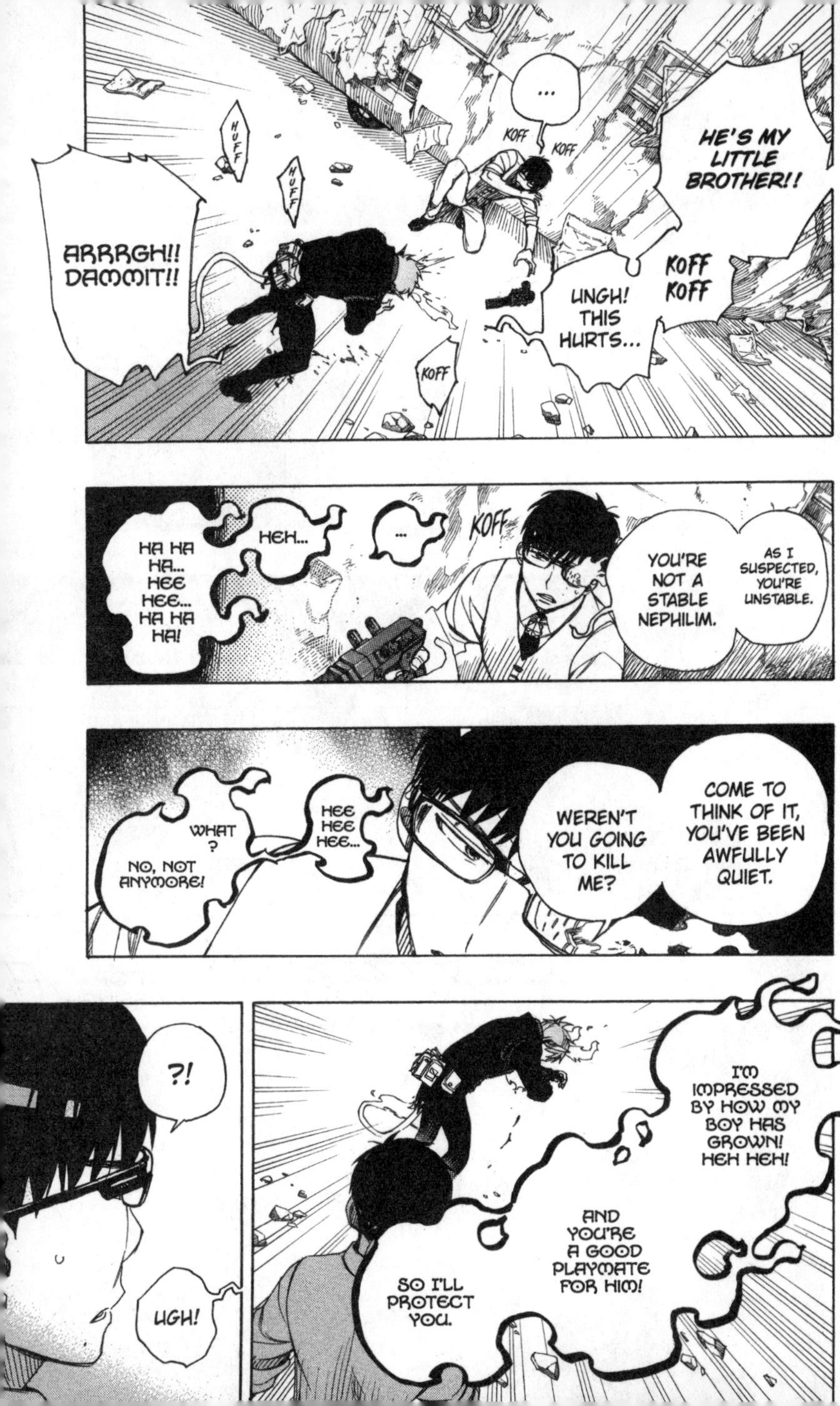
HE'S MY LITTLE BROTHER!!
...
KOFF
KOFF
HUFF
HUFF
ARRRGH!! DAMMIT!!
KOFF KOFF
UNGH! THIS HURTS...
KOFF
AS I SUSPECTED, YOU'RE UNSTABLE.
YOU'RE NOT A STABLE NEPHILIM.
KOFF
...
HEH...
HA HA HA... HEE HEE... HA HA HA!
COME TO THINK OF IT, YOU'VE BEEN AWFULLY QUIET.
WEREN'T YOU GOING TO KILL ME?
HEE HEE HEE...
WHAT?
NO, NOT ANYMORE!
I'M IMPRESSED BY HOW MY BOY HAS GROWN! HEH HEH!
AND YOU'RE A GOOD PLAYMATE FOR HIM!
SO I'LL PROTECT YOU.
?!
UGH!

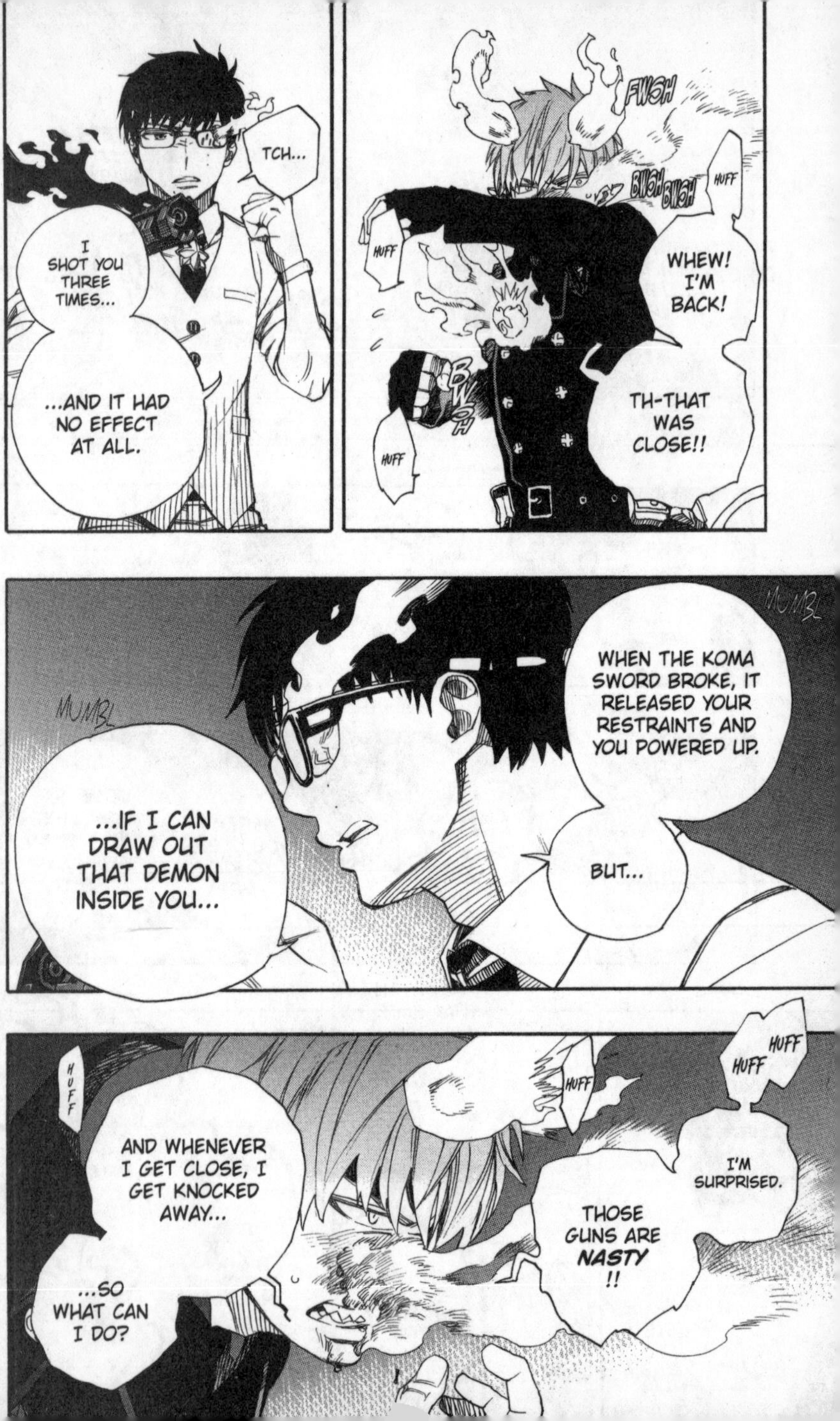
FWSH
BWSH BWSH
HUFF
HUFF
WHEW! I'M BACK!
TH-THAT WAS CLOSE!!
BWOSH
HUFF
TCH...
I SHOT YOU THREE TIMES...
...AND IT HAD NO EFFECT AT ALL.
MUMBL
WHEN THE KOMA SWORD BROKE, IT RELEASED YOUR RESTRAINTS AND YOU POWERED UP.
BUT...
MUMBL
...IF I CAN DRAW OUT THAT DEMON INSIDE YOU...
HUFF
HUFF
HUFF
I'M SURPRISED.
THOSE GUNS ARE NASTY!!
HUFF
AND WHENEVER I GET CLOSE, I GET KNOCKED AWAY...
...SO WHAT CAN I DO?

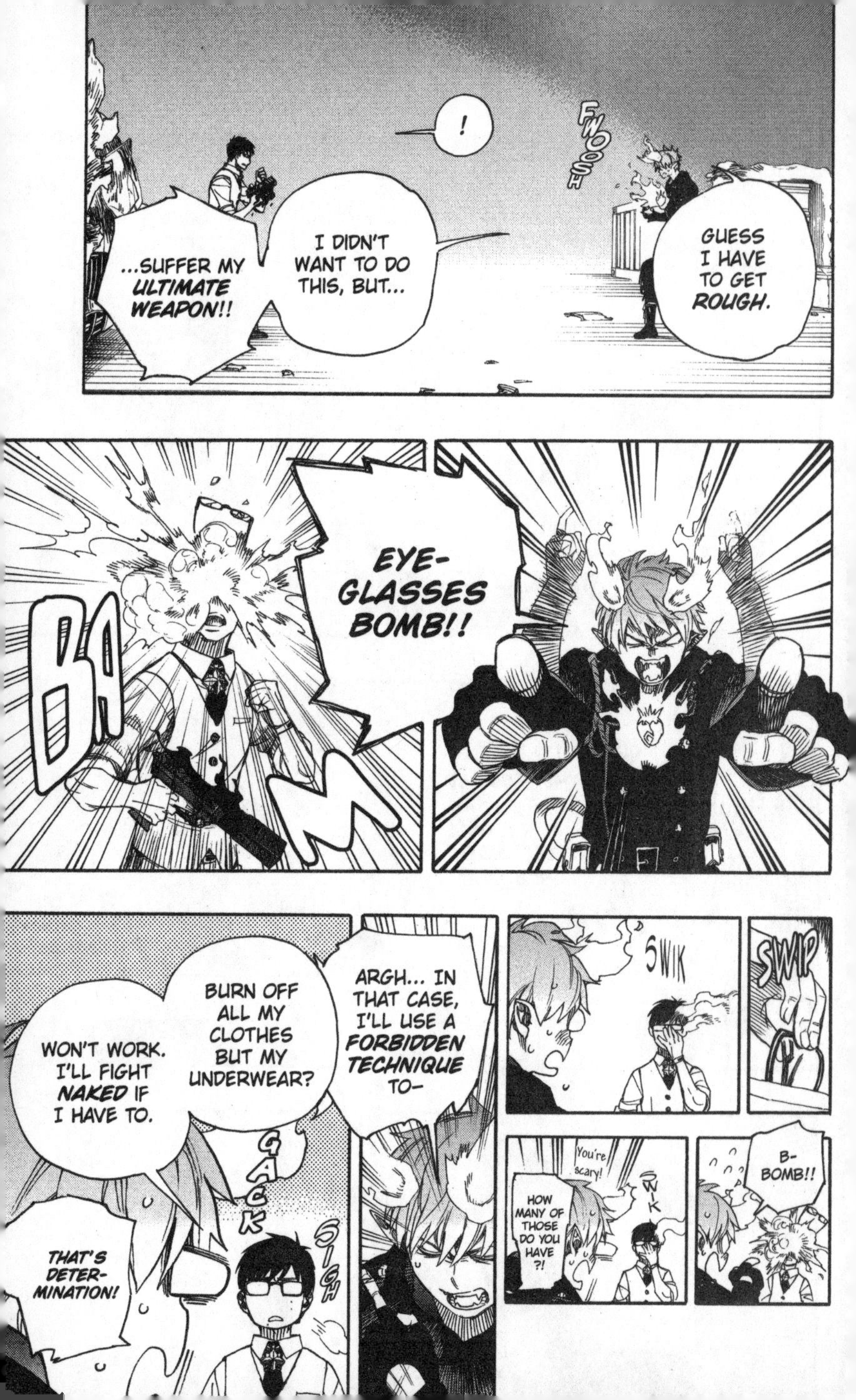
FWOOSH
GUESS I HAVE TO GET ***ROUGH.***
!
I DIDN'T WANT TO DO THIS, BUT...
...SUFFER MY ***ULTIMATE WEAPON!!***
EYE-GLASSES BOMB!!
BAM
SWIP
SWIK
B-BOMB!!
You're scary!
SWIK
HOW MANY OF THOSE DO YOU HAVE ?!
ARGH... IN THAT CASE, I'LL USE A ***FORBIDDEN TECHNIQUE*** TO-
BURN OFF ALL MY CLOTHES BUT MY UNDERWEAR?
WON'T WORK. I'LL FIGHT ***NAKED*** IF I HAVE TO.
GACK
SIGH
THAT'S DETER-MINATION!

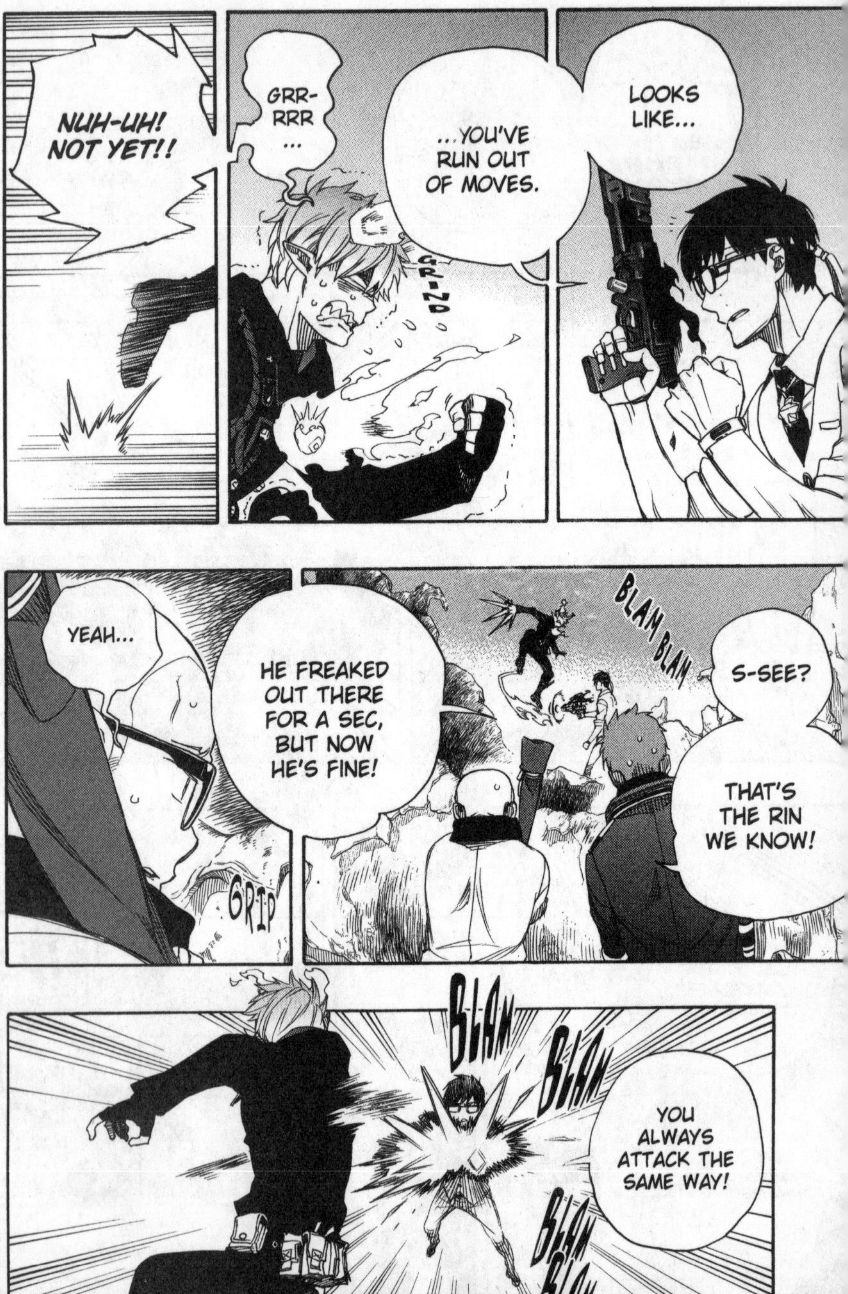
LOOKS LIKE...
...YOU'VE RUN OUT OF MOVES.
GRR-RRR ...
GRIND
NUH-UH! NOT YET!!
BLAM BLAM
S-SEE?
THAT'S THE RIN WE KNOW!
HE FREAKED OUT THERE FOR A SEC, BUT NOW HE'S FINE!
YEAH...
GRIP
YOU ALWAYS ATTACK THE SAME WAY!
BLAM
BLAM
BLAM
BLAM

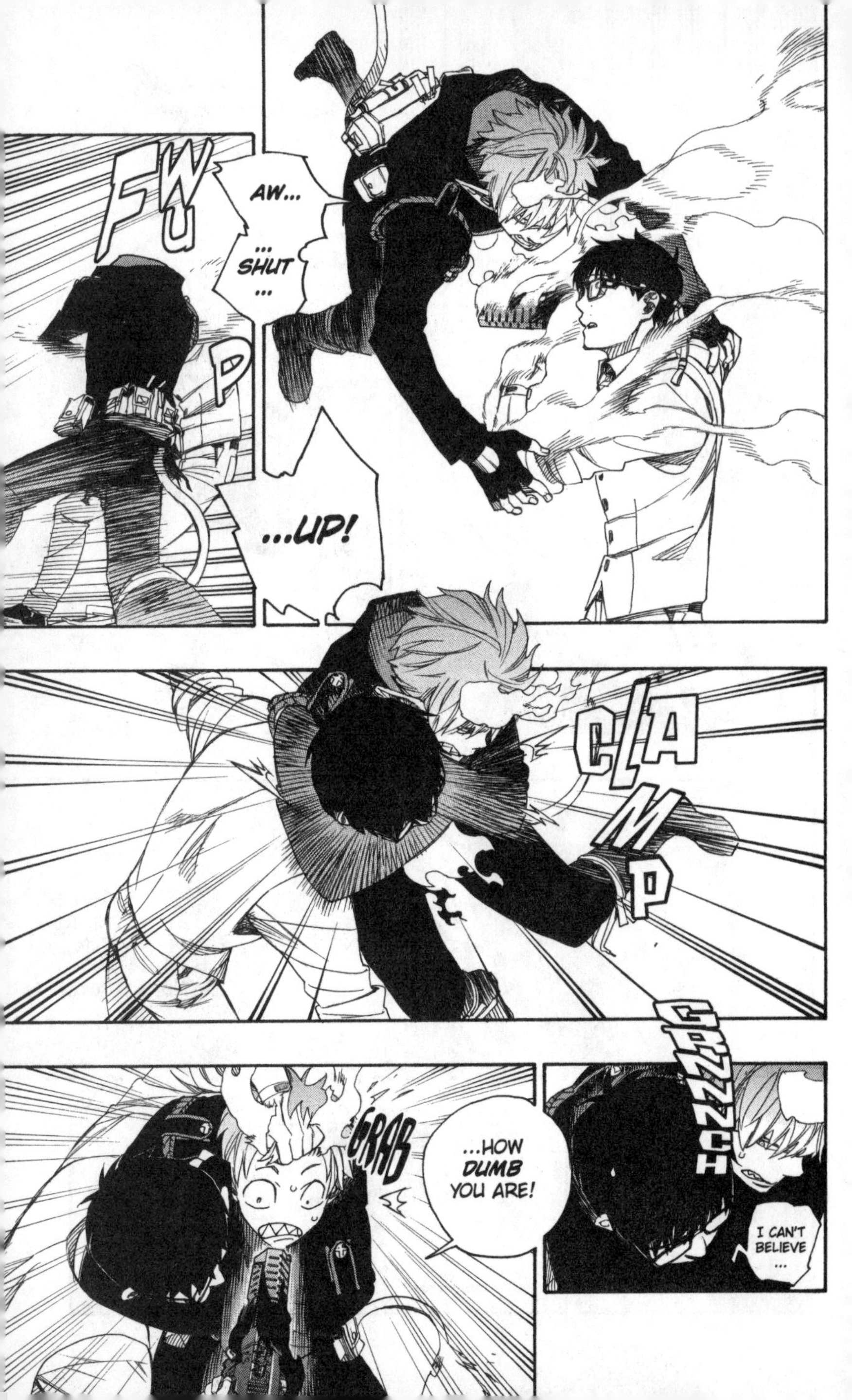
AW...
...SHUT...
...UP!
FWUP
CLAMP
GRNNNCH
I CAN'T BELIEVE...
GRAB
...HOW DUMB YOU ARE!

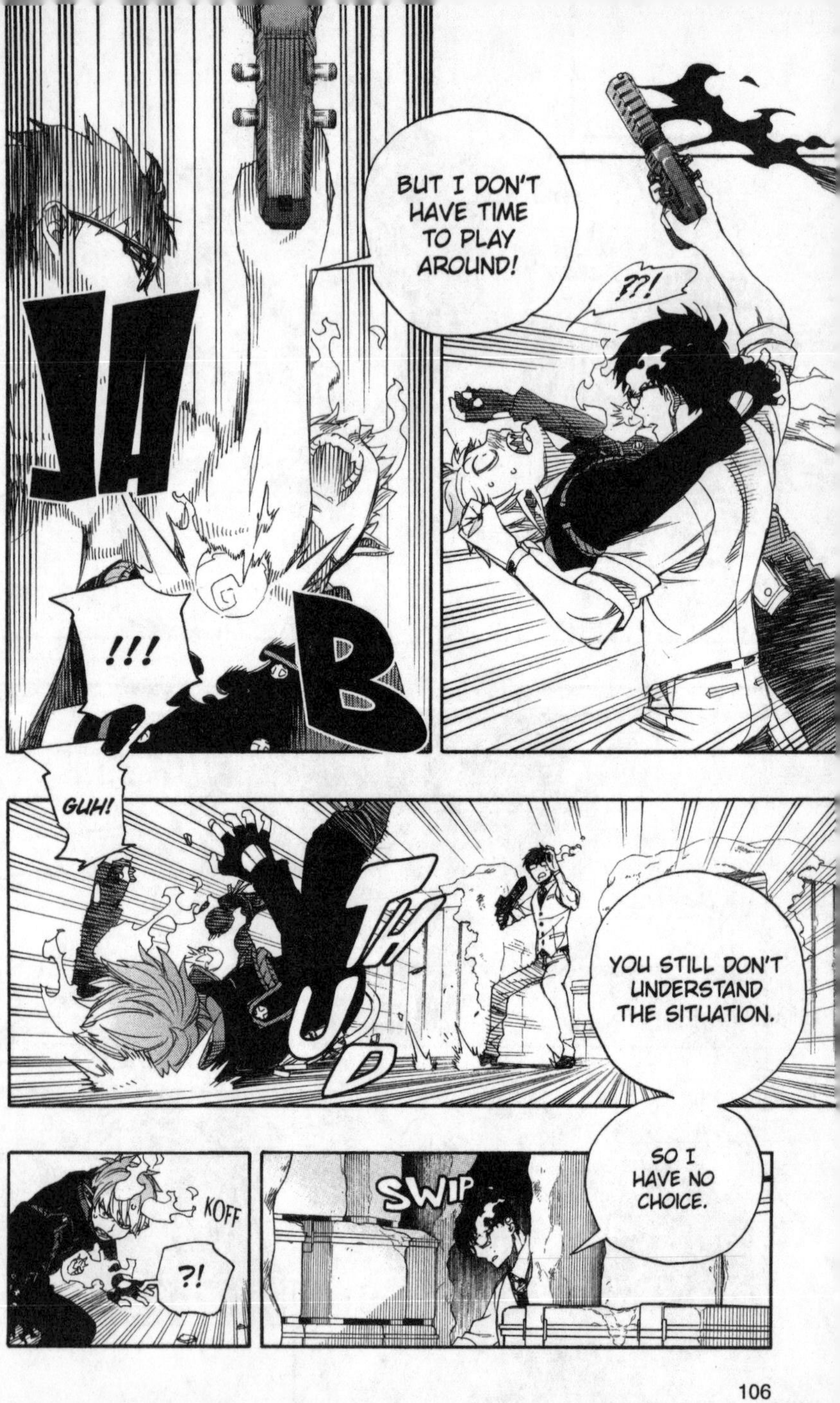
??!
BUT I DON'T HAVE TIME TO PLAY AROUND!
JAB
!!!
GUH!
THUD
YOU STILL DON'T UNDERSTAND THE SITUATION.
SO I HAVE NO CHOICE.
SWIP
KOFF
?!

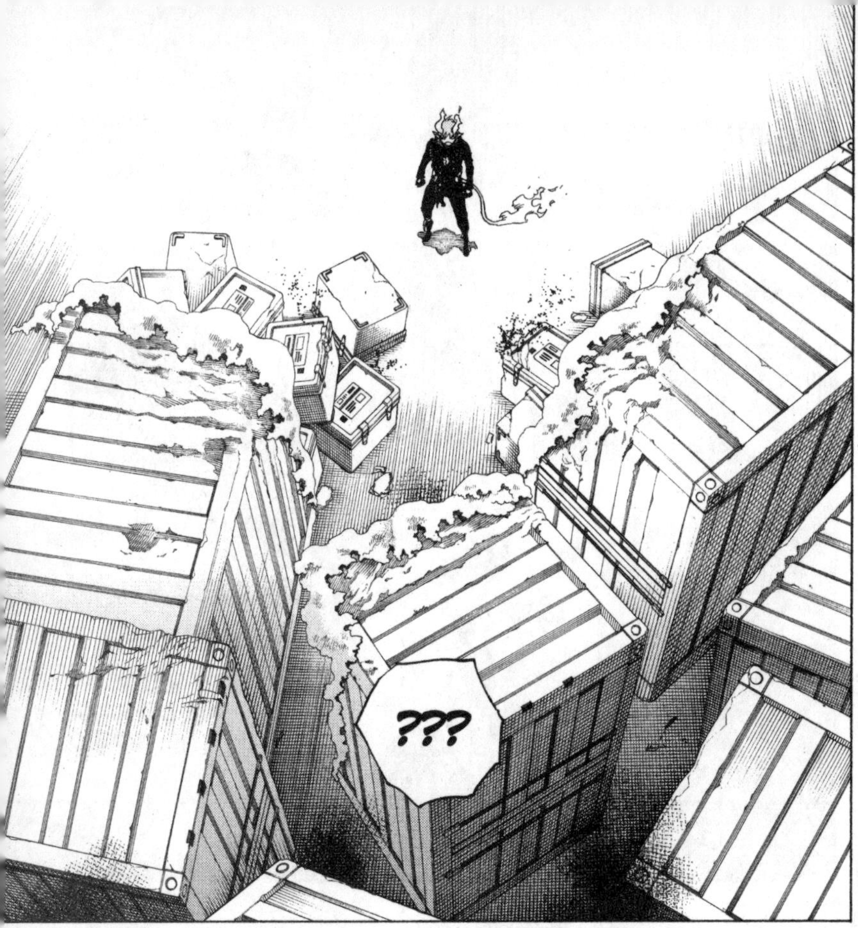
???

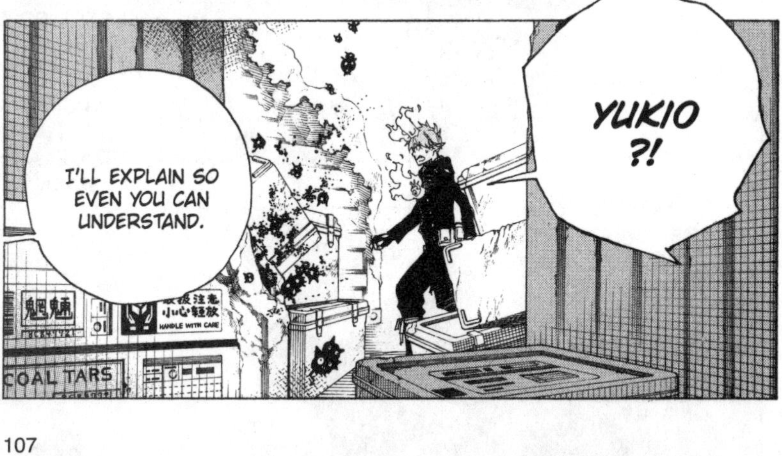
YUKIO ?!
I'LL EXPLAIN SO EVEN YOU CAN UNDERSTAND.
HANDLE WITH CARE
COAL TARS

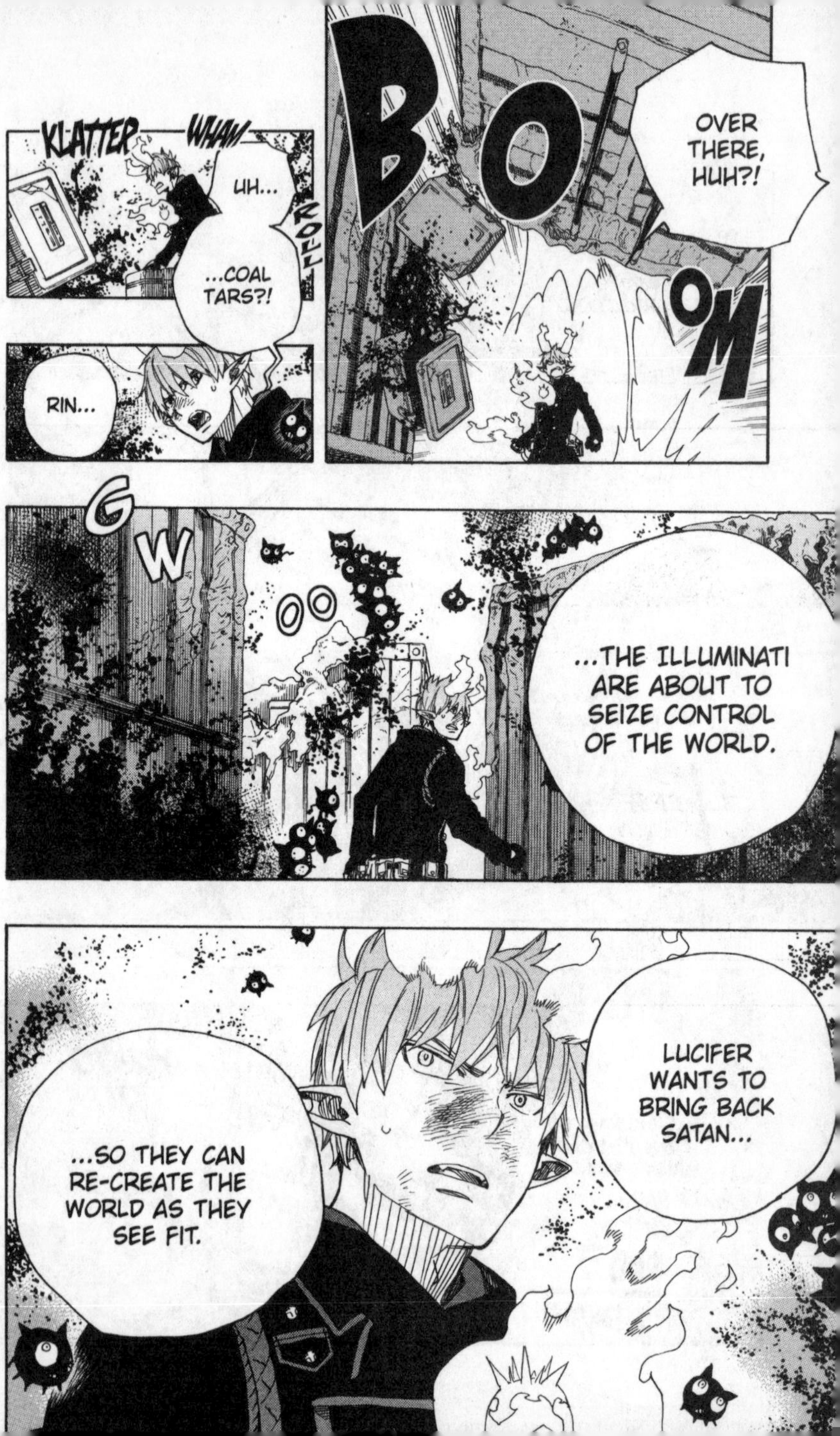
BOOM
OVER THERE, HUH?!
KLATTER
WHAM
UH...
ROLL
...COAL TARS?!
RIN...
GWOO
...THE ILLUMINATI ARE ABOUT TO SEIZE CONTROL OF THE WORLD.
LUCIFER WANTS TO BRING BACK SATAN...
...SO THEY CAN RE-CREATE THE WORLD AS THEY SEE FIT.

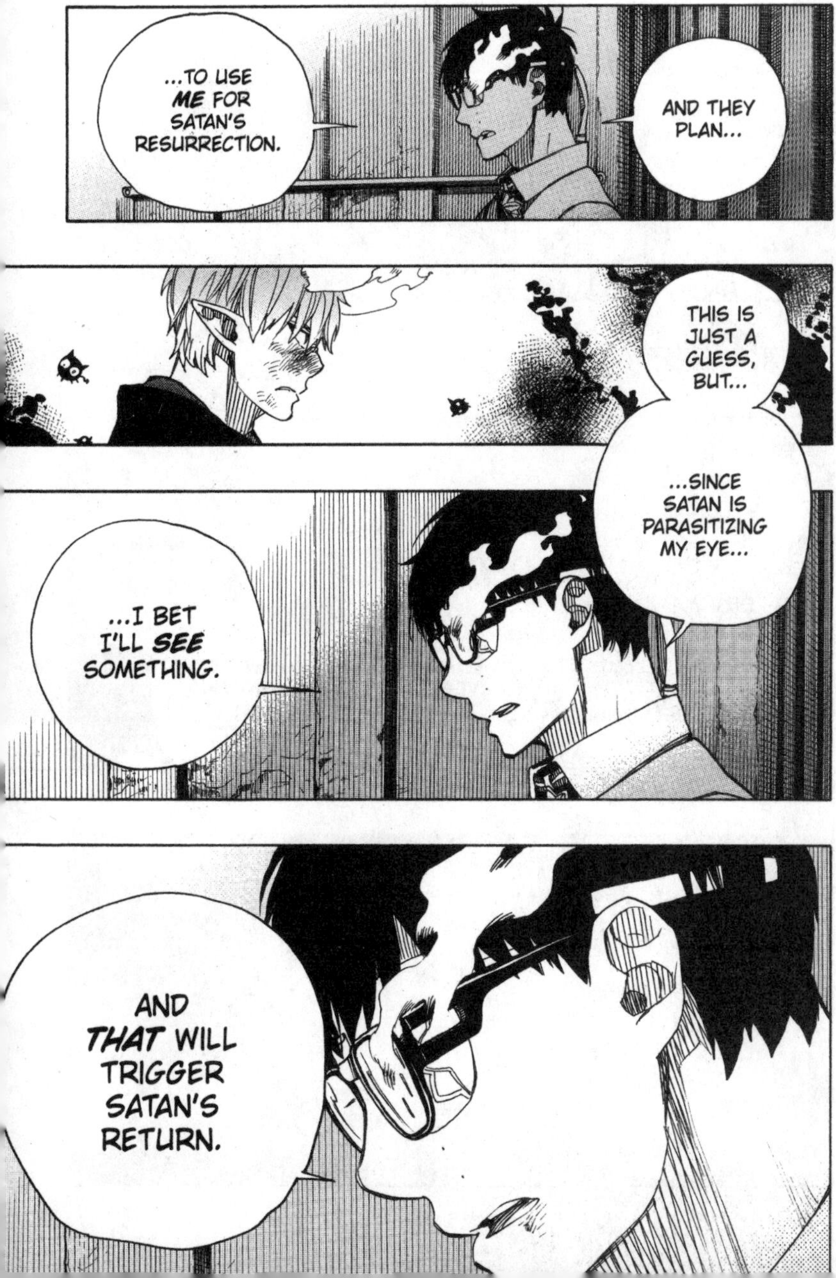
AND THEY PLAN...
...TO USE *ME* FOR SATAN'S RESURRECTION.
THIS IS JUST A GUESS, BUT...
...SINCE SATAN IS PARASITIZING MY EYE...
...I BET I'LL *SEE* SOMETHING.
AND *THAT* WILL TRIGGER SATAN'S RETURN.

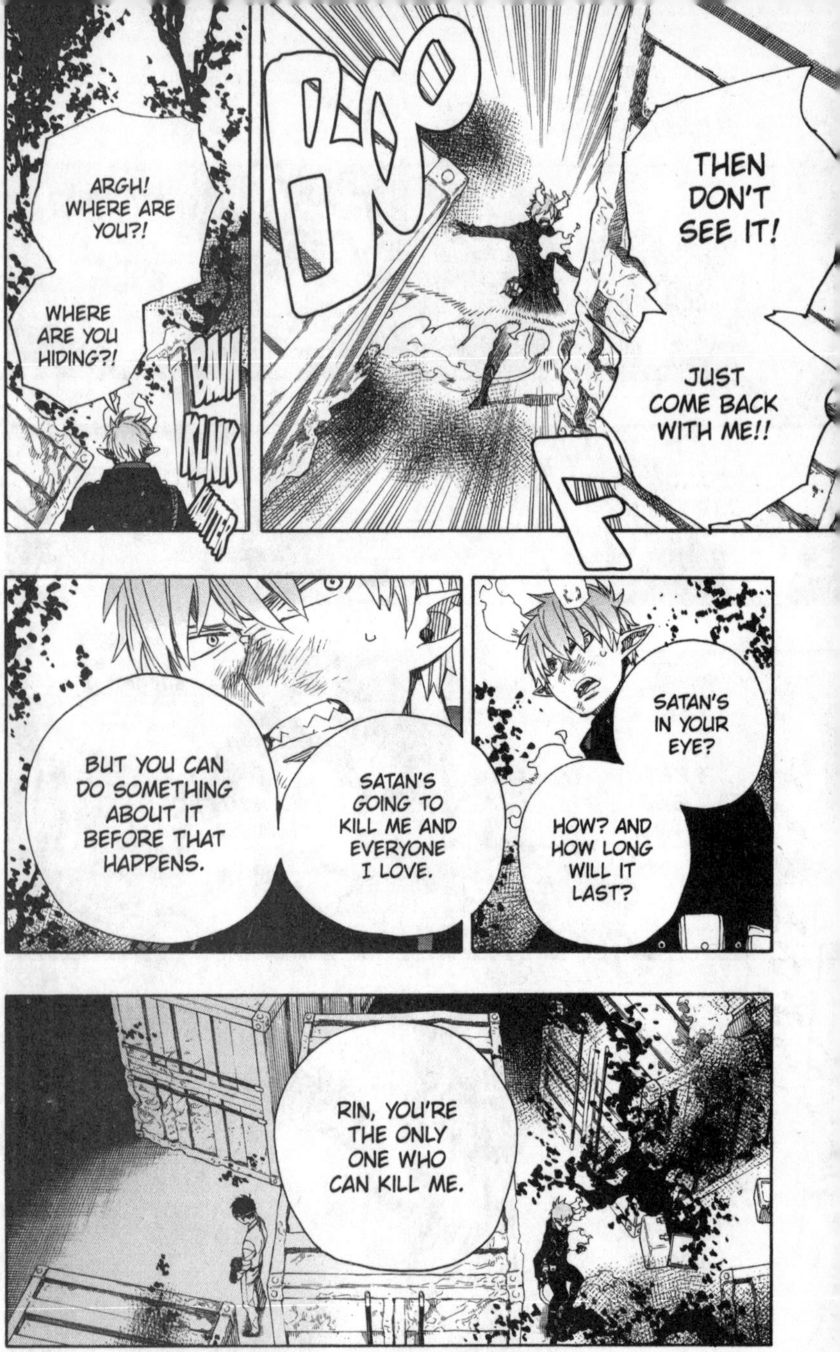
THEN DON'T SEE IT!
JUST COME BACK WITH ME!!
ARGH! WHERE ARE YOU?!
WHERE ARE YOU HIDING?!
BAM
KLINK
KLATTER
SATAN'S IN YOUR EYE?
HOW? AND HOW LONG WILL IT LAST?
SATAN'S GOING TO KILL ME AND EVERYONE I LOVE.
BUT YOU CAN DO SOMETHING ABOUT IT BEFORE THAT HAPPENS.
RIN, YOU'RE THE ONLY ONE WHO CAN KILL ME.

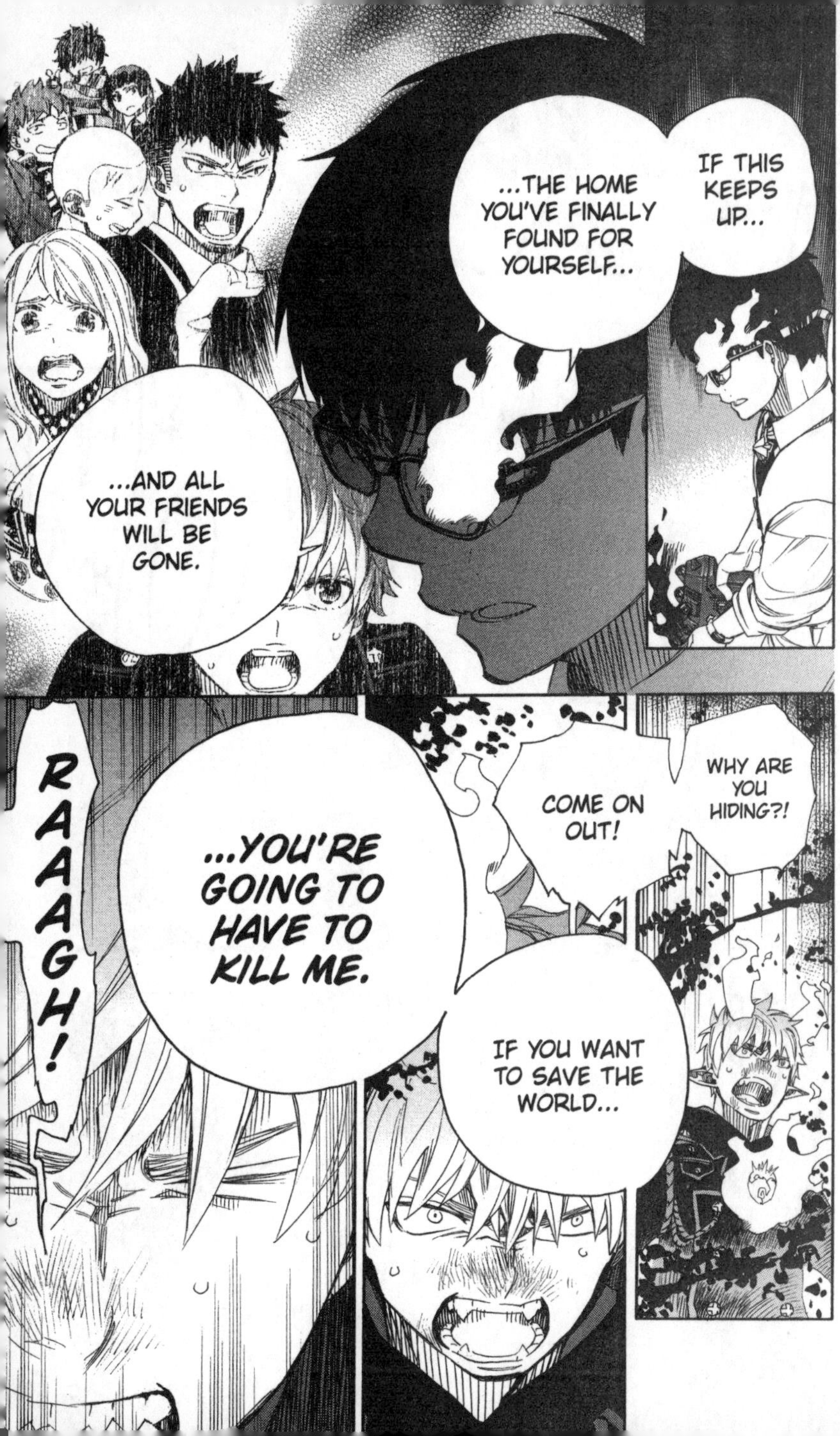
IF THIS KEEPS UP...
...THE HOME YOU'VE FINALLY FOUND FOR YOURSELF...
...AND ALL YOUR FRIENDS WILL BE GONE.
WHY ARE YOU HIDING?!
COME ON OUT!
IF YOU WANT TO SAVE THE WORLD...
...YOU'RE GOING TO HAVE TO KILL ME.
RAAAAGH!

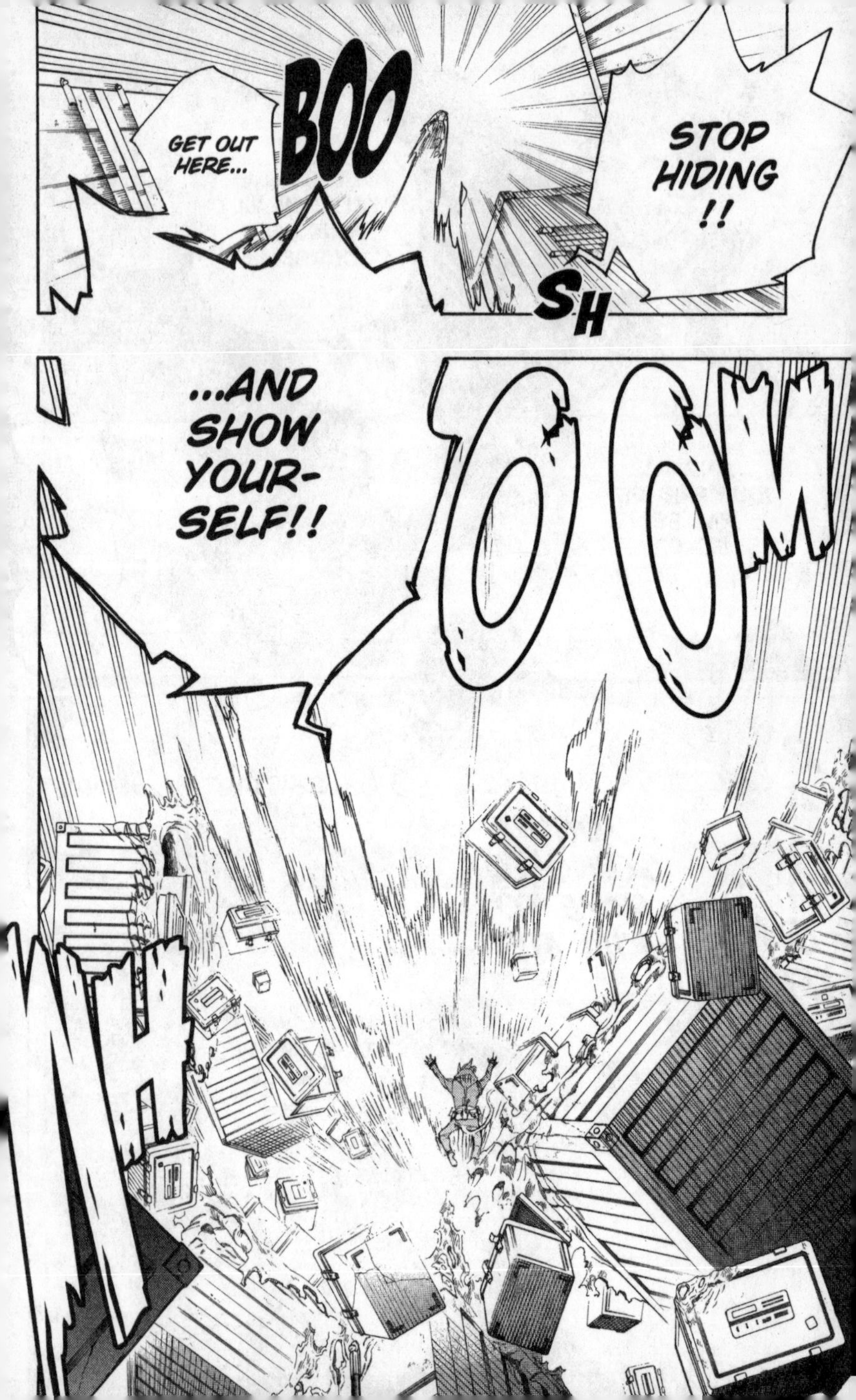
STOP HIDING!!
GET OUT HERE...
BOO
SH
...AND SHOW YOURSELF!!
OOM
WH

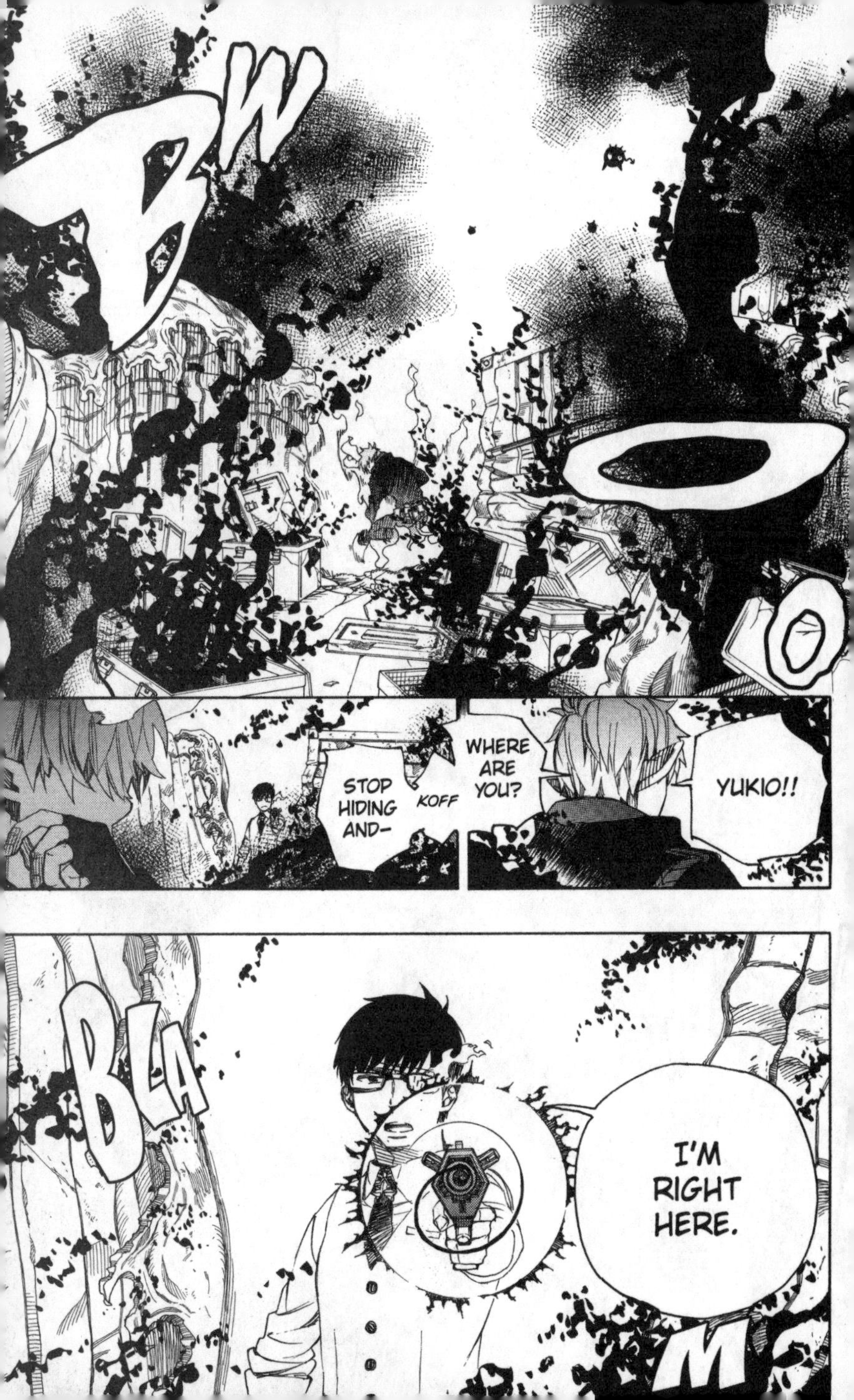
YUKIO!!
WHERE ARE YOU?
KOFF
STOP HIDING AND–
I'M RIGHT HERE.
BLA

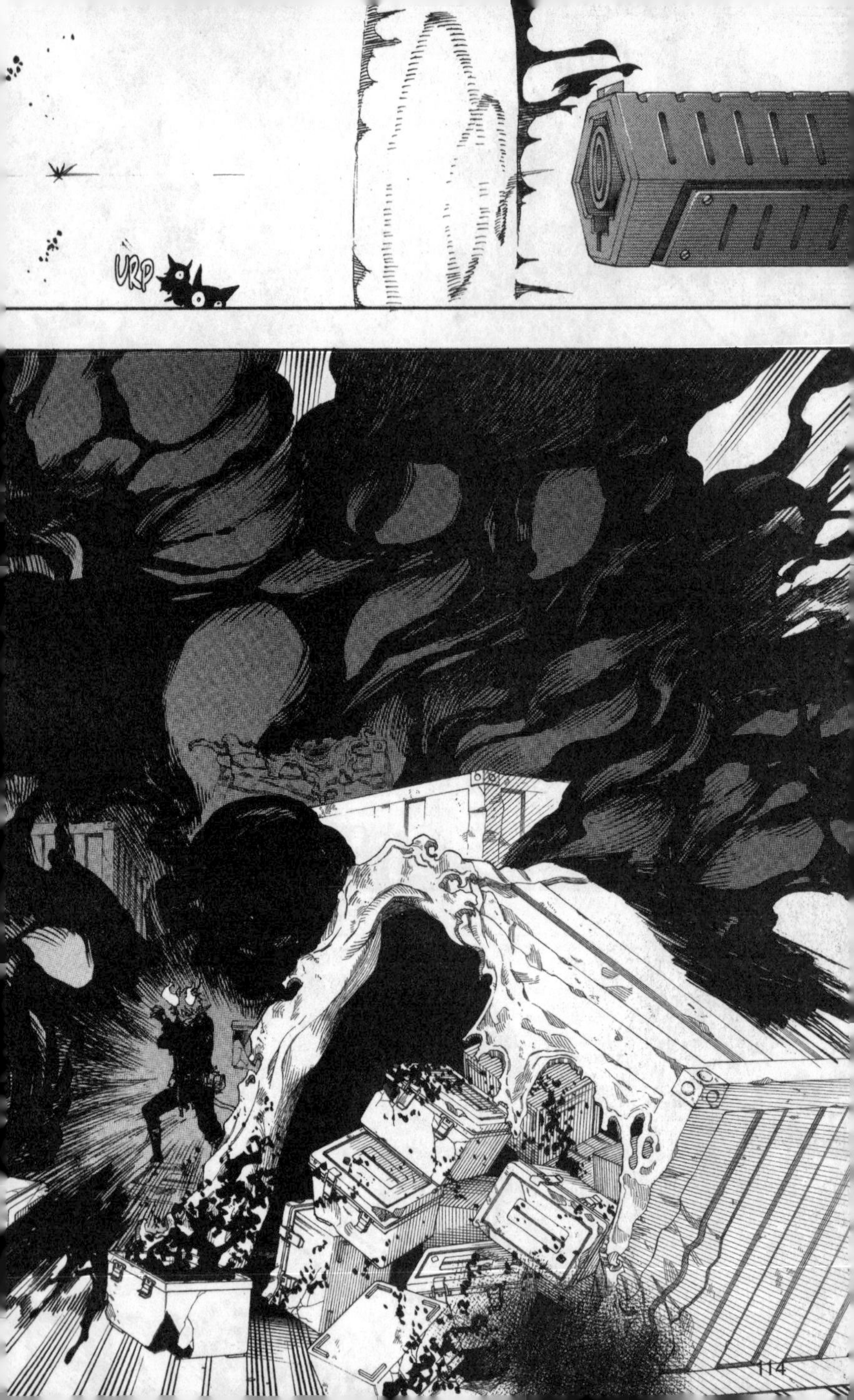
URP

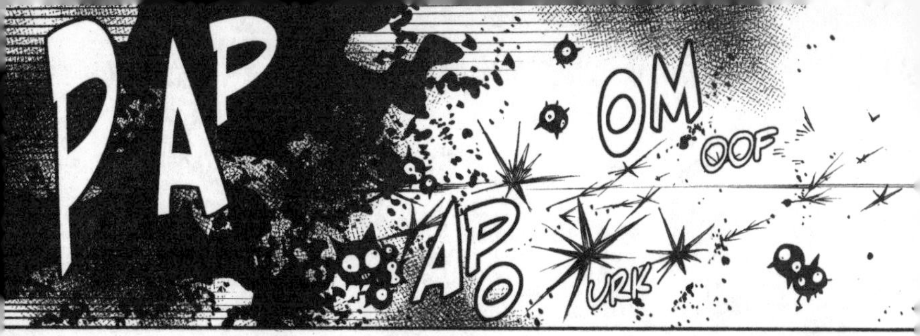
OOF
OM
URK
APO
PAP
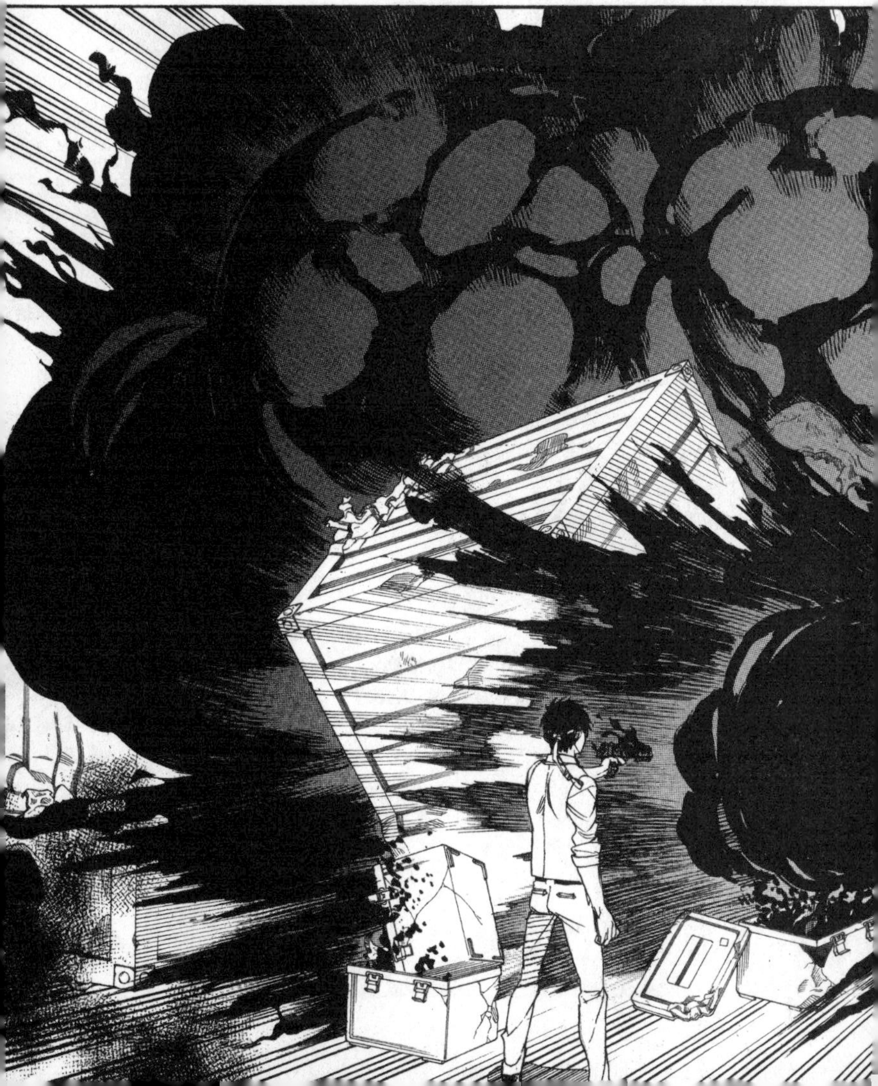

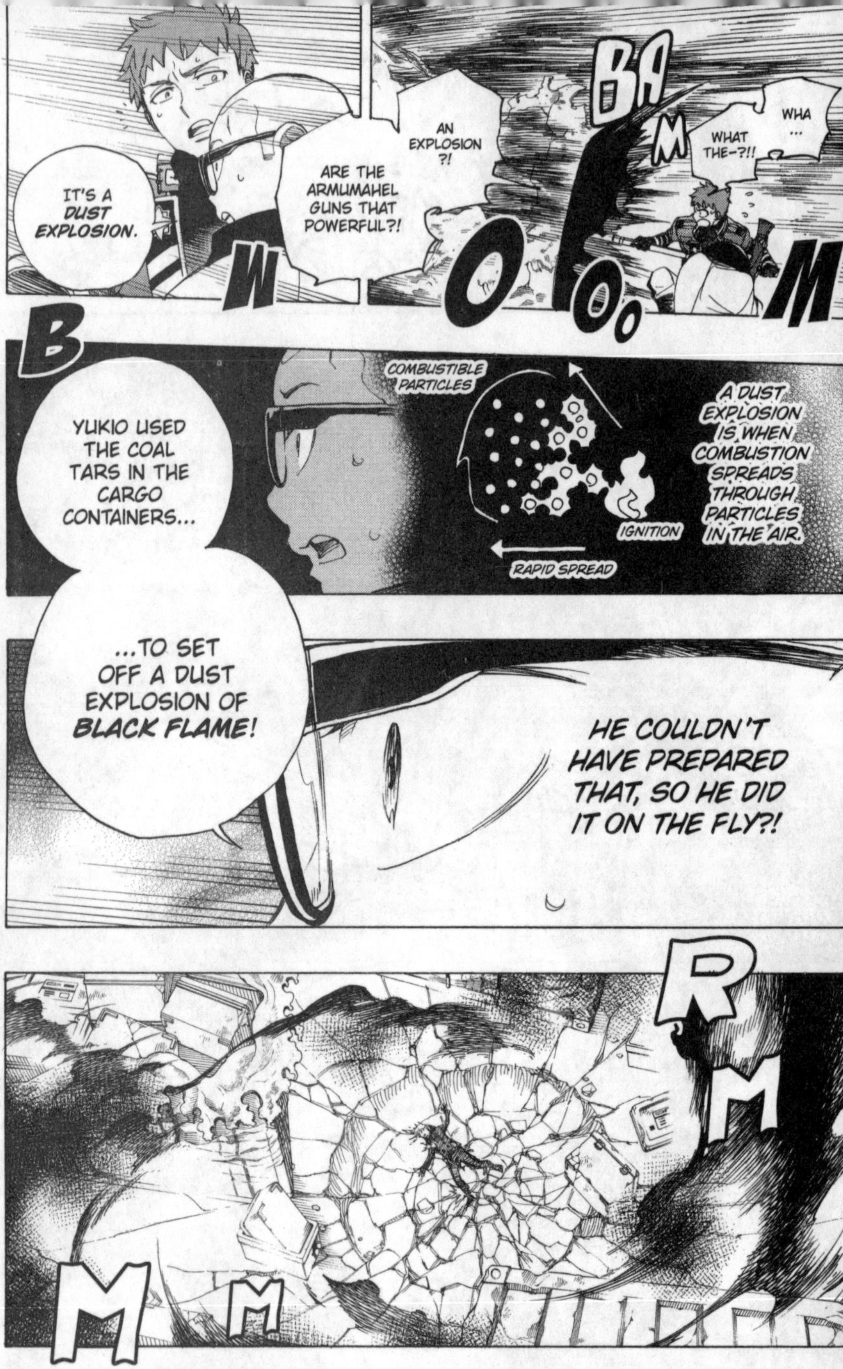

BAM
WHA...
WHAT THE-?!!
AN EXPLOSION?!
ARE THE ARMUMAHEL GUNS THAT POWERFUL?!
IT'S A DUST EXPLOSION.
BWOOOM
A DUST EXPLOSION IS WHEN COMBUSTION SPREADS THROUGH PARTICLES IN THE AIR.
COMBUSTIBLE PARTICLES
IGNITION
RAPID SPREAD
YUKIO USED THE COAL TARS IN THE CARGO CONTAINERS...
...TO SET OFF A DUST EXPLOSION OF BLACK FLAME!
HE COULDN'T HAVE PREPARED THAT, SO HE DID IT ON THE FLY?!
RMMMM

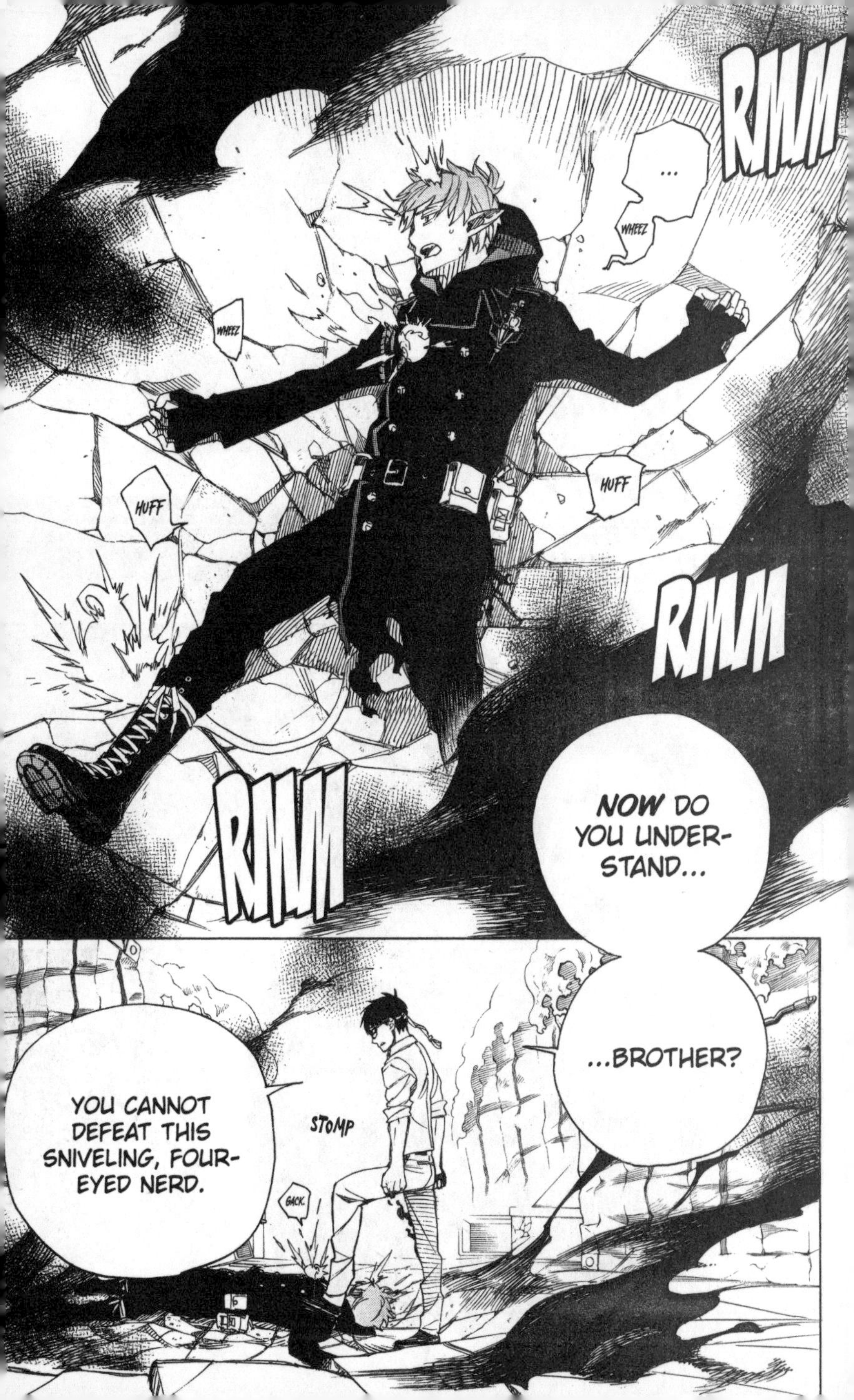
RMM
...
WHEEZ
WHEEZ
HUFF
HUFF
RMM
NOW DO YOU UNDERSTAND...
RMM
...BROTHER?
STOMP
YOU CANNOT DEFEAT THIS SNIVELING, FOUR-EYED NERD.
GACK

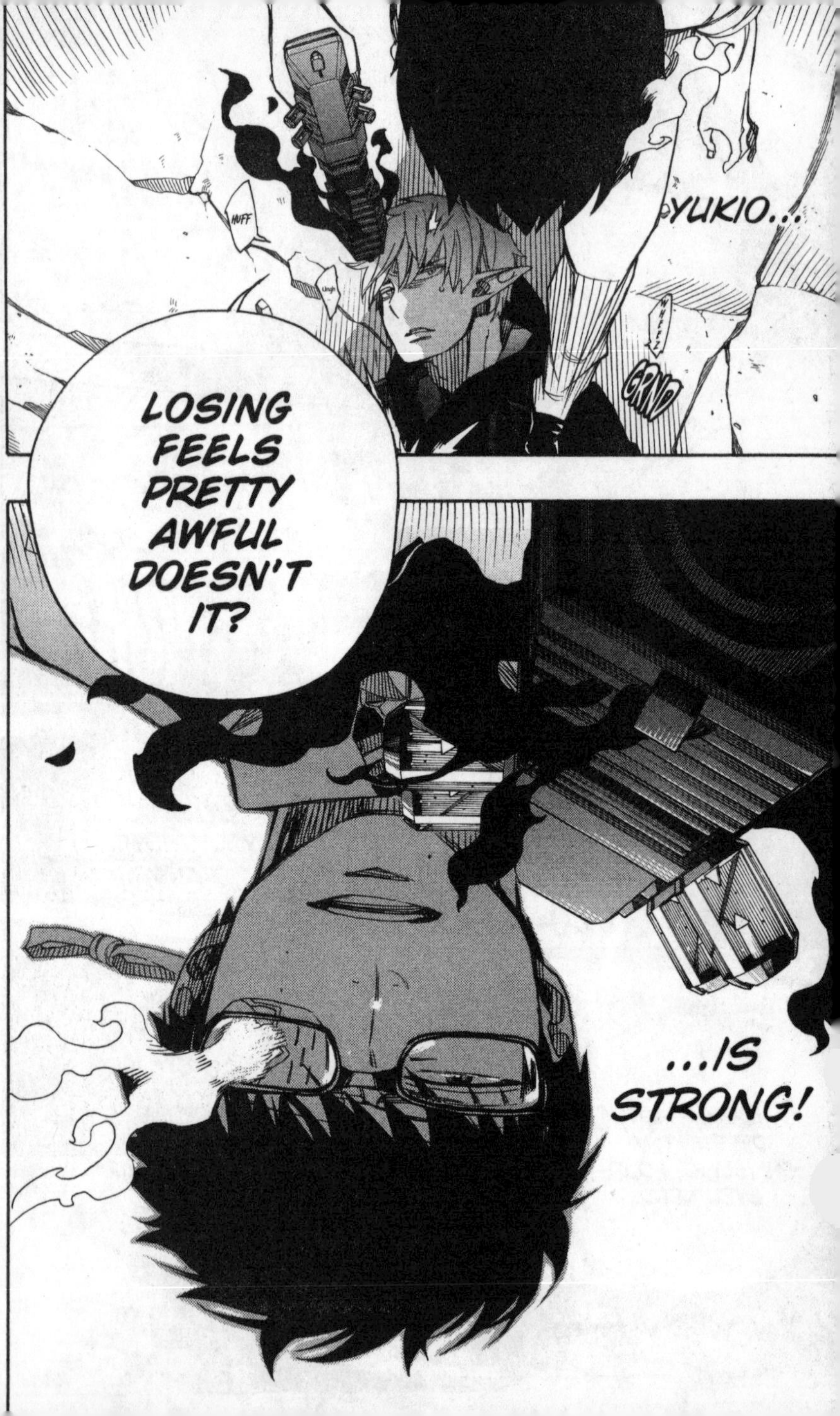
YUKIO...
WHEEZ
GRND
HUFF
Ungh
LOSING FEELS PRETTY AWFUL DOESN'T IT?
...IS STRONG!

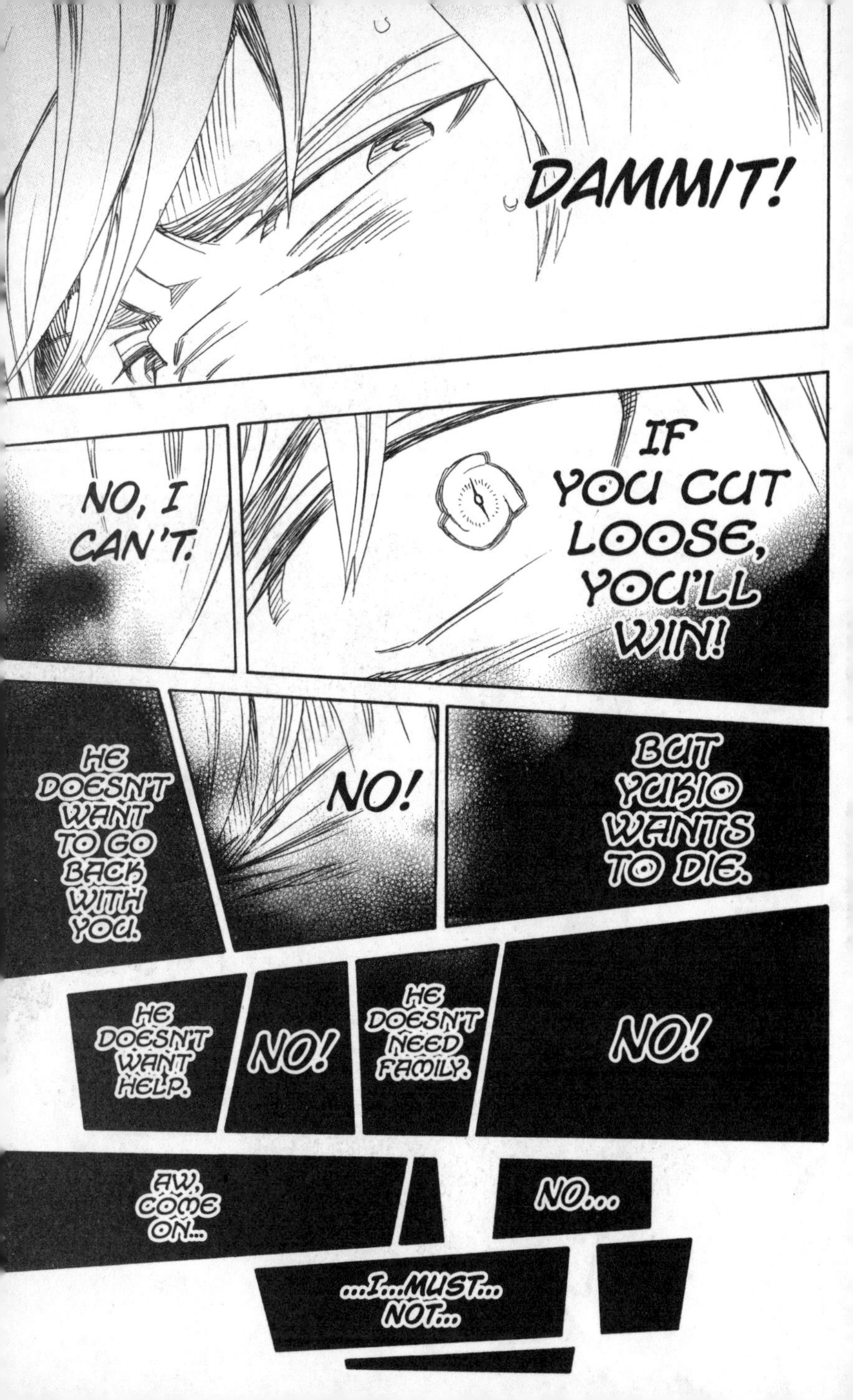
DAMMIT!
IF YOU CUT LOOSE, YOU'LL WIN!
NO, I CAN'T.
BUT YUKIO WANTS TO DIE.
NO!
HE DOESN'T WANT TO GO BACK WITH YOU.
NO!
HE DOESN'T NEED FAMILY.
NO!
HE DOESN'T WANT HELP.
NO...
AW, COME ON...
...I...MUST... NOT...

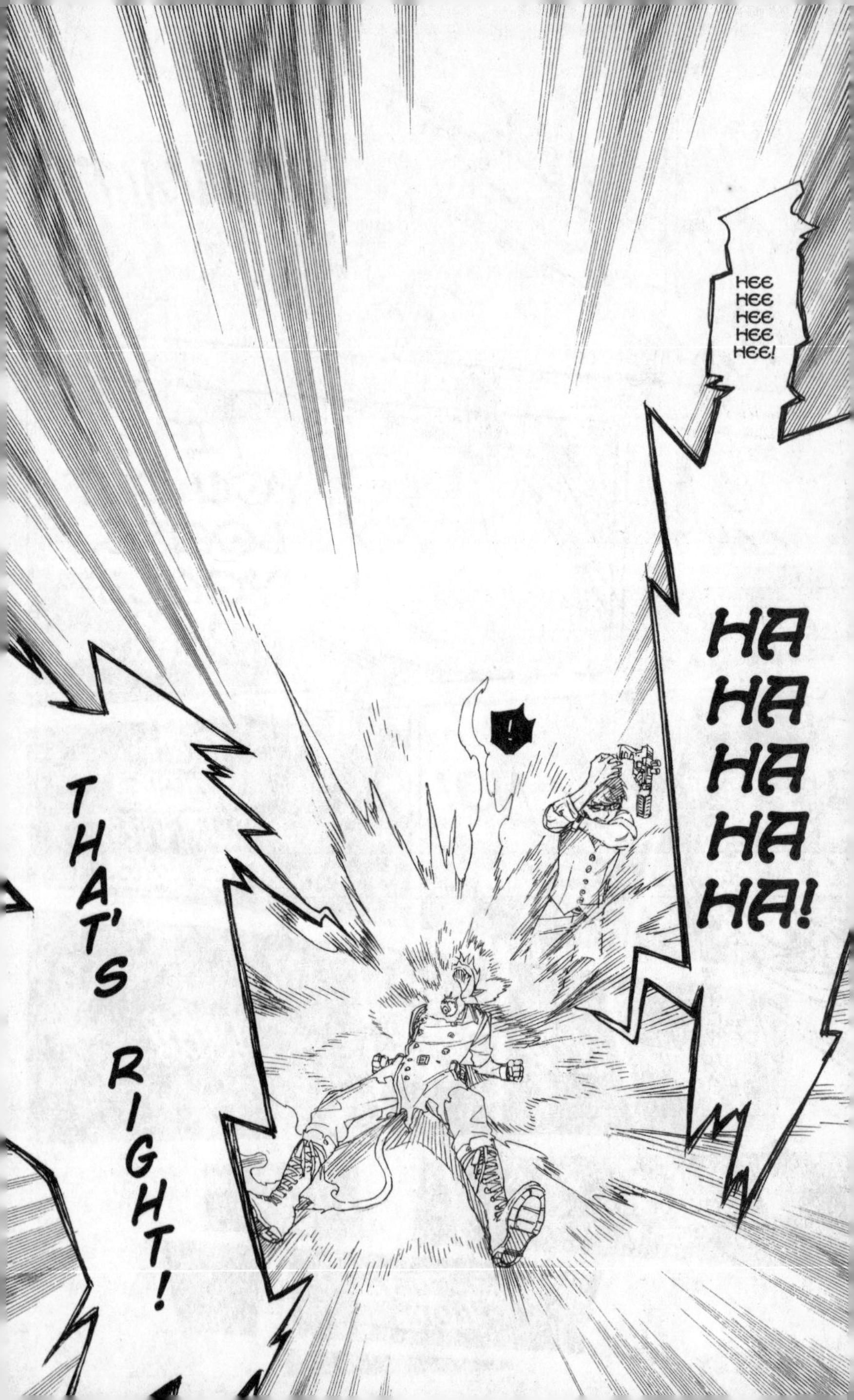
HEE HEE HEE HEE HEE!
HA HA HA HA HA!
!
THAT'S RIGHT!

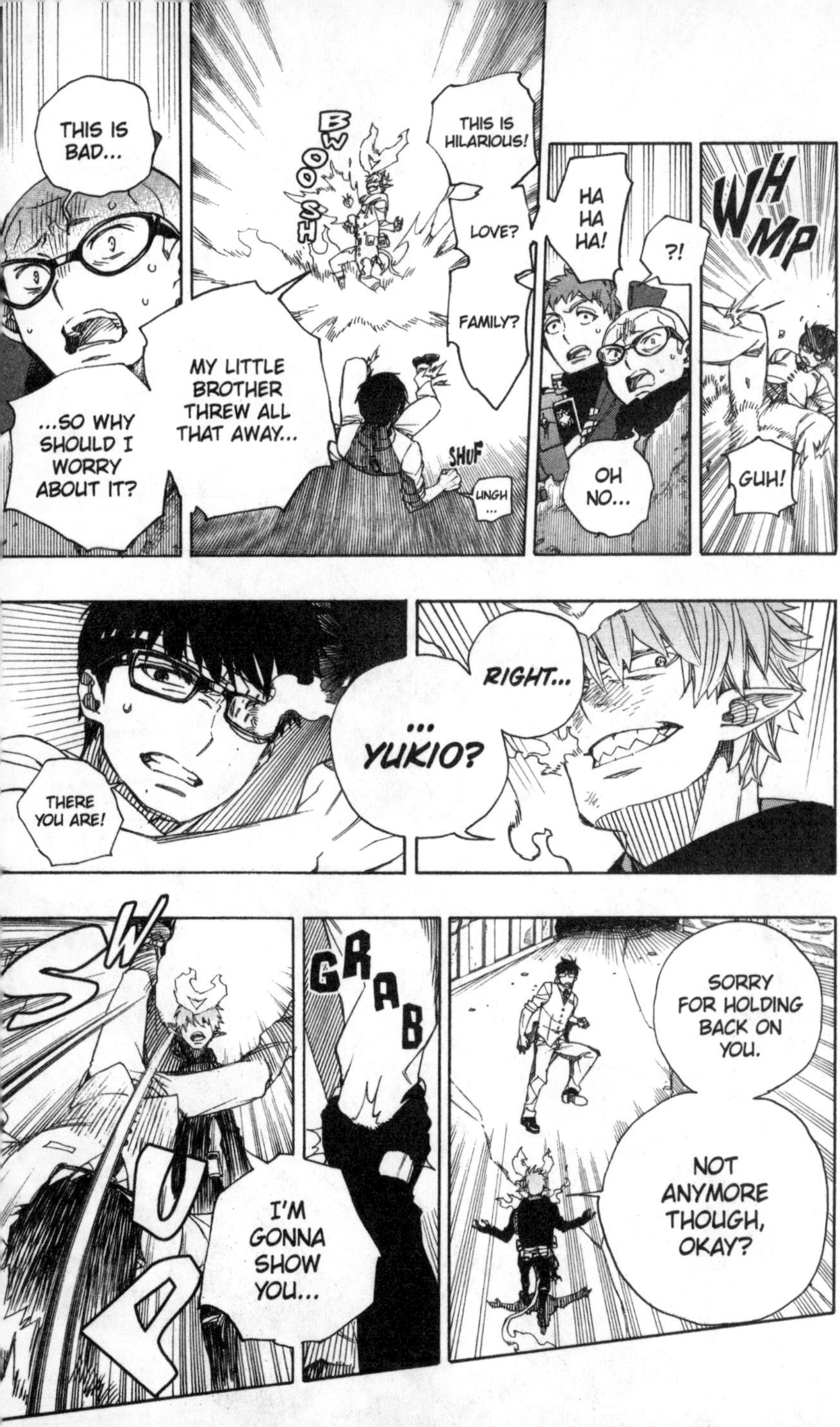
WHMP
?!
GUH!
HA HA HA!
OH NO...
THIS IS HILARIOUS!
LOVE?
FAMILY?
BWOOSH
MY LITTLE BROTHER THREW ALL THAT AWAY...
SHUF
UNGH...
THIS IS BAD...
...SO WHY SHOULD I WORRY ABOUT IT?
RIGHT...
...YUKIO?
THERE YOU ARE!
SORRY FOR HOLDING BACK ON YOU.
NOT ANYMORE THOUGH, OKAY?
GRAB
I'M GONNA SHOW YOU...
SWUP

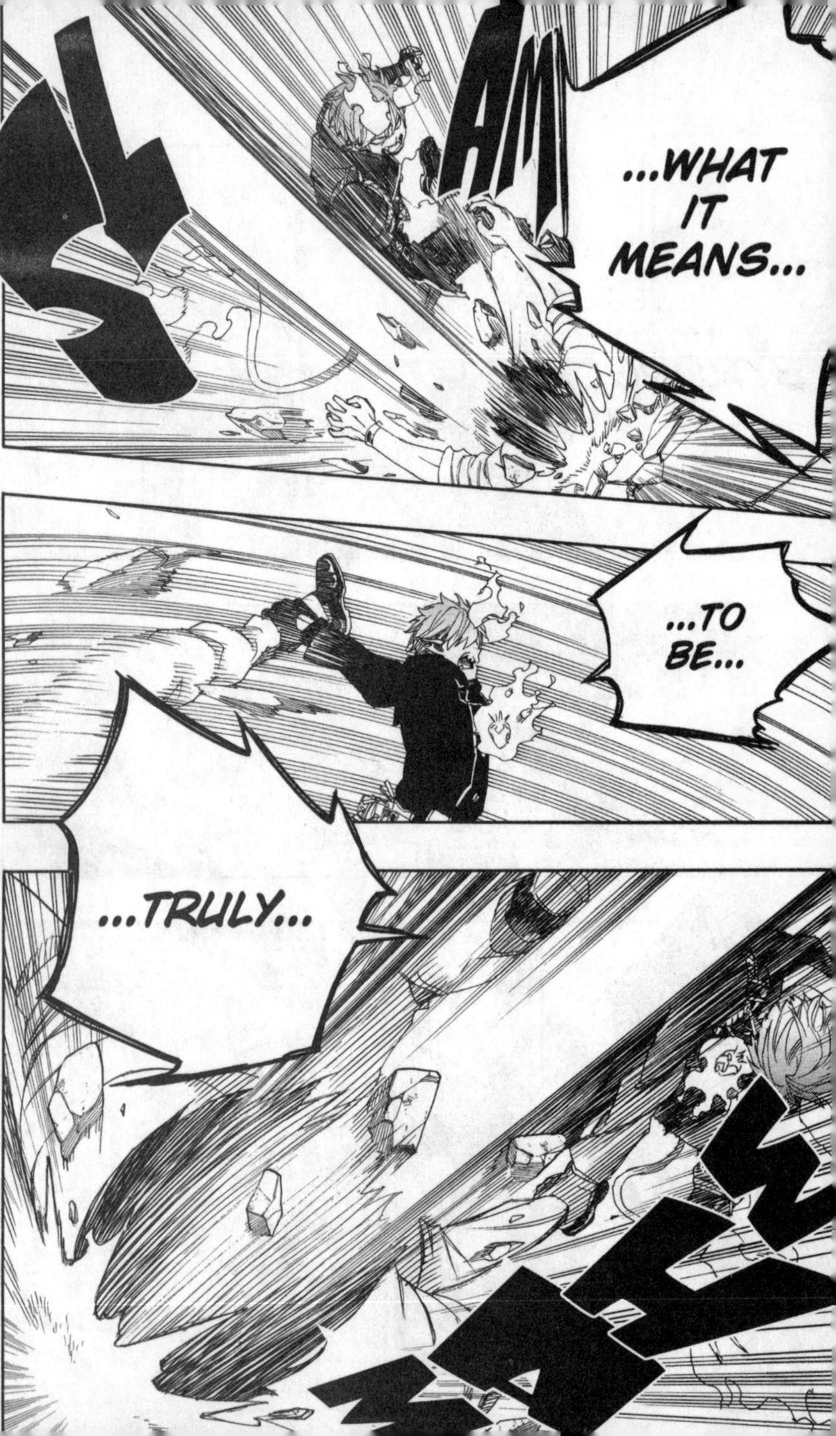
...WHAT IT MEANS...
...TO BE...
...TRULY...

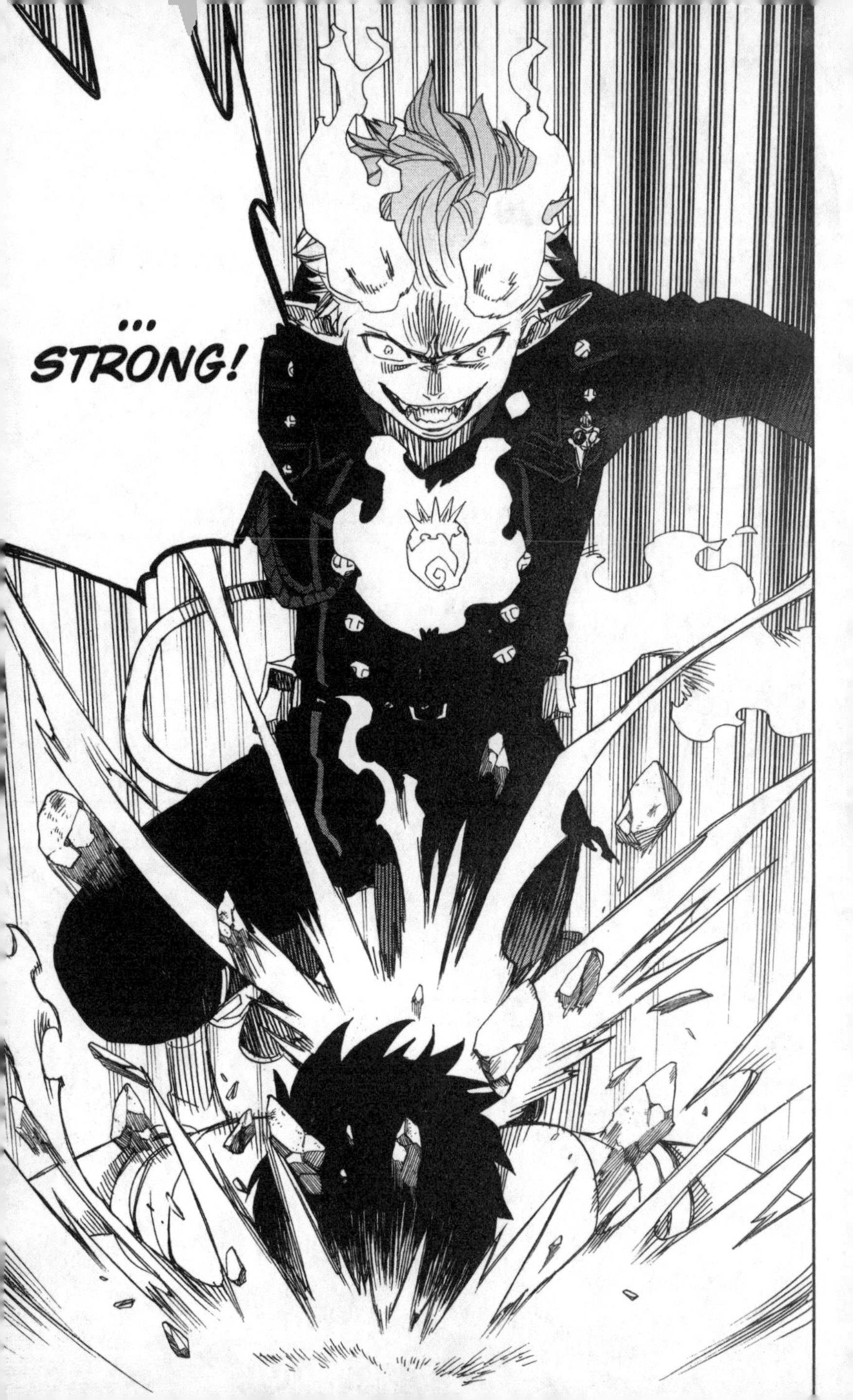
...STRONG!

Blue Exorcist Chapter 123: Of One Cloth—All-Out War

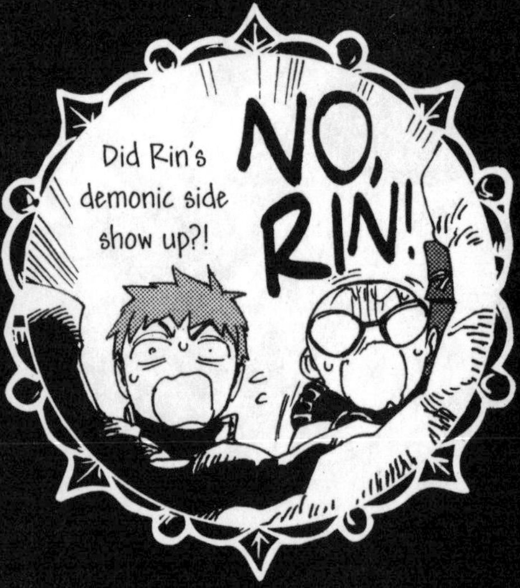
NO, RIN!
Did Rin's demonic side show up?!

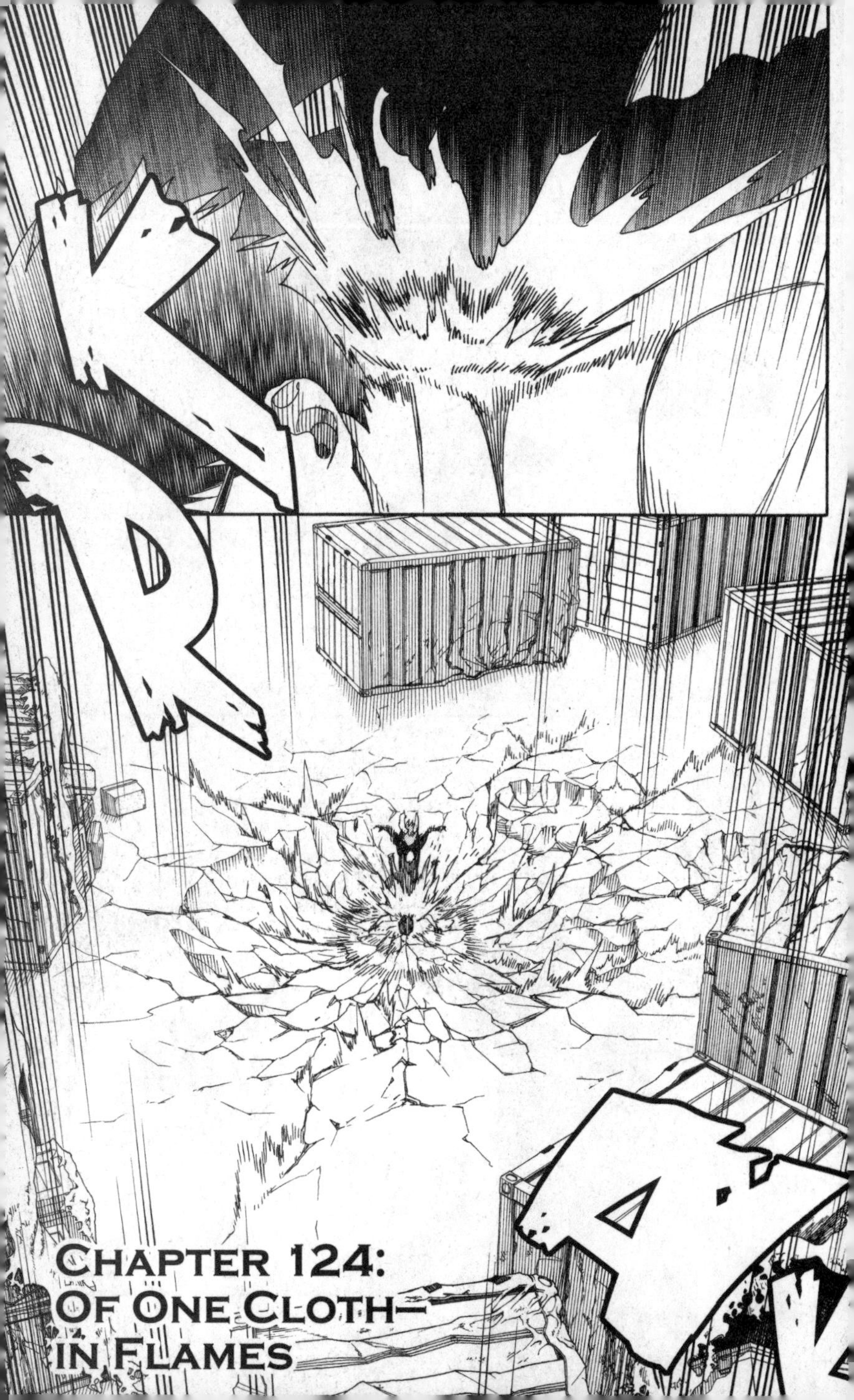
Chapter 124:
Of One Cloth—
in Flames

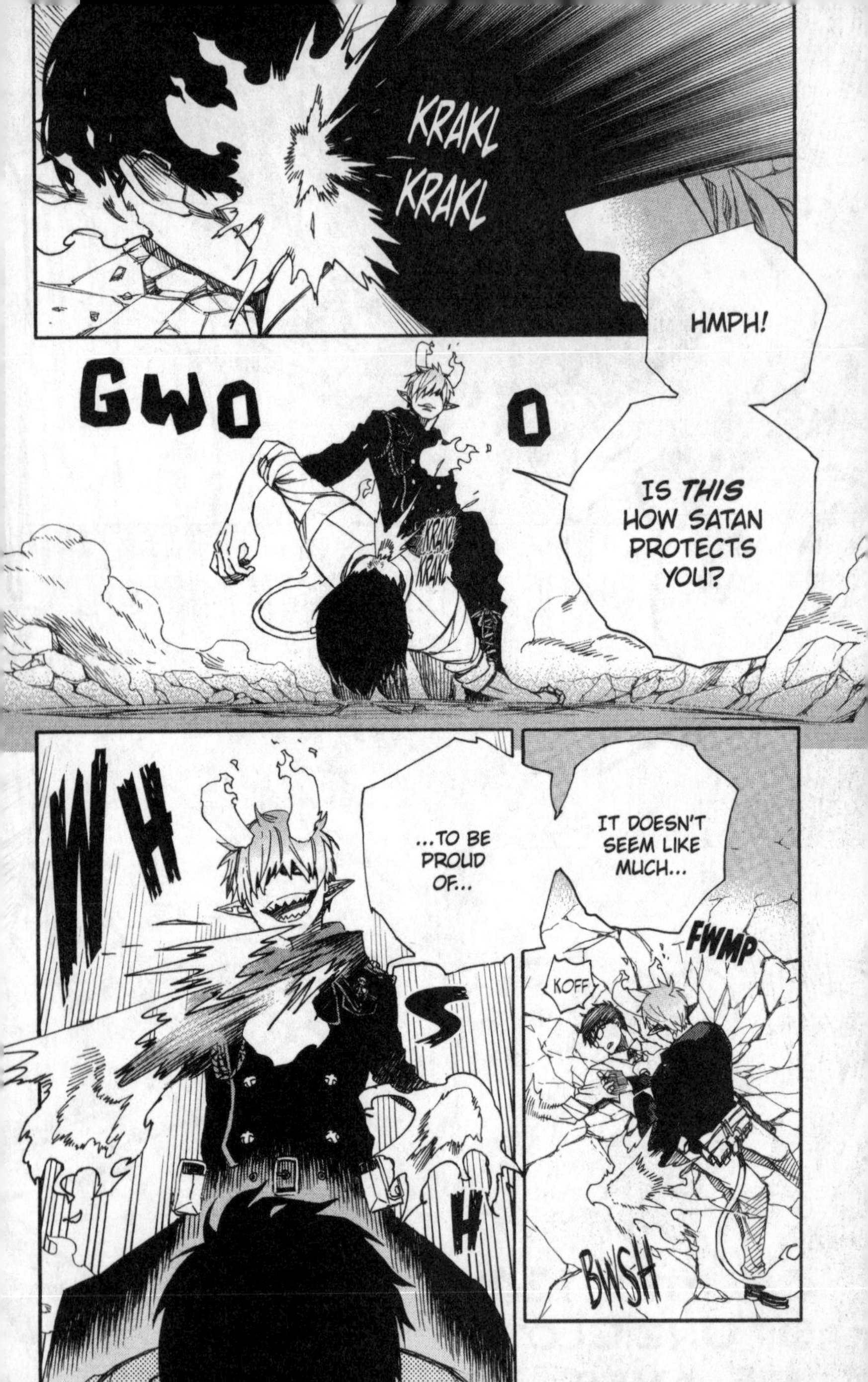
KRAKL
KRAKL
HMPH!
IS THIS HOW SATAN PROTECTS YOU?
GWO O
KRAKL KRAKL
IT DOESN'T SEEM LIKE MUCH...
FWMP
KOFF
BWSH
...TO BE PROUD OF...
WH S H

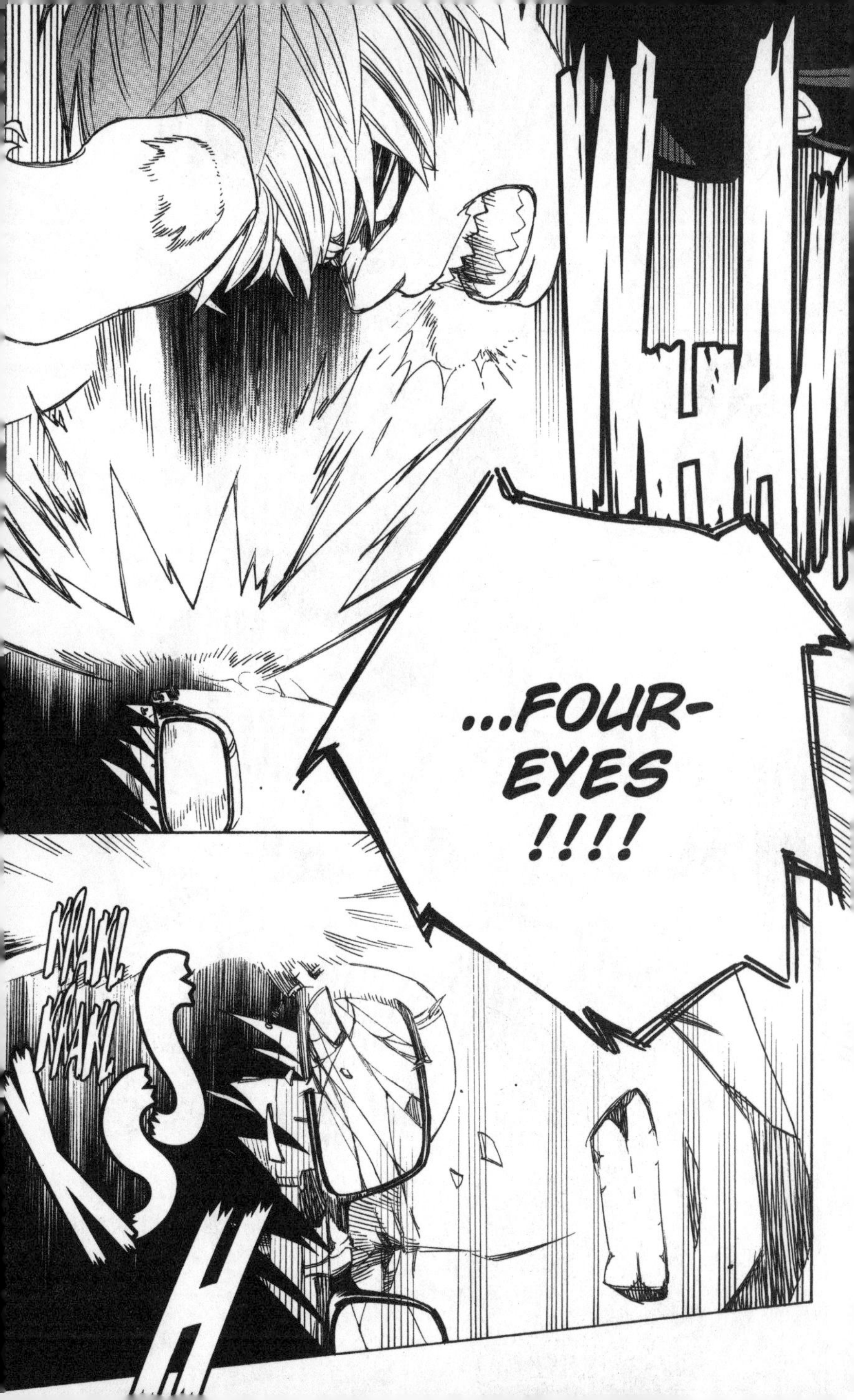
...FOUR-EYES !!!!

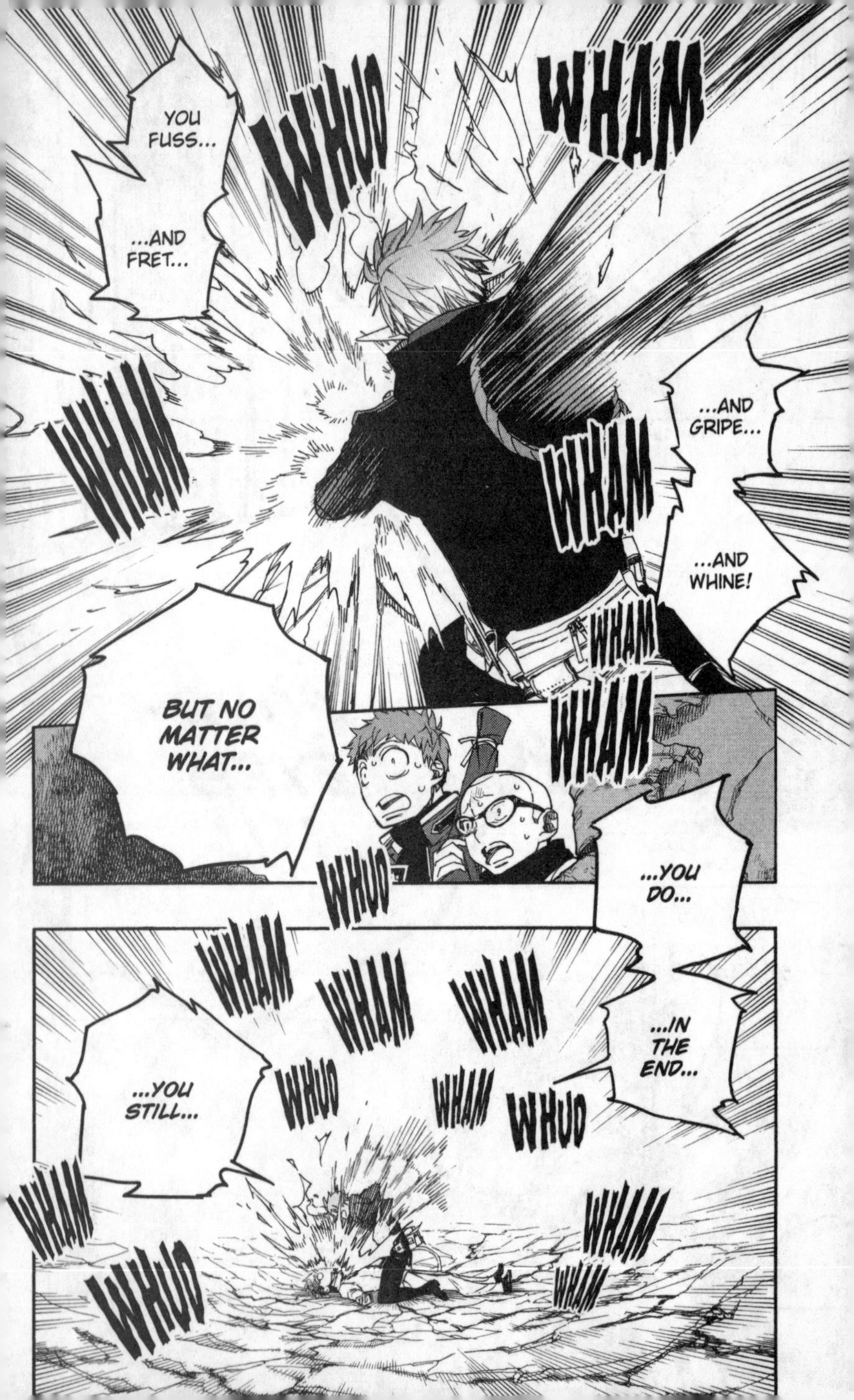
WHAM
WHUD
YOU FUSS...
...AND FRET...
WHAM
...AND GRIPE...
WHAM
...AND WHINE!
WHAM
WHAM
BUT NO MATTER WHAT...
WHUD
...YOU DO...
...IN THE END...
WHAM
WHAM
WHAM
WHUD
WHAM
WHUD
...YOU STILL...
WHAM
WHAM
WHAM
WHUD

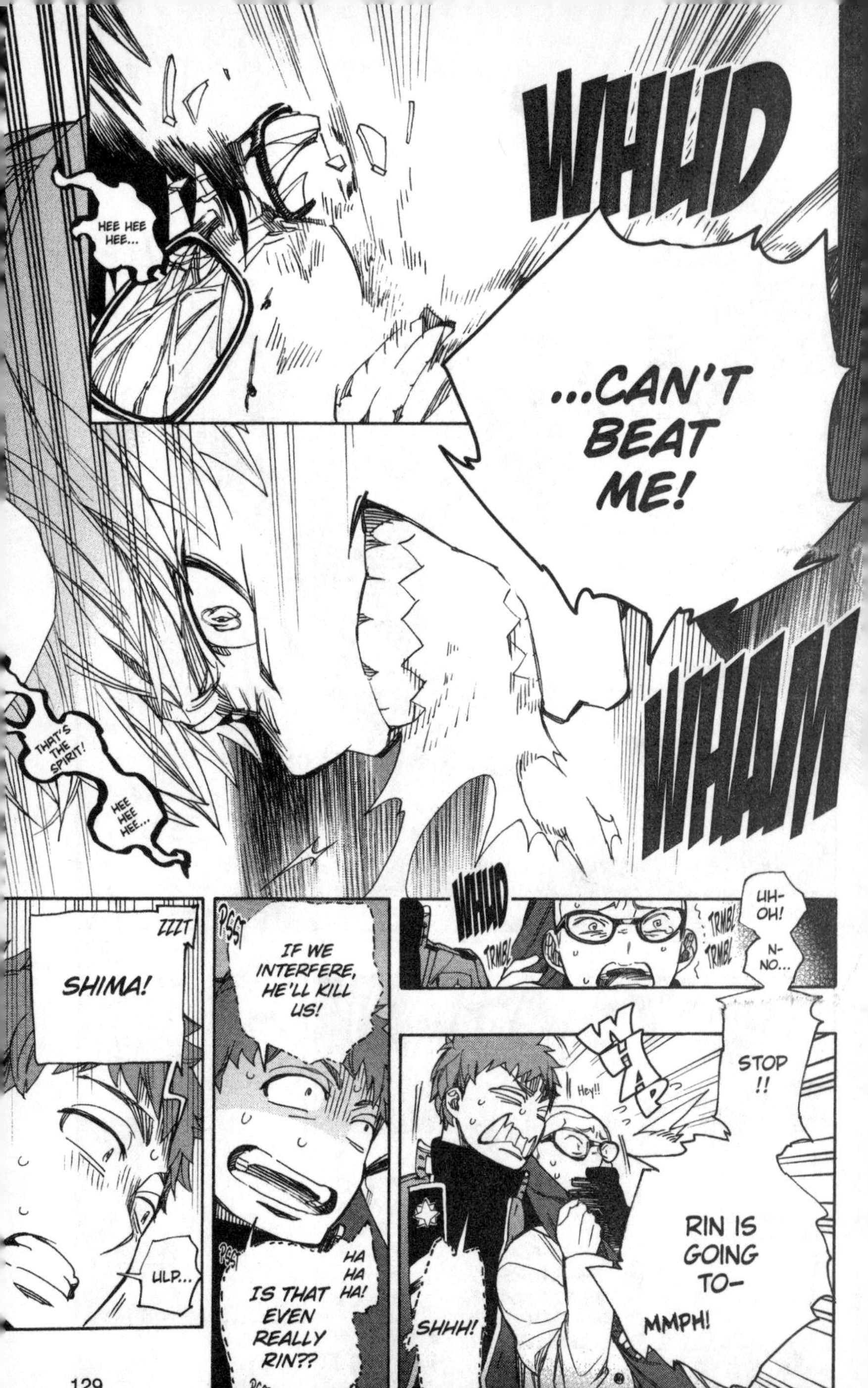
WHUD
HEE HEE HEE...
...CAN'T BEAT ME!
WHAM
THAT'S THE SPIRIT!
HEE HEE HEE...
WHUD
UH-OH!
N-NO...
TRMBL
TRMBL TRMBL
PSST
IF WE INTERFERE, HE'LL KILL US!
ZZZT
SHIMA!
STOP!!
WHAP
Hey!!
RIN IS GOING TO-
MMPH!
SHHH!
HA HA HA HA!
IS THAT EVEN REALLY RIN??
PSST
ULP...

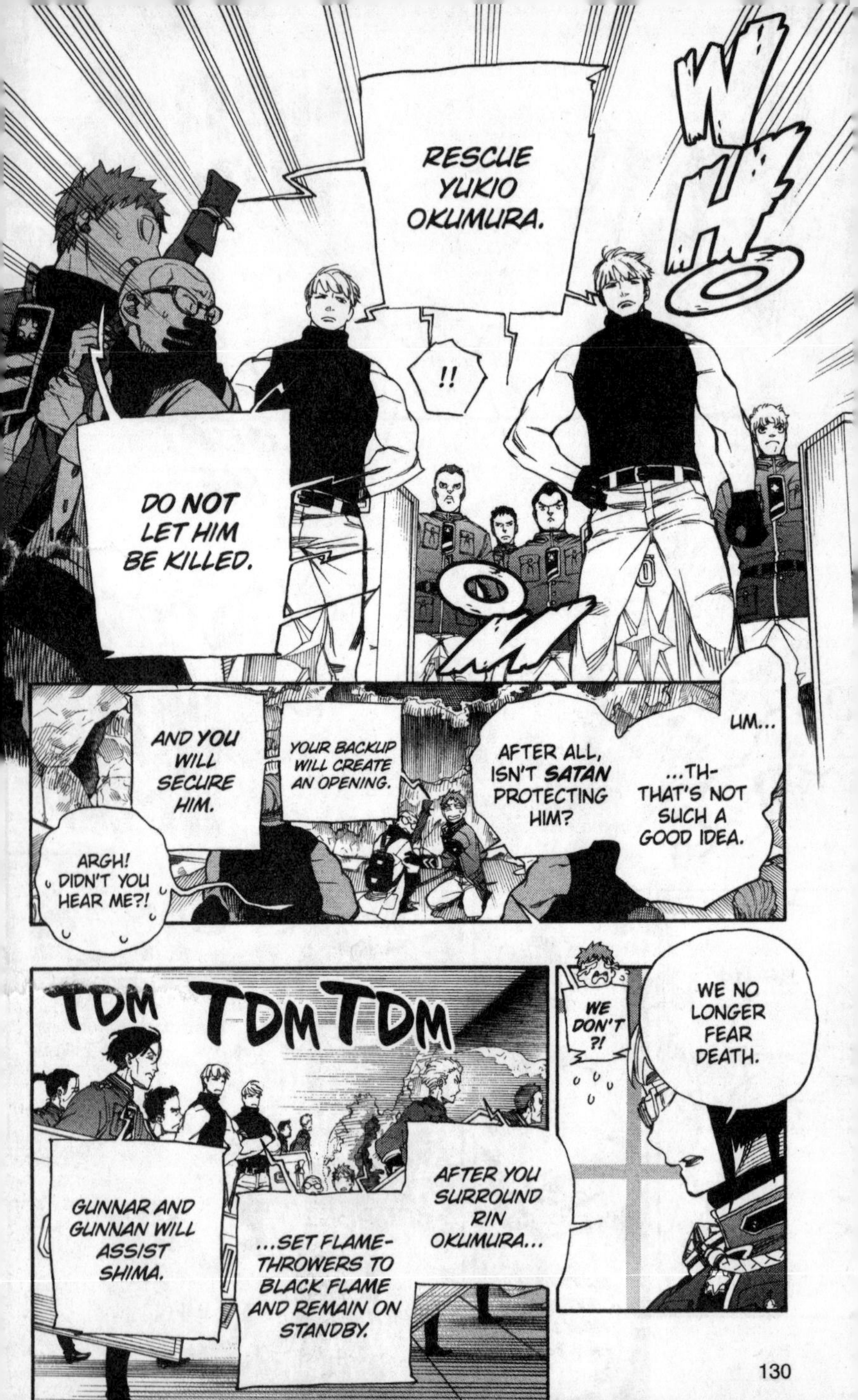
WHO
RESCUE YUKIO OKUMURA.
!!
DO NOT LET HIM BE KILLED.
OM
UM...
...TH- THAT'S NOT SUCH A GOOD IDEA.
AFTER ALL, ISN'T SATAN PROTECTING HIM?
YOUR BACKUP WILL CREATE AN OPENING.
AND YOU WILL SECURE HIM.
ARGH! DIDN'T YOU HEAR ME?!
WE NO LONGER FEAR DEATH.
WE DON'T ?!
TDM TDM TDM
AFTER YOU SURROUND RIN OKUMURA...
...SET FLAME-THROWERS TO BLACK FLAME AND REMAIN ON STANDBY.
GUNNAR AND GUNNAN WILL ASSIST SHIMA.

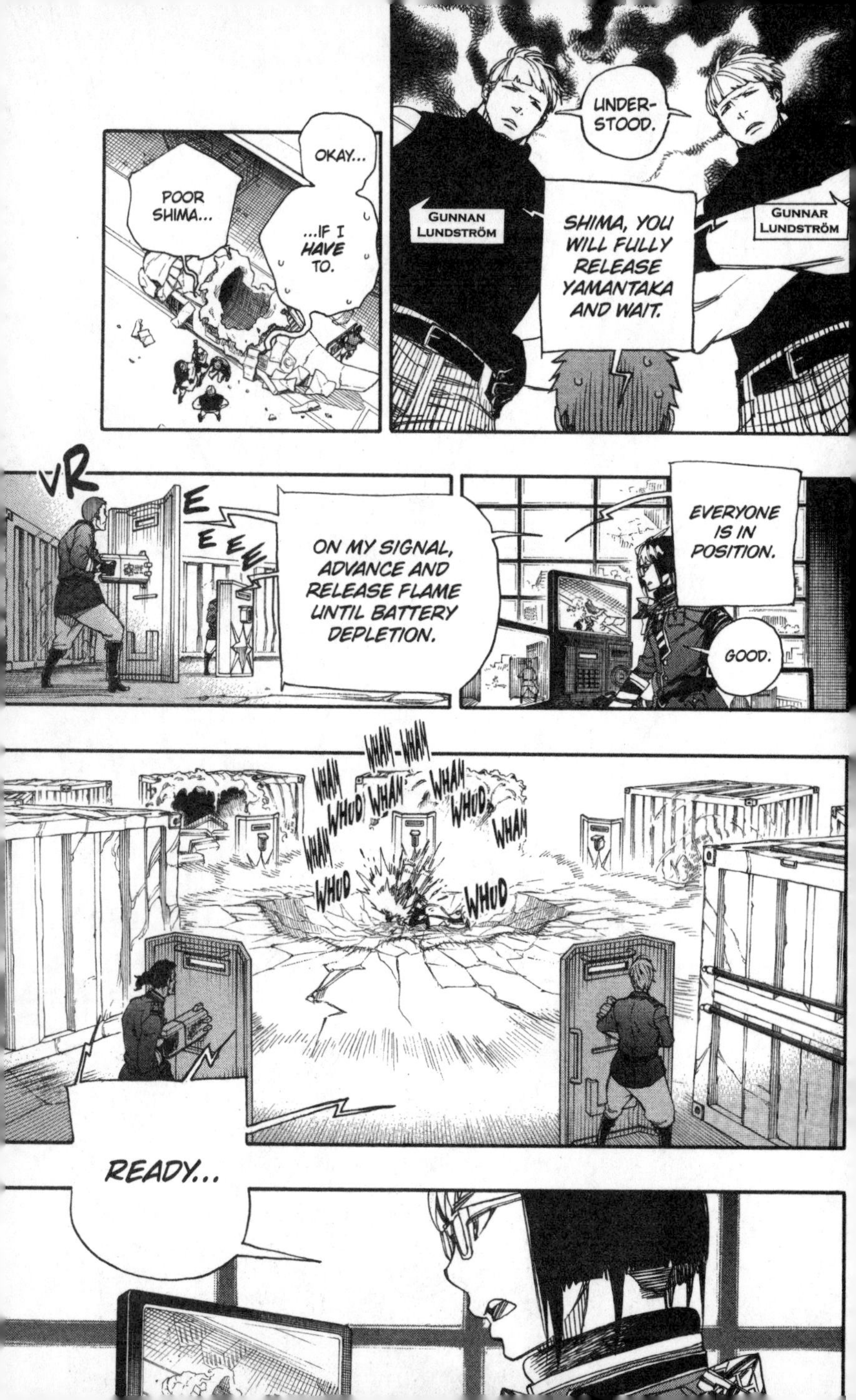
GUNNAR LUNDSTRÖM
SHIMA, YOU WILL FULLY RELEASE YAMANTAKA AND WAIT.
GUNNAN LUNDSTRÖM
UNDER-STOOD.
OKAY...
...IF I HAVE TO.
POOR SHIMA...
EVERYONE IS IN POSITION.
GOOD.
ON MY SIGNAL, ADVANCE AND RELEASE FLAME UNTIL BATTERY DEPLETION.
VR
EEEE
WHAM-WHAM
WHAM WHUD
WHAM WHUD
WHAM WHUD
WHAM
WHAM
WHUD
WHUD
READY...

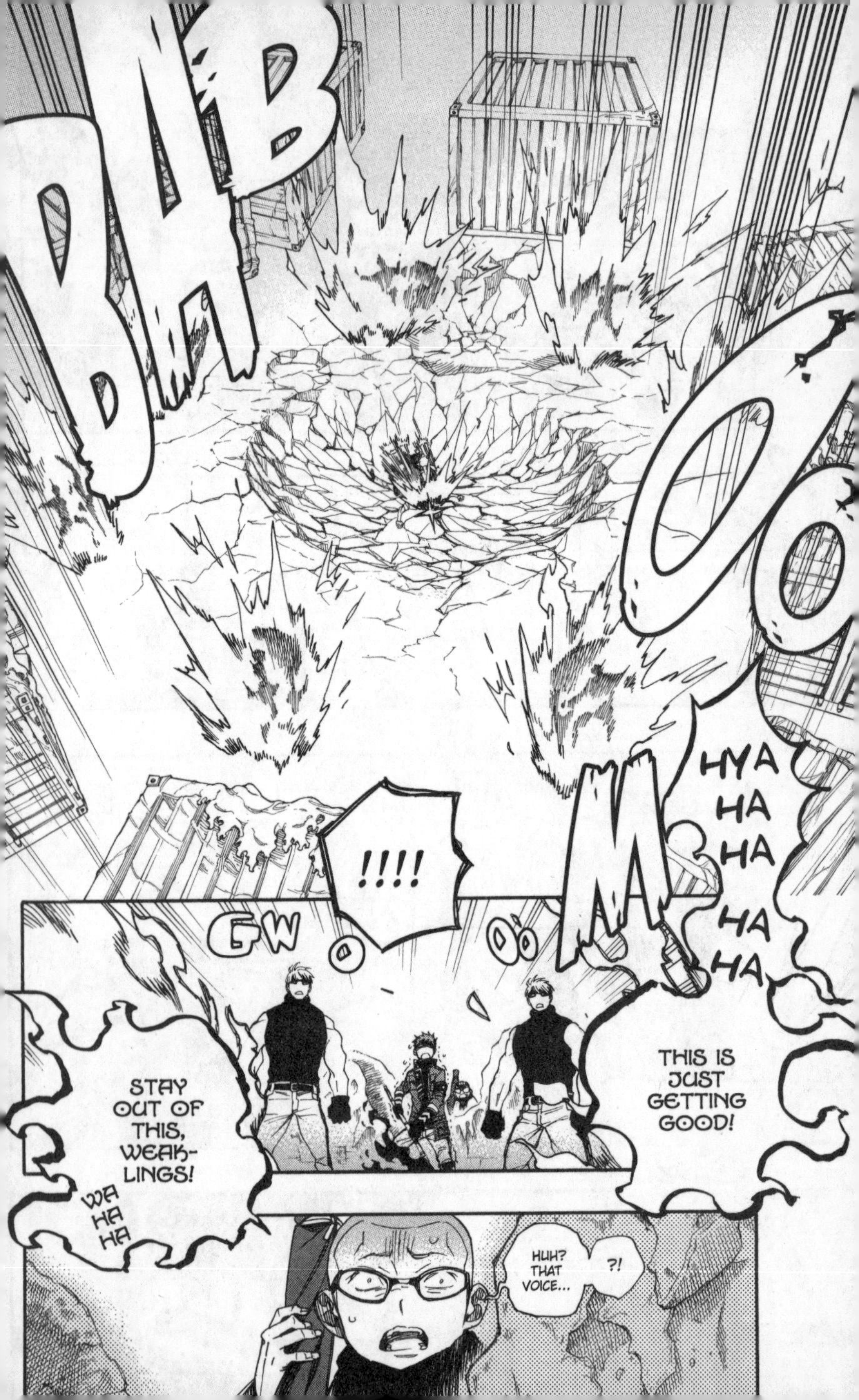
BADOOM
HYA HA HA HA HA HA
!!!!
GWOOO
THIS IS JUST GETTING GOOD!
STAY OUT OF THIS, WEAK-LINGS!
WA HA HA
?!
HUH? THAT VOICE...

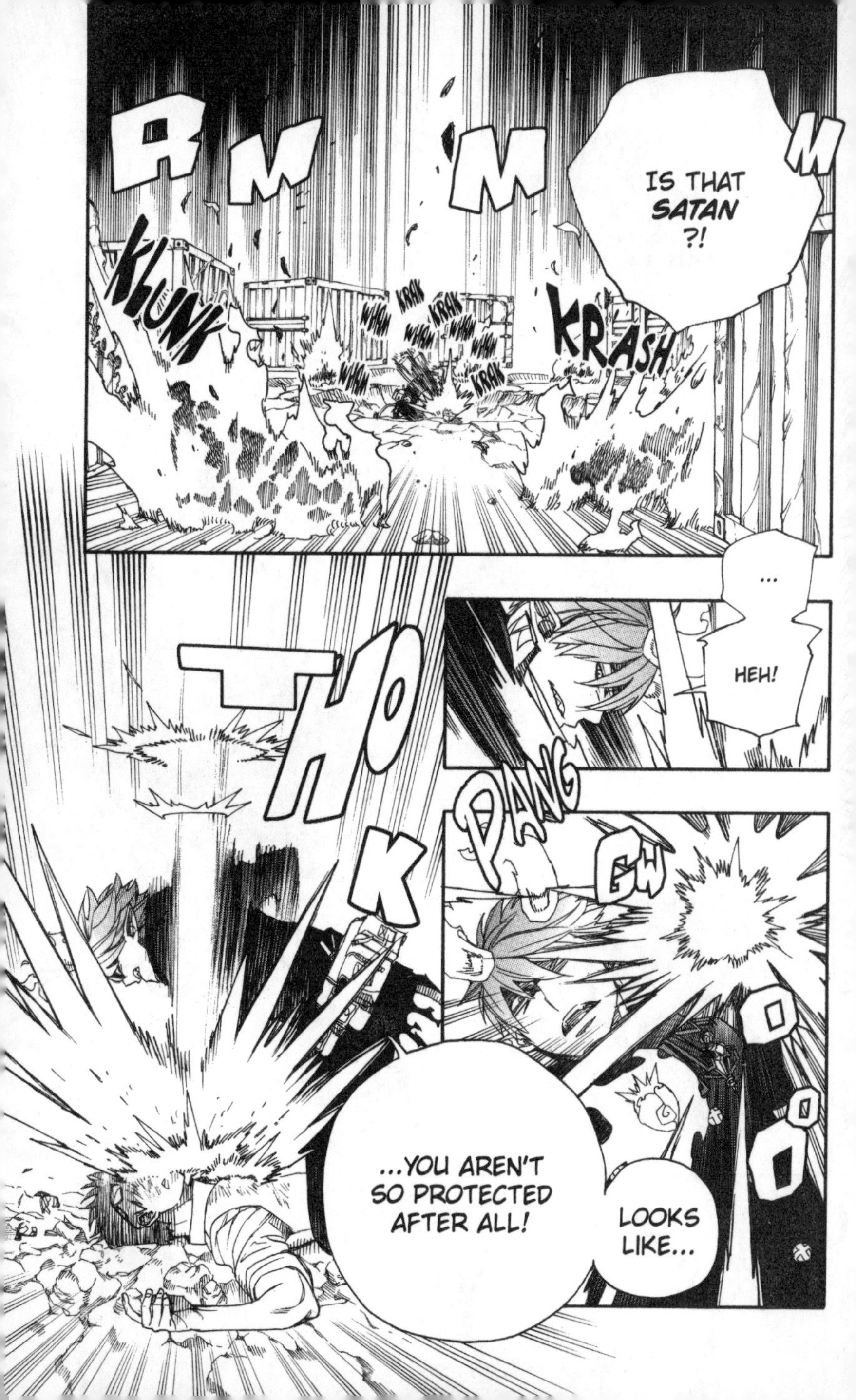
IS THAT SATAN ?!
RMMMMM
KLUNK
KRASH
...
HEH!
THOK
PANG
GH
OOO
LOOKS LIKE...
...YOU AREN'T SO PROTECTED AFTER ALL!

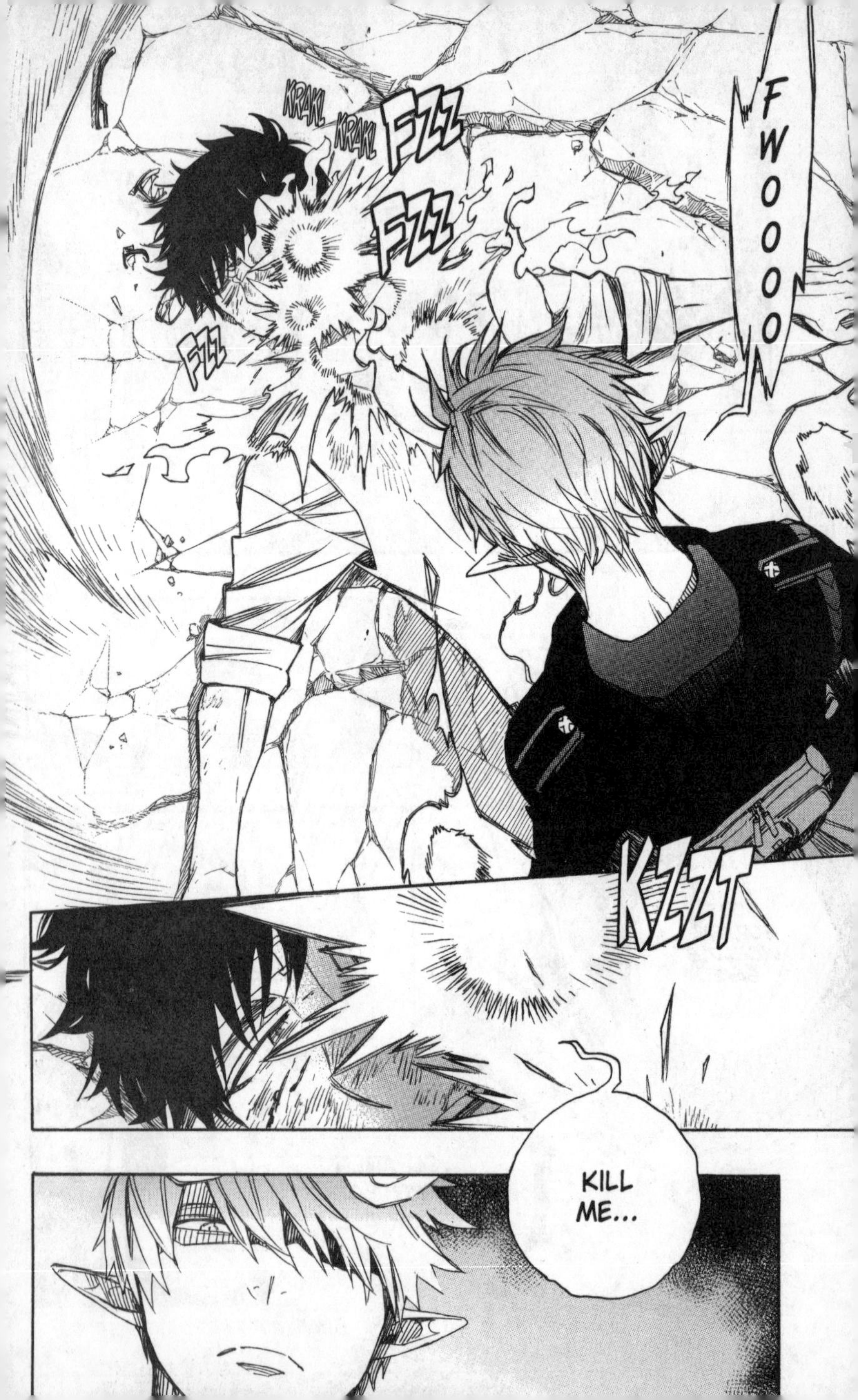
FWOOOO
KRAKL KRAKL
FZZZ
FZZZ
FZZZ
KZZZT
KILL ME...

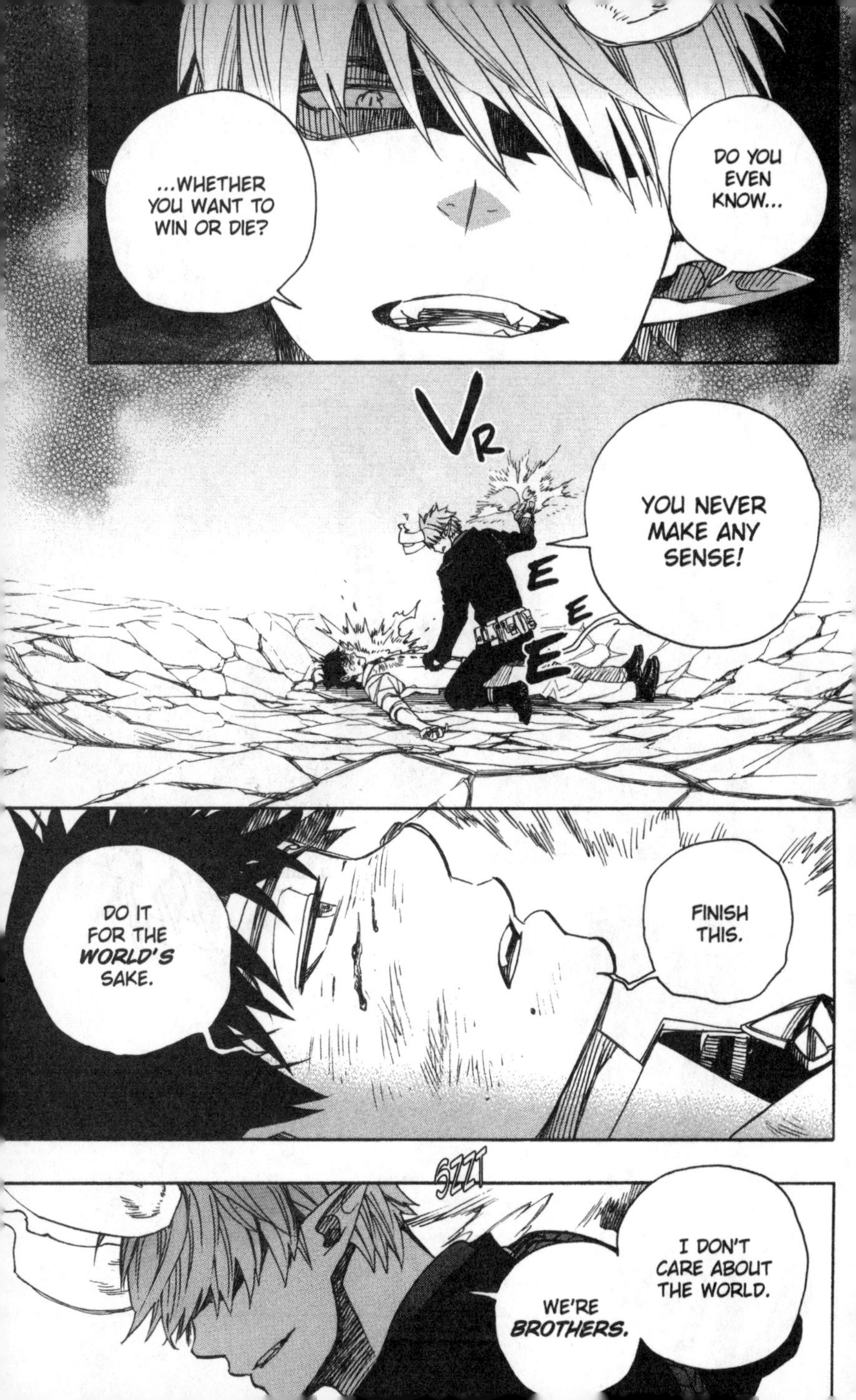
DO YOU EVEN KNOW...
...WHETHER YOU WANT TO WIN OR DIE?
VR
EEE
YOU NEVER MAKE ANY SENSE!
FINISH THIS.
DO IT FOR THE *WORLD'S* SAKE.
SZZT
I DON'T CARE ABOUT THE WORLD.
WE'RE *BROTHERS.*

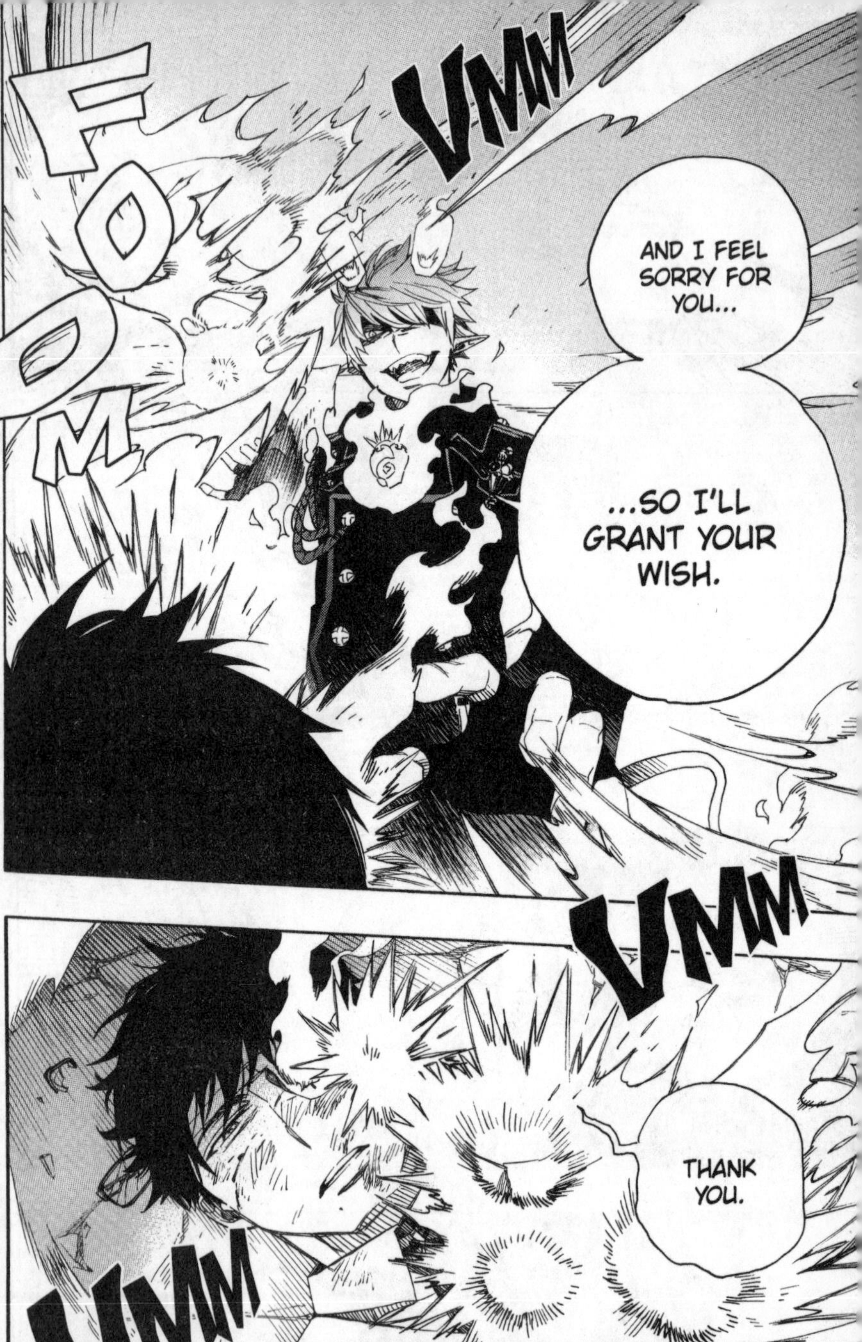
VMM
AND I FEEL SORRY FOR YOU...
...SO I'LL GRANT YOUR WISH.
FOOOM
VMM
THANK YOU.
VMM

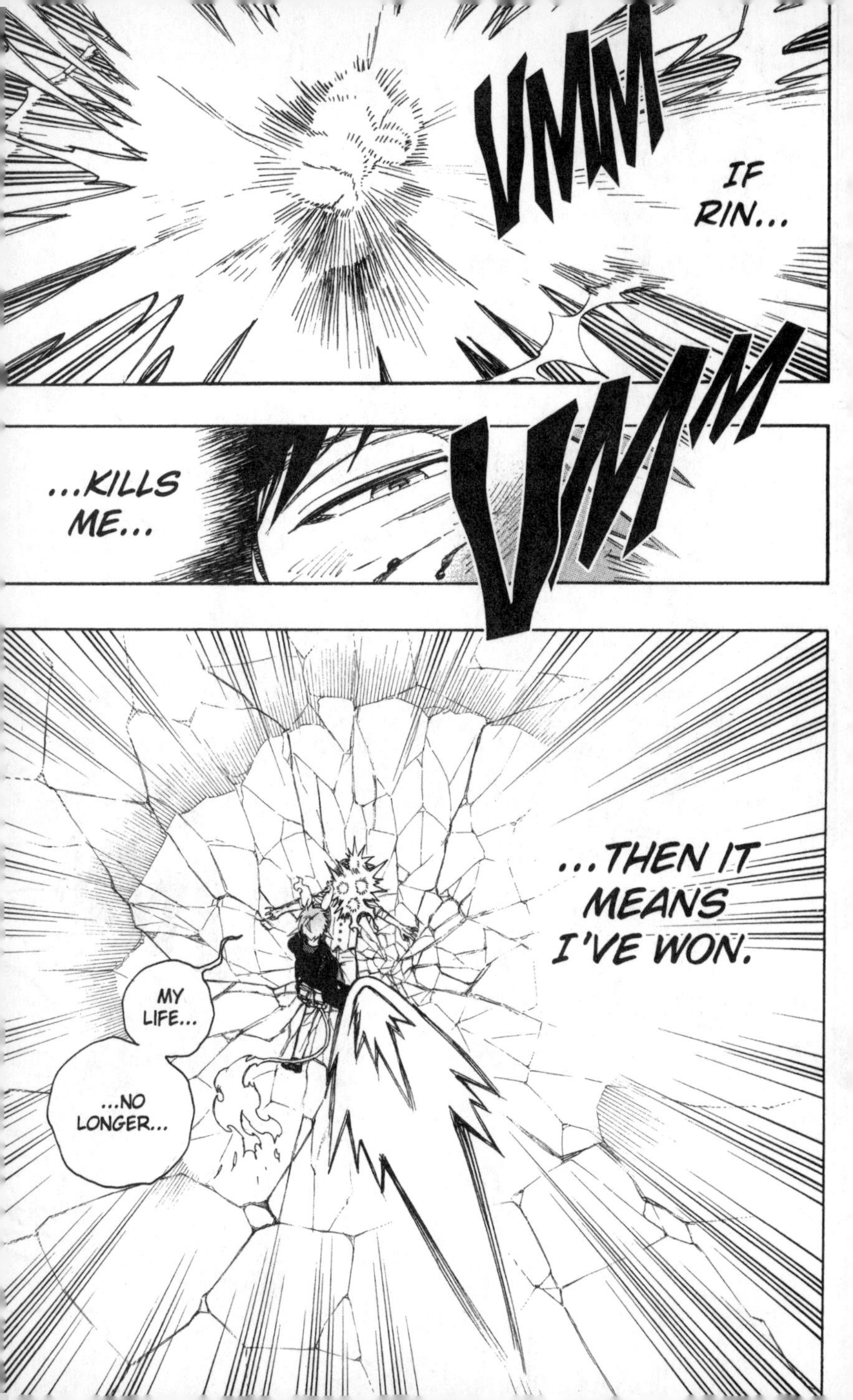
VMM
IF RIN...
VMMM
...KILLS ME...
...THEN IT MEANS I'VE WON.
MY LIFE...
...NO LONGER...

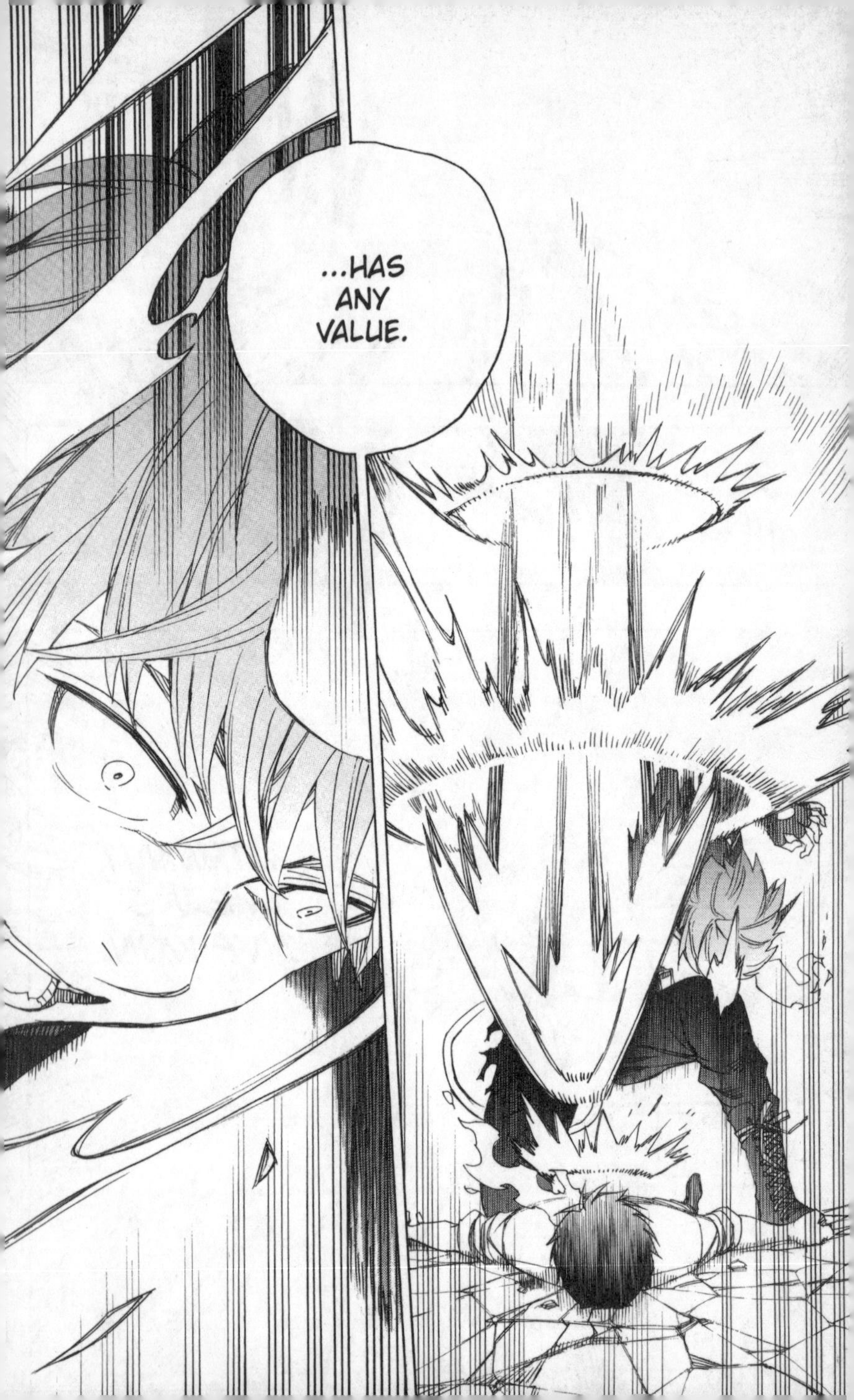
...HAS ANY VALUE.

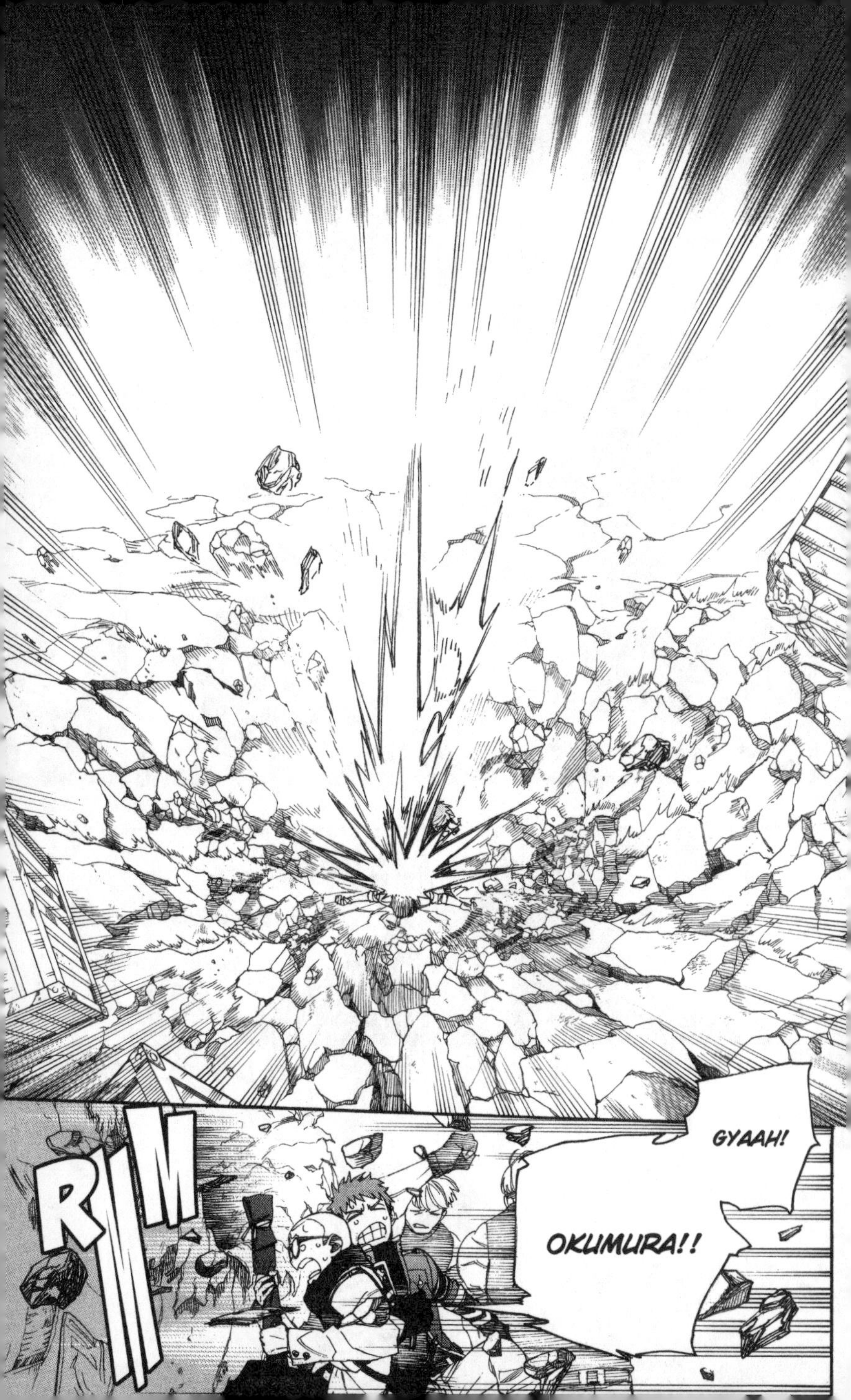
GYAAH!
OKUMURA!!
RMM

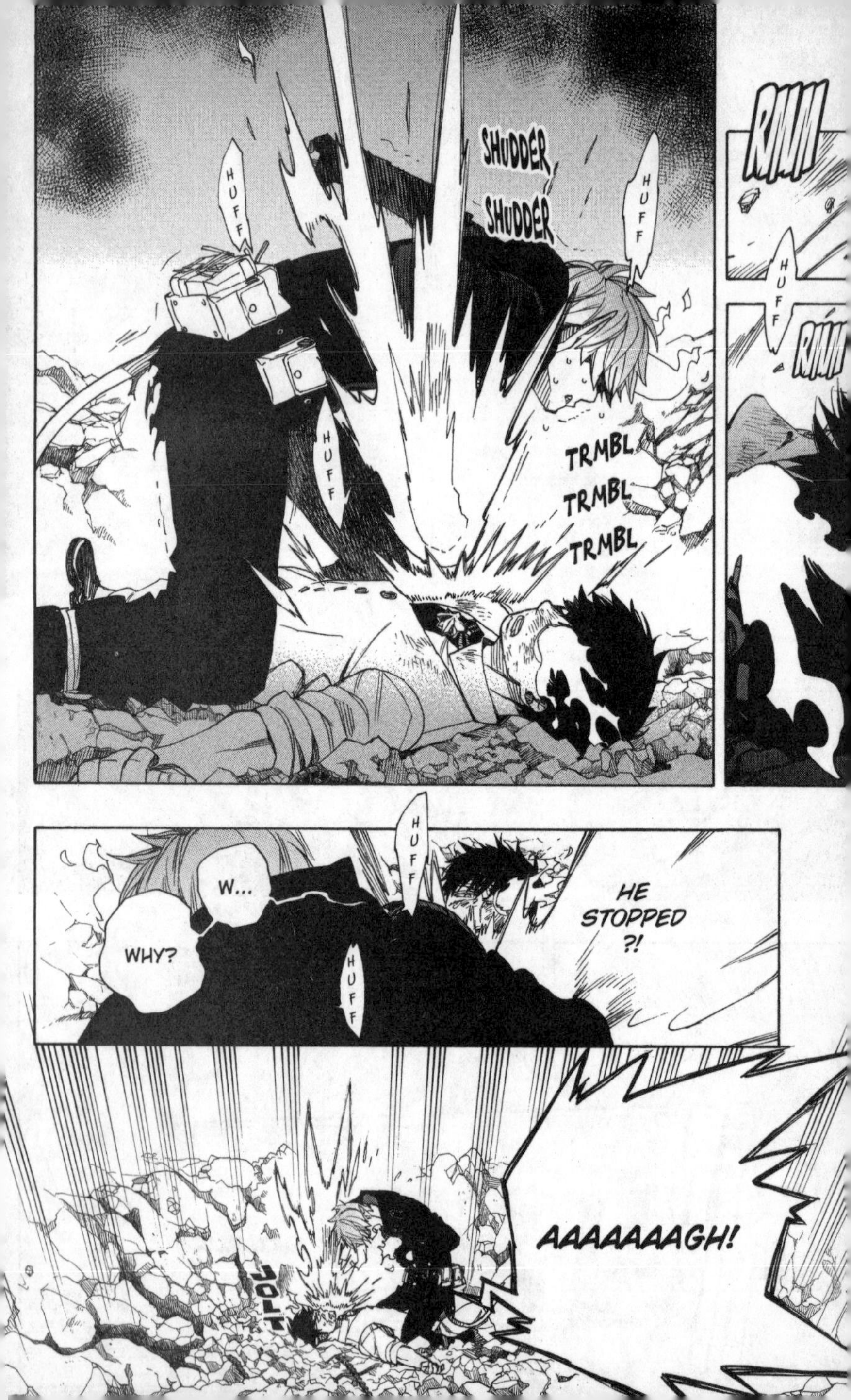
RMM
HUFF
RMM
HUFF
SHUDDER, SHUDDER
HUFF
TRMBL
TRMBL
TRMBL
HUFF
HE STOPPED?!
HUFF
W...
WHY?
HUFF
AAAAAAAGH!
JOLT

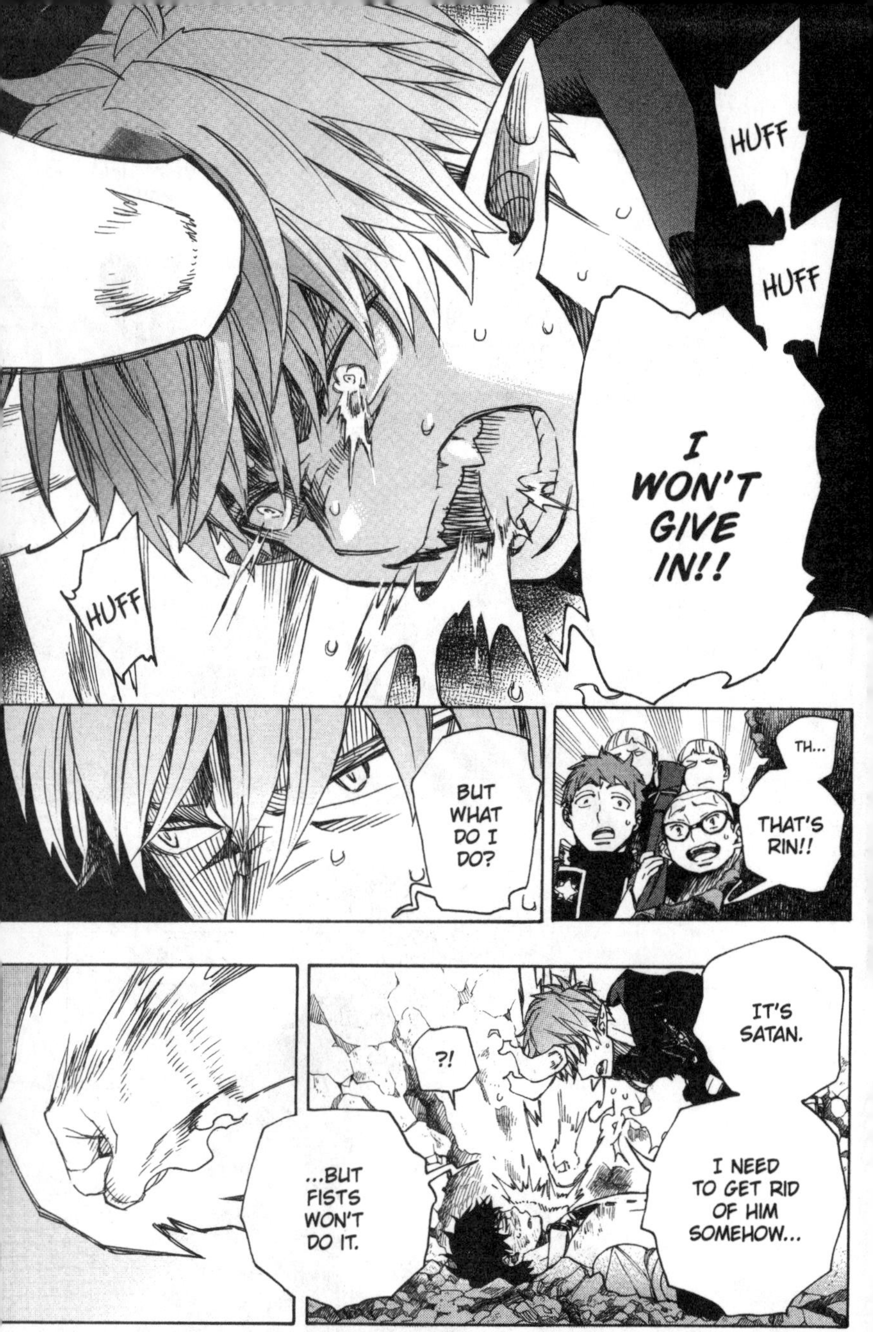
HUFF
HUFF
I WON'T GIVE IN!!
HUFF
TH...
THAT'S RIN!!
BUT WHAT DO I DO?
IT'S SATAN.
?!
I NEED TO GET RID OF HIM SOMEHOW...
...BUT FISTS WON'T DO IT.

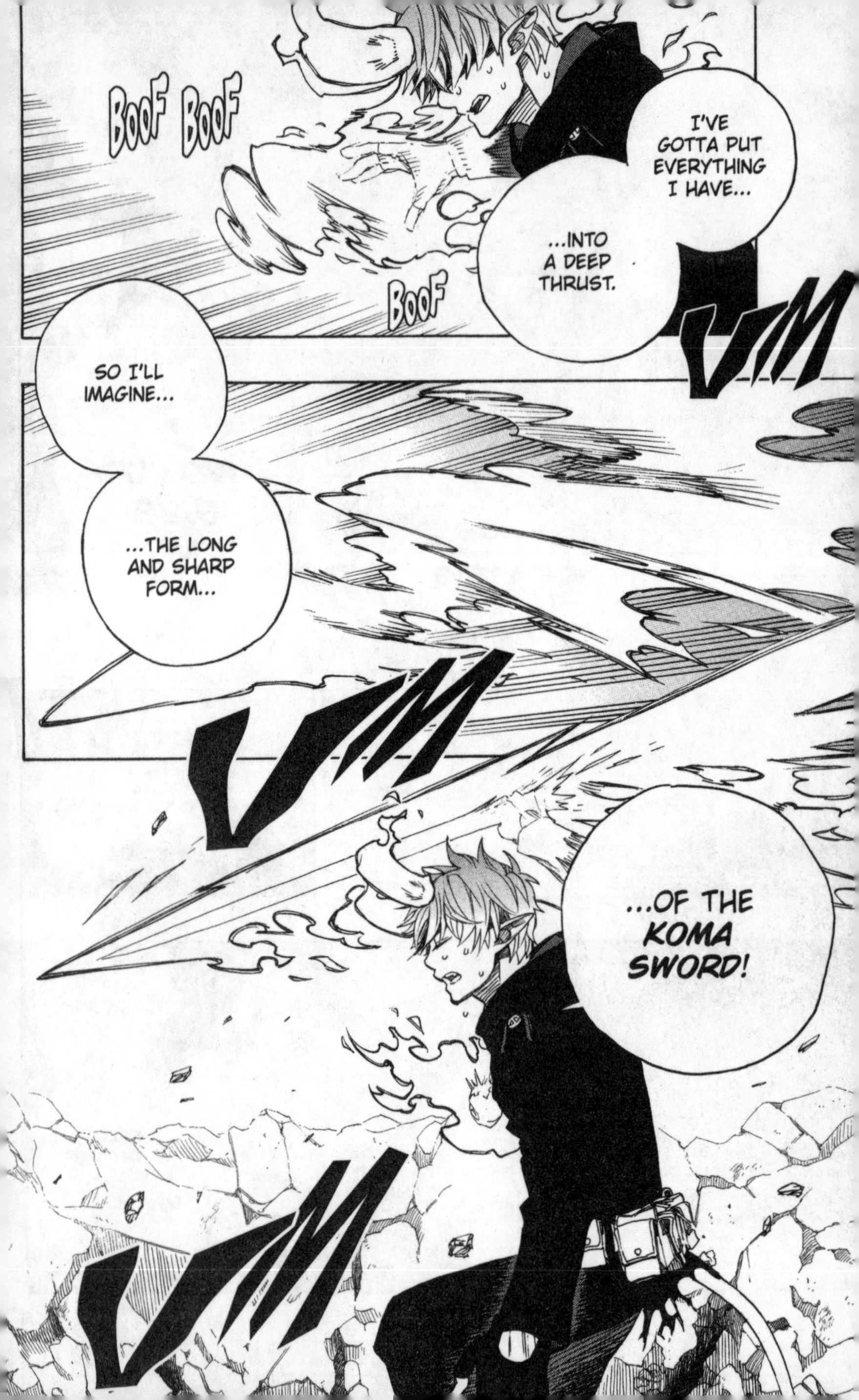
I'VE GOTTA PUT EVERYTHING I HAVE...
BOOF BOOF
...INTO A DEEP THRUST.
BOOF
VM
SO I'LL IMAGINE...
...THE LONG AND SHARP FORM...
VM
...OF THE KOMA SWORD!
VM

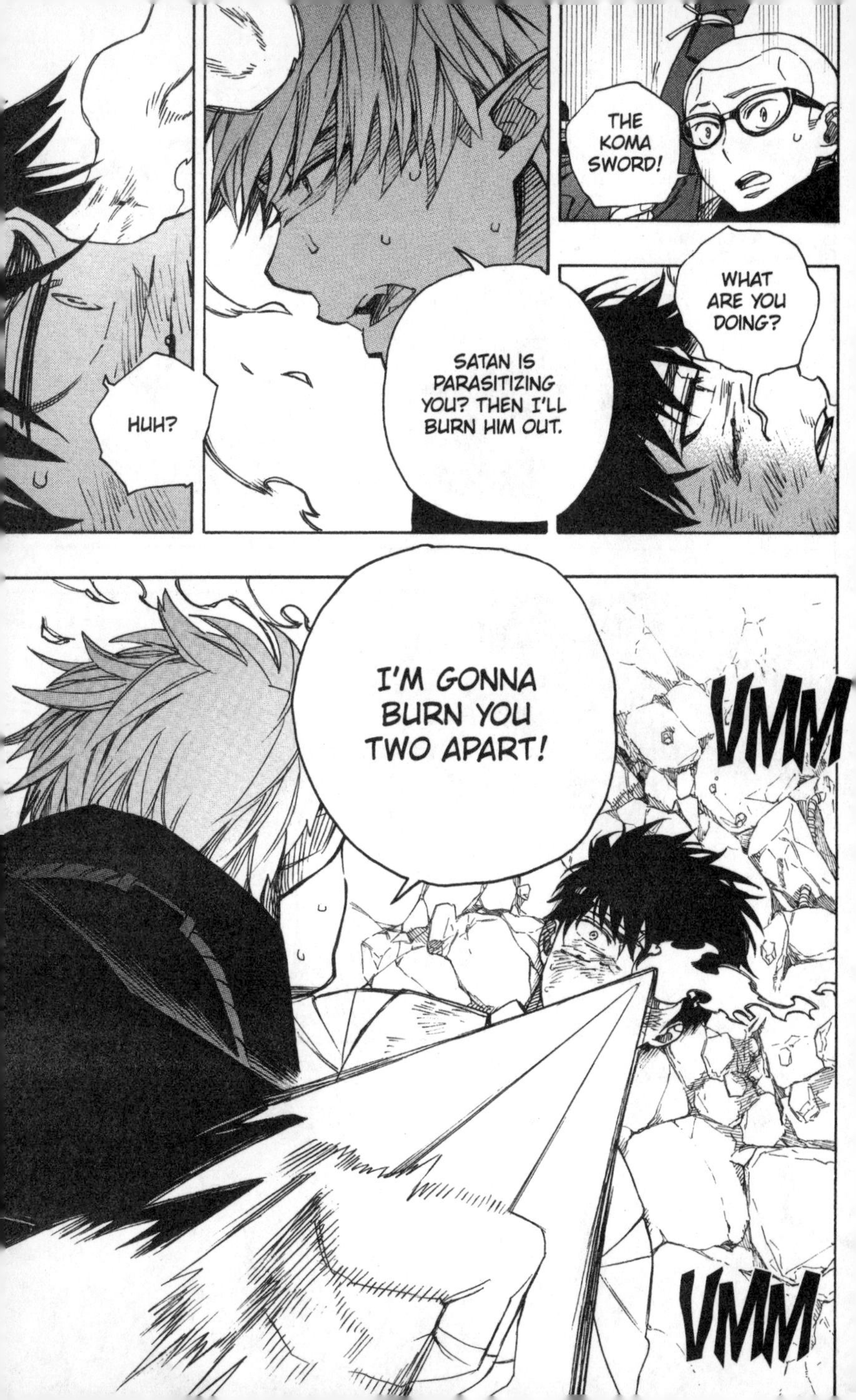
THE KOMA SWORD!
WHAT ARE YOU DOING?
SATAN IS PARASITIZING YOU? THEN I'LL BURN HIM OUT.
HUH?
I'M GONNA BURN YOU TWO APART!
VMM
VMM

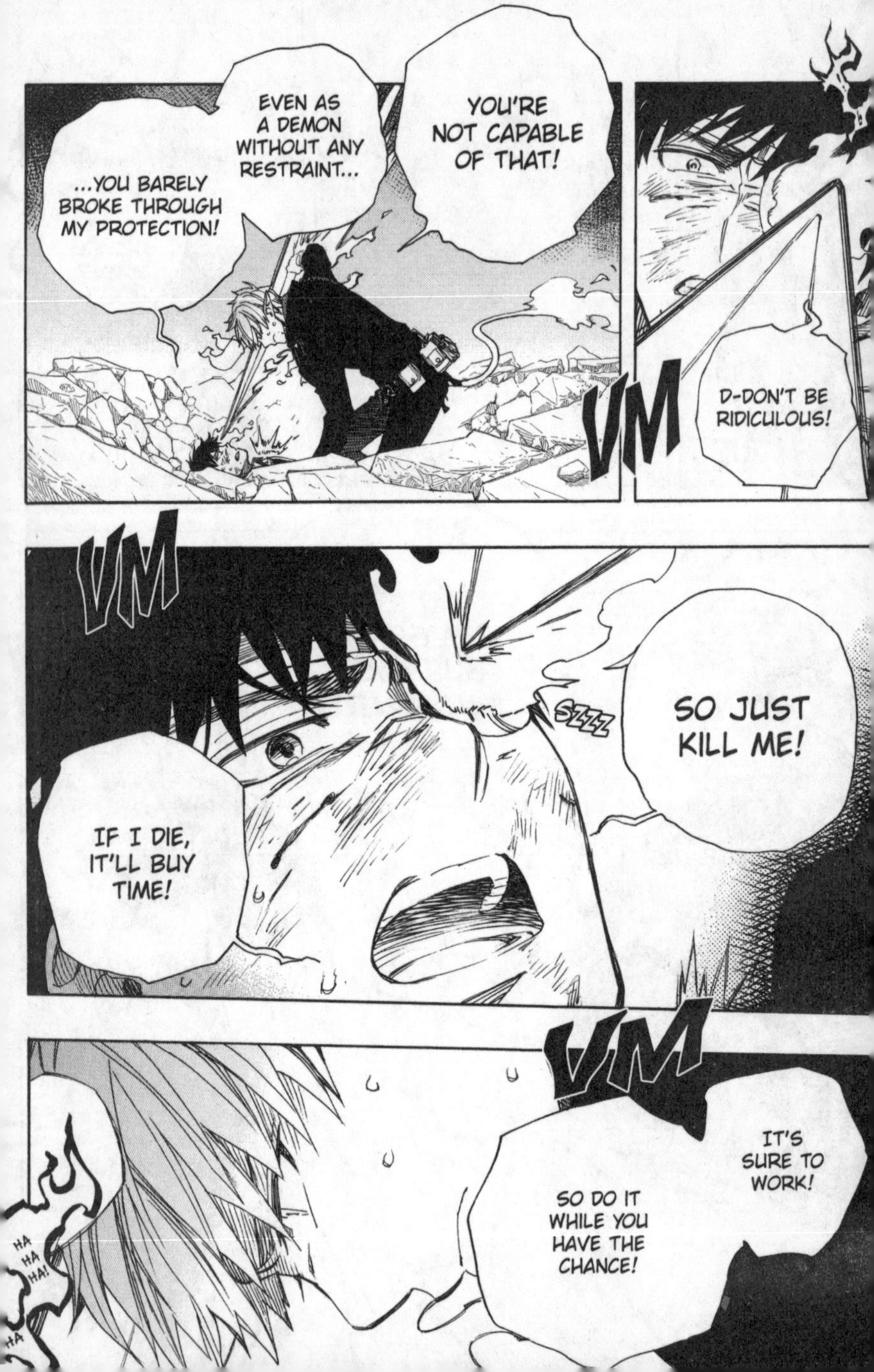
D-DON'T BE RIDICULOUS!
VM
EVEN AS A DEMON WITHOUT ANY RESTRAINT...
...YOU BARELY BROKE THROUGH MY PROTECTION!
YOU'RE NOT CAPABLE OF THAT!
VM
SZZZ
SO JUST KILL ME!
IF I DIE, IT'LL BUY TIME!
VM
IT'S SURE TO WORK!
SO DO IT WHILE YOU HAVE THE CHANCE!
HA HA HA!
HA

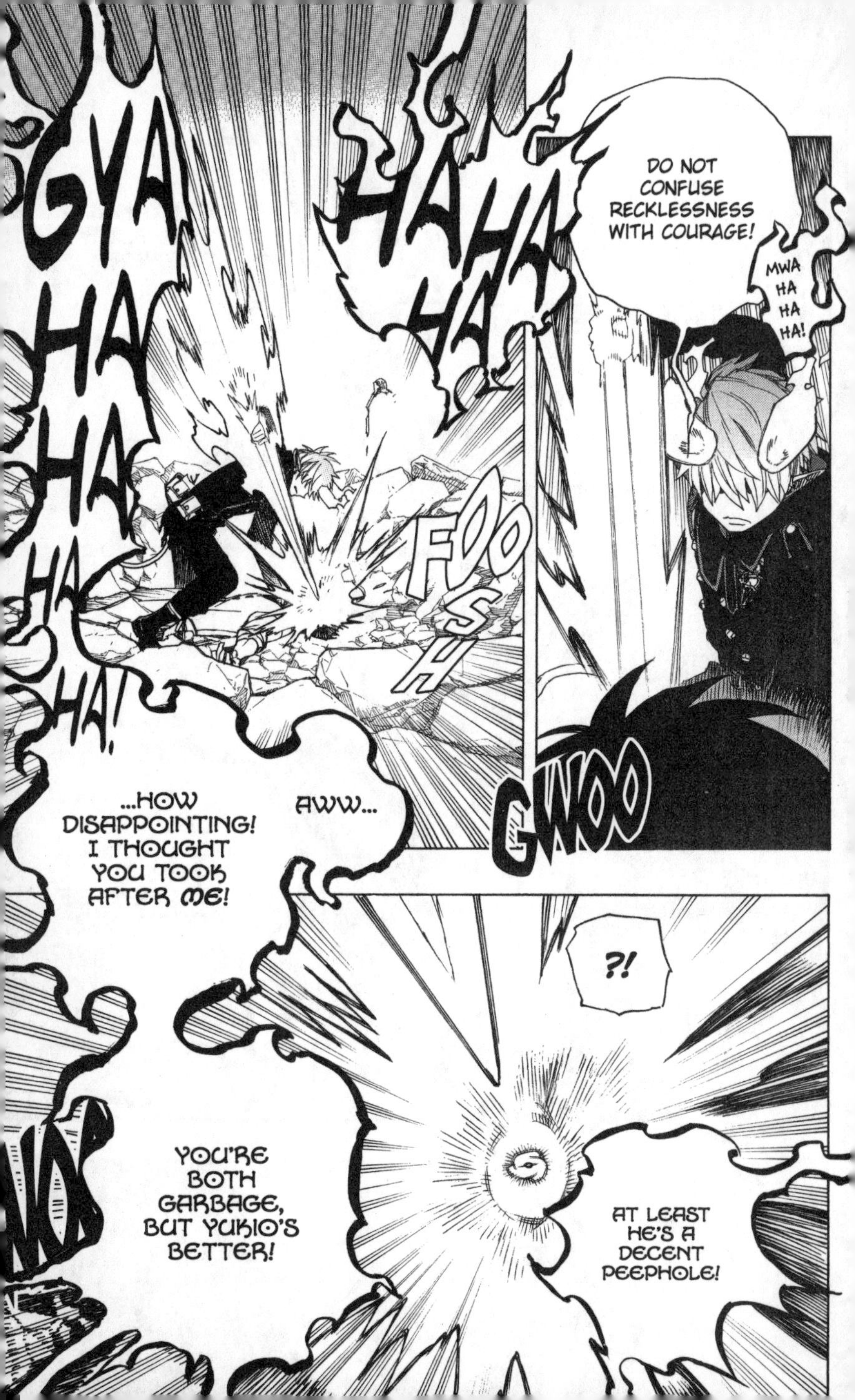

DO NOT CONFUSE RECKLESSNESS WITH COURAGE!
MWA HA HA HA!
GWOO
HAHAHA
GYAHAHAHAHA!
FOOSH
AWW...
...HOW DISAPPOINTING! I THOUGHT YOU TOOK AFTER ME!
?!
YOU'RE BOTH GARBAGE, BUT YUKIO'S BETTER!
AT LEAST HE'S A DECENT PEEPHOLE!

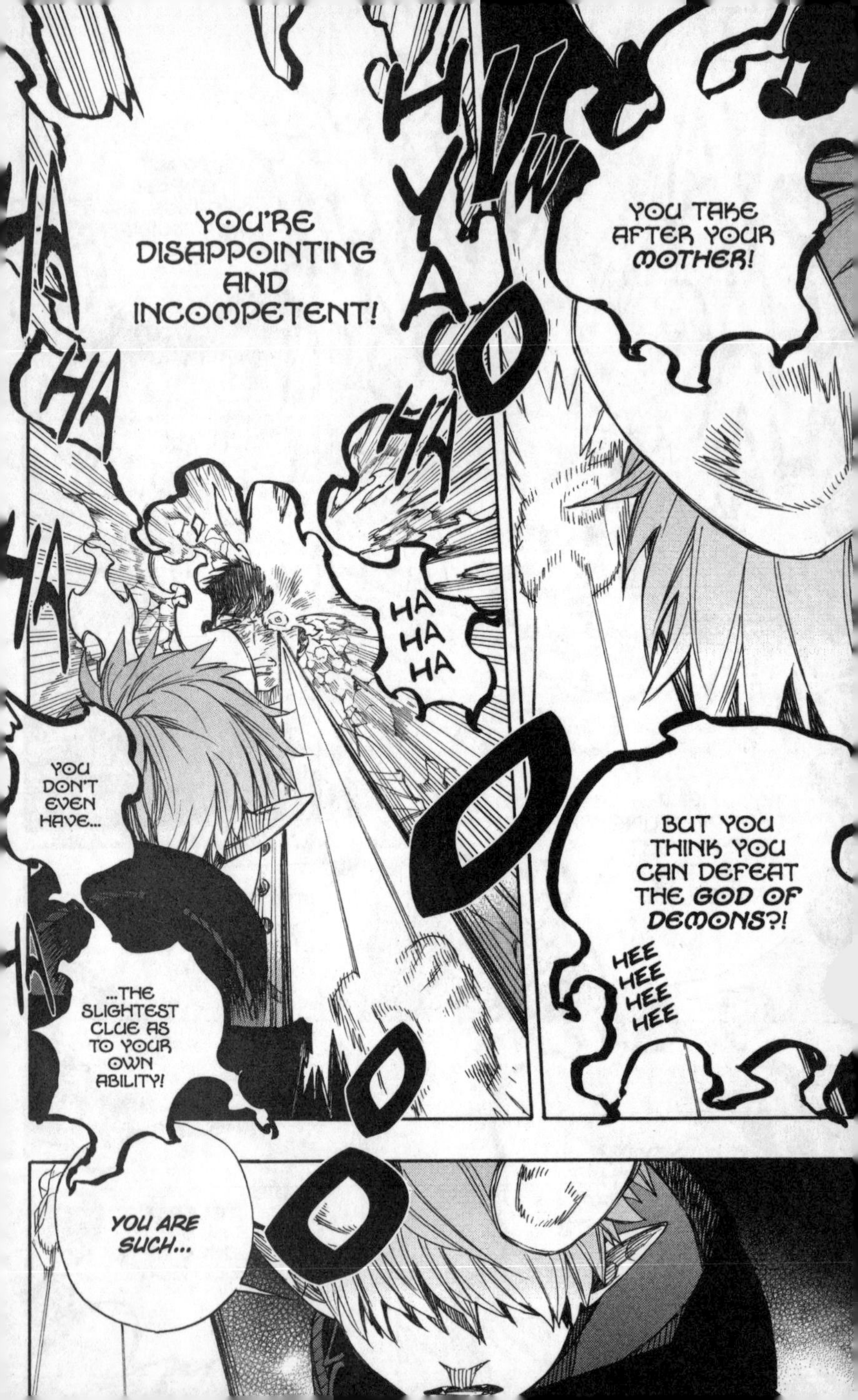
YOU TAKE AFTER YOUR MOTHER!
YOU'RE DISAPPOINTING AND INCOMPETENT!
HA HA HA
BUT YOU THINK YOU CAN DEFEAT THE GOD OF DEMONS?!
HEE HEE HEE HEE
YOU DON'T EVEN HAVE...
...THE SLIGHTEST CLUE AS TO YOUR OWN ABILITY!
YOU ARE SUCH...

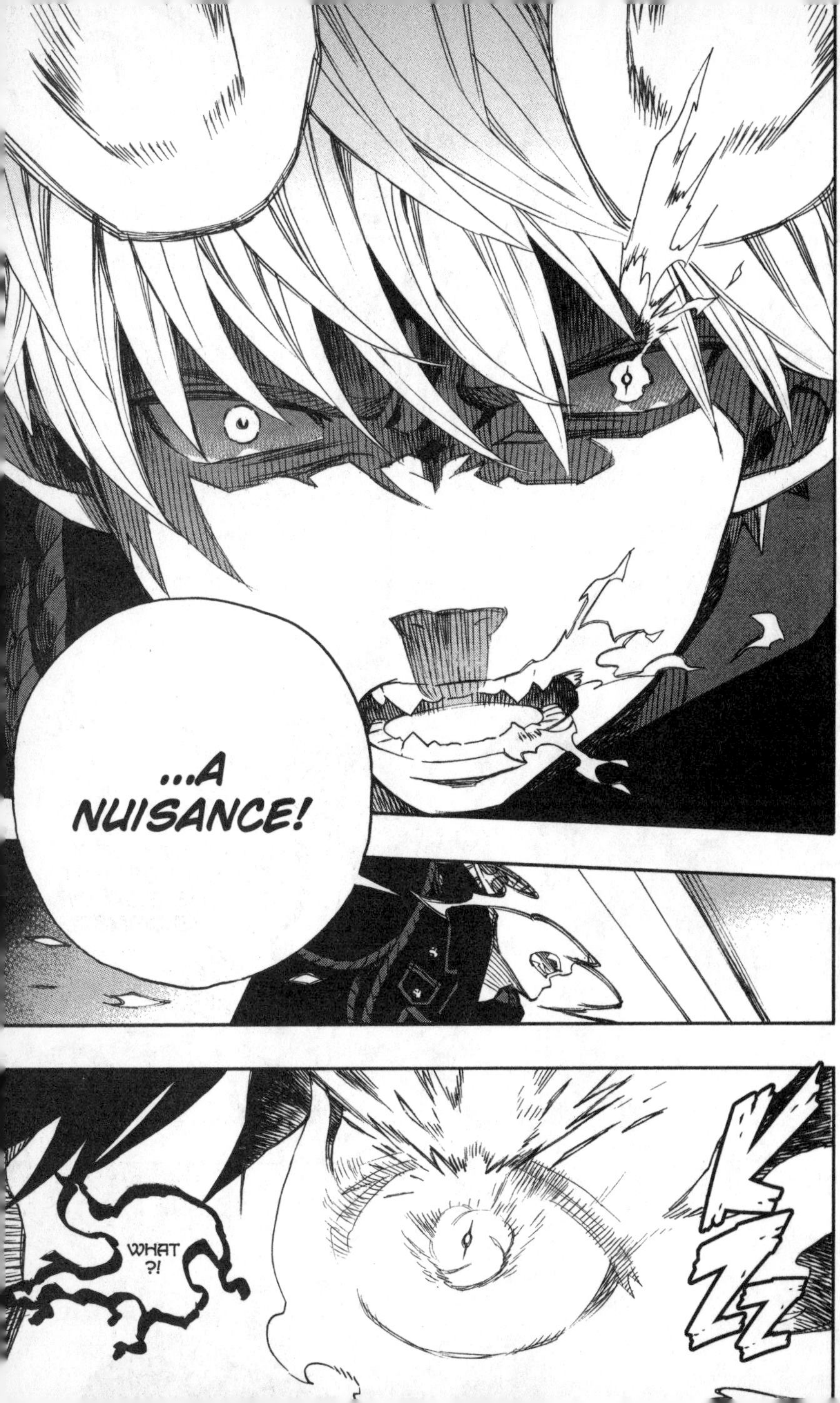
...A NUISANCE!
WHAT ?!

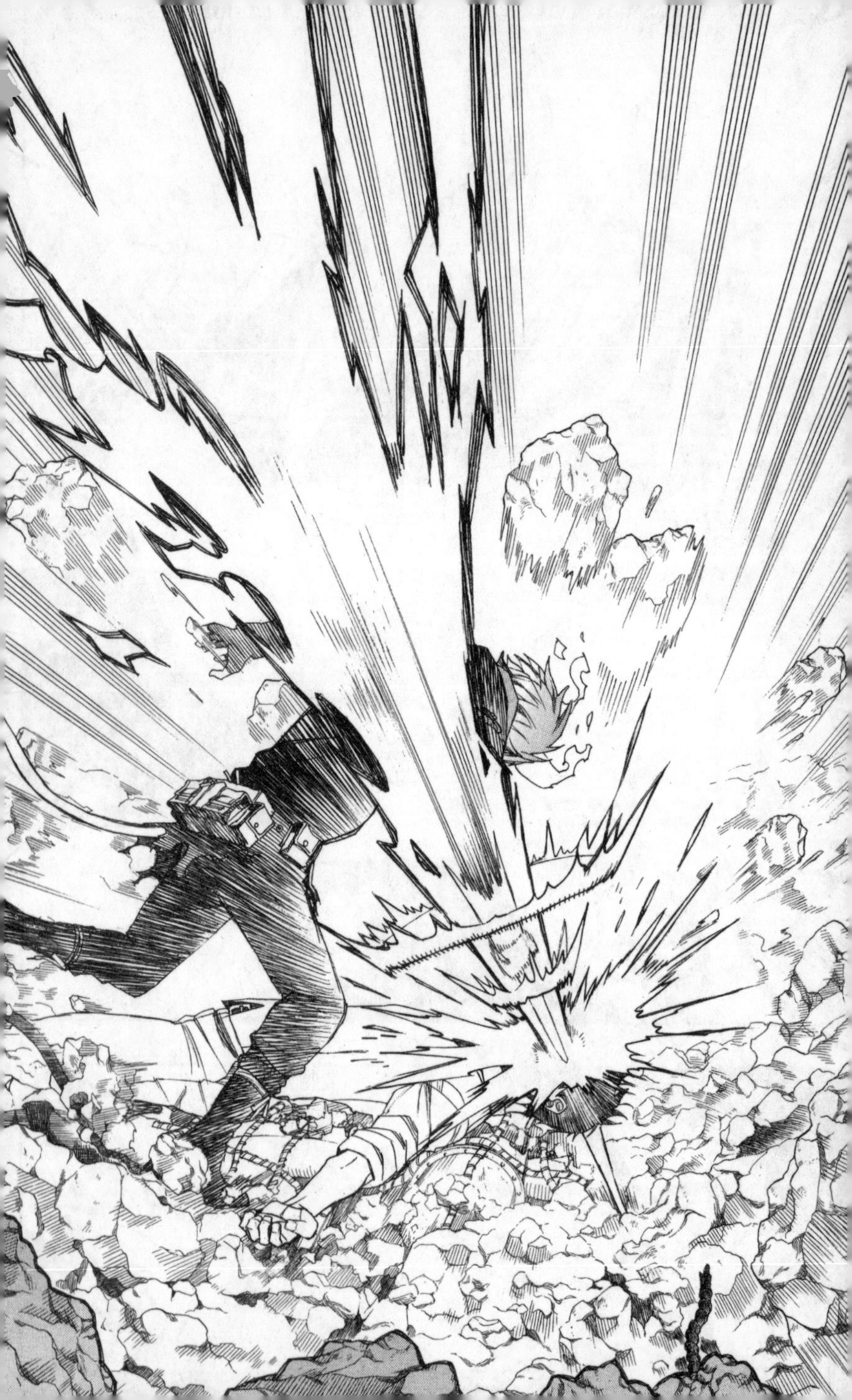

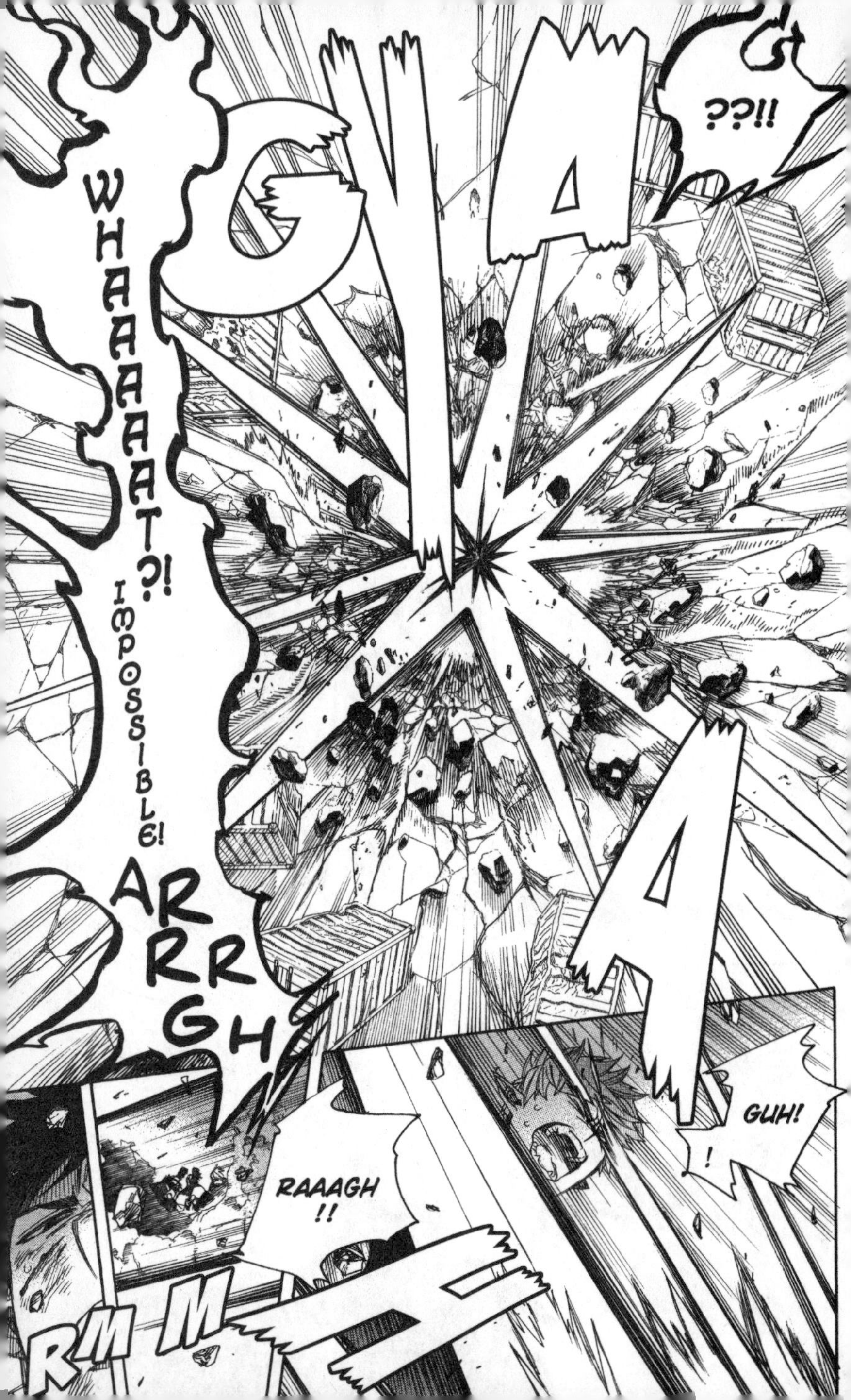
??!!
GYAA
WHAAAAAAT?! IMPOSSIBLE!
ARRRGH
GUH!
!
RAAAGH!!
RMMM

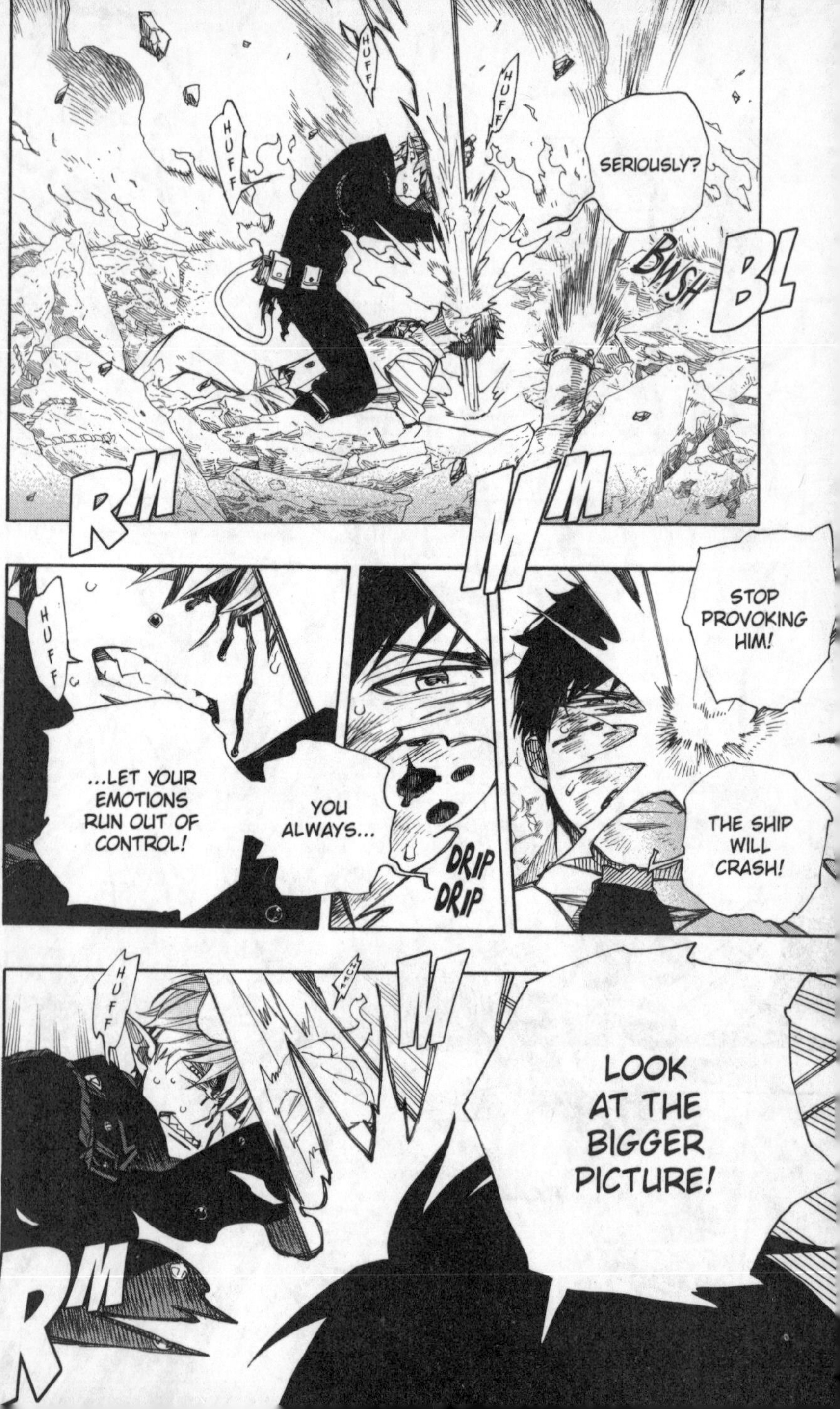
SERIOUSLY?
BL
BWSH
HUFF
HUFF
HUFF
M
M
RM
STOP PROVOKING HIM!
THE SHIP WILL CRASH!
YOU ALWAYS...
DRIP DRIP
HUFF
...LET YOUR EMOTIONS RUN OUT OF CONTROL!
LOOK AT THE BIGGER PICTURE!
M
HUFF
RM

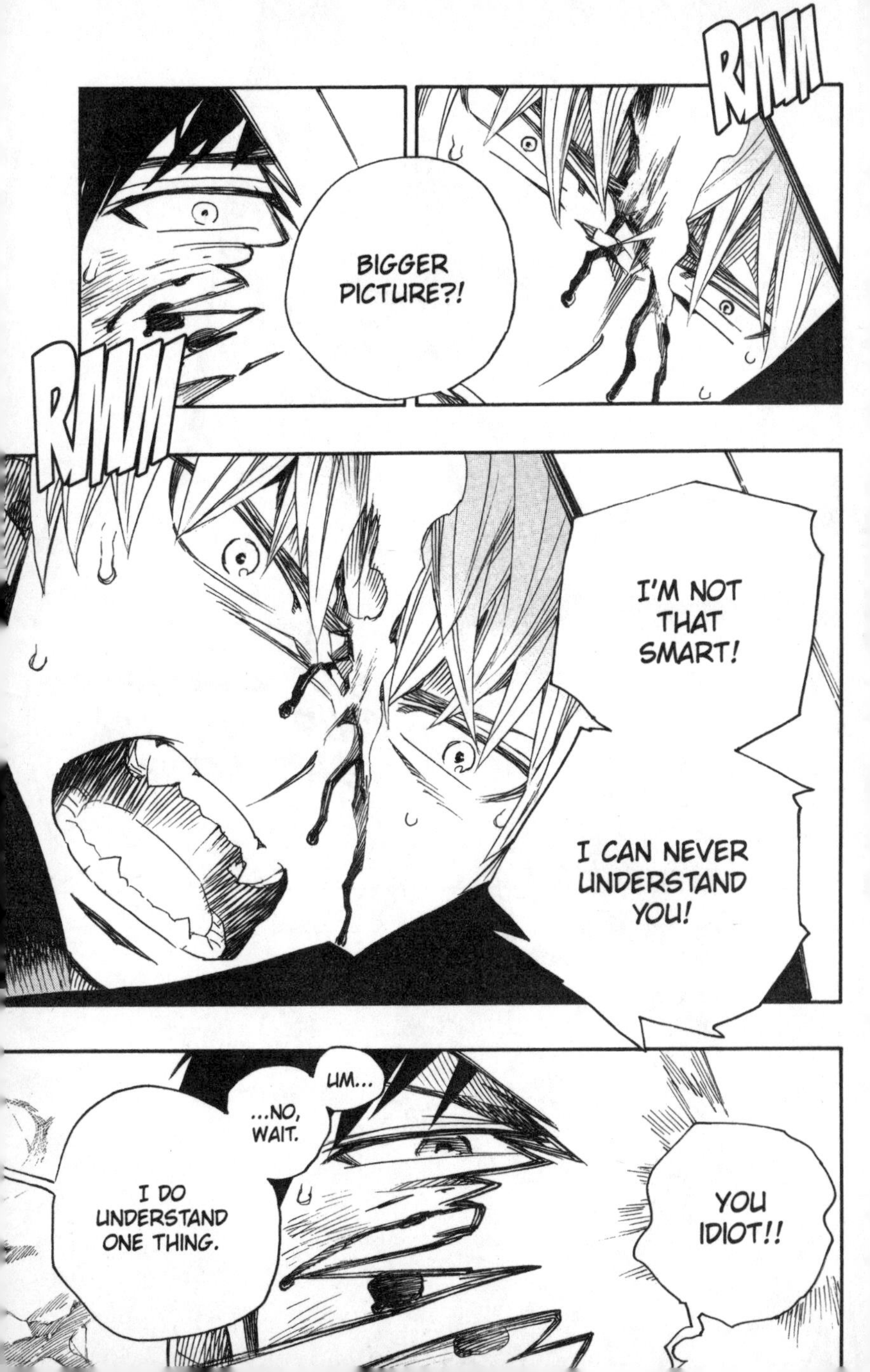
RMM
BIGGER PICTURE?!
RMM
I'M NOT THAT SMART!
I CAN NEVER UNDERSTAND YOU!
YOU IDIOT!!
UM...
...NO, WAIT.
I DO UNDERSTAND ONE THING.

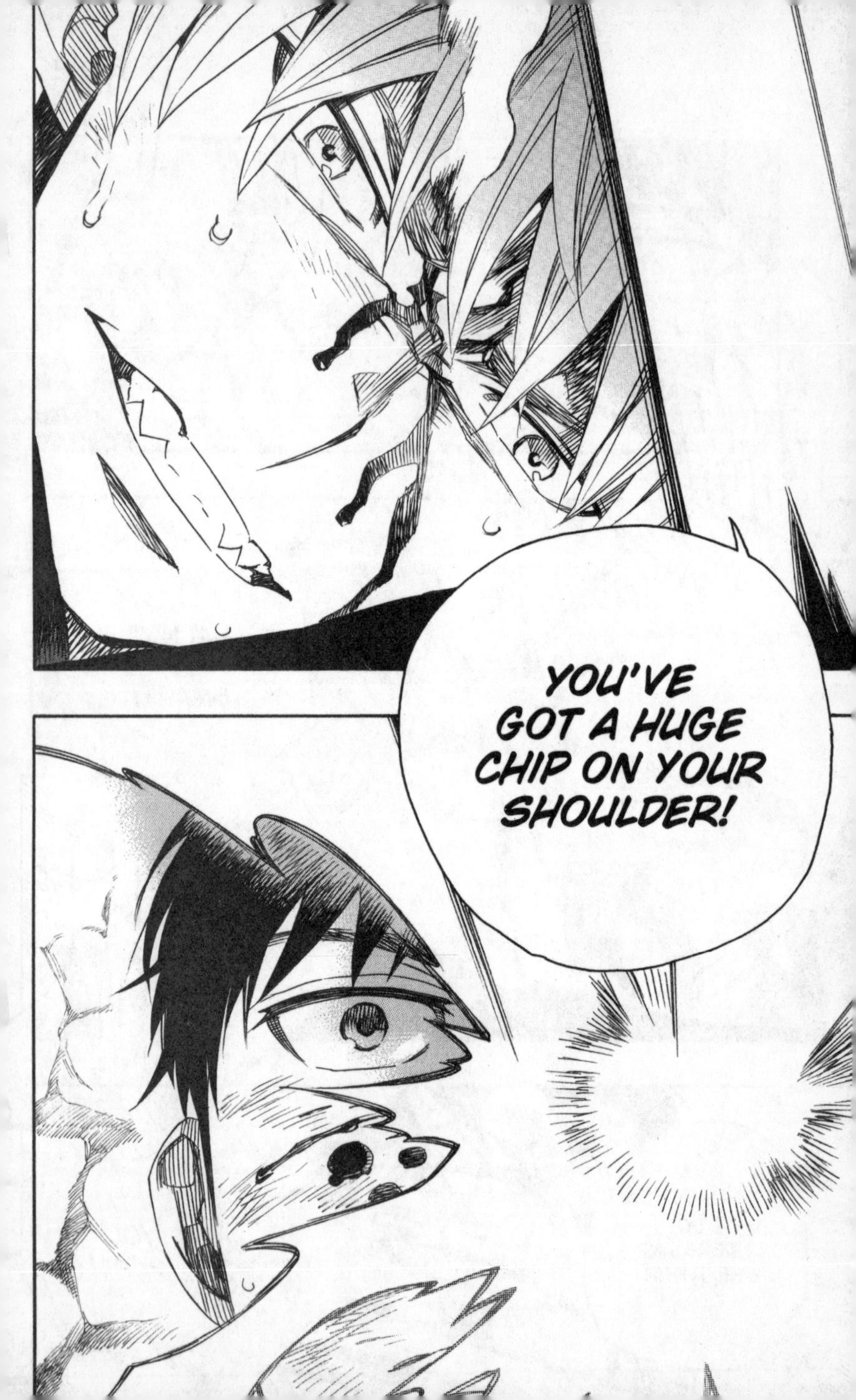
YOU'VE GOT A HUGE CHIP ON YOUR SHOULDER!

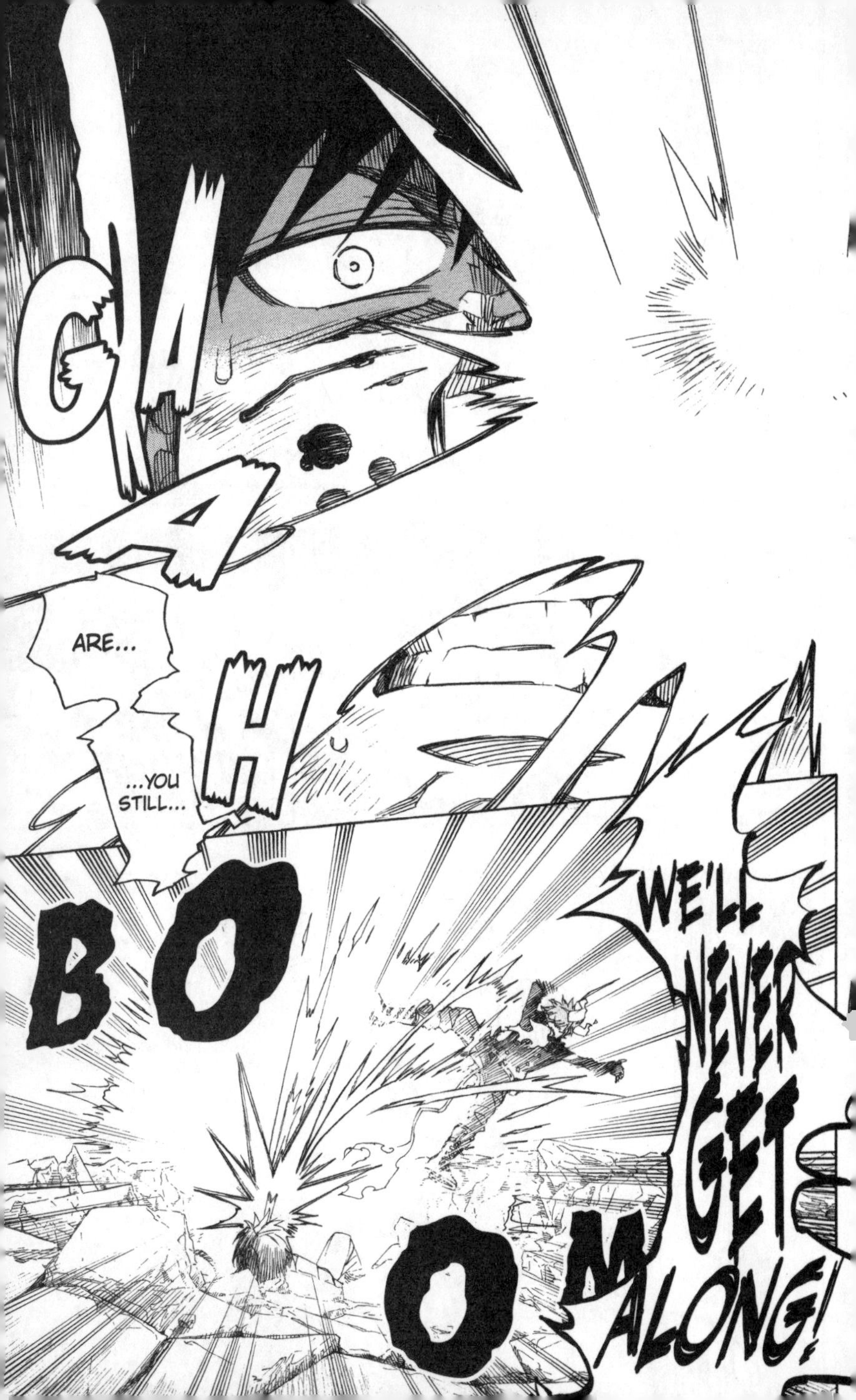
GAAH
ARE...
...YOU STILL...
WE'LL NEVER GET ALONG!
BOOOM

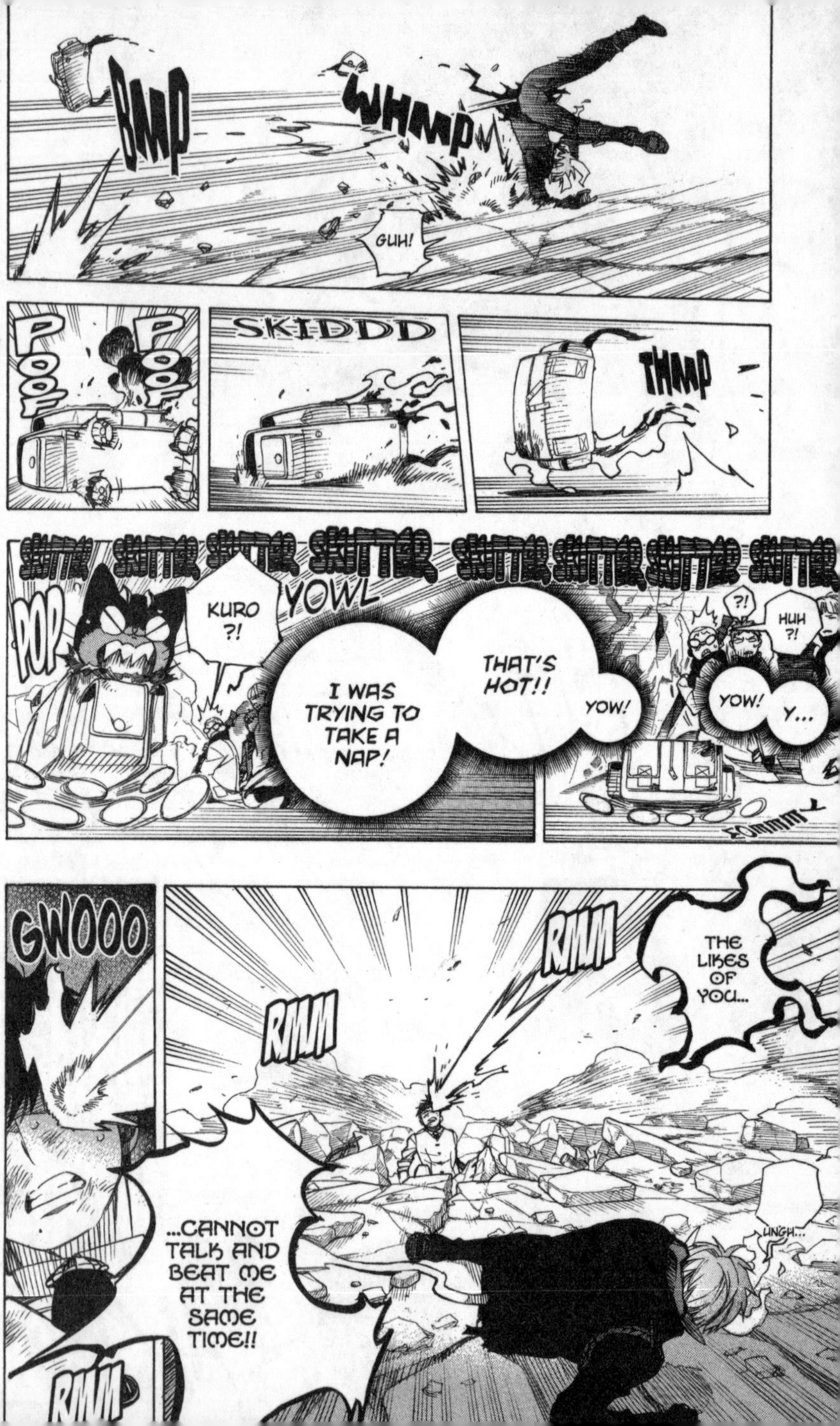
WHMP
BMP
GUH!
THMP
SKIDDD
POOF
POOF
SKITTER SKITTER SKITTER SKITTER
?!
HUH ?!
YOW!
Y...
YOW!
THAT'S HOT!!
SKITTER SKITTER SKITTER SKITTER
YOWL
KURO ?!
POP
I WAS TRYING TO TAKE A NAP!
THE LIKES OF YOU...
RMM
RMM
UNGH...
...CANNOT TALK AND BEAT ME AT THE SAME TIME!!
GWOOO
RMM

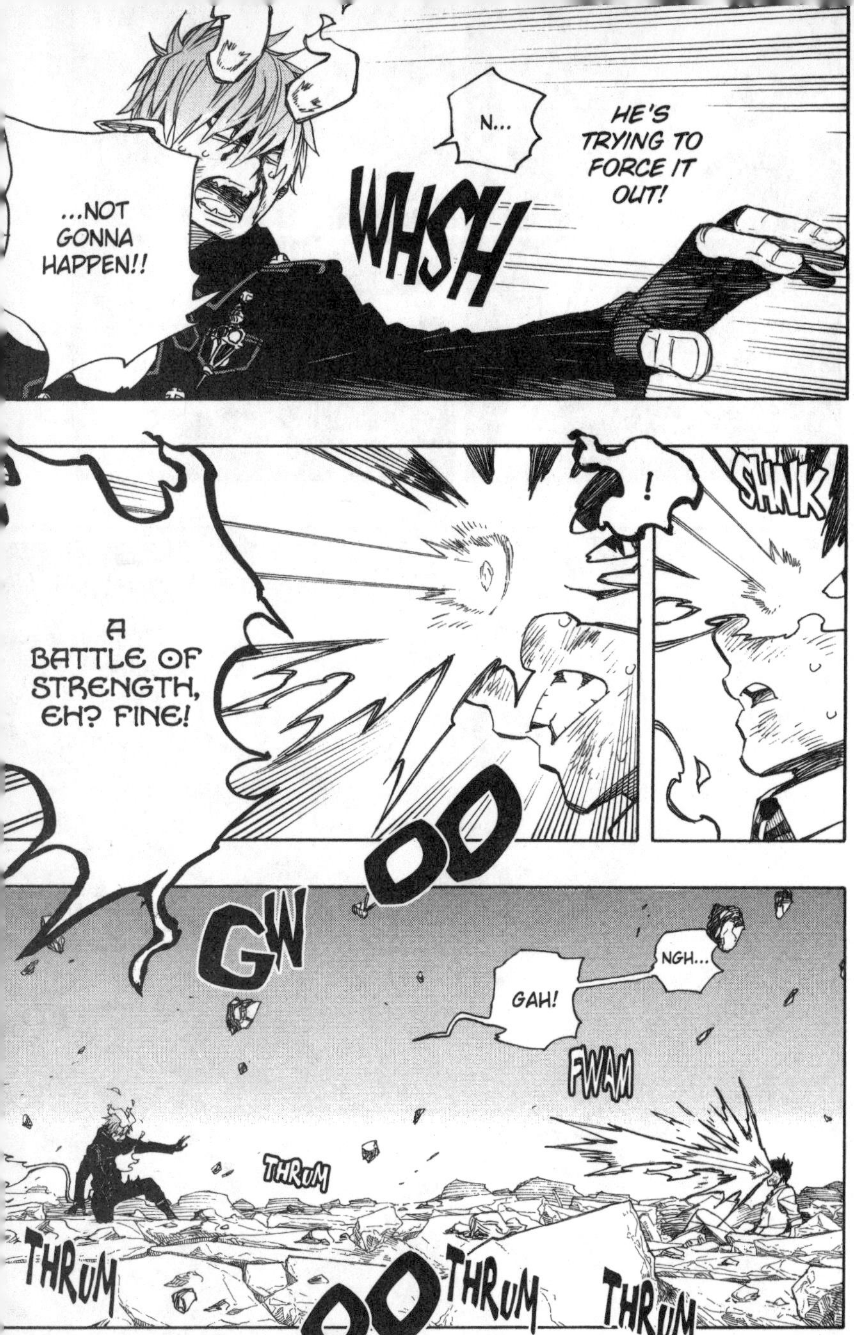
HE'S TRYING TO FORCE IT OUT!
N...
WHSH
...NOT GONNA HAPPEN!!
SHNK
!
A BATTLE OF STRENGTH, EH? FINE!
GW
OO
NGH...
GAH!
FWAM
THRUM
THRUM
THRUM
OO
THRUM

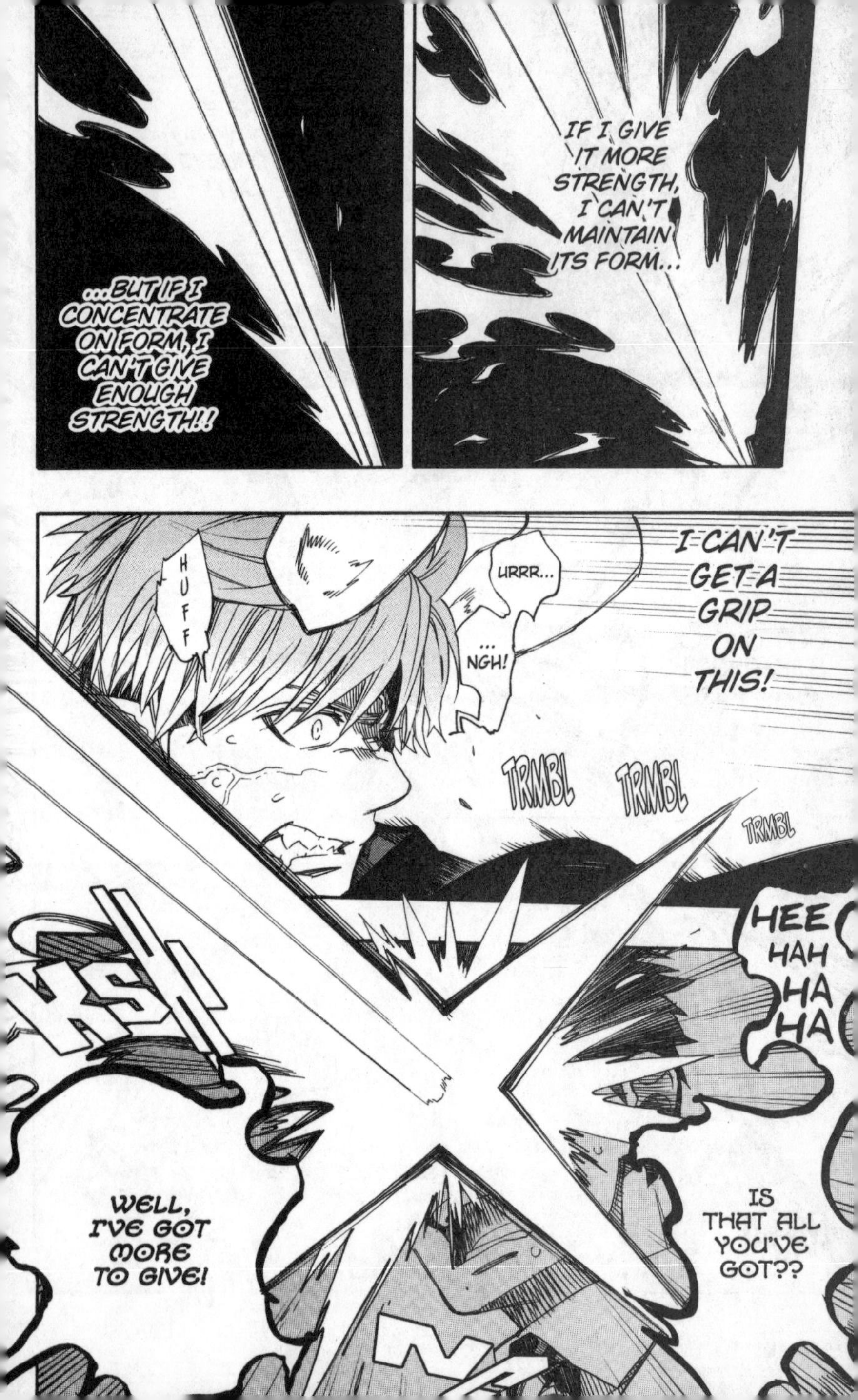
IF I GIVE IT MORE STRENGTH, I CAN'T MAINTAIN ITS FORM...
...BUT IF I CONCENTRATE ON FORM, I CAN'T GIVE ENOUGH STRENGTH!!
I CAN'T GET A GRIP ON THIS!
URRR...
...NGH!
HUFF
TRMBL
TRMBL
TRMBL
HEE HAH HA HA
IS THAT ALL YOU'VE GOT??
WELL, I'VE GOT MORE TO GIVE!

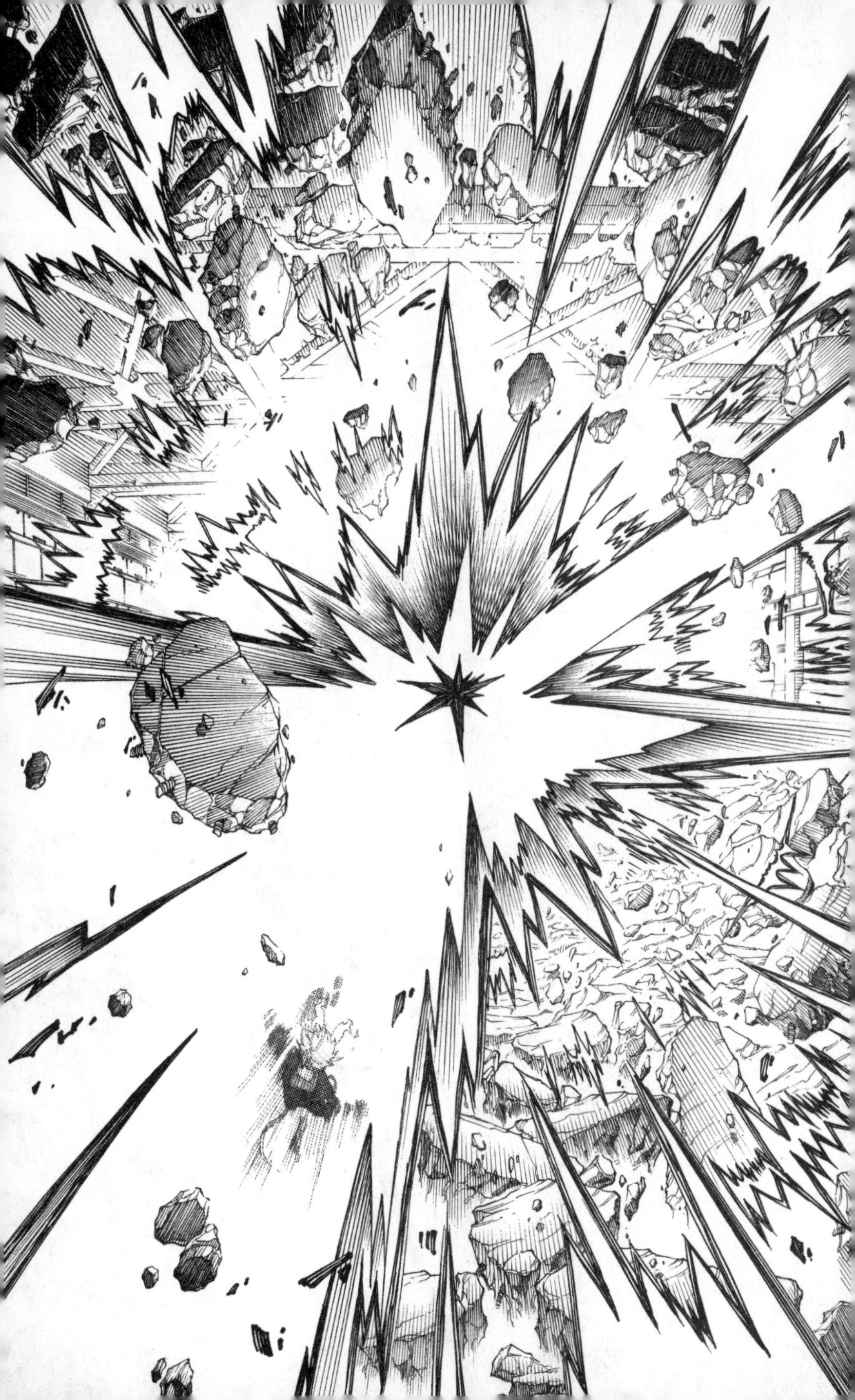

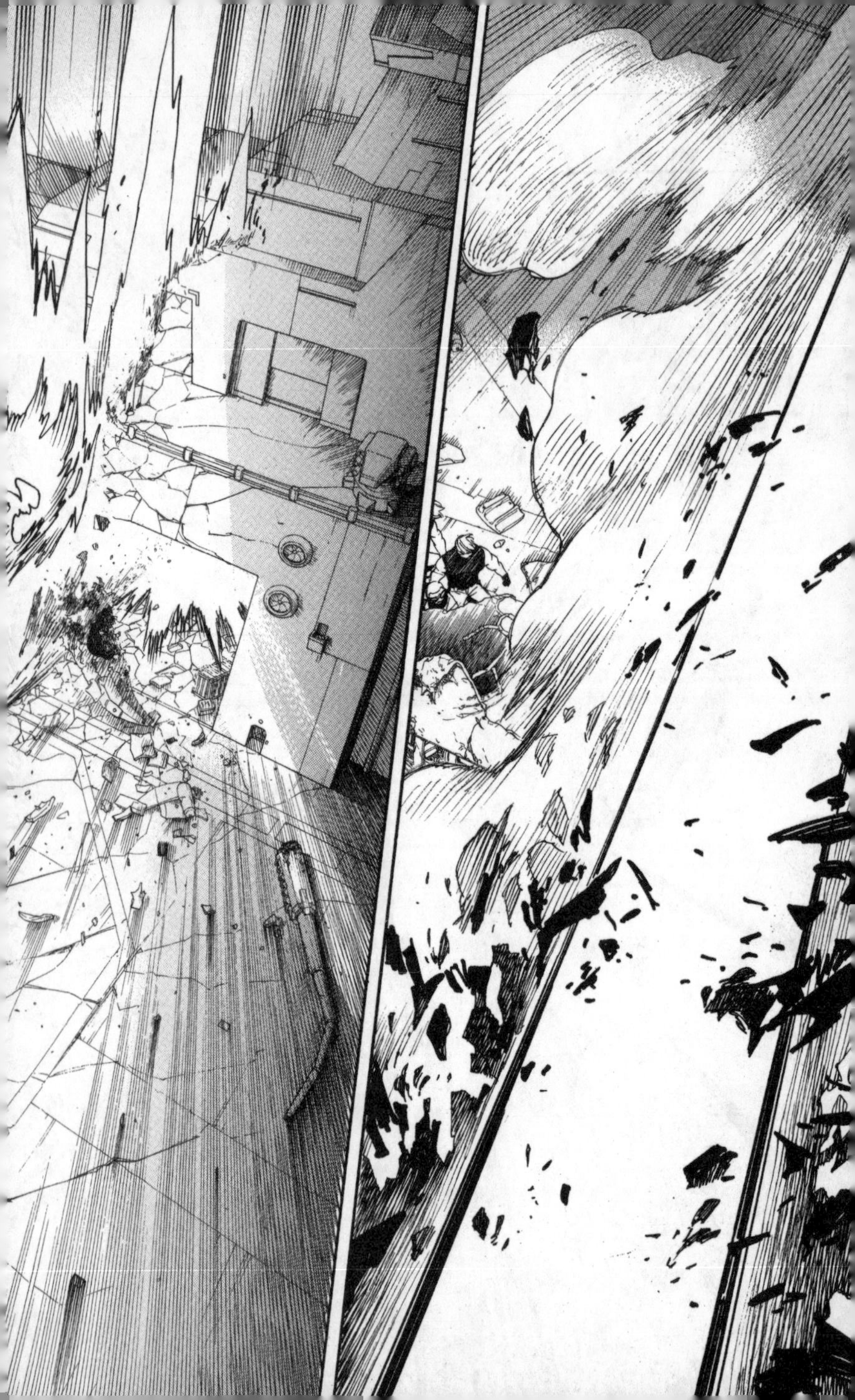

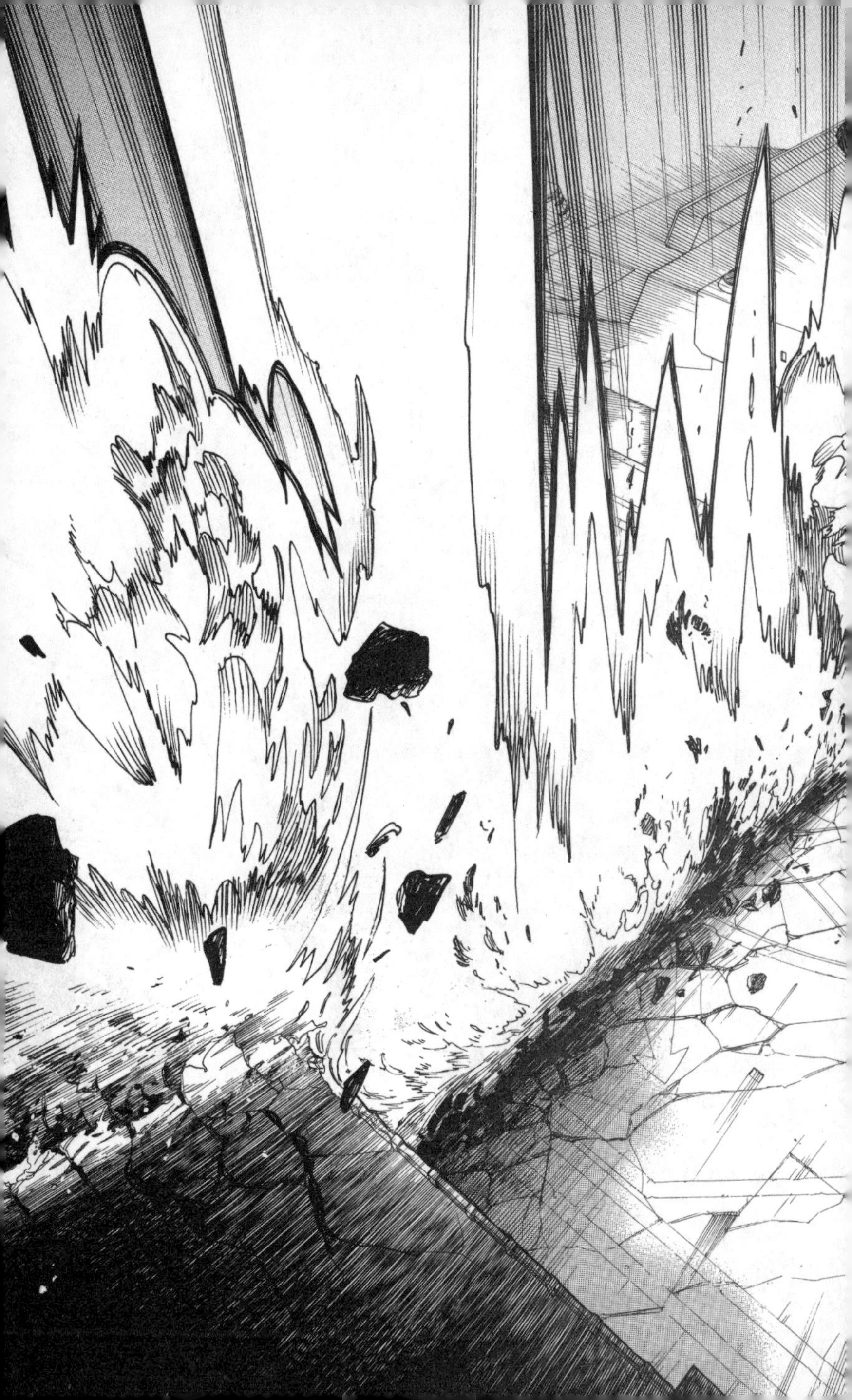

Blue Exorcist Chapter 124: Of One Cloth—In Flames

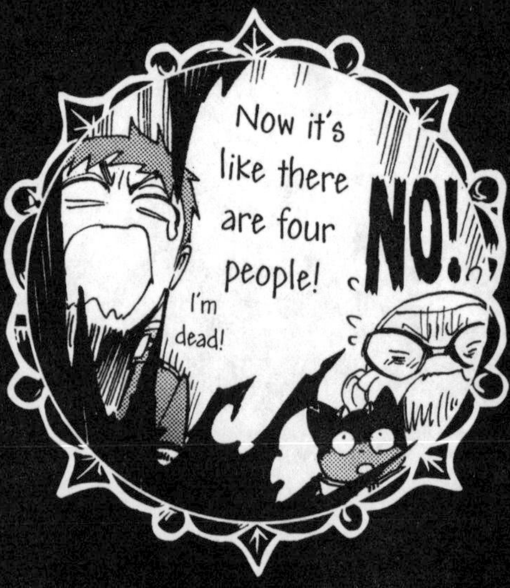
NO!
Now it's like there are four people!
I'm dead!

Chapter 125: Of One Cloth—Disrupt

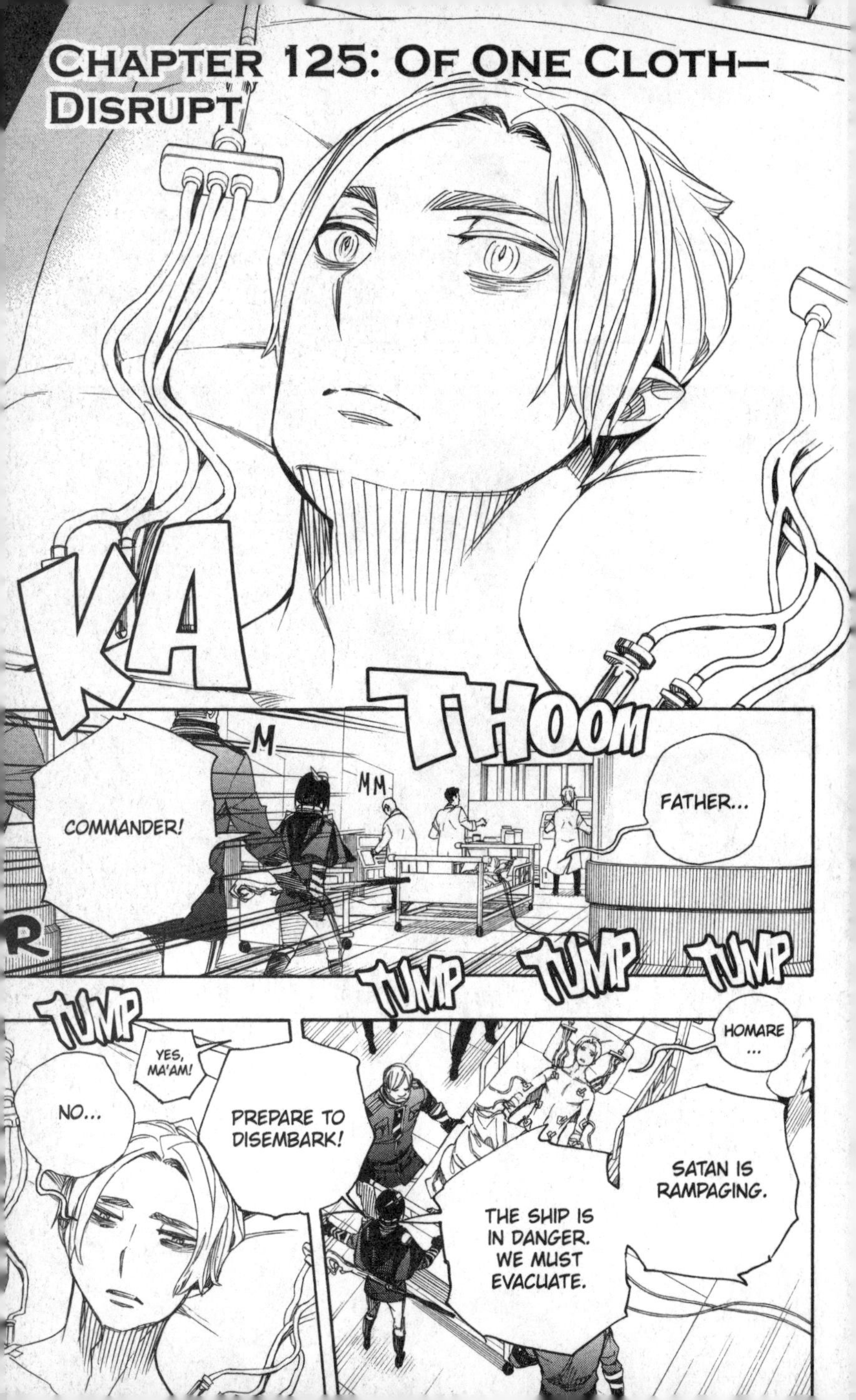
KA
THOOM
FATHER...
MMM
COMMANDER!
R
TUMP
TUMP
TUMP
TUMP
HOMARE...
SATAN IS RAMPAGING.
THE SHIP IS IN DANGER. WE MUST EVACUATE.
PREPARE TO DISEMBARK!
YES, MA'AM!
NO...

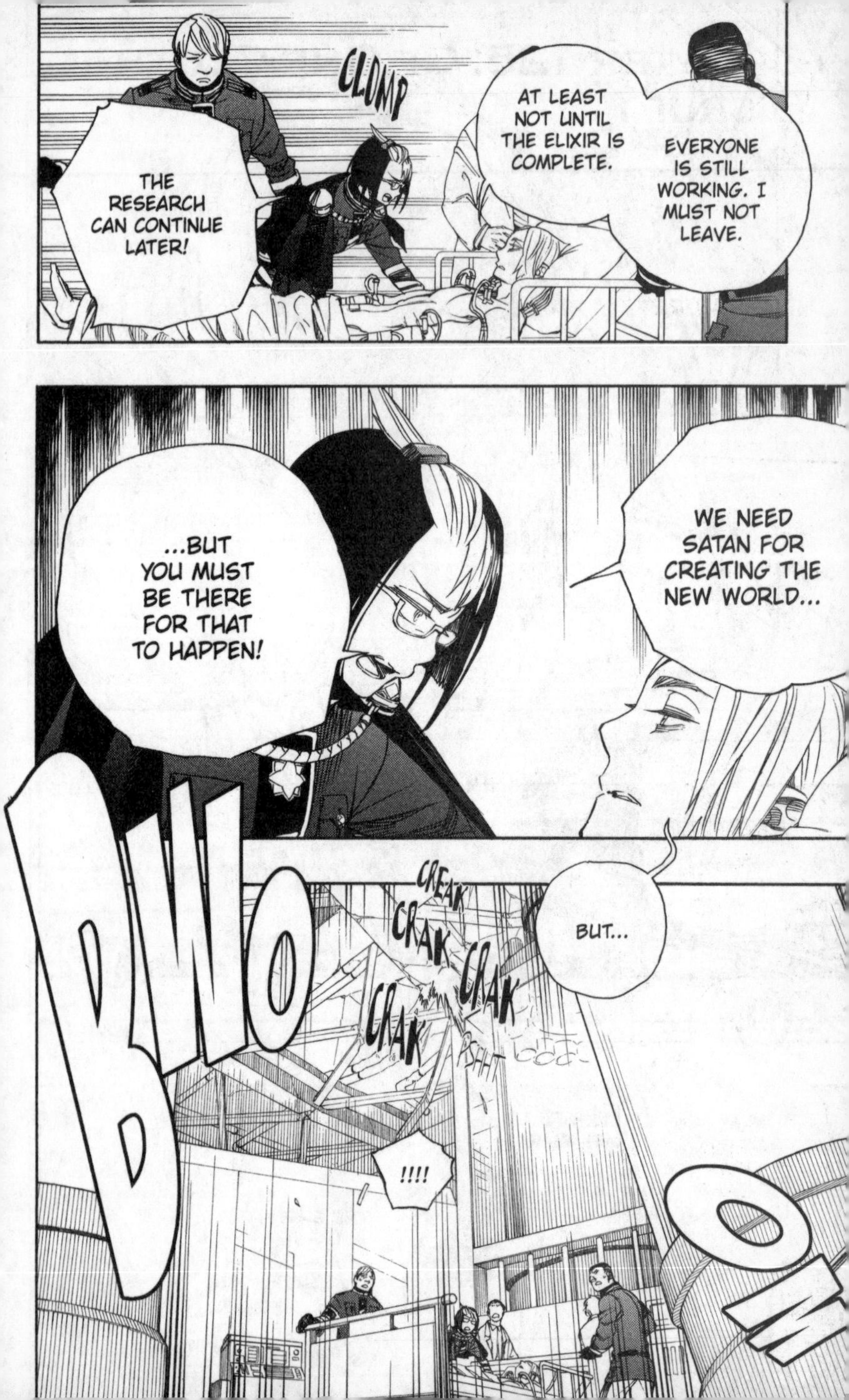
EVERYONE IS STILL WORKING. I MUST NOT LEAVE.
AT LEAST NOT UNTIL THE ELIXIR IS COMPLETE.
CLOMP
THE RESEARCH CAN CONTINUE LATER!
WE NEED SATAN FOR CREATING THE NEW WORLD...
...BUT YOU MUST BE THERE FOR THAT TO HAPPEN!
BUT...
CREAK
CRAK
CRAK
CRAK
!!!!
BWO
OM

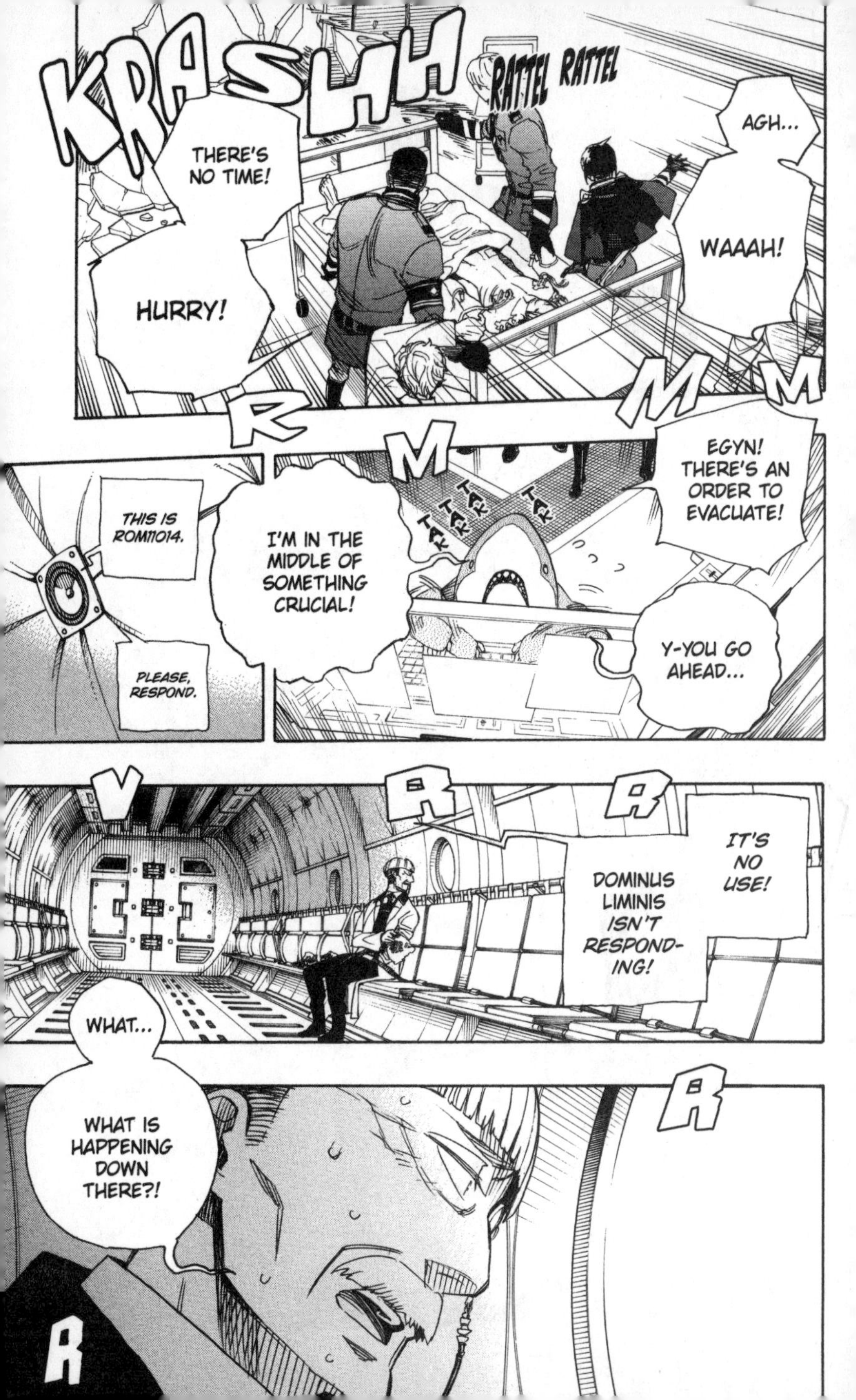
RATTEL RATTEL
KRASHH
AGH...
WAAAH!
THERE'S NO TIME!
HURRY!
R
M
M
M
EGYN! THERE'S AN ORDER TO EVACUATE!
TAK TAK TAK TAK
I'M IN THE MIDDLE OF SOMETHING CRUCIAL!
Y-YOU GO AHEAD...
THIS IS ROM11014.
PLEASE, RESPOND.
R
R
V
IT'S NO USE!
DOMINUS LIMINIS ISN'T RESPONDING!
WHAT...
R
WHAT IS HAPPENING DOWN THERE?!
R

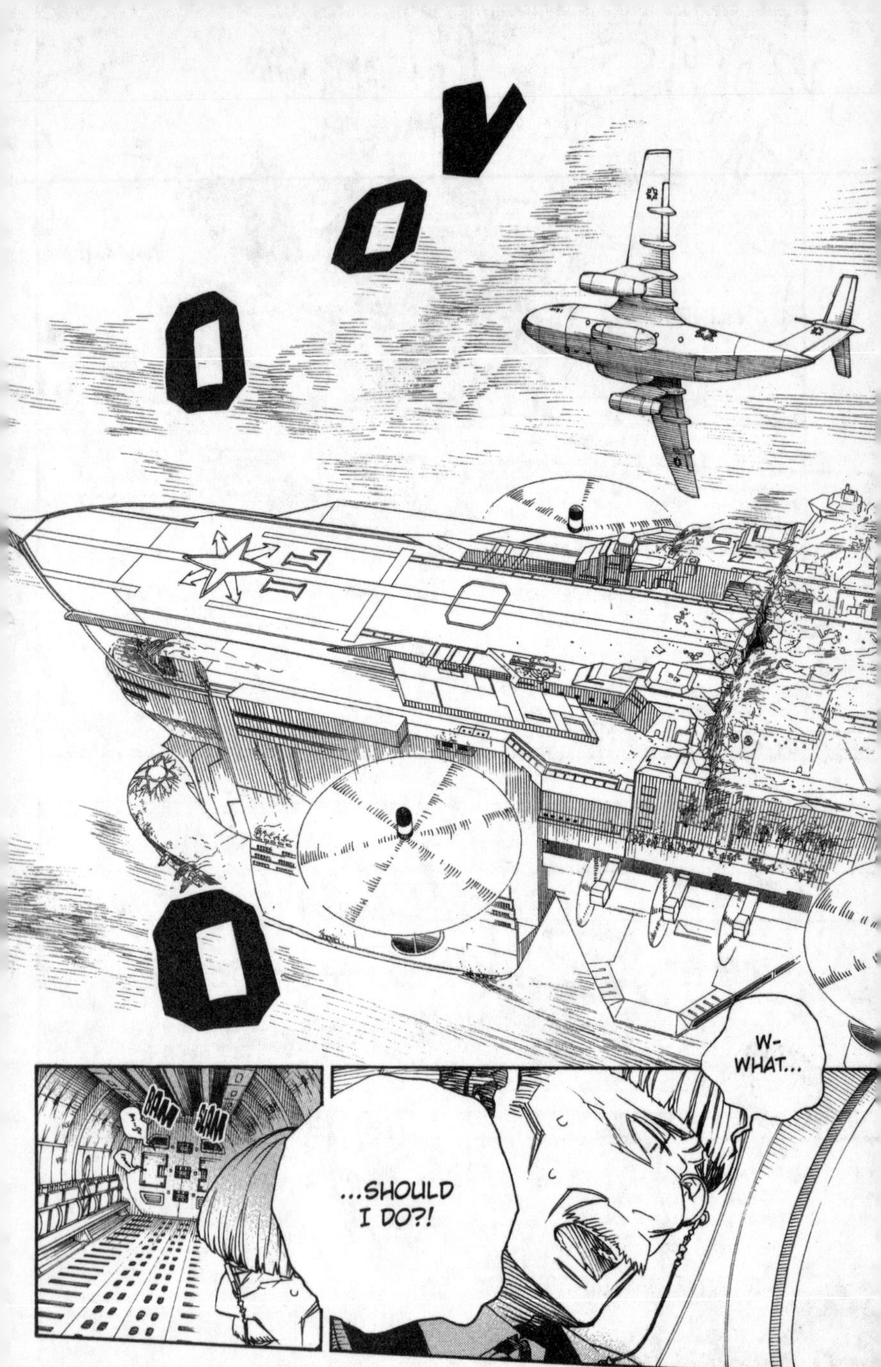
VOOO
W-
WHAT...
...SHOULD
I DO?!
BAAM
SLAM

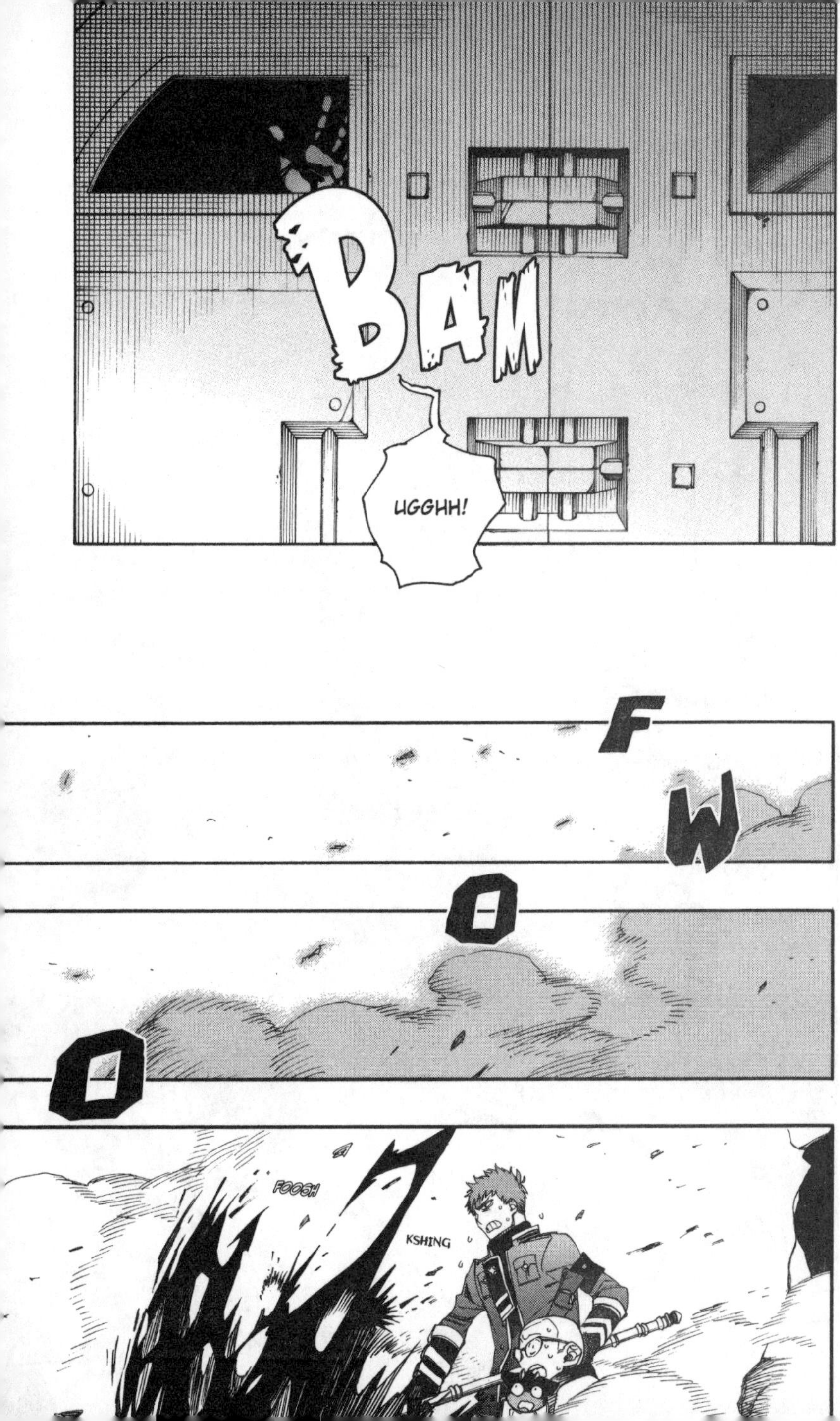
BAM
UGGHH!
FWOO
FOOSH
KSHING

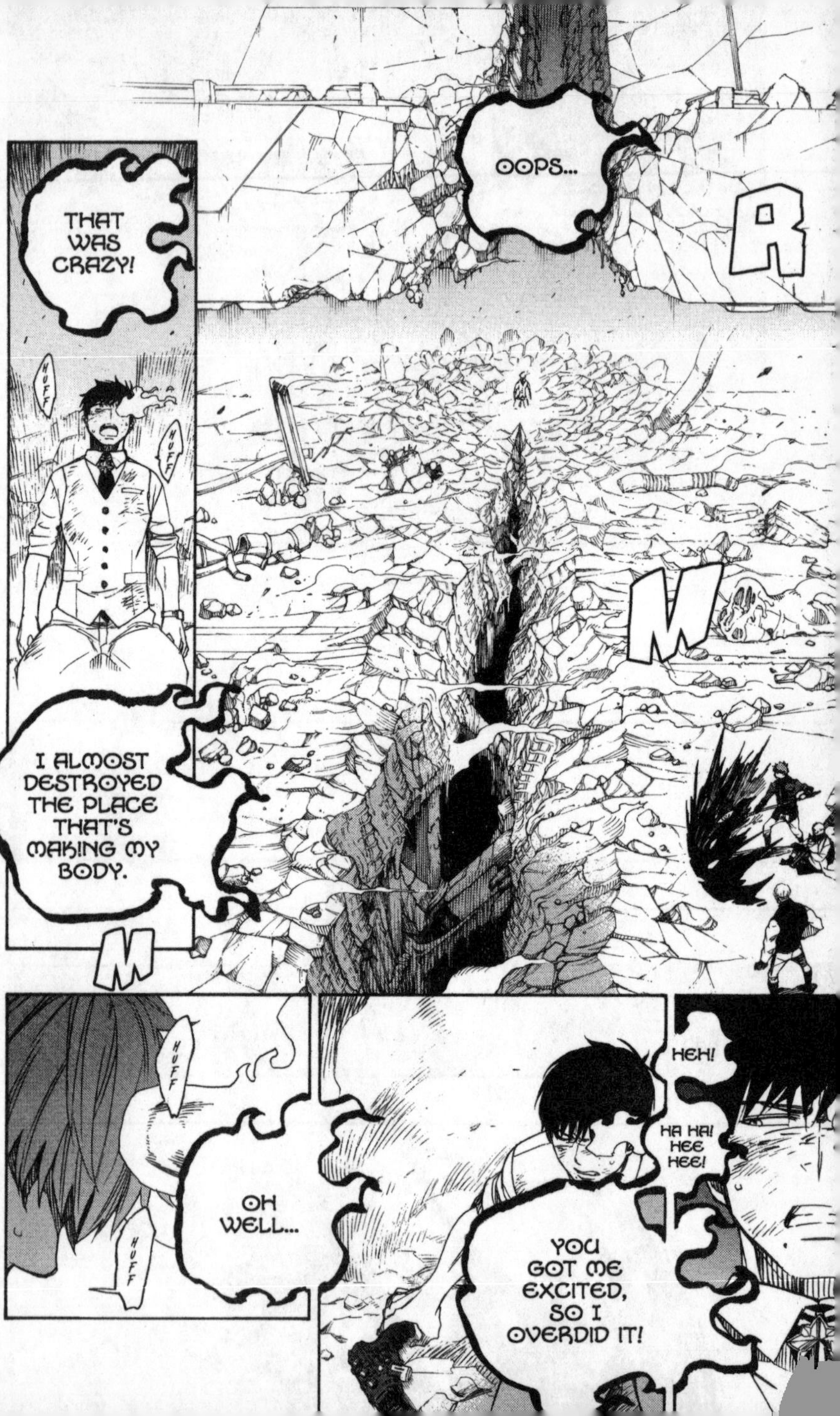
OOPS...
R
M
M
THAT WAS CRAZY!
HUFF
HUFF
I ALMOST DESTROYED THE PLACE THAT'S MAKING MY BODY.
HEH!
HA HA! HEE HEE!
YOU GOT ME EXCITED, SO I OVERDID IT!
OH WELL...
HUFF
HUFF

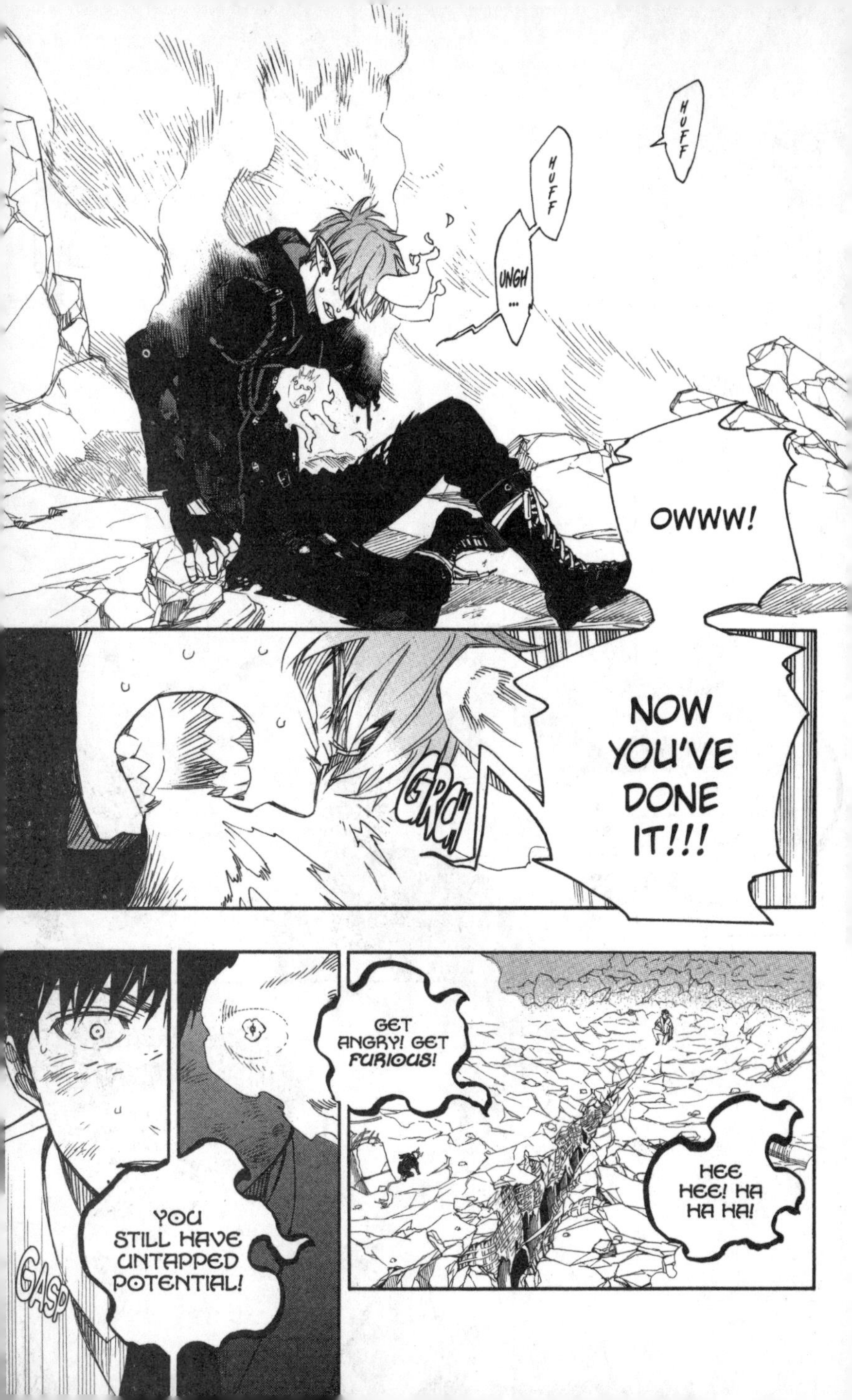
HUFF
HUFF
UNGH...
OWWW!
NOW YOU'VE DONE IT!!!
GRCH
GET ANGRY! GET FURIOUS!
HEE HEE! HA HA HA!
YOU STILL HAVE UNTAPPED POTENTIAL!
GASP

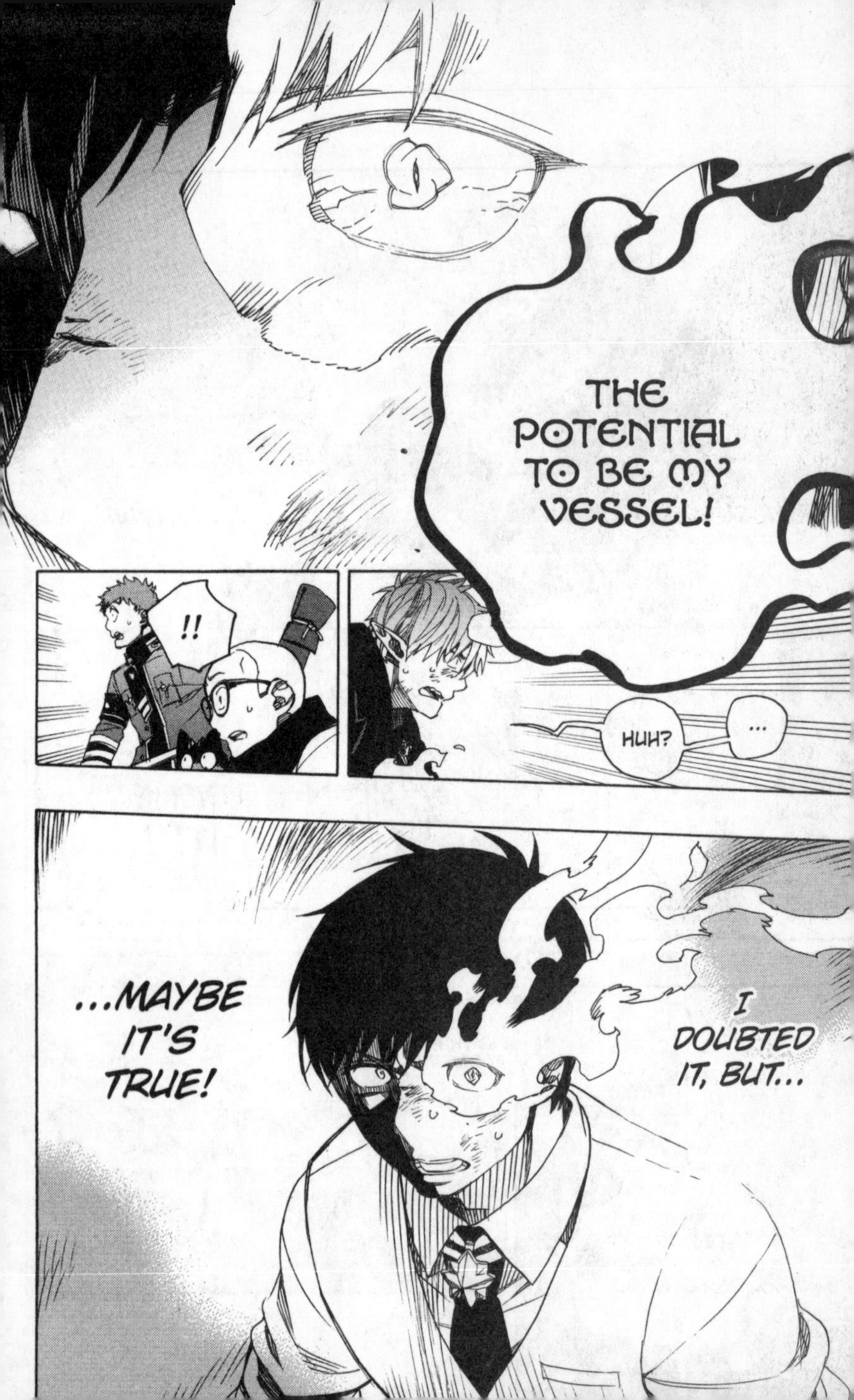
THE POTENTIAL TO BE MY VESSEL!
...
HUH?
!!
I DOUBTED IT, BUT...
...MAYBE IT'S TRUE!

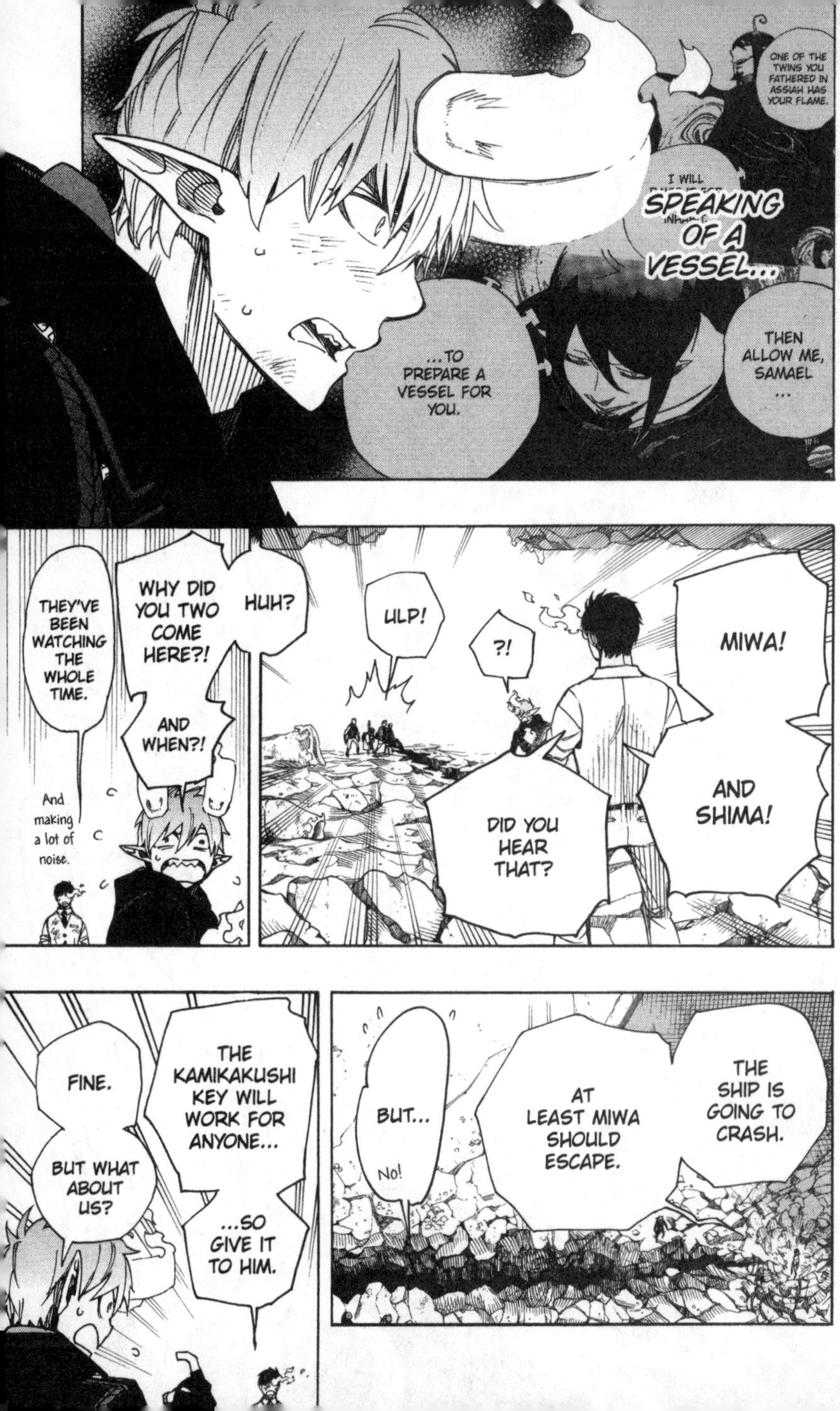
ONE OF THE TWINS YOU FATHERED IN ASSIAH HAS YOUR FLAME.
I WILL
SPEAKING OF A VESSEL...
THEN ALLOW ME, SAMAEL ...
...TO PREPARE A VESSEL FOR YOU.
MIWA!
AND SHIMA!
?!
ULP!
DID YOU HEAR THAT?
HUH?
WHY DID YOU TWO COME HERE?!
AND WHEN?!
THEY'VE BEEN WATCHING THE WHOLE TIME.
And making a lot of noise.
THE SHIP IS GOING TO CRASH.
AT LEAST MIWA SHOULD ESCAPE.
BUT...
No!
THE KAMIKAKUSHI KEY WILL WORK FOR ANYONE...
...SO GIVE IT TO HIM.
FINE.
BUT WHAT ABOUT US?

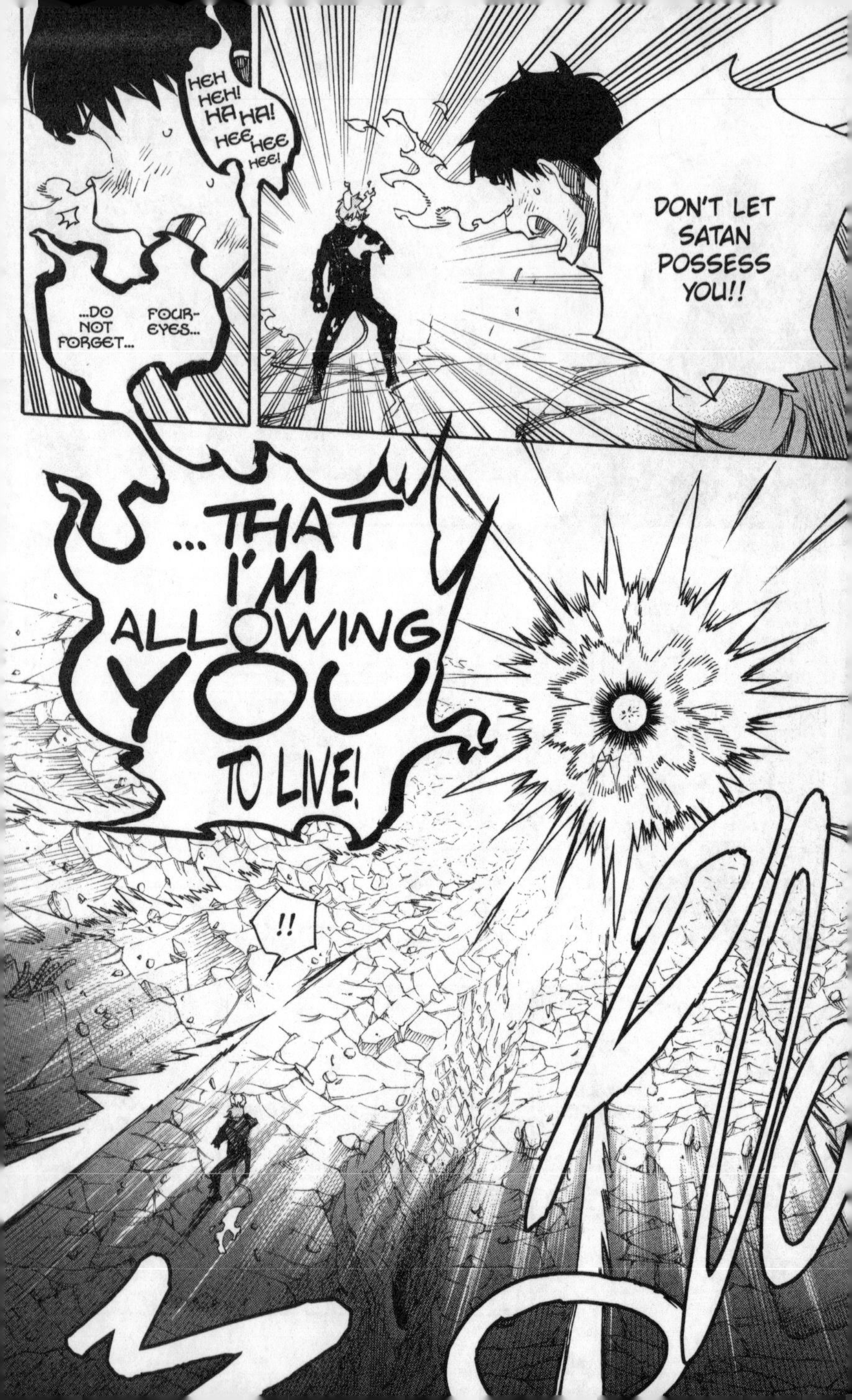
DON'T LET SATAN POSSESS YOU!!
HEH HEH! HA HA! HEE HEE HEE!
FOUR-EYES...
...DO NOT FORGET...
...THAT I'M ALLOWING YOU TO LIVE!
!!

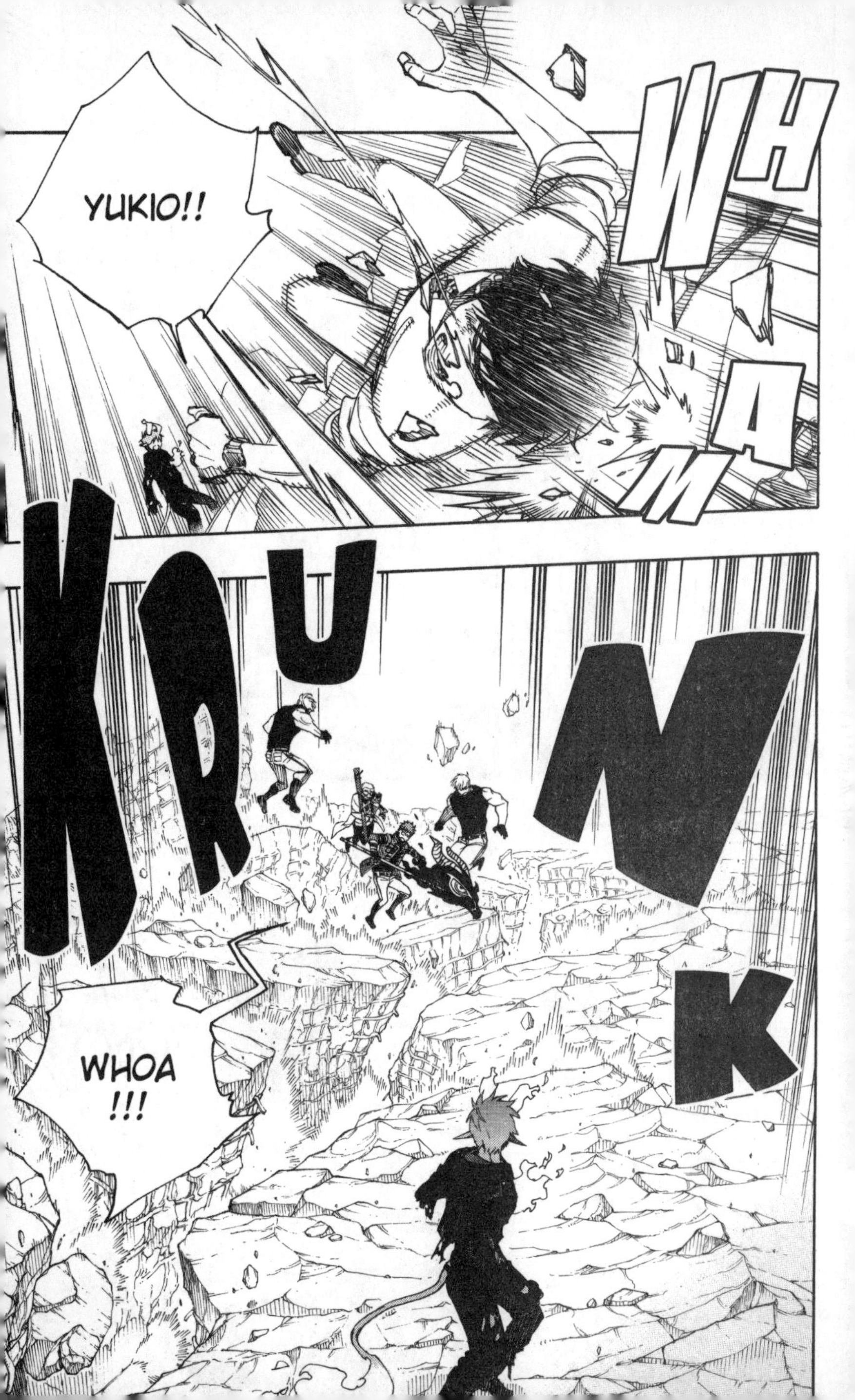
WHAM
YUKIO!!
KRUNK
WHOA !!!

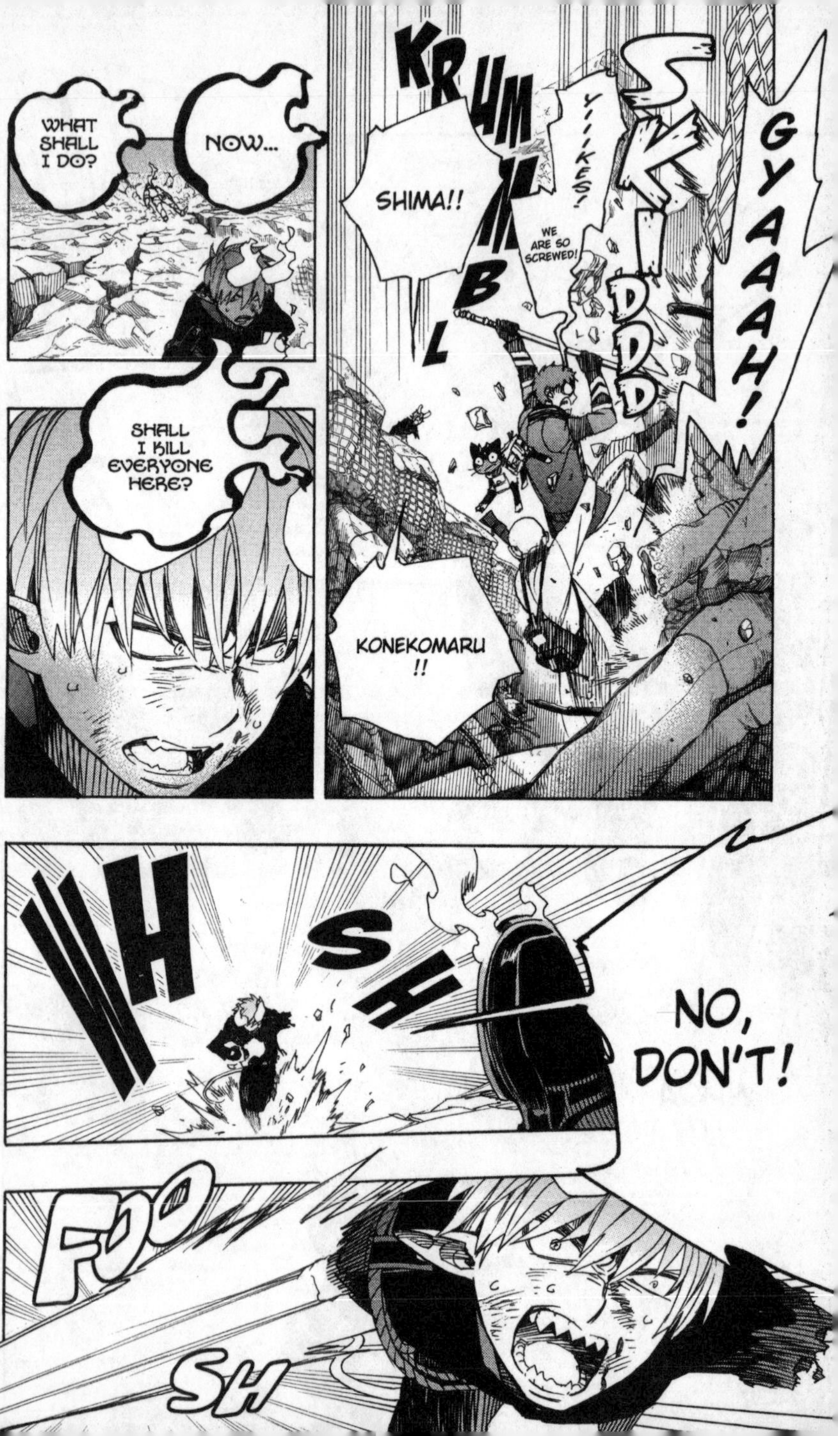
GYAAAH!
SKIDDD
Y-I-IKES!
WE ARE SO SCREWED!
KRUMBL
SHIMA!!
KONEKOMARU !!
WHAT SHALL I DO?
NOW...
SHALL I KILL EVERYONE HERE?
NO, DON'T!
WH
SH
FOO
SH

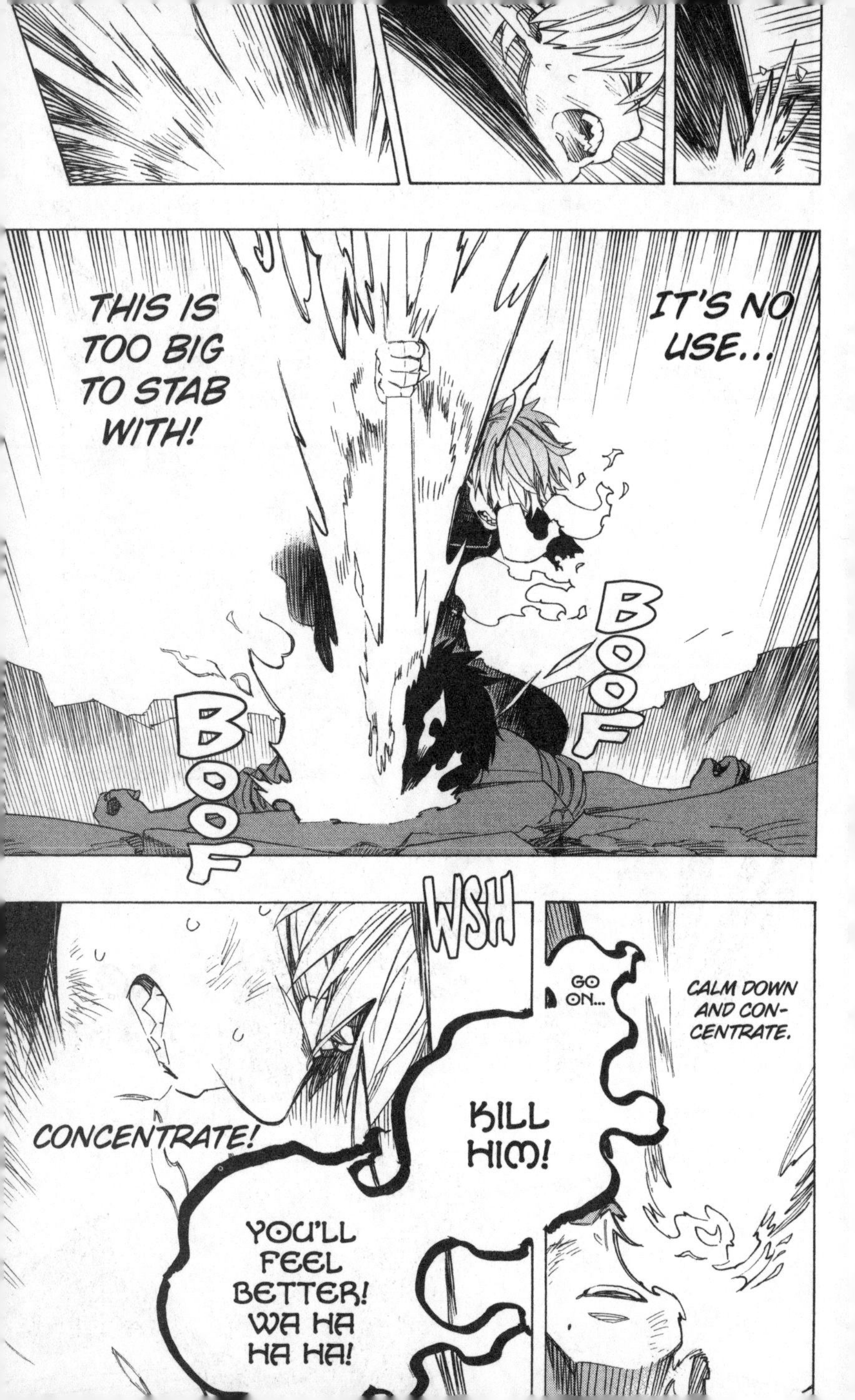
IT'S NO USE...
THIS IS TOO BIG TO STAB WITH!
BOOF
BOOF
CALM DOWN AND CONCENTRATE.
GO ON...
KILL HIM!
YOU'LL FEEL BETTER! WA HA HA HA!
WSH
CONCENTRATE!

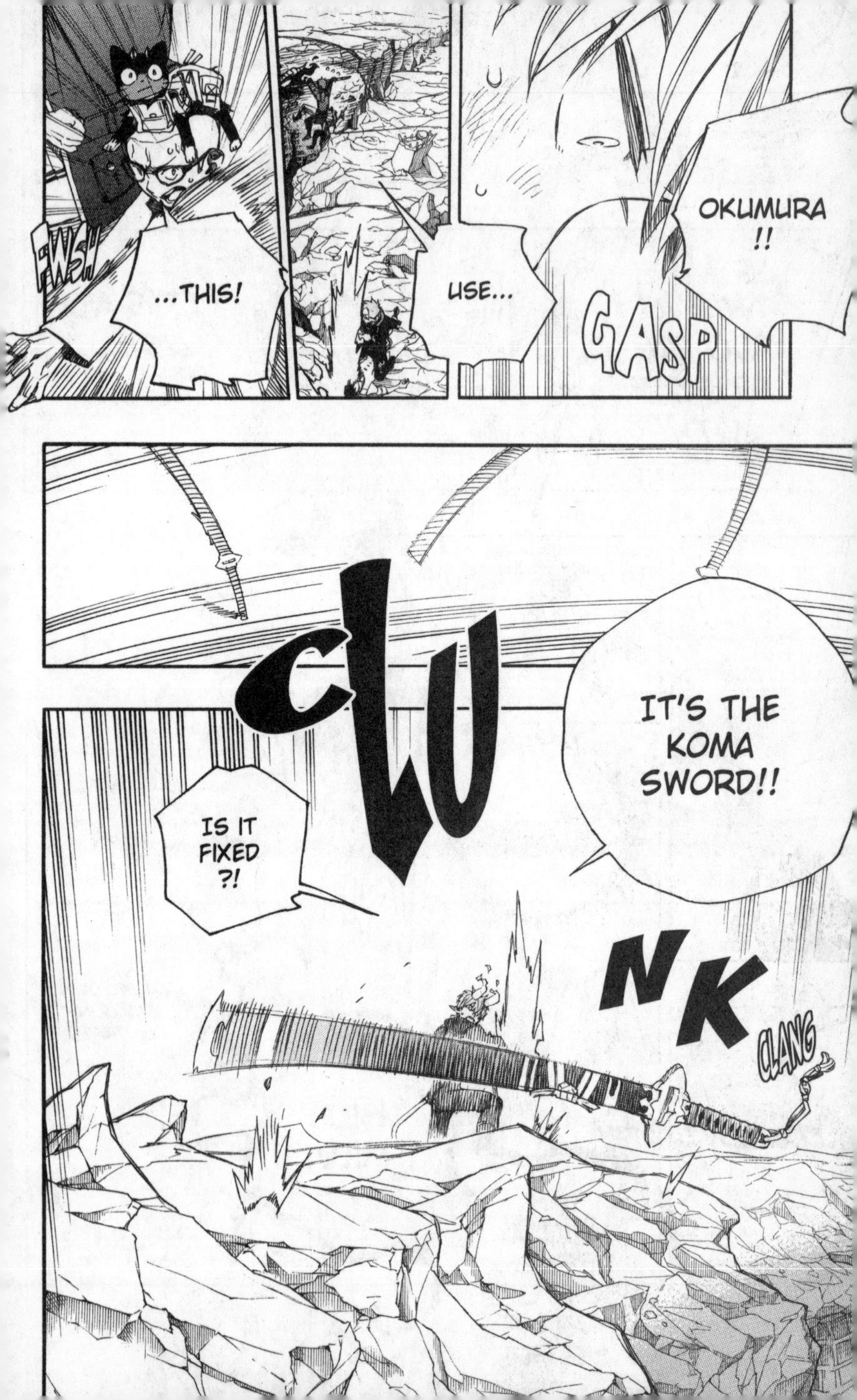
OKUMURA !!
GASP
USE...
...THIS!
FWSH
CLUNK
IT'S THE KOMA SWORD!!
IS IT FIXED ?!
CLANG

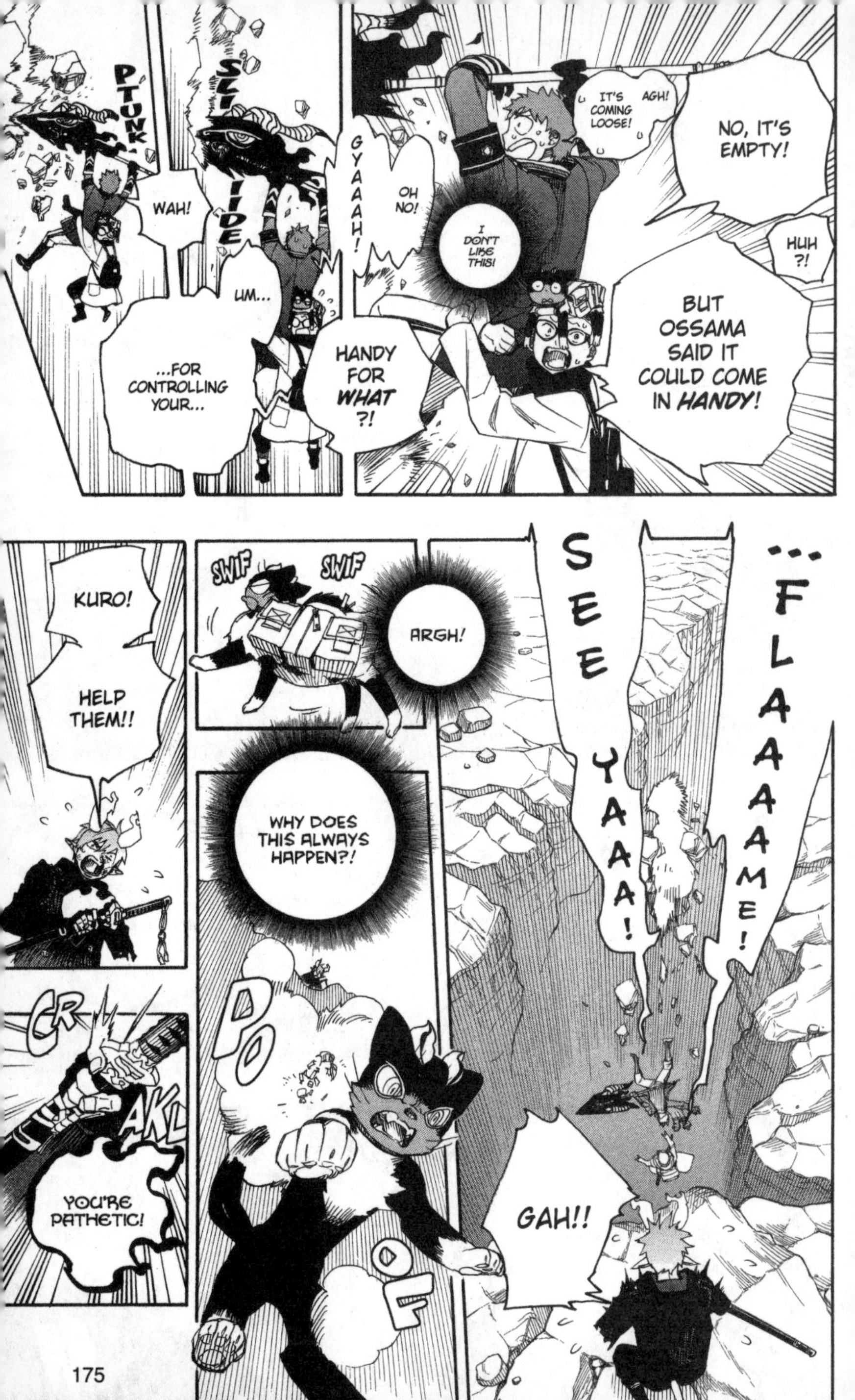
AGH!
IT'S COMING LOOSE!
NO, IT'S EMPTY!
HUH ?!
BUT OSSAMA SAID IT COULD COME IN *HANDY*!
I DON'T LIKE THIS!
HANDY FOR *WHAT* ?!
OH NO!
GYAAAAH!
SLI IIDE
UM...
...FOR CONTROLLING YOUR...
PTUNK
WAH!
...FLAAAAAME!
SEE YAAA!
GAH!!
SWIF
SWIF
ARGH!
WHY DOES THIS ALWAYS HAPPEN?!
DO
OF
KURO!
HELP THEM!!
CR
AKL
YOU'RE PATHETIC!

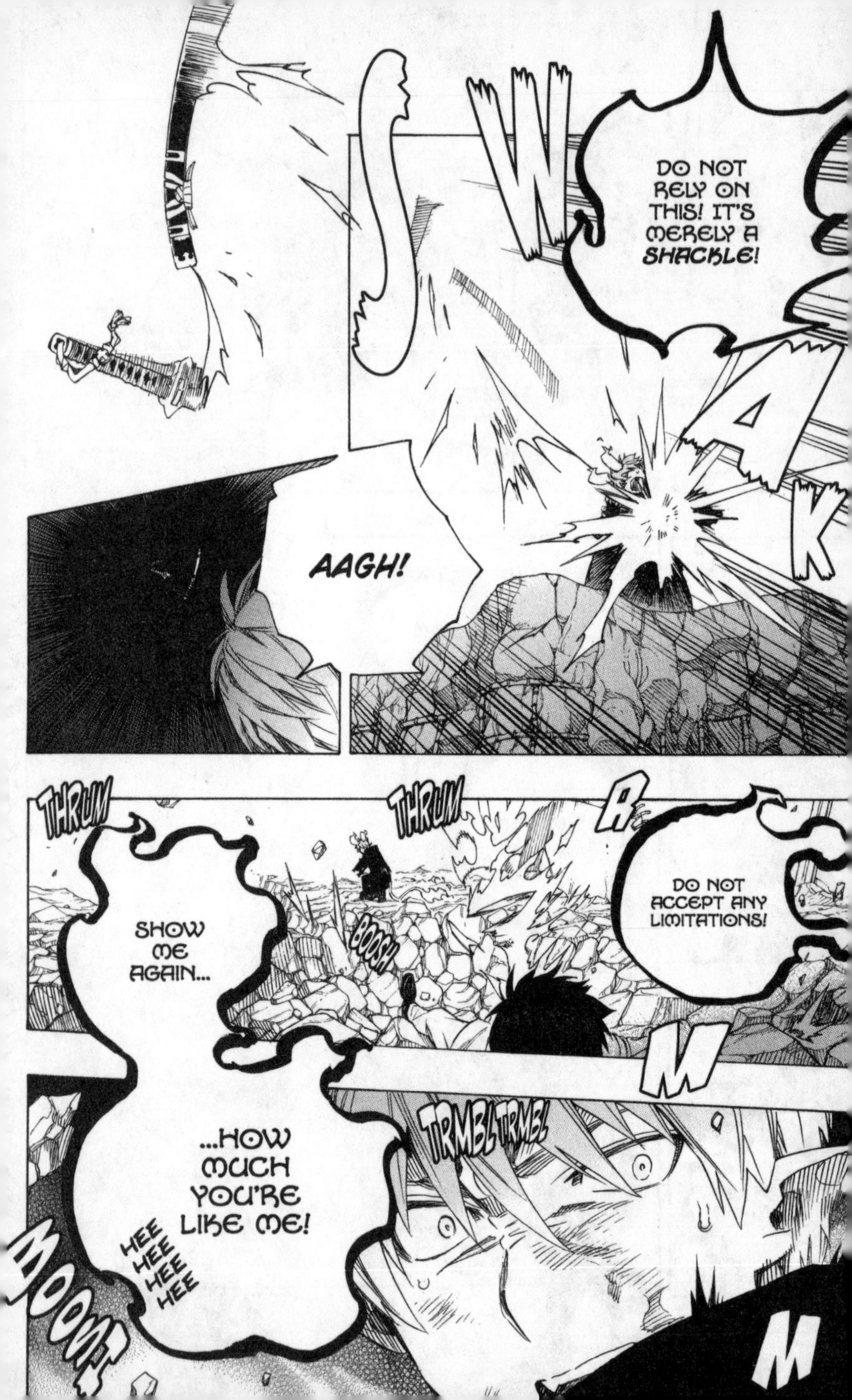
SWAK
DO NOT RELY ON THIS! IT'S MERELY A *SHACKLE!*
AAGH!
DO NOT ACCEPT ANY LIMITATIONS!
THRUM
THRUM
BOOSH
SHOW ME AGAIN...
TRMBL TRMBL
...HOW MUCH YOU'RE LIKE ME!
HEE HEE HEE HEE

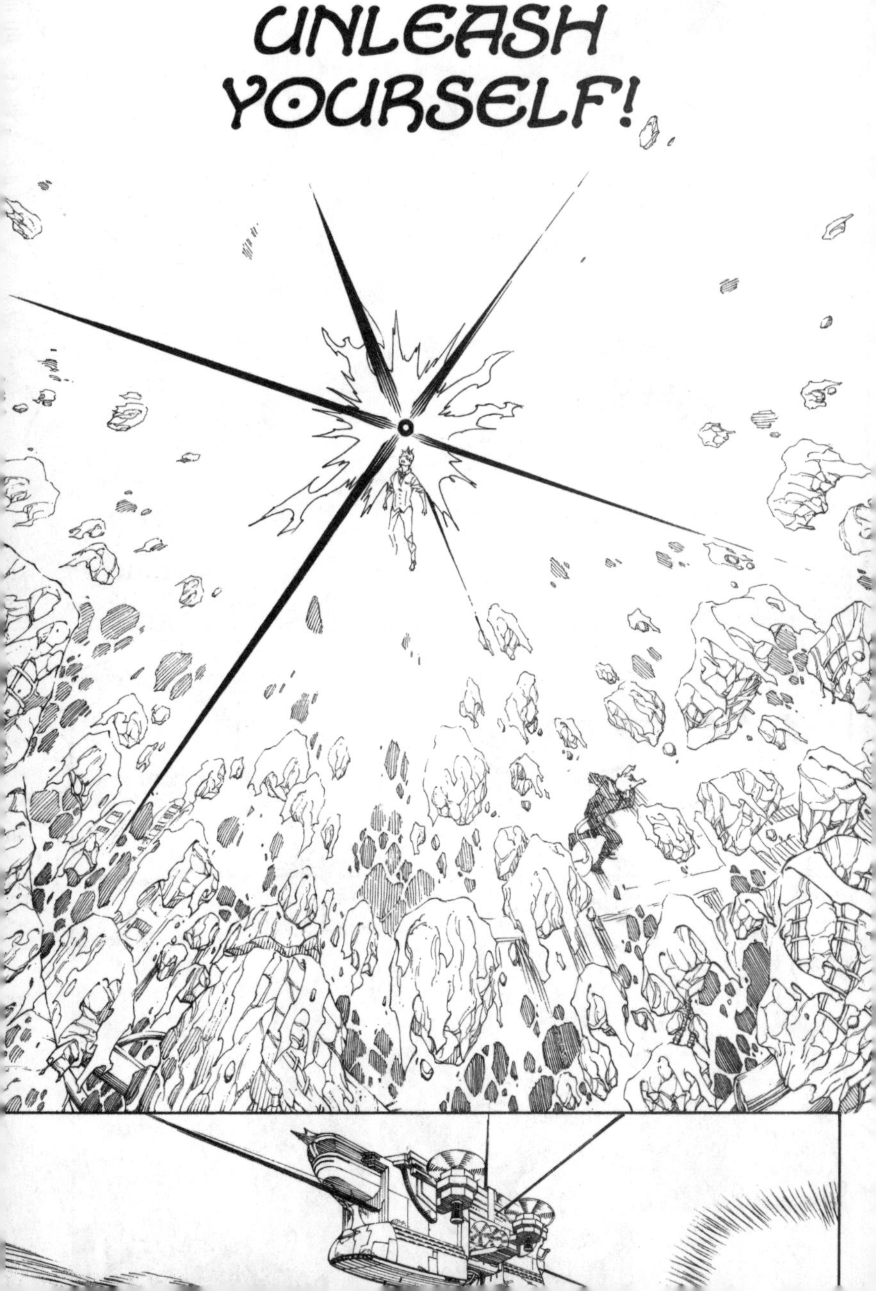
UNLEASH YOURSELF!

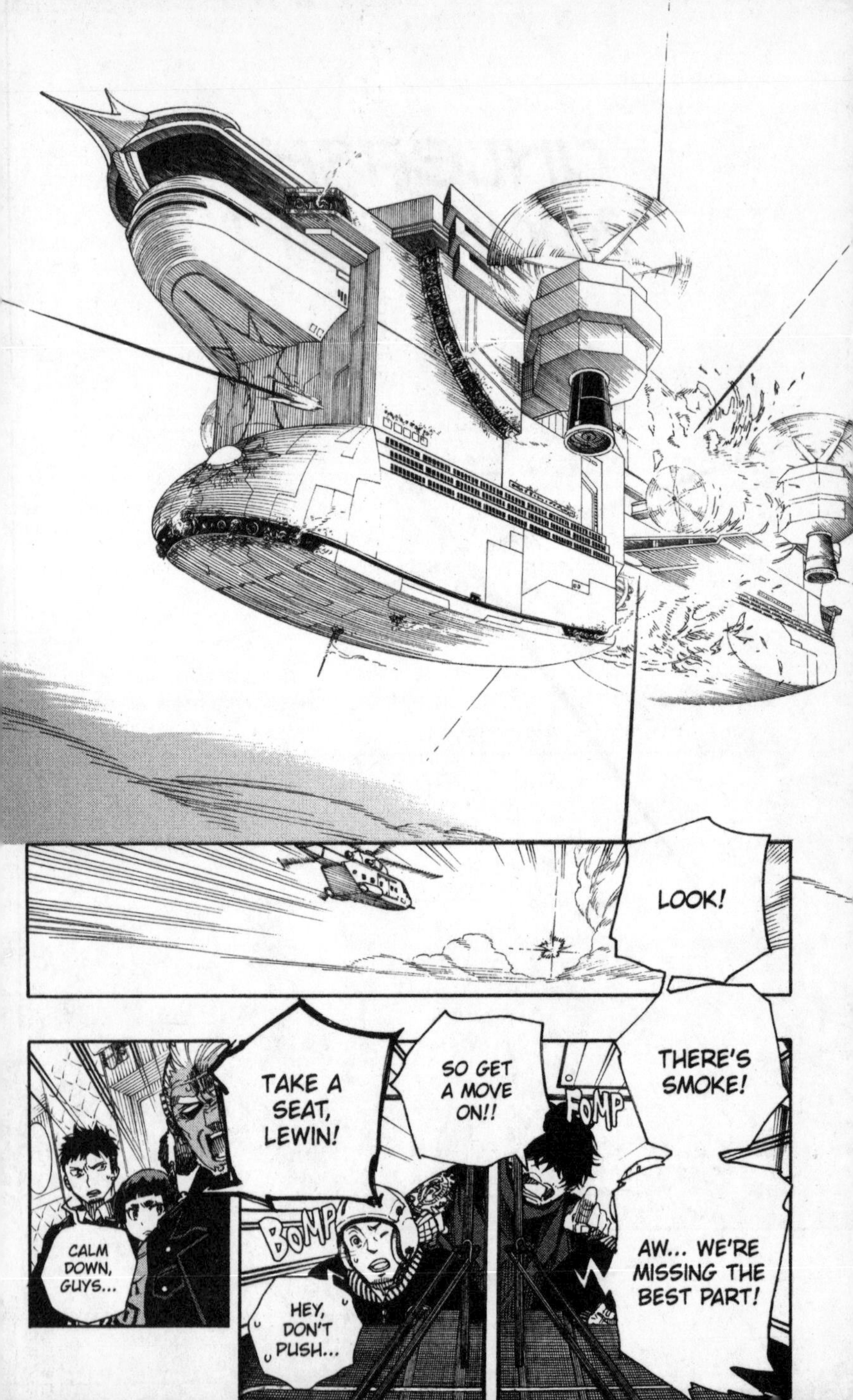

LOOK!
THERE'S SMOKE!
FOMP
AW... WE'RE MISSING THE BEST PART!
SO GET A MOVE ON!!
BOMP
HEY, DON'T PUSH...
TAKE A SEAT, LEWIN!
CALM DOWN, GUYS...

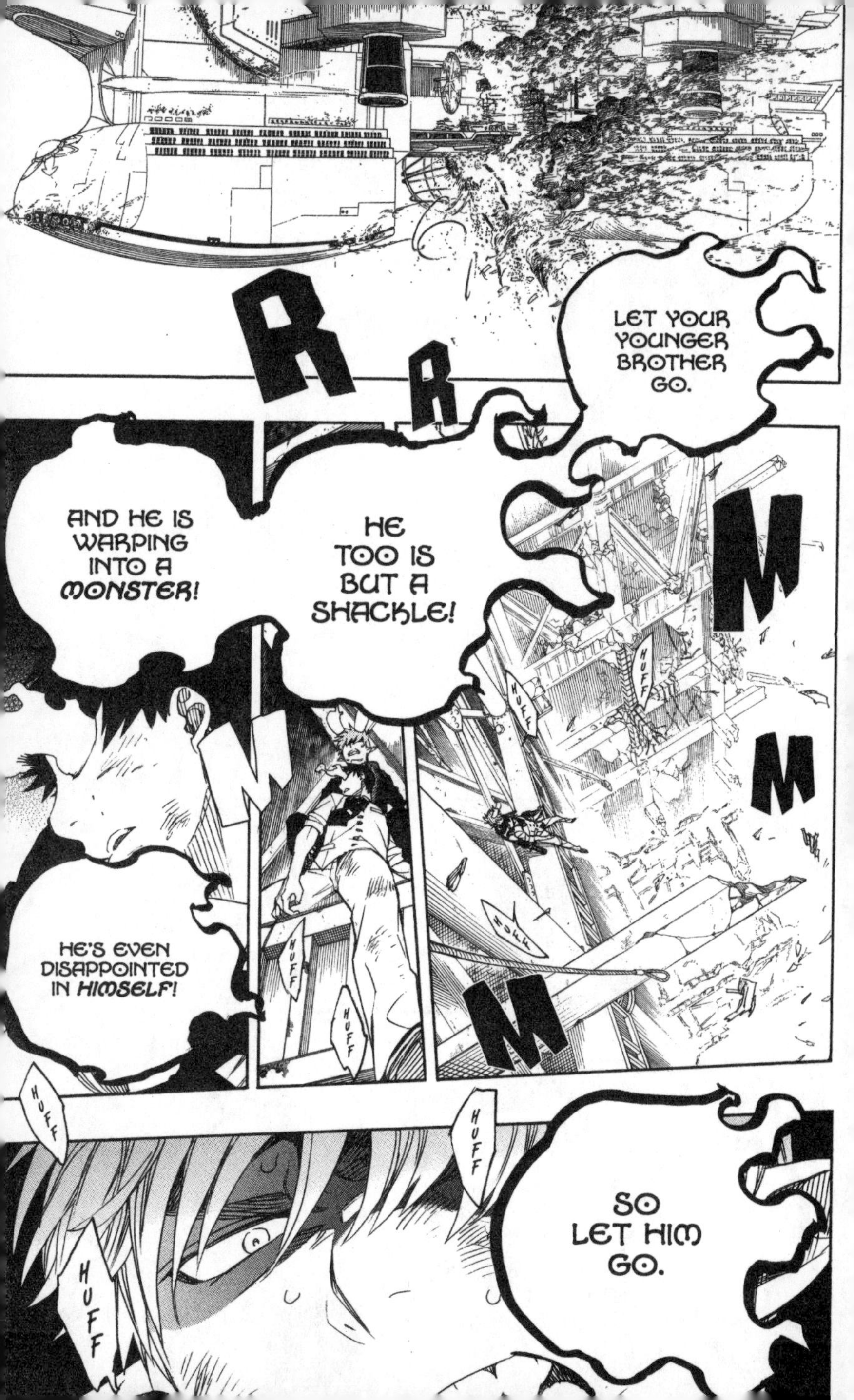
LET YOUR YOUNGER BROTHER GO.
R R
HE TOO IS BUT A SHACKLE!
AND HE IS WARPING INTO A *MONSTER!*
M M M M
HUFF
HUFF
HUFF
HE'S EVEN DISAPPOINTED IN *HIMSELF!*
HUFF
HUFF
SO LET HIM GO.
HUFF
HUFF
HUFF

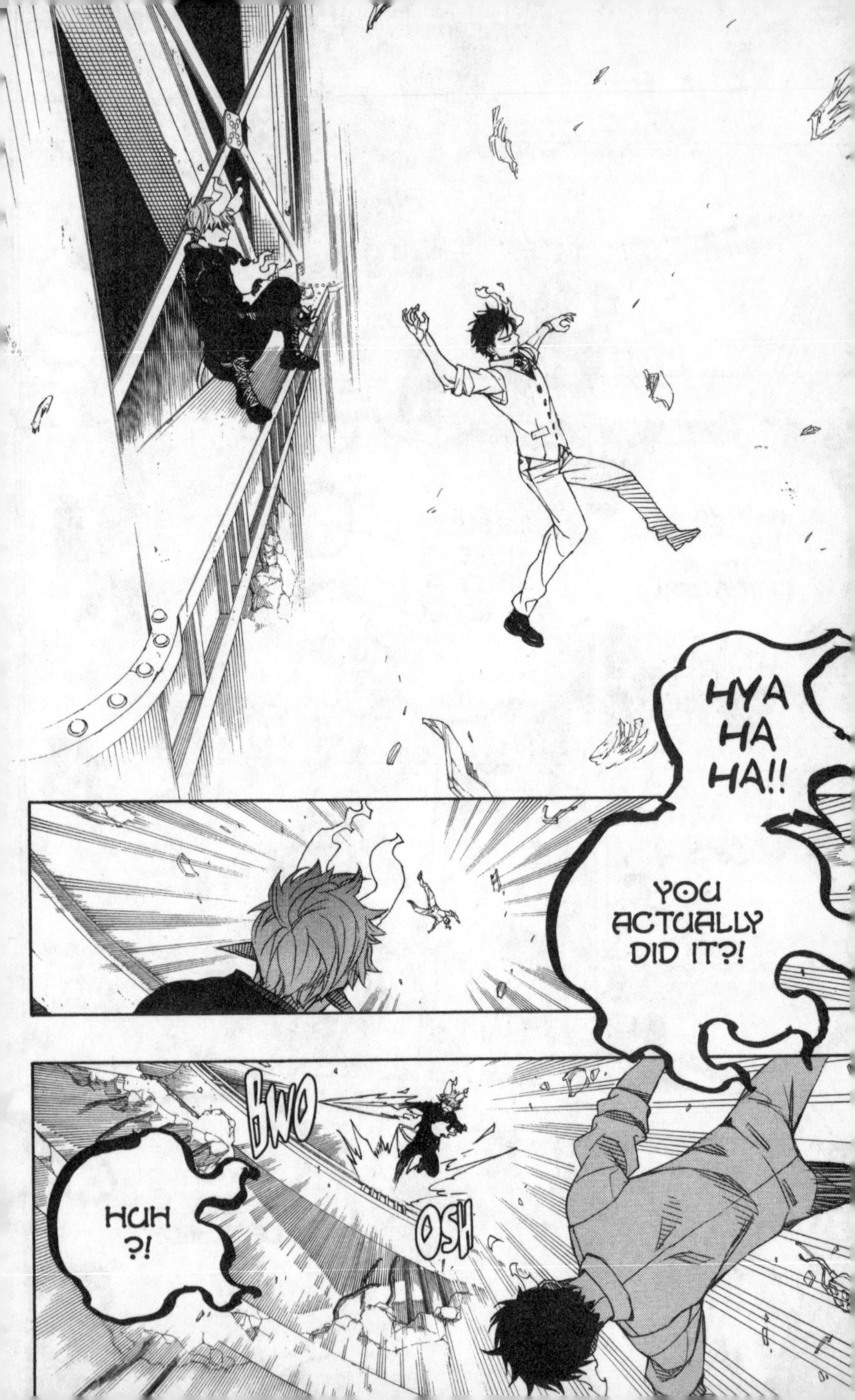
HYA HA HA!!
YOU ACTUALLY DID IT?!
BWO
OSH
HUH ?!

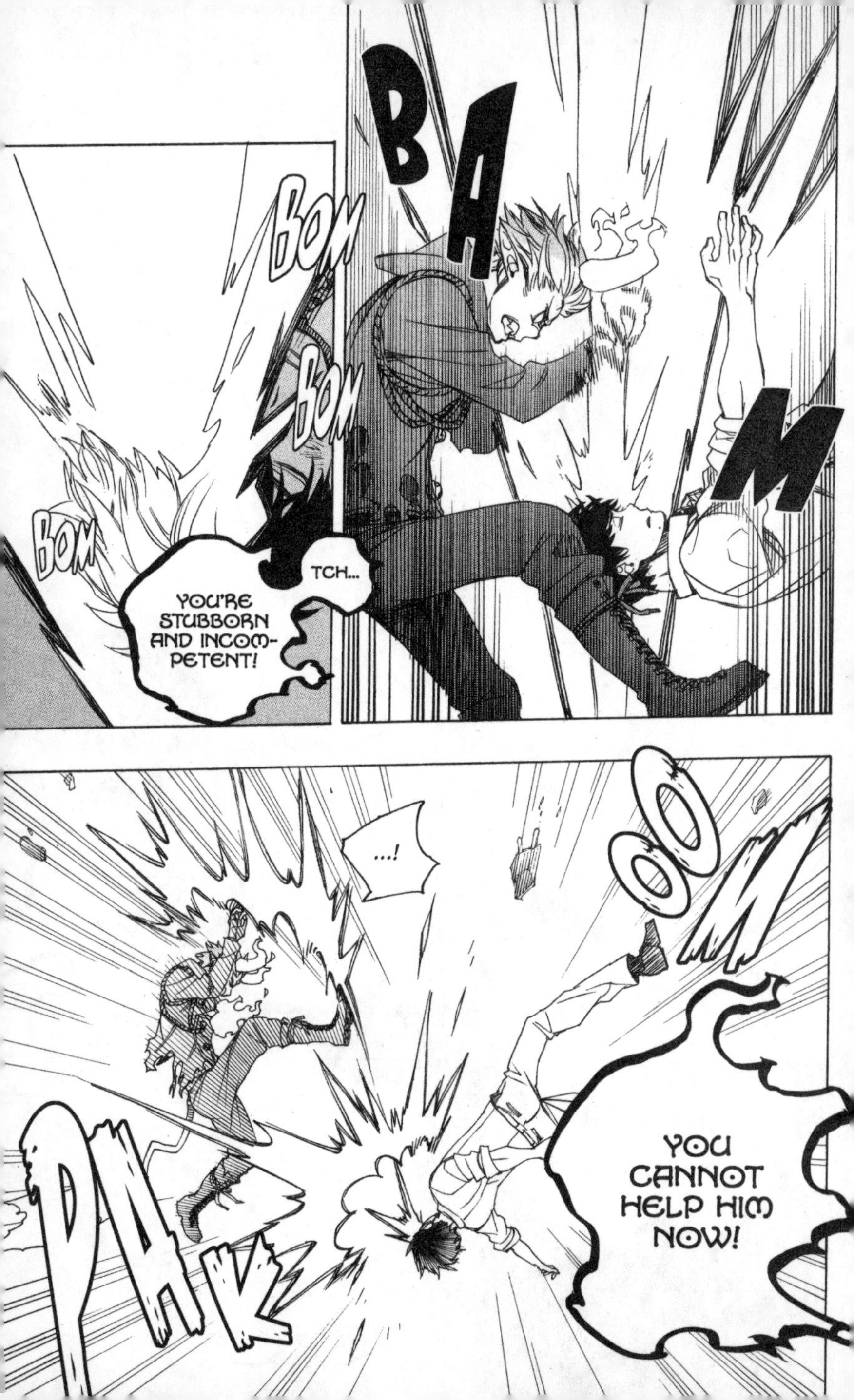
BAM
BOM
BOM
BOM
TCH... YOU'RE STUBBORN AND INCOMPETENT!
BOOM
...!
YOU CANNOT HELP HIM NOW!
PAK

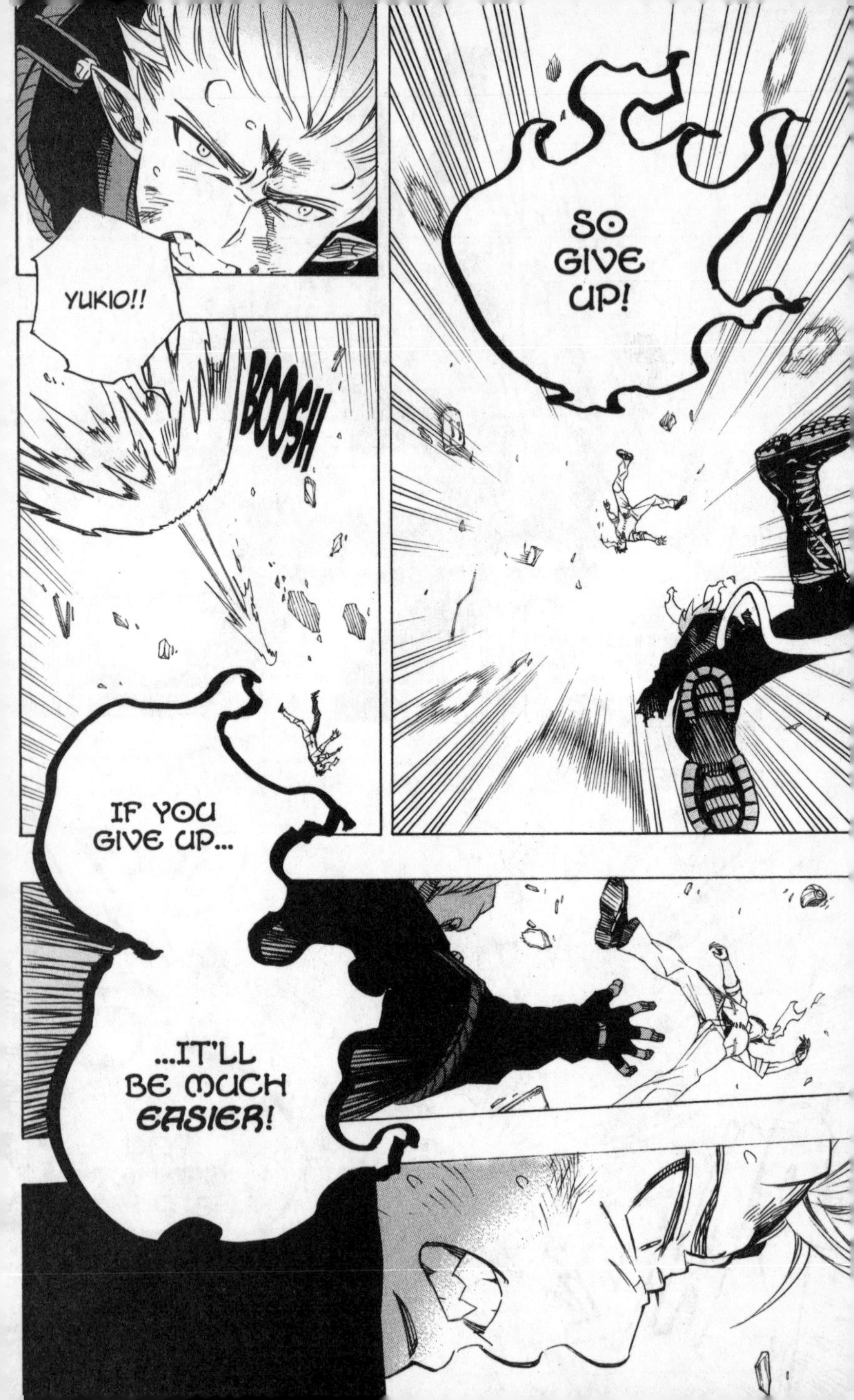
SO GIVE UP!
YUKIO!!
BOOSH
IF YOU GIVE UP...
...IT'LL BE MUCH EASIER!

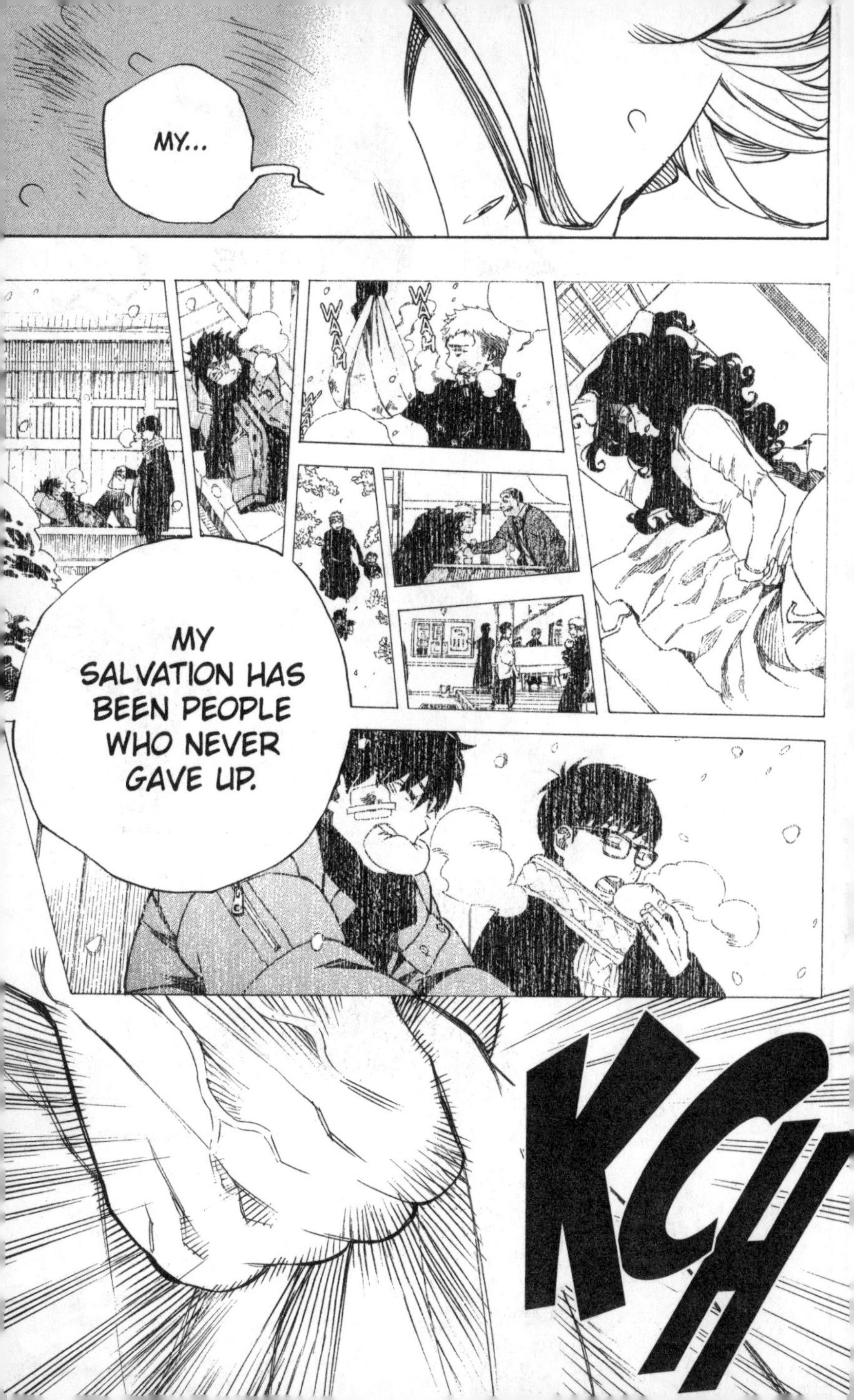
MY...
WAAH
WAAH
MY SALVATION HAS BEEN PEOPLE WHO NEVER GAVE UP.
KCH

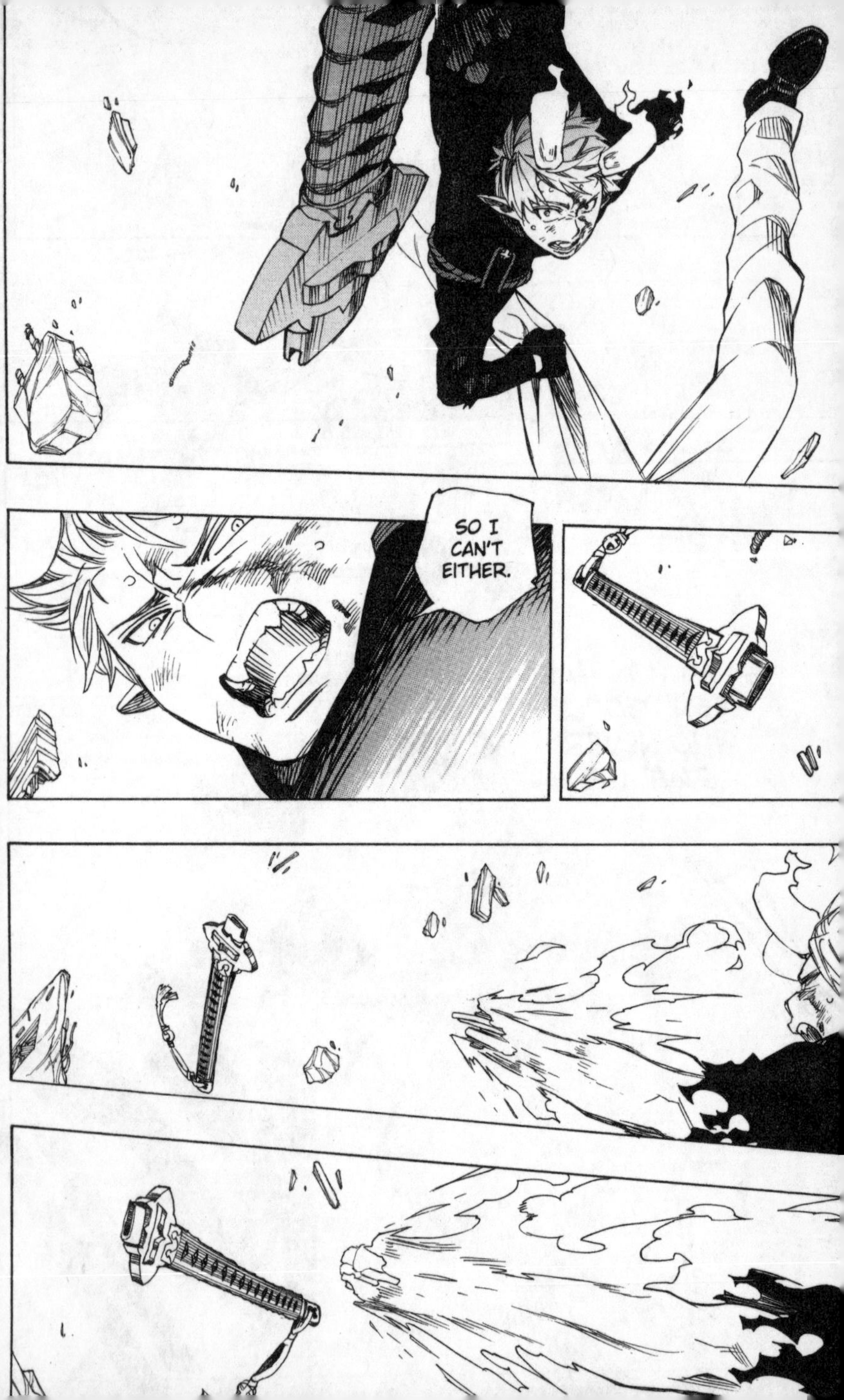
SO I CAN'T EITHER.

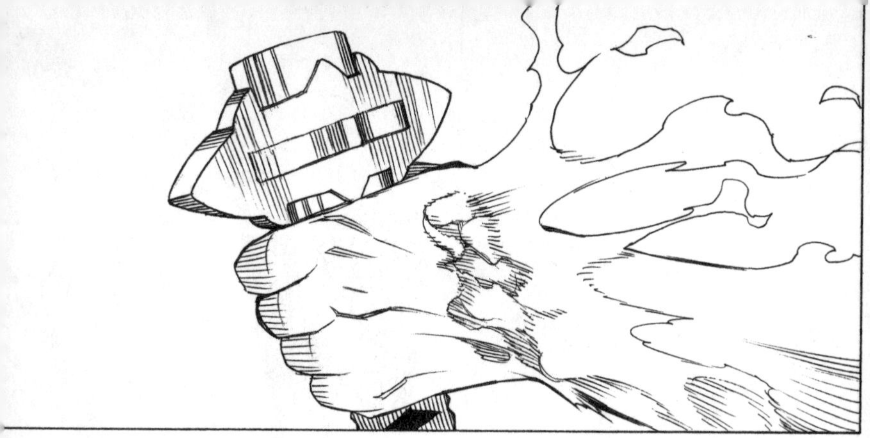

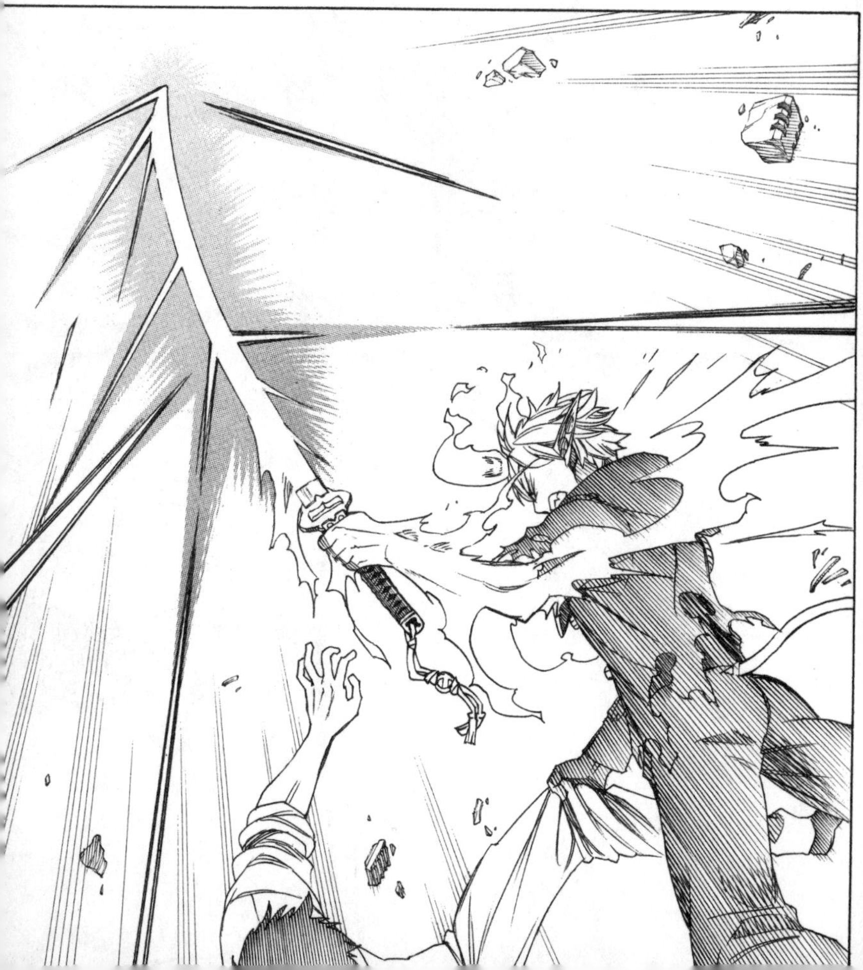

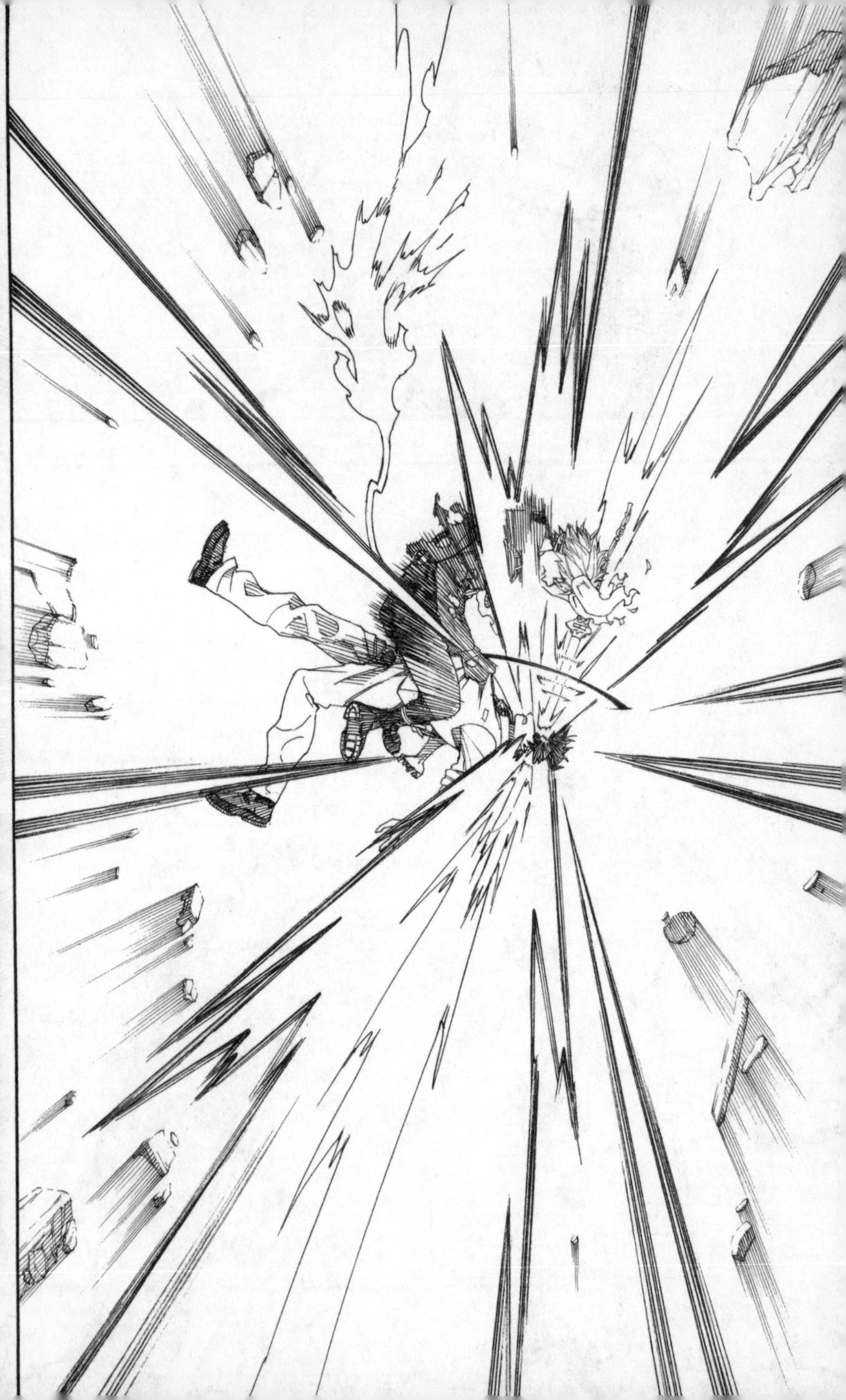

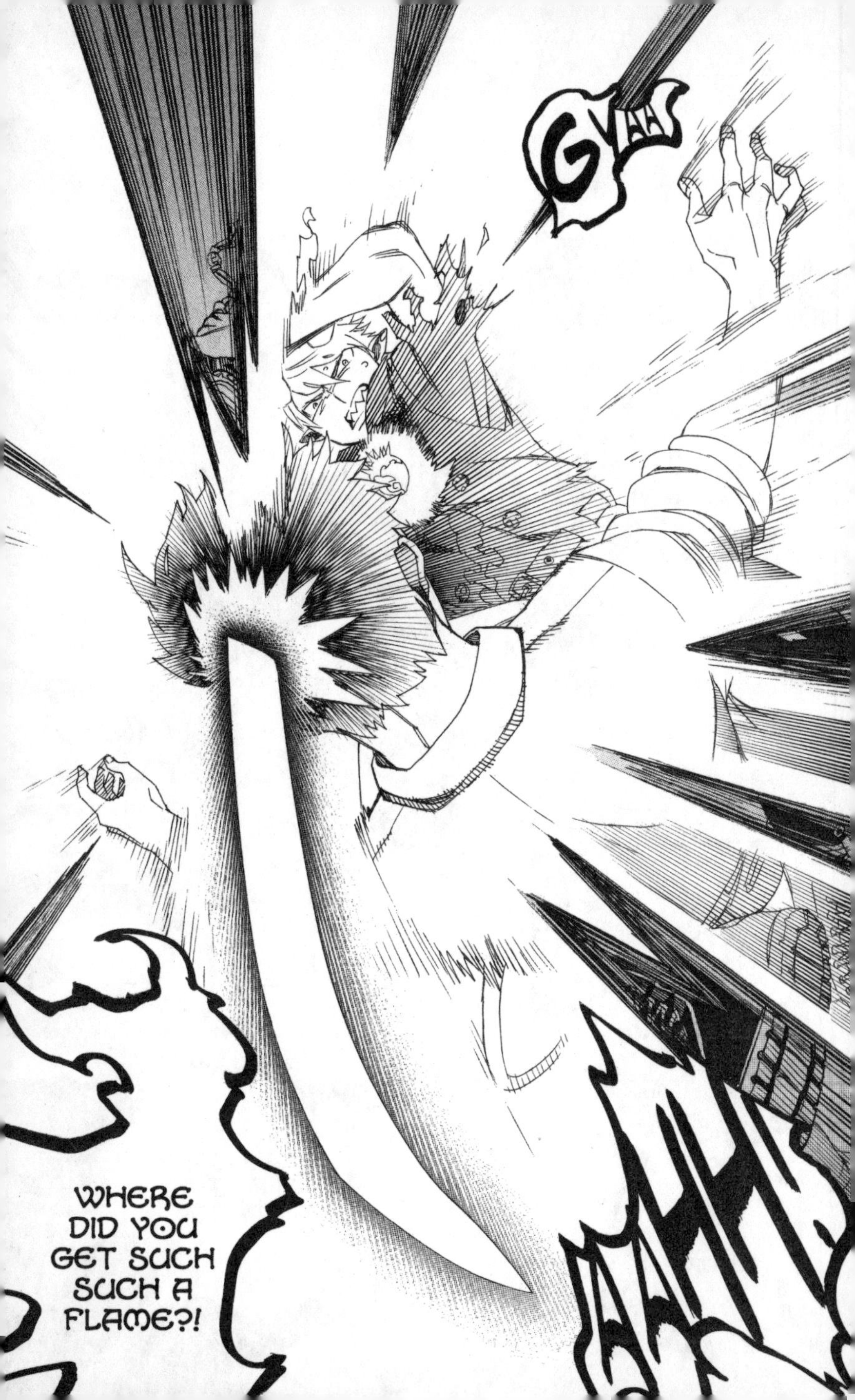
GYAAH
WHERE DID YOU GET SUCH SUCH A FLAME?!

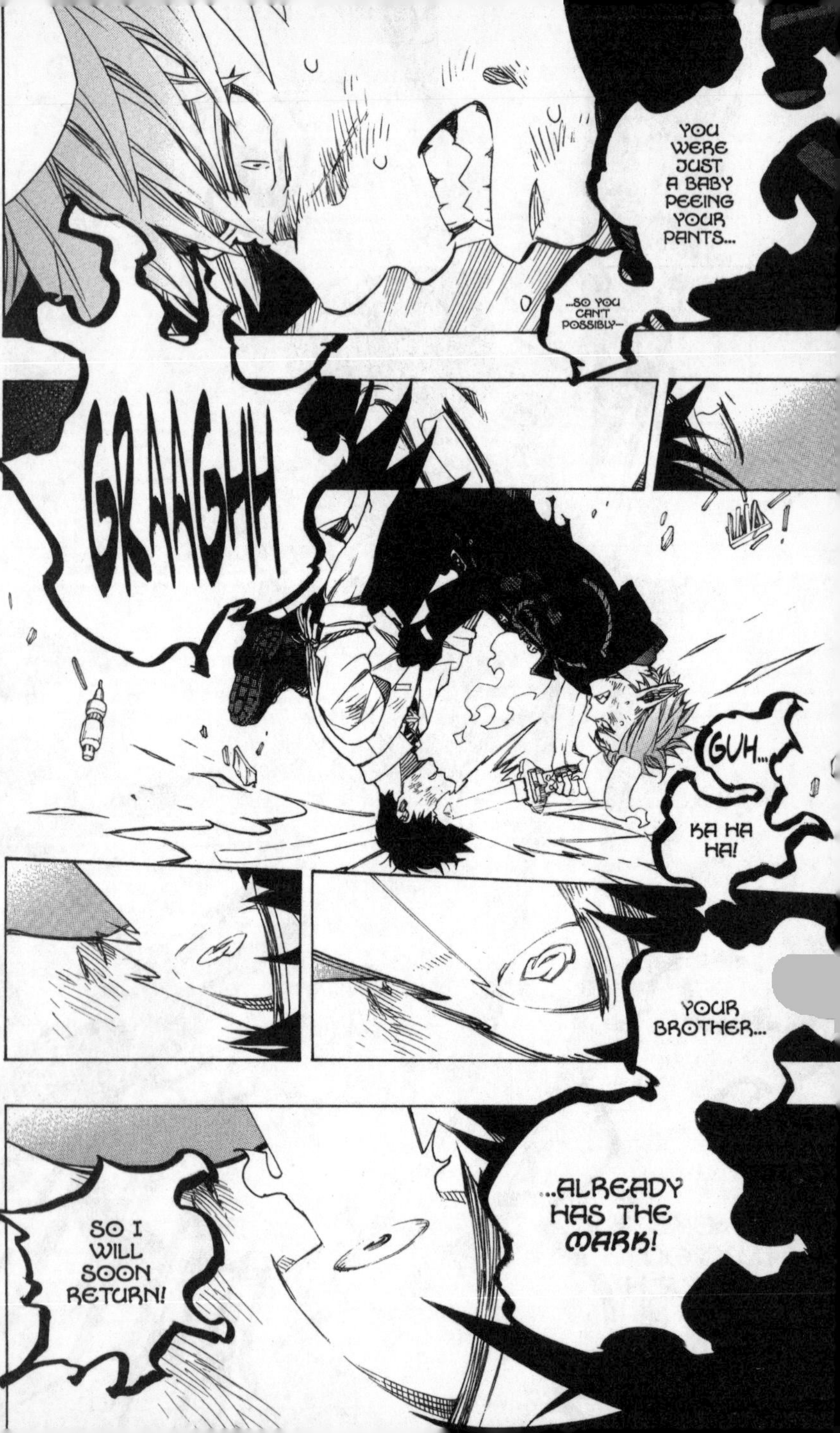
YOU WERE JUST A BABY PEEING YOUR PANTS...
...SO YOU CAN'T POSSIBLY—
GRAAGHH
GUH...
KA HA HA!
YOUR BROTHER...
...ALREADY HAS THE MARK!
SO I WILL SOON RETURN!

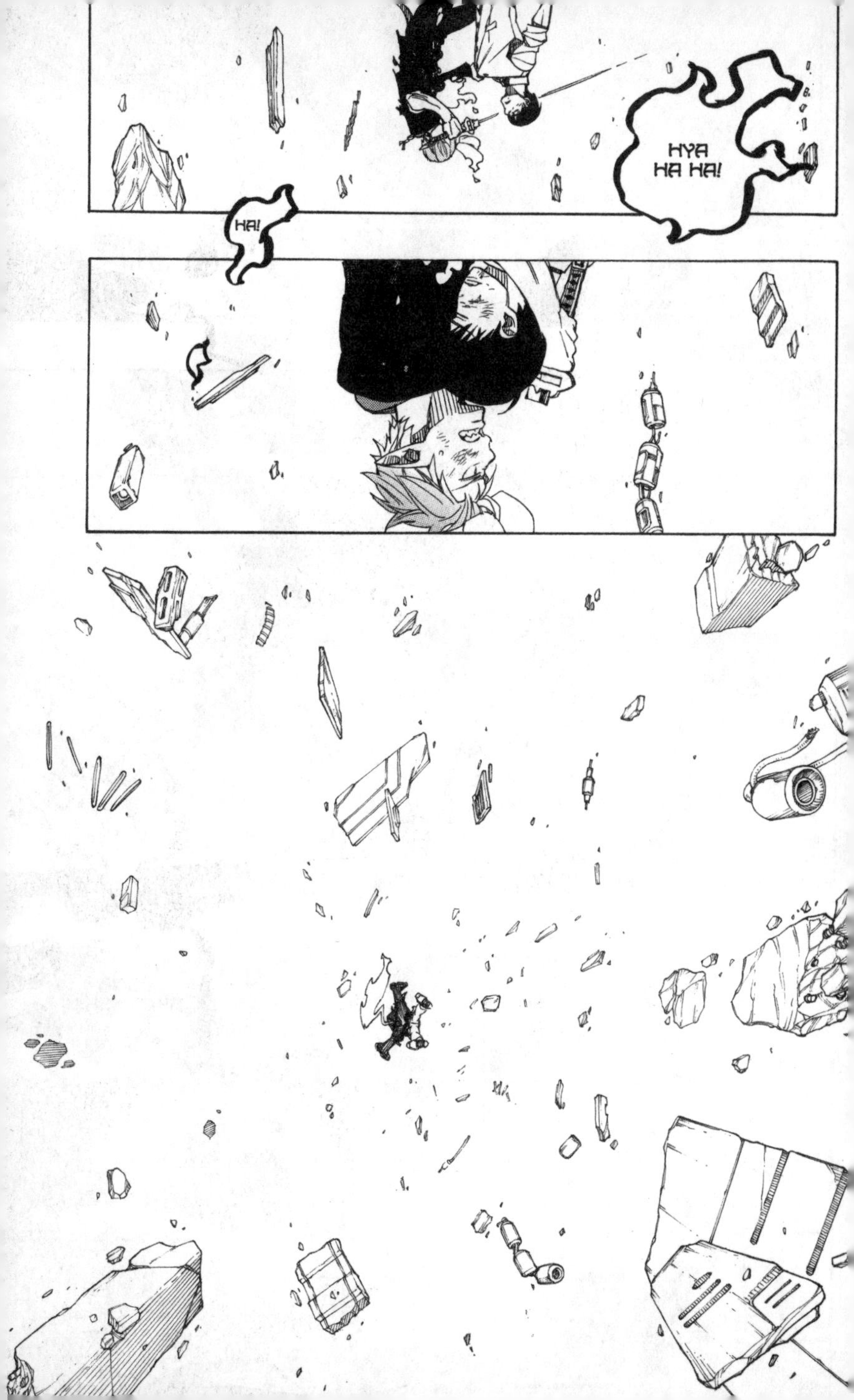
HYA HA HA!
HA!

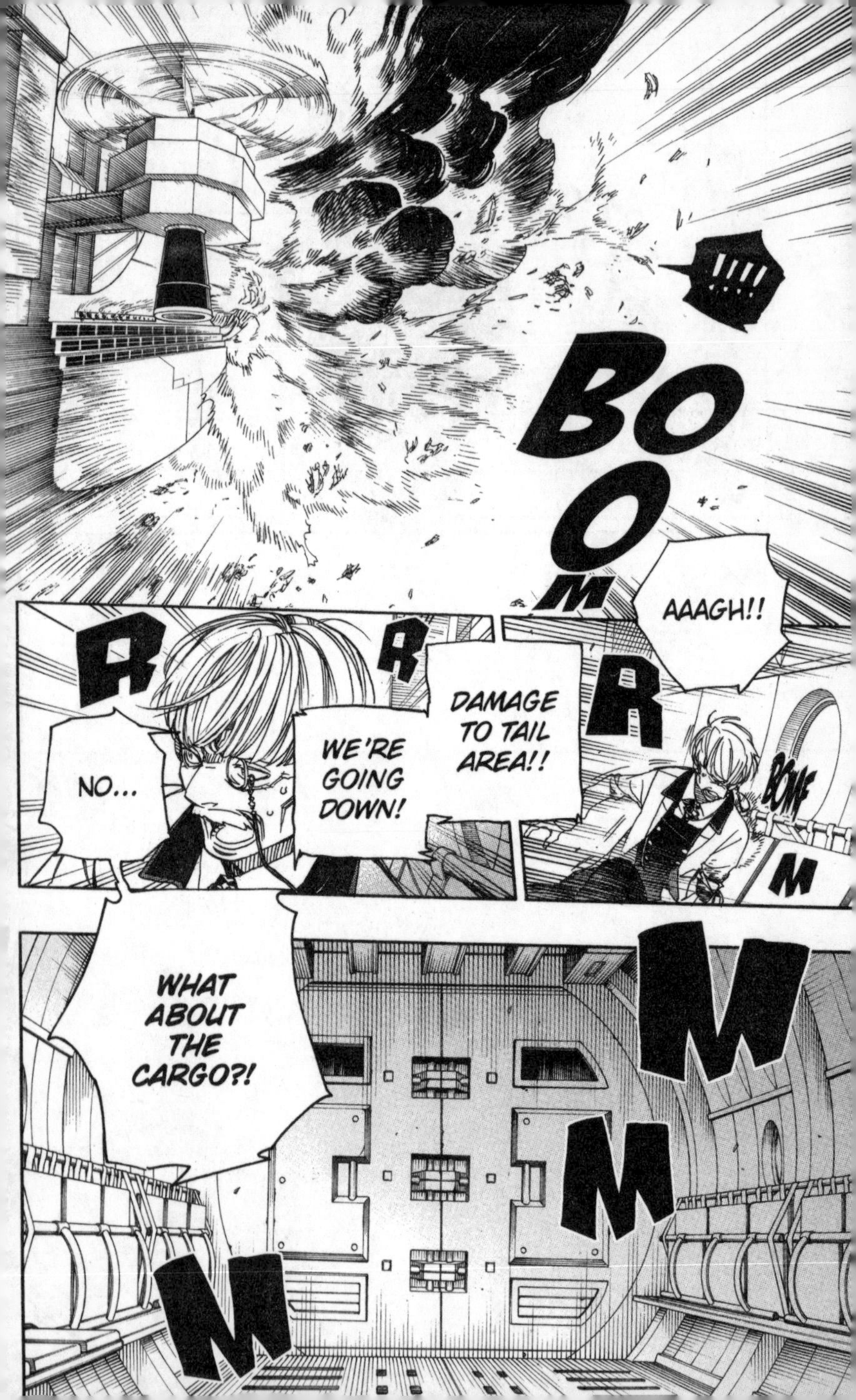
!!!!
BOOM
AAAGH!!
RRR
BOMF
DAMAGE TO TAIL AREA!!
WE'RE GOING DOWN!
NO...
MMMM
WHAT ABOUT THE CARGO?!

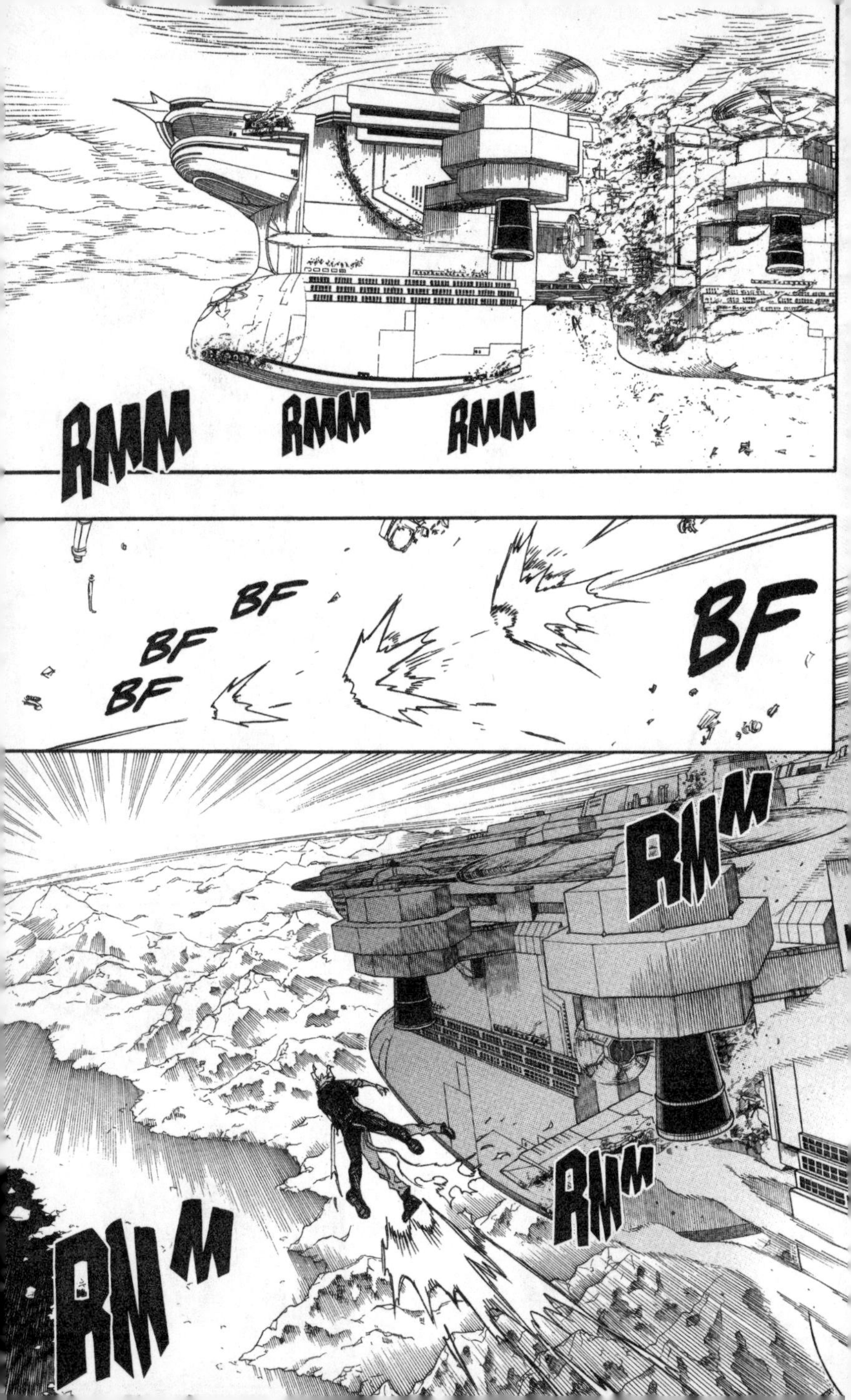
RMM
RMM
RMM
BF
BF
BF
BF
RMM
RMM
RMM

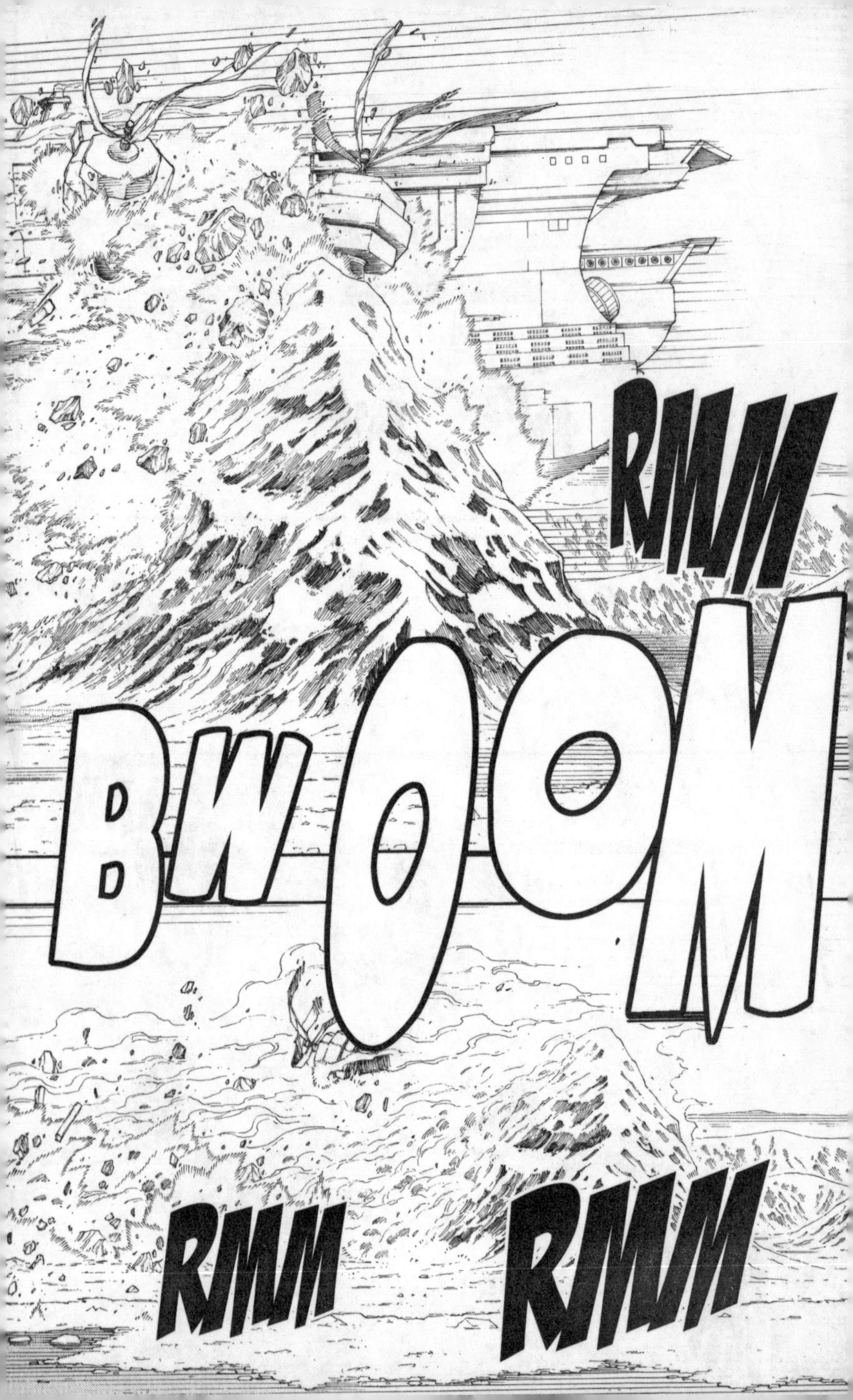
RMM
BWOOM
RMM
RMM

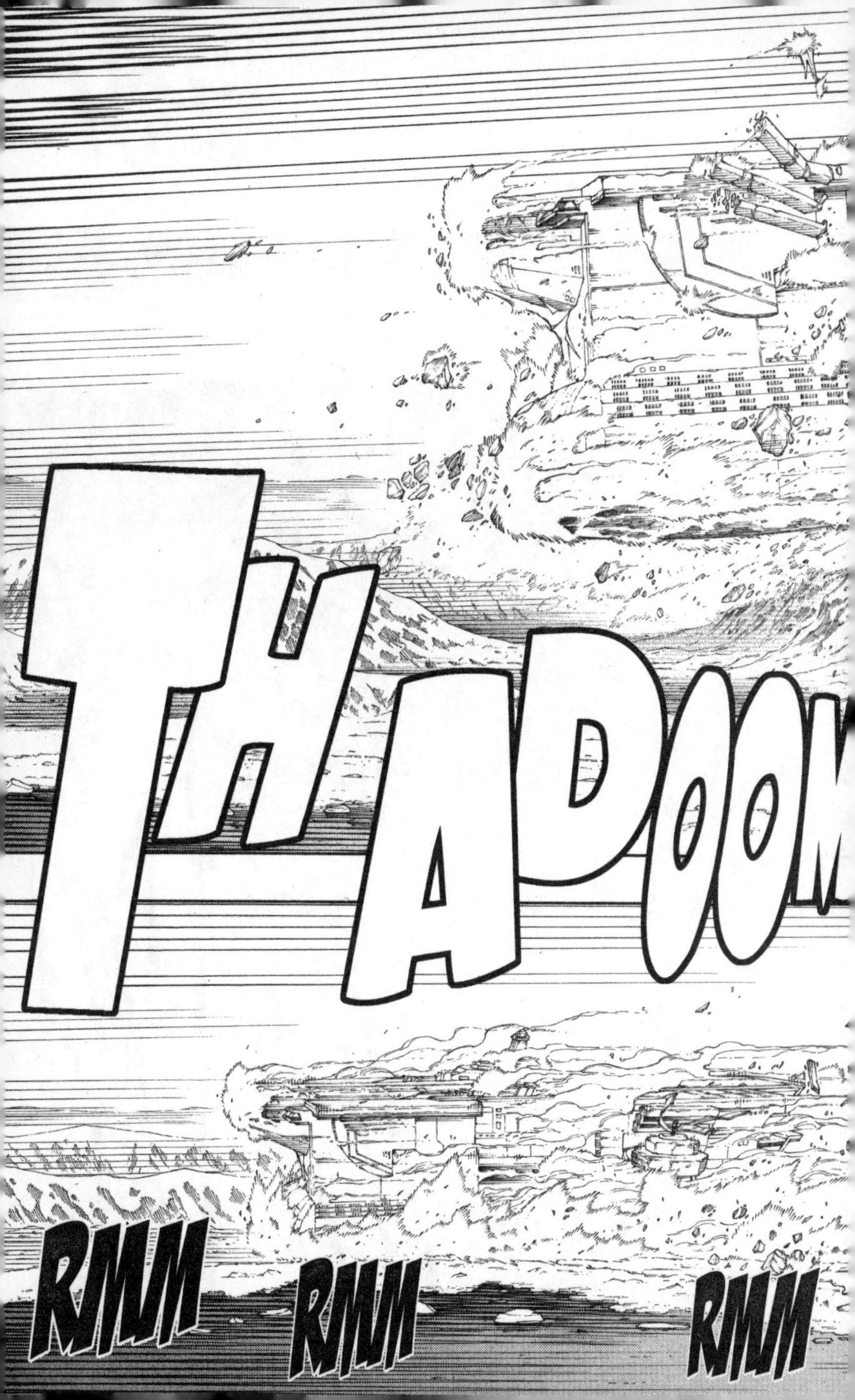
THADOOM
RMM
RMM
RMM

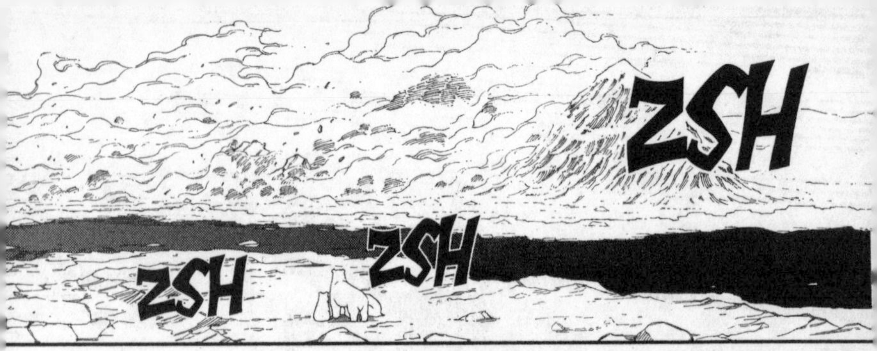
ZSH
ZSH
ZSH
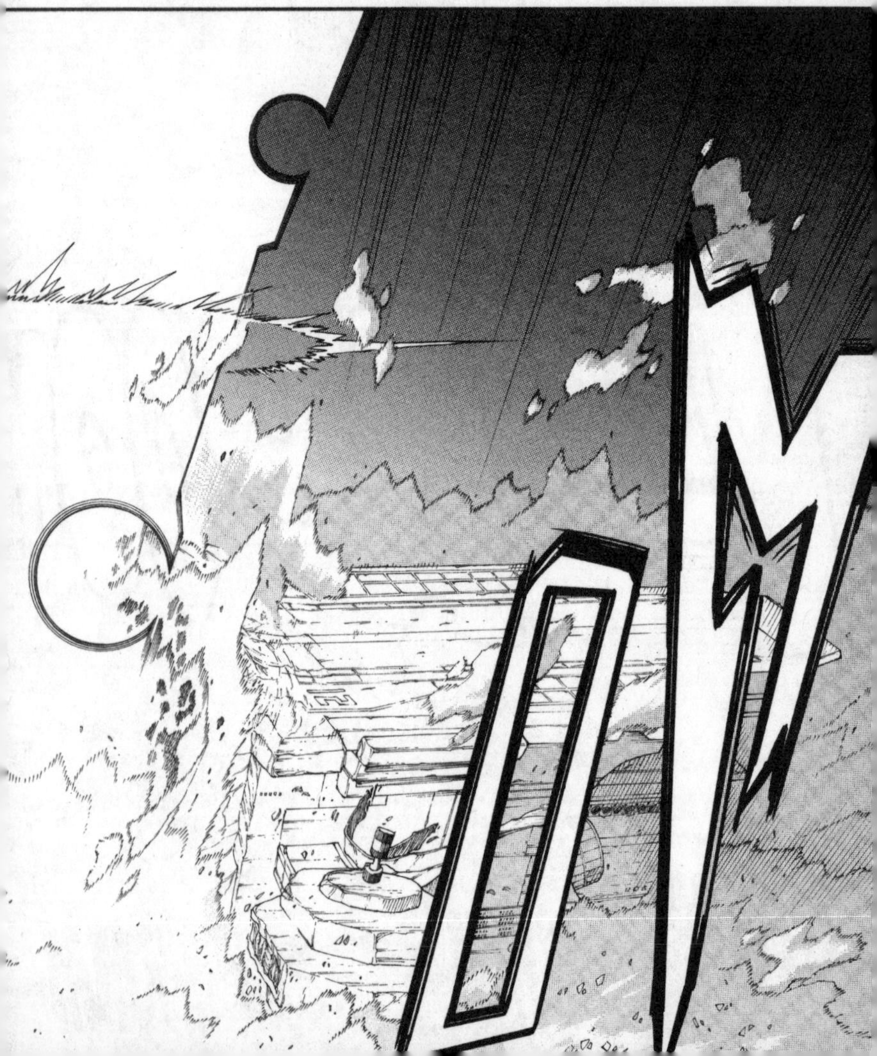

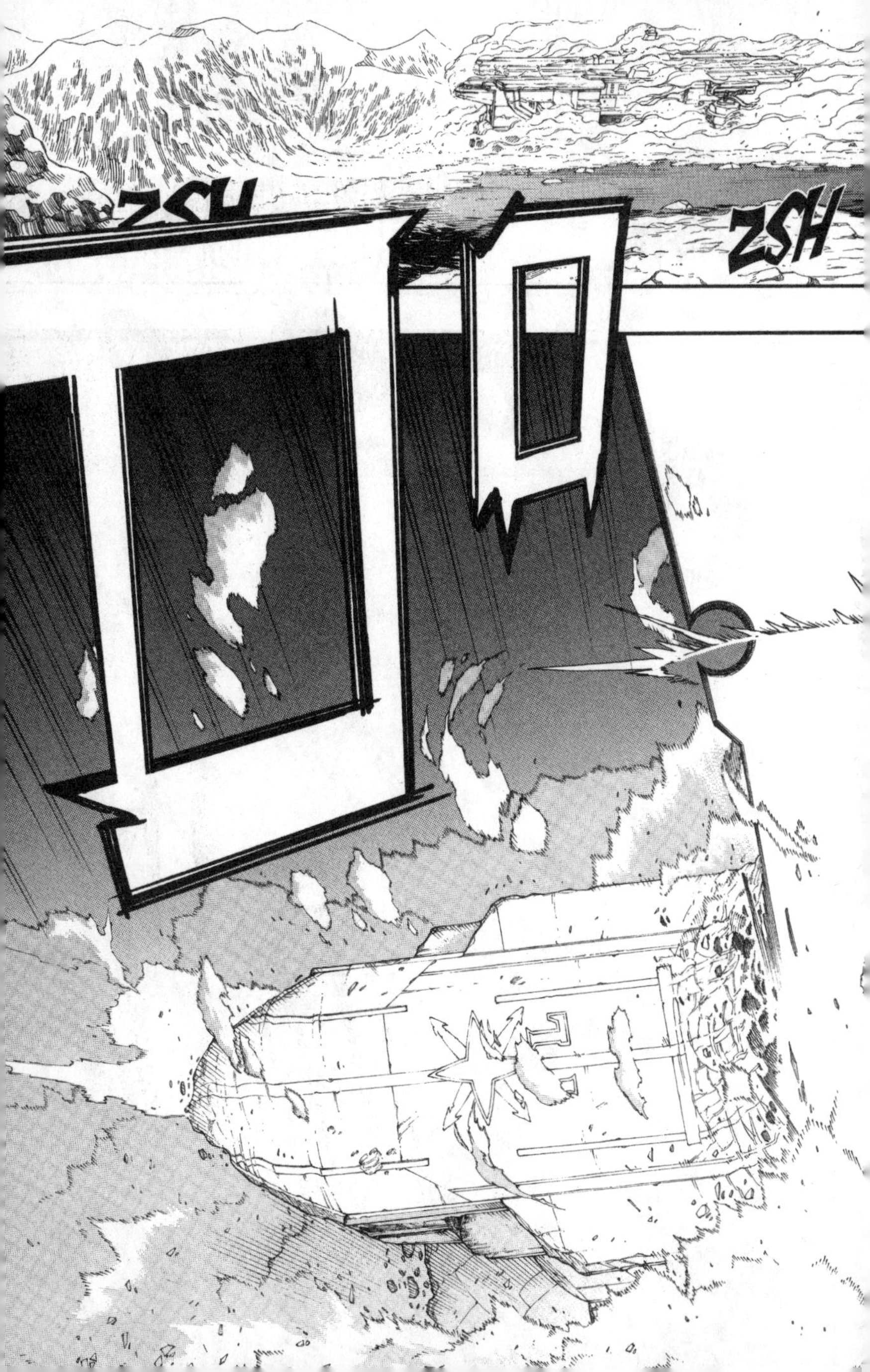
ZSH

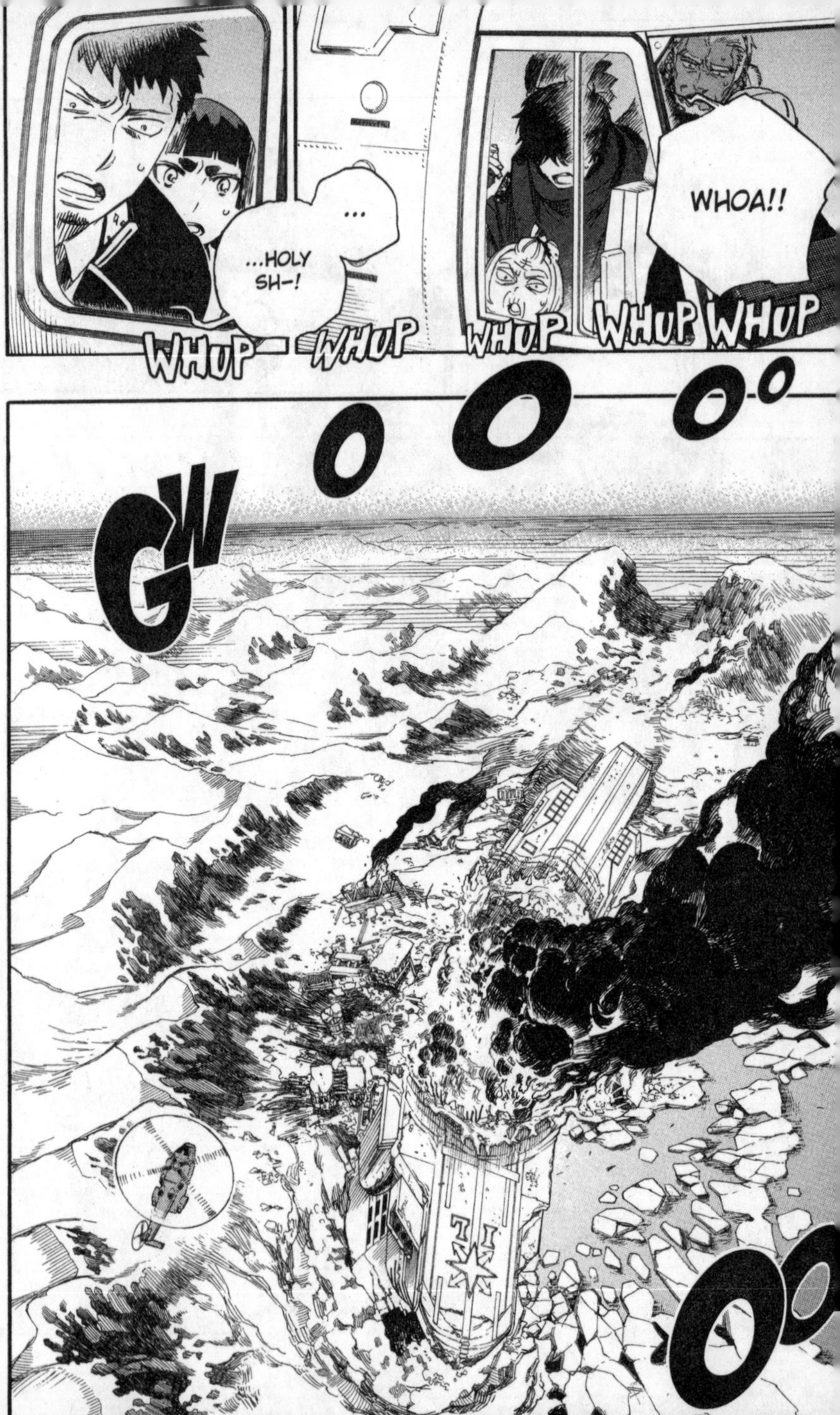
WHOA!!
...
...HOLY SH-!
WHUP WHUP WHUP WHUP WHUP
GWOOOOOO

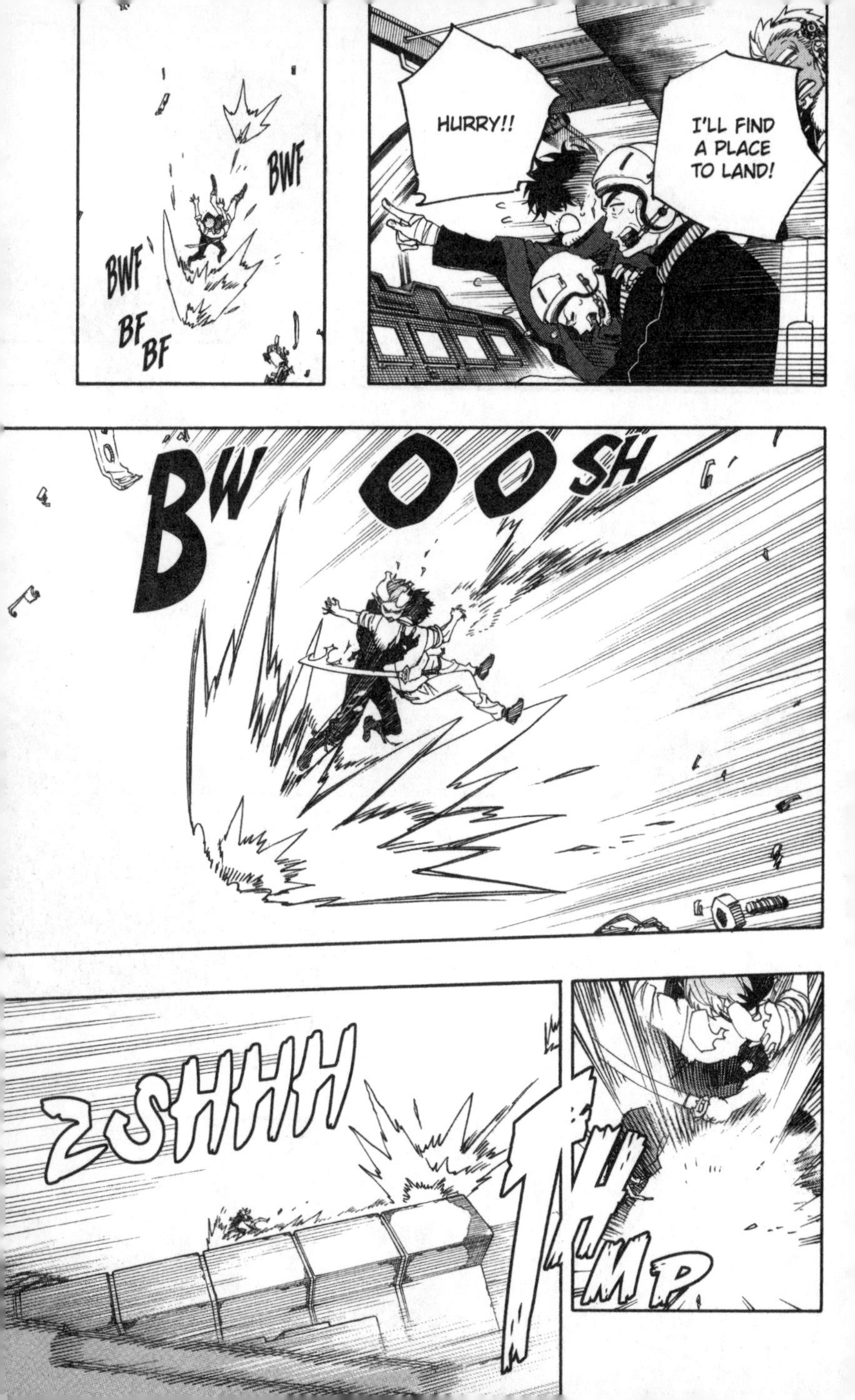
I'LL FIND A PLACE TO LAND!
HURRY!!
BWF
BWF
BF BF
BWOOSH
THUMP
ZSHHH

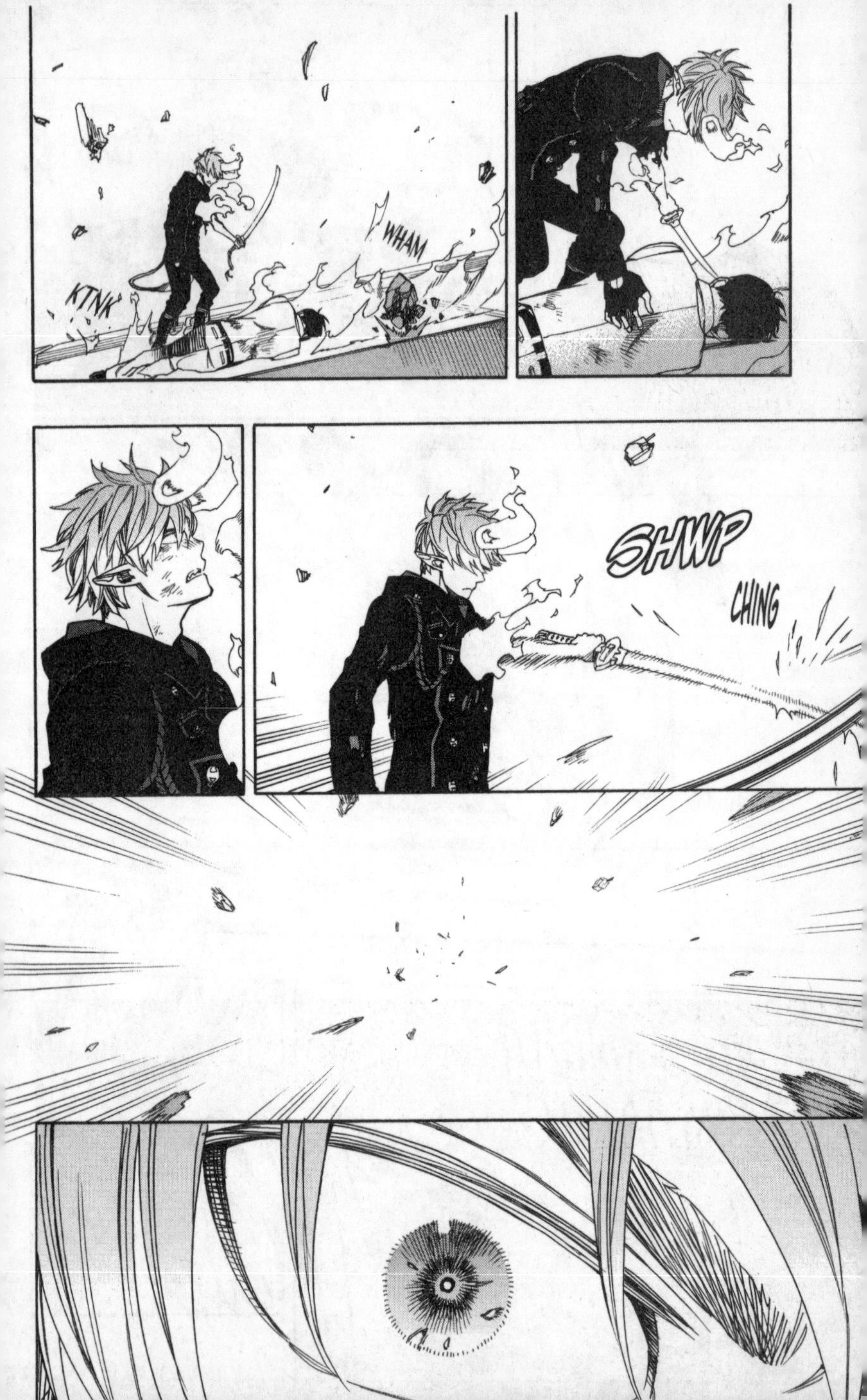
WHAM
KTNK
SHWP
CHING

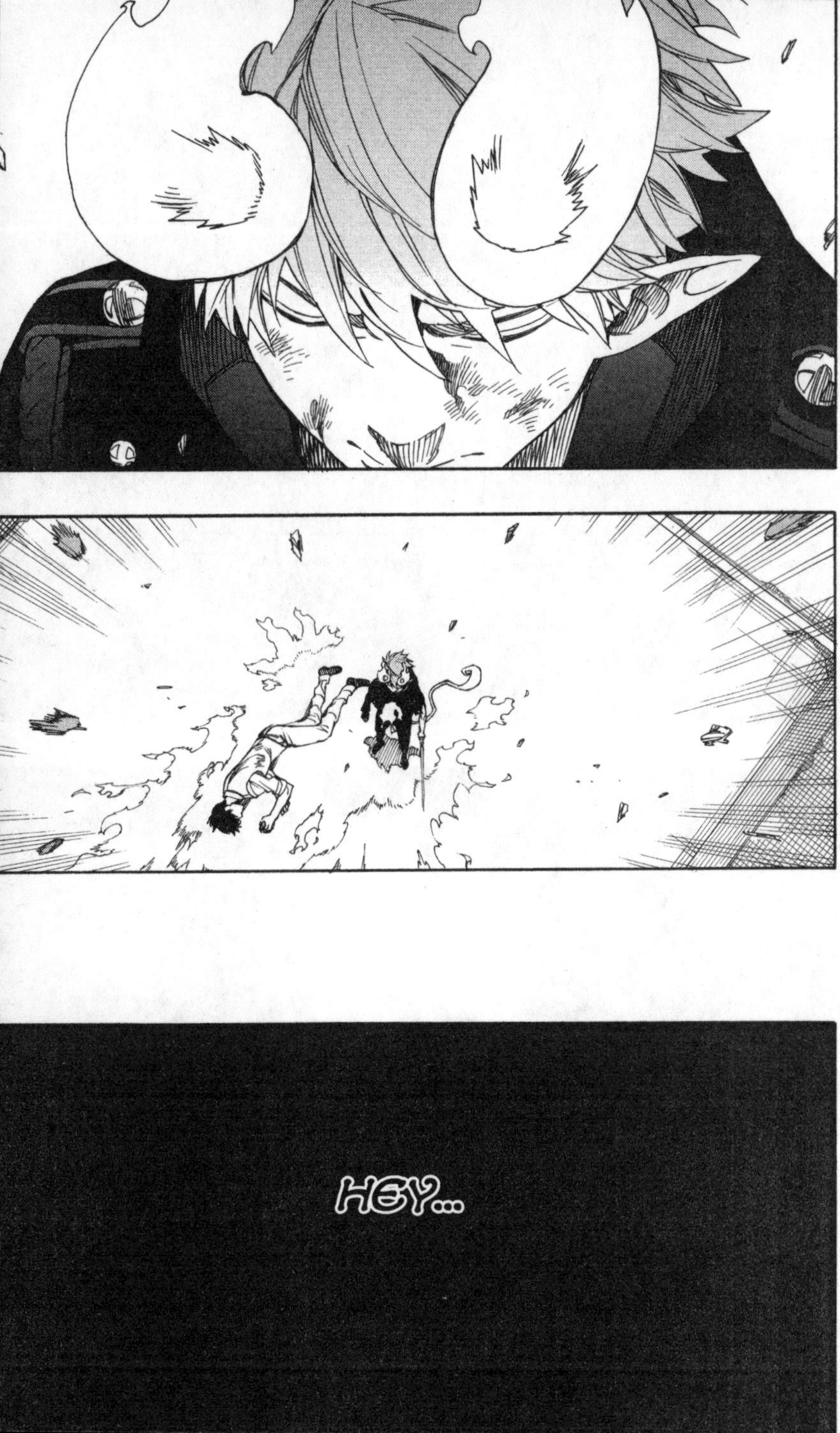
HEY...

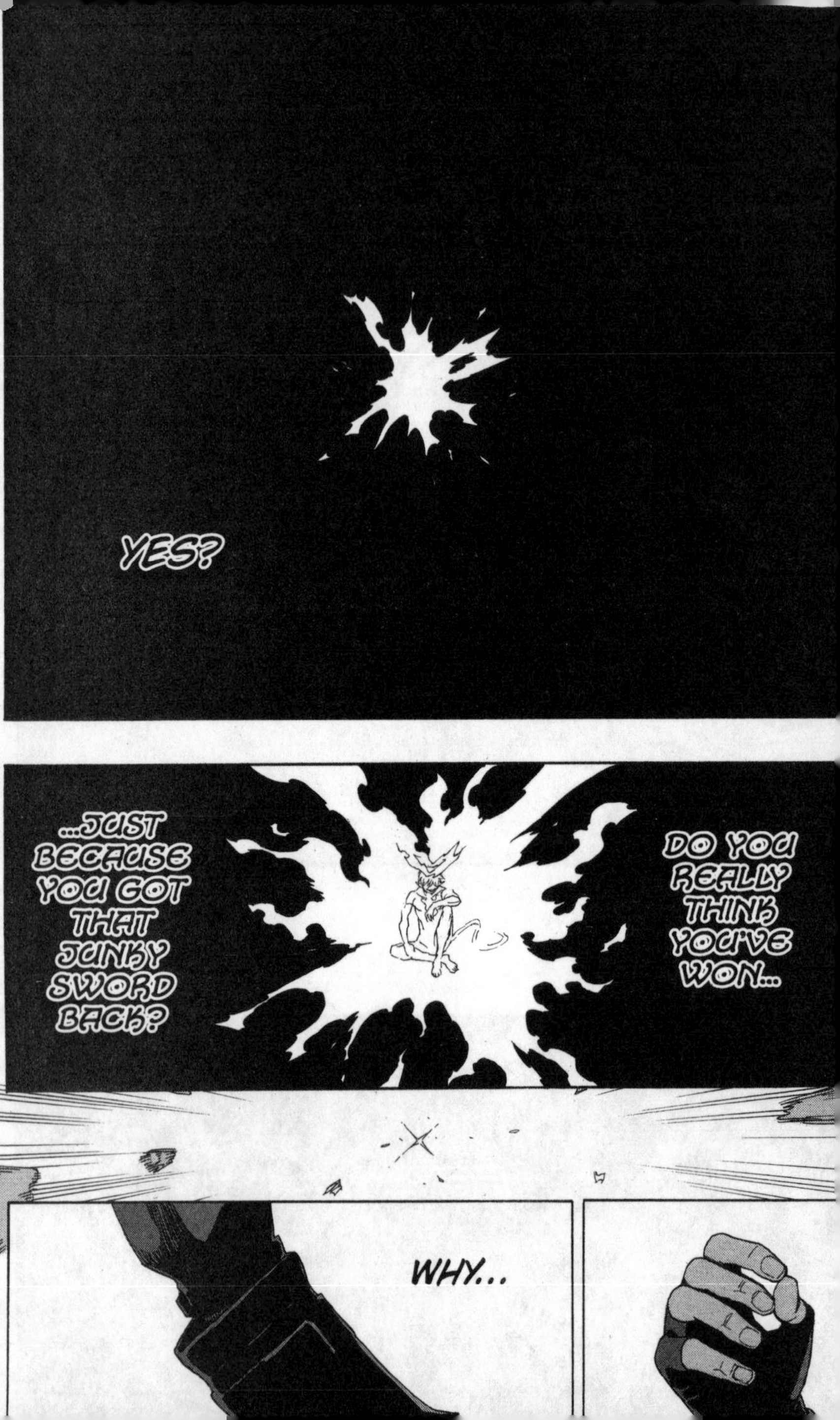
YES?
DO YOU REALLY THINK YOU'VE WON...
...JUST BECAUSE YOU GOT THAT JUNKY SWORD BACK?
WHY...

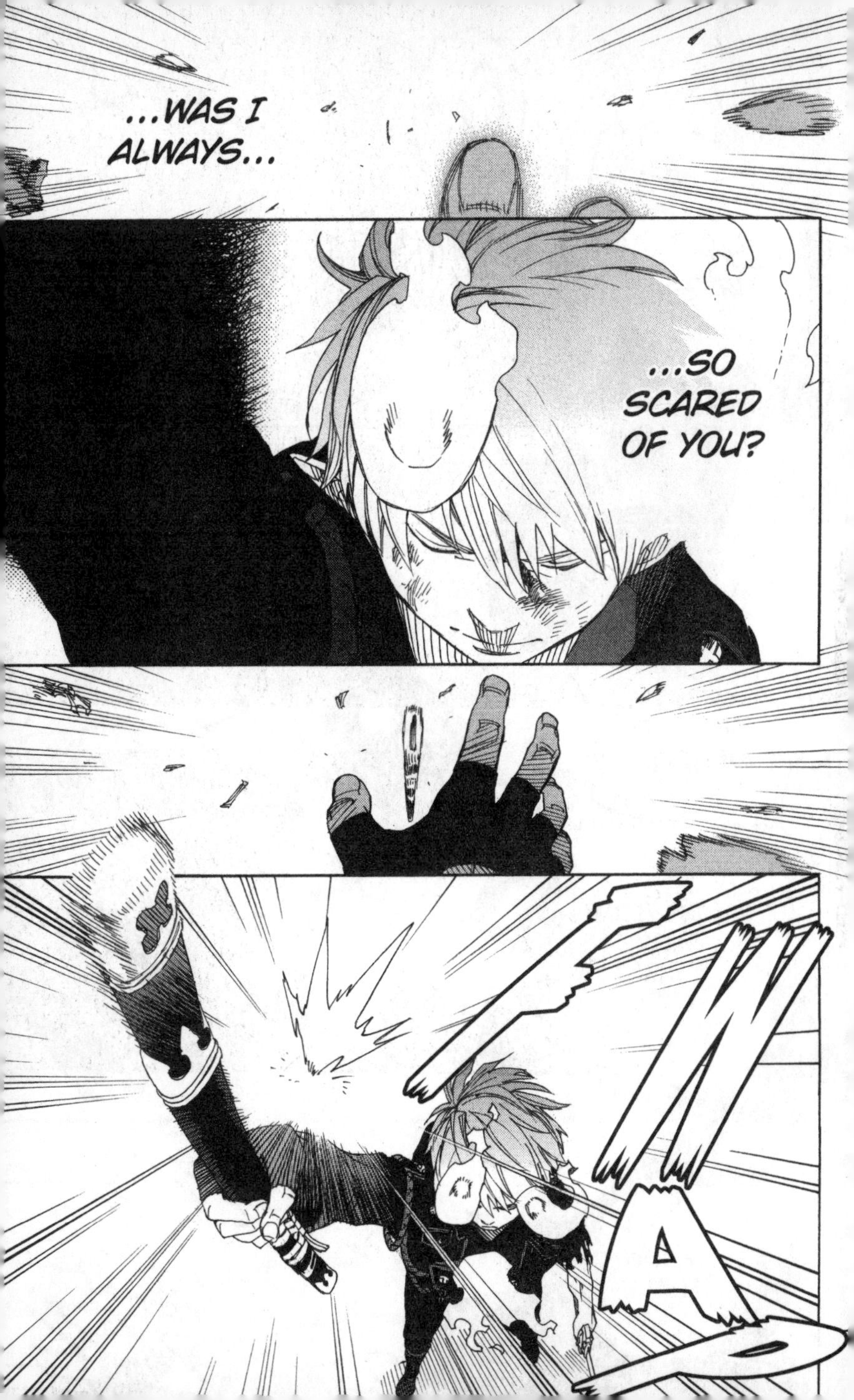
...WAS I ALWAYS...
...SO SCARED OF YOU?

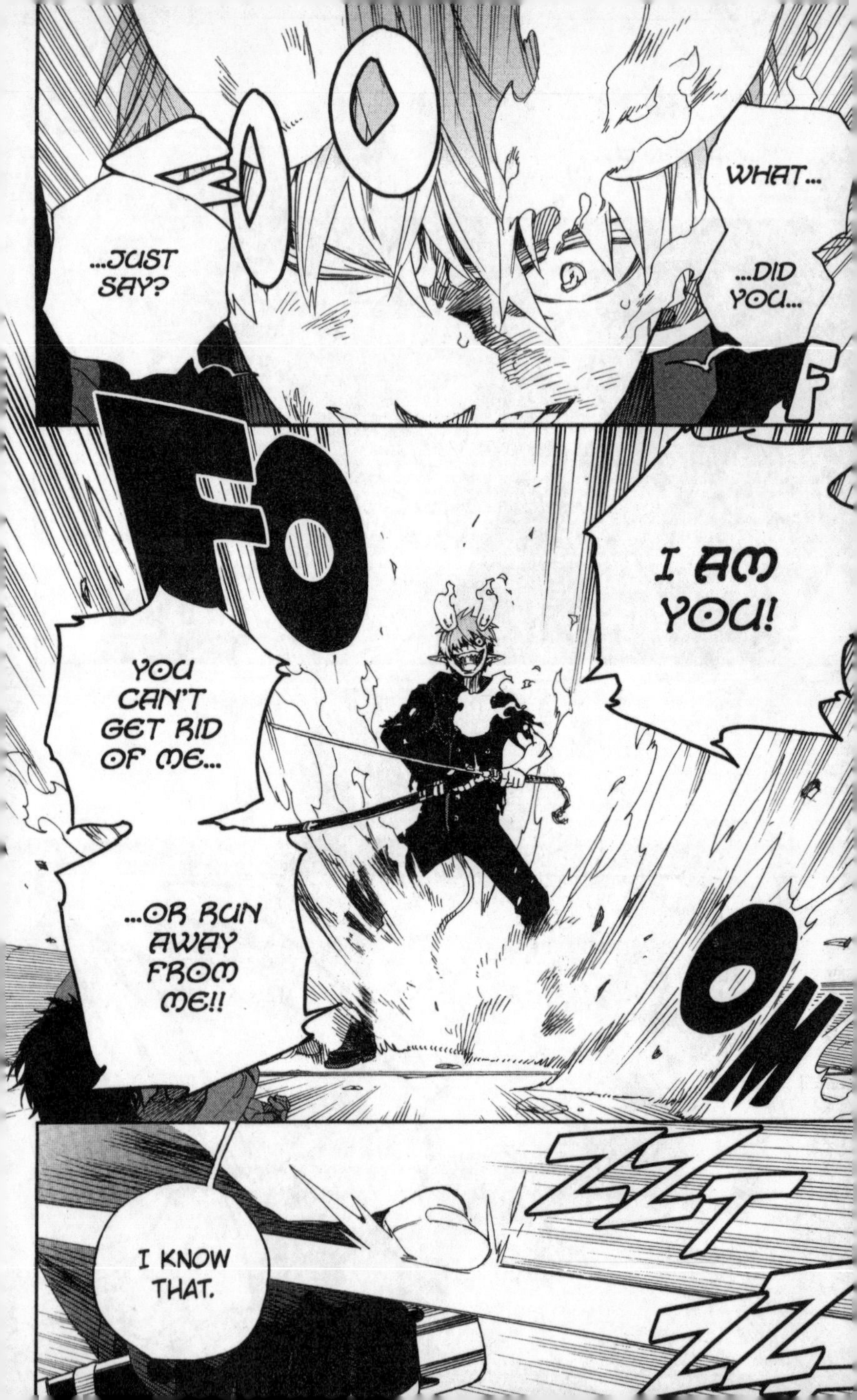
WHAT...
...DID YOU...
...JUST SAY?
F
FO
I AM YOU!
YOU CAN'T GET RID OF ME...
...OR RUN AWAY FROM ME!!
OM
ZZT
ZZ
I KNOW THAT.

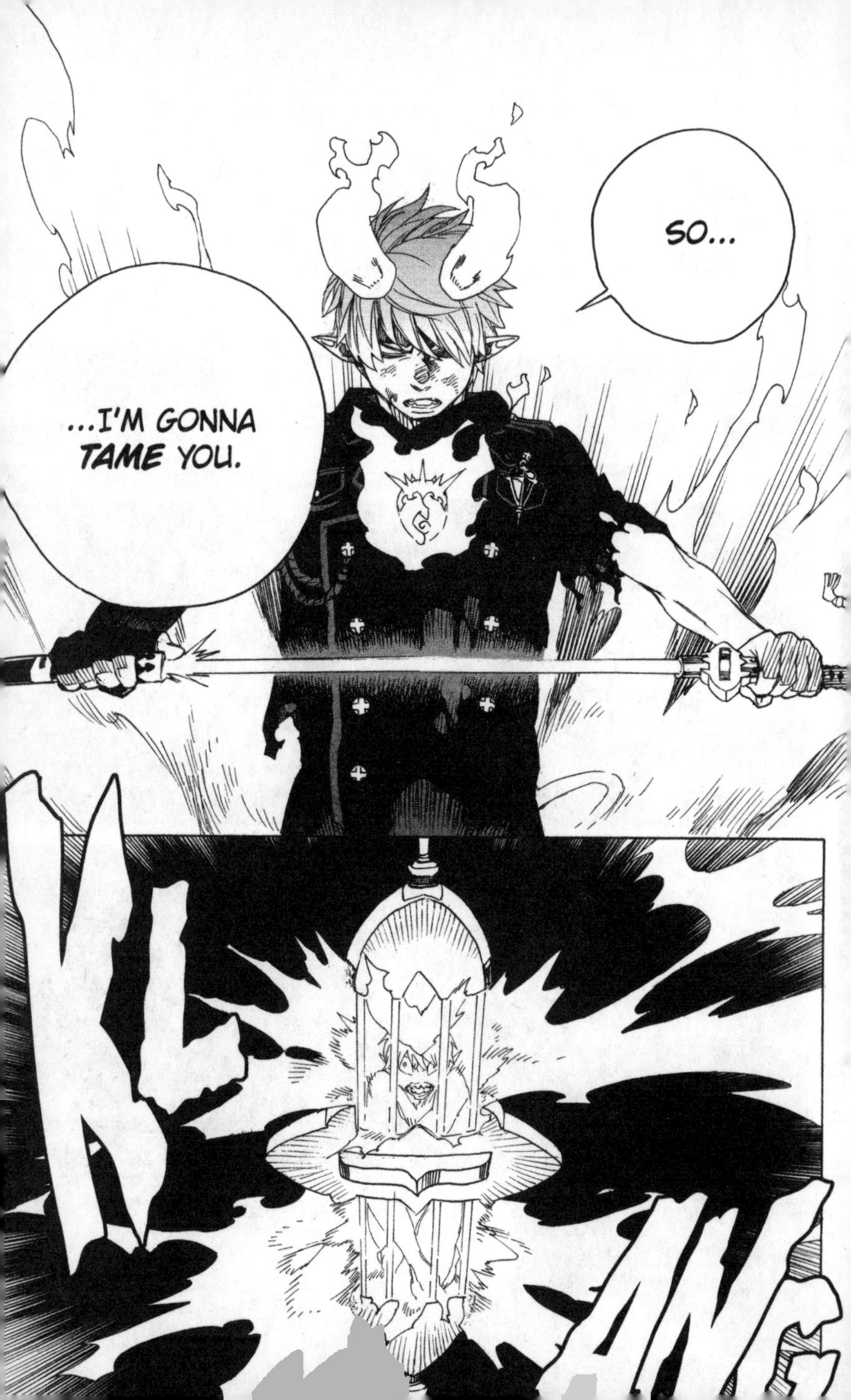
SO...
...I'M GONNA TAME YOU.

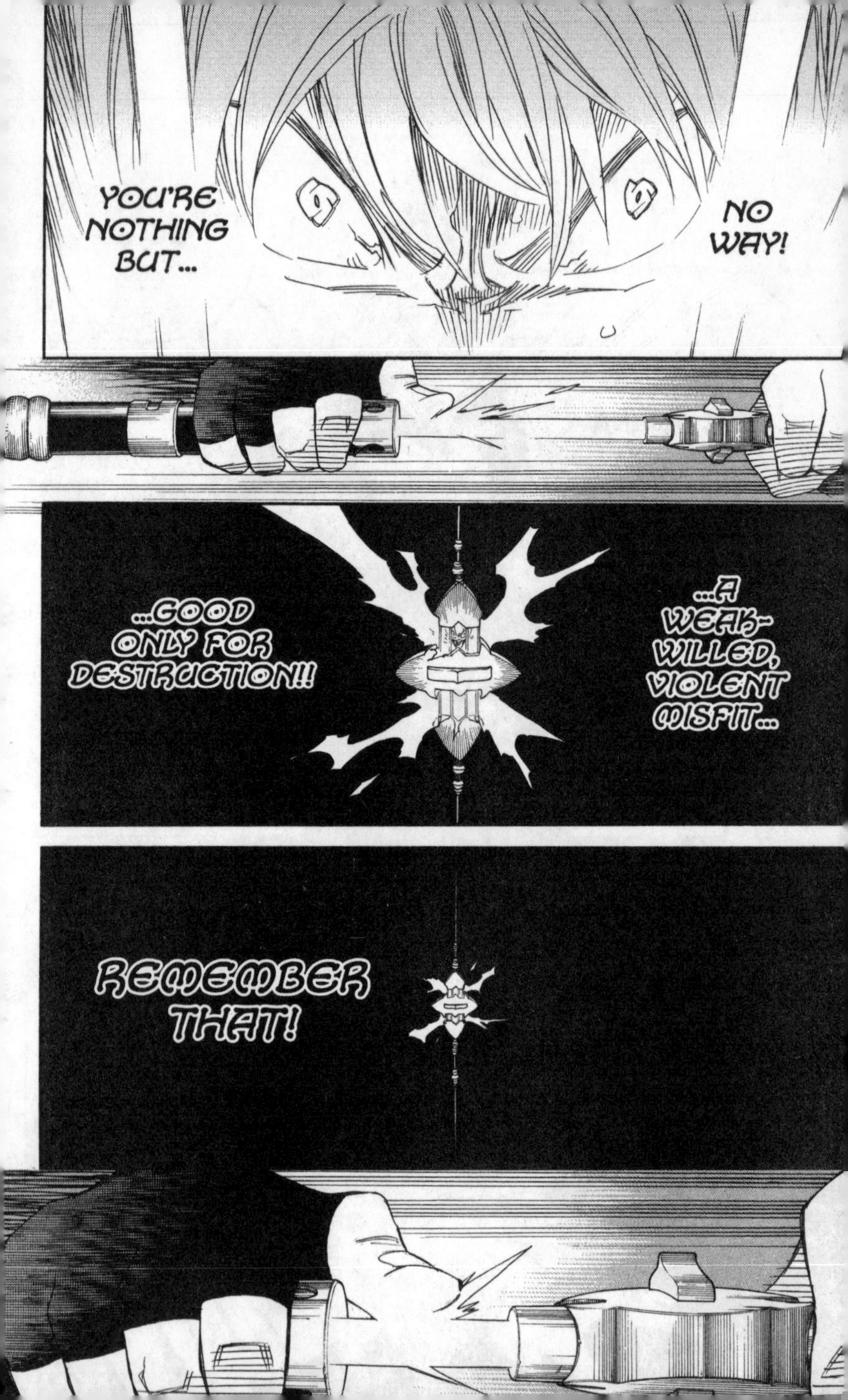
NO WAY!
YOU'RE NOTHING BUT...
...A WEAK-WILLED, VIOLENT MISFIT...
...GOOD ONLY FOR DESTRUCTION!!
REMEMBER THAT!

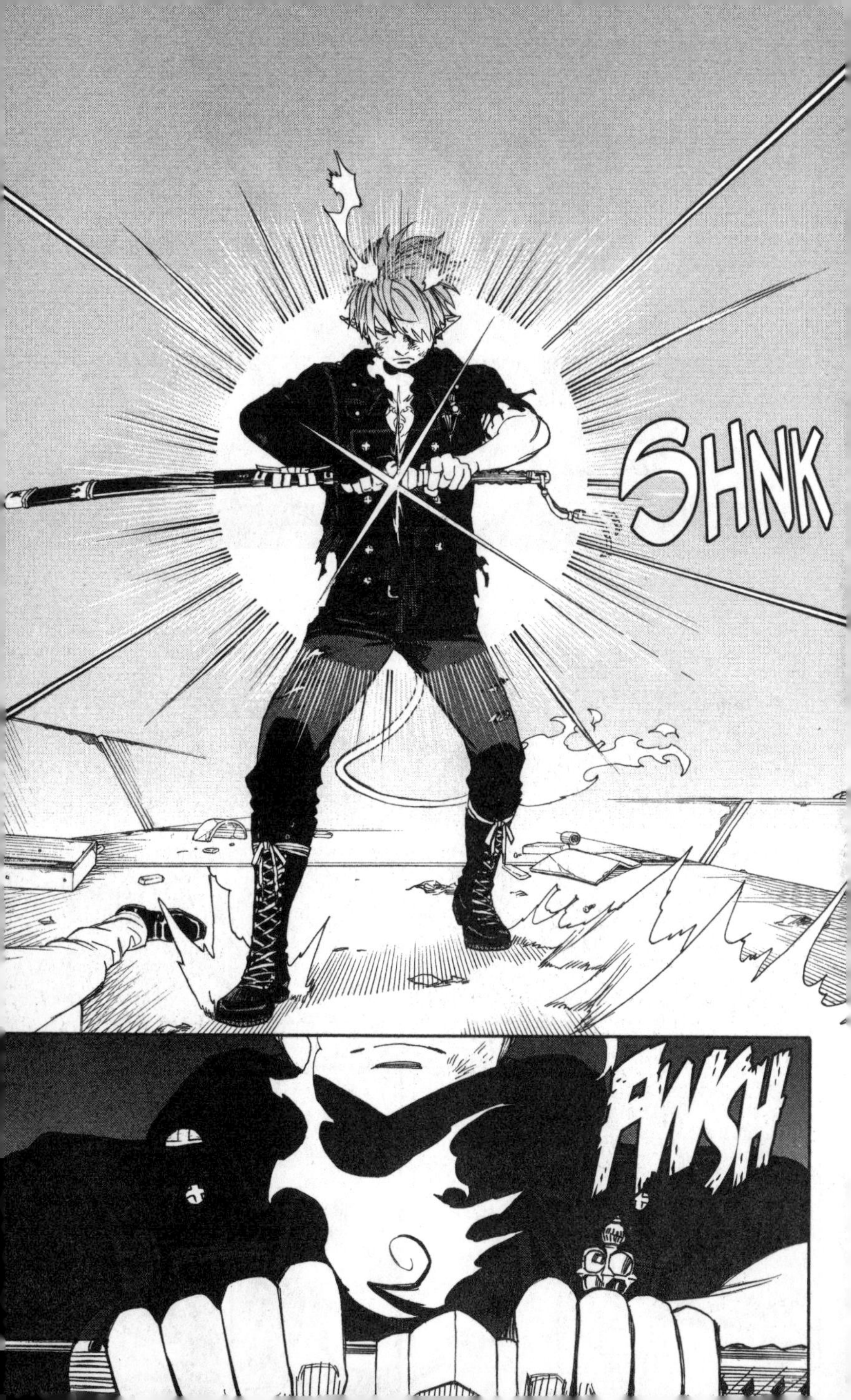
SHNK
FWSH

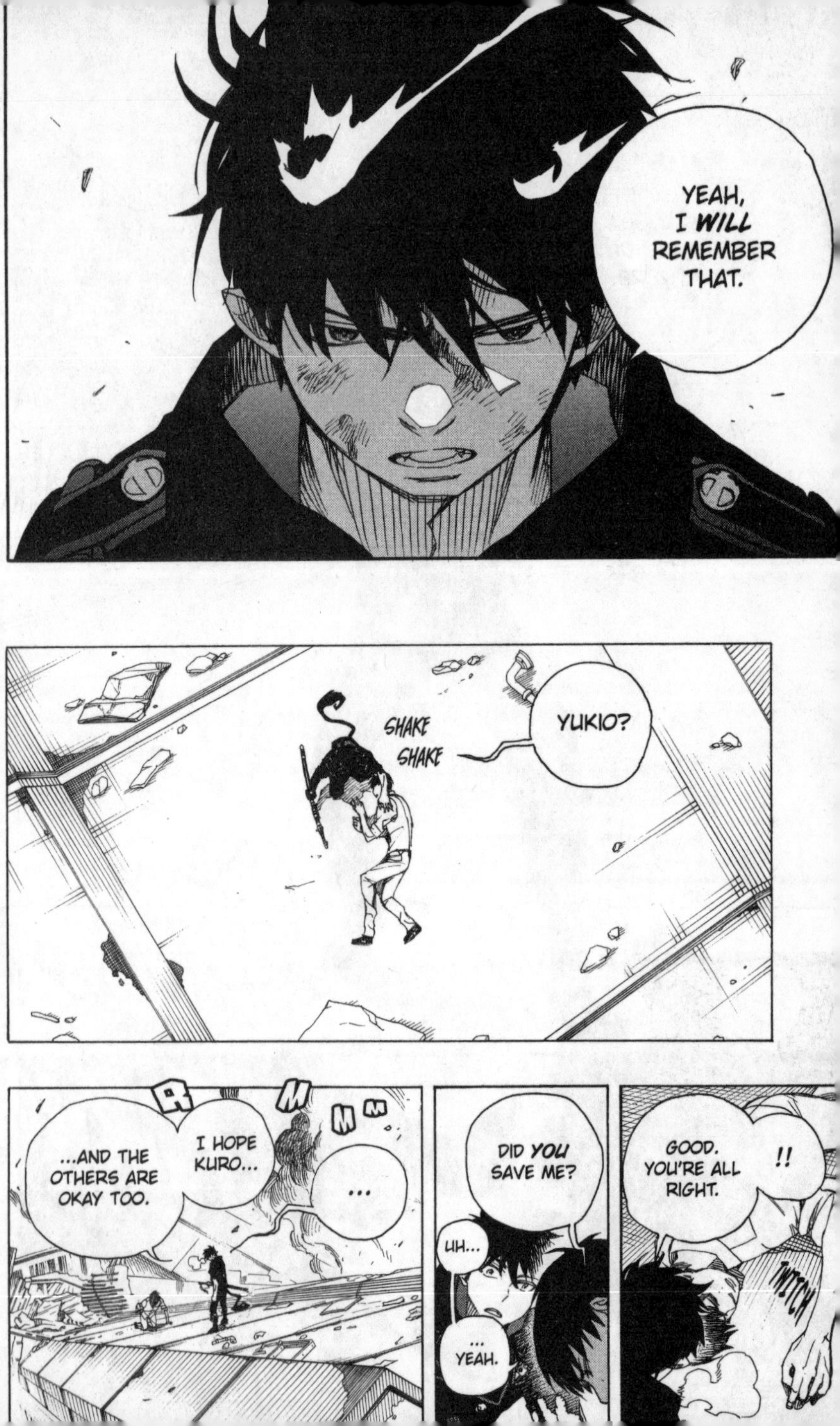
YEAH, I *WILL* REMEMBER THAT.
YUKIO?
SHAKE SHAKE
!!
GOOD. YOU'RE ALL RIGHT.
TWITCH
DID *YOU* SAVE ME?
UH...
...YEAH.
RUMMM
...
I HOPE KURO...
...AND THE OTHERS ARE OKAY TOO.

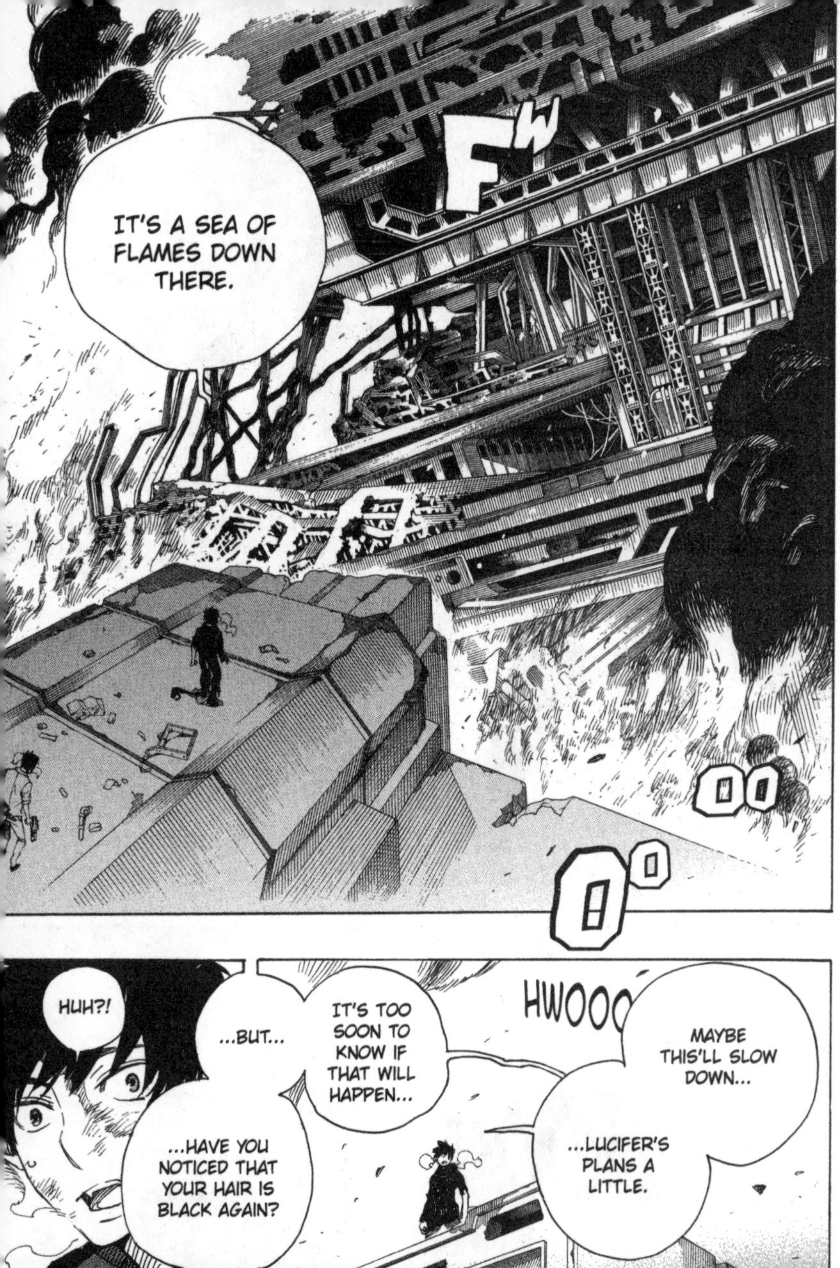
FW
IT'S A SEA OF FLAMES DOWN THERE.
HWOOO
MAYBE THIS'LL SLOW DOWN...
...LUCIFER'S PLANS A LITTLE.
IT'S TOO SOON TO KNOW IF THAT WILL HAPPEN...
...BUT...
...HAVE YOU NOTICED THAT YOUR HAIR IS BLACK AGAIN?
HUH?!

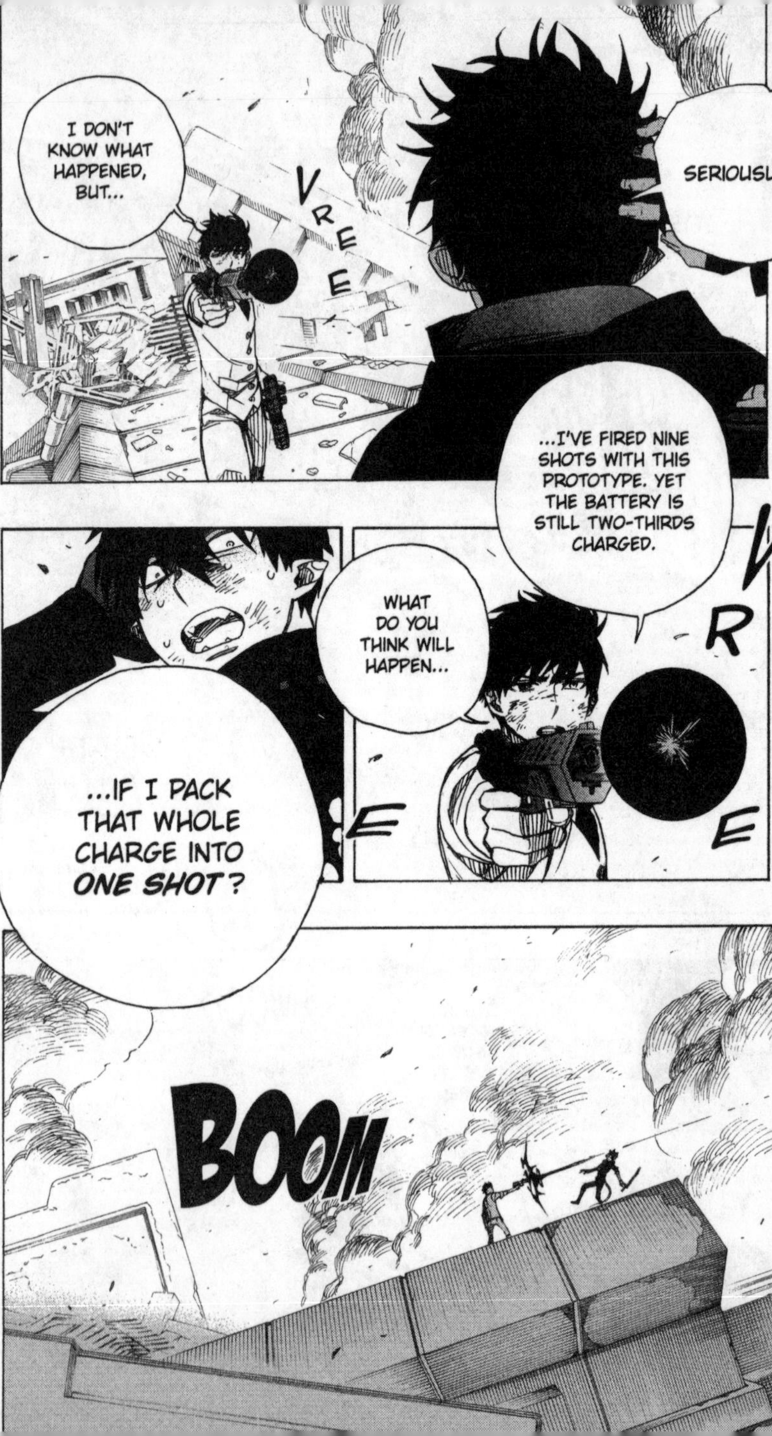
SERIOUSLY?
I DON'T KNOW WHAT HAPPENED, BUT...
VREE
...I'VE FIRED NINE SHOTS WITH THIS PROTOTYPE. YET THE BATTERY IS STILL TWO-THIRDS CHARGED.
WHAT DO YOU THINK WILL HAPPEN...
VREE
...IF I PACK THAT WHOLE CHARGE INTO ONE SHOT?
BOOM

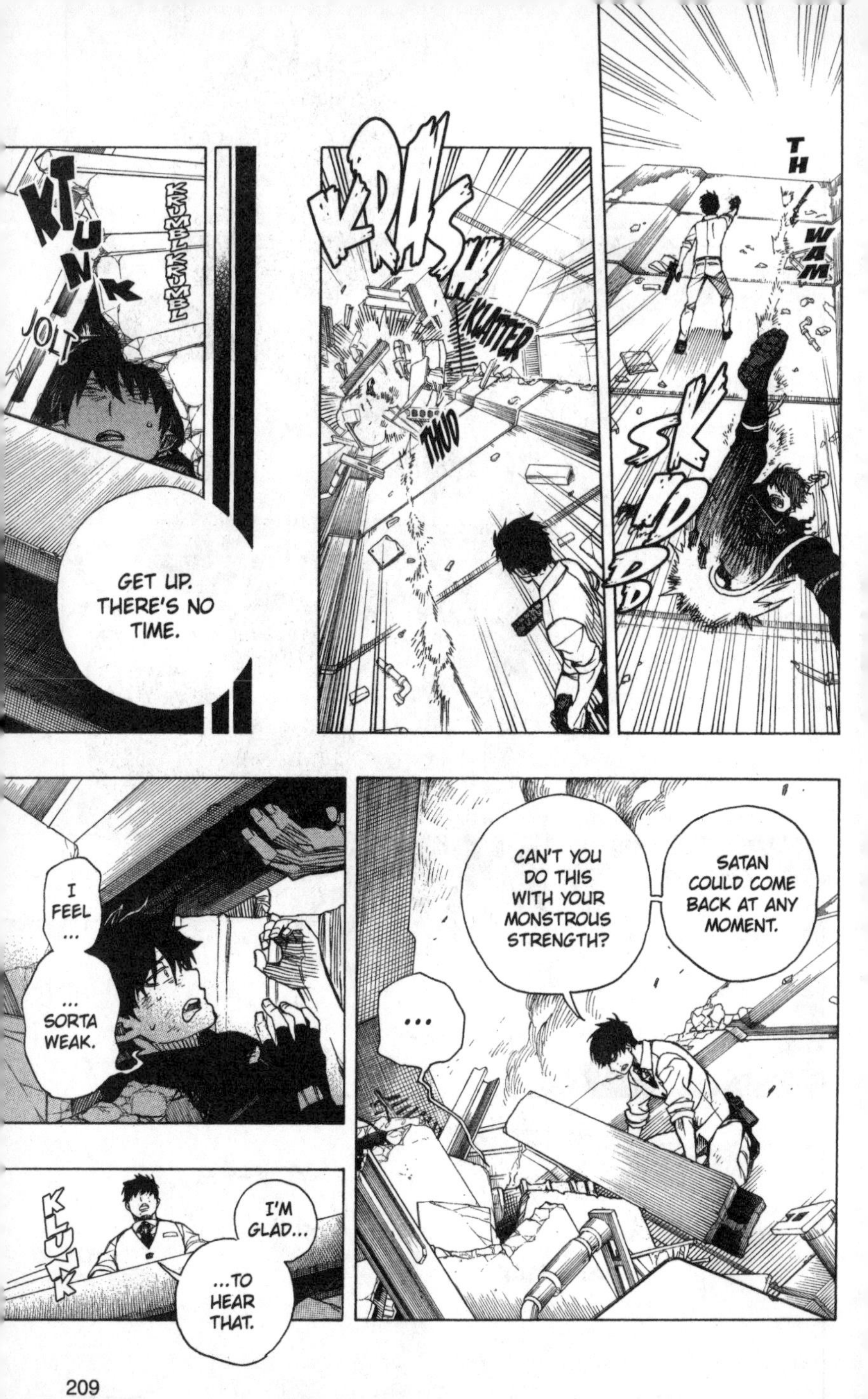

TH
WAM
SKDDD
KRASH
KLATTER
THUD
KTUNK
KRUMBLKRUMBL
JOLT
GET UP. THERE'S NO TIME.
SATAN COULD COME BACK AT ANY MOMENT.
CAN'T YOU DO THIS WITH YOUR MONSTROUS STRENGTH?
...
I FEEL ...
... SORTA WEAK.
KLUNK
I'M GLAD...
...TO HEAR THAT.

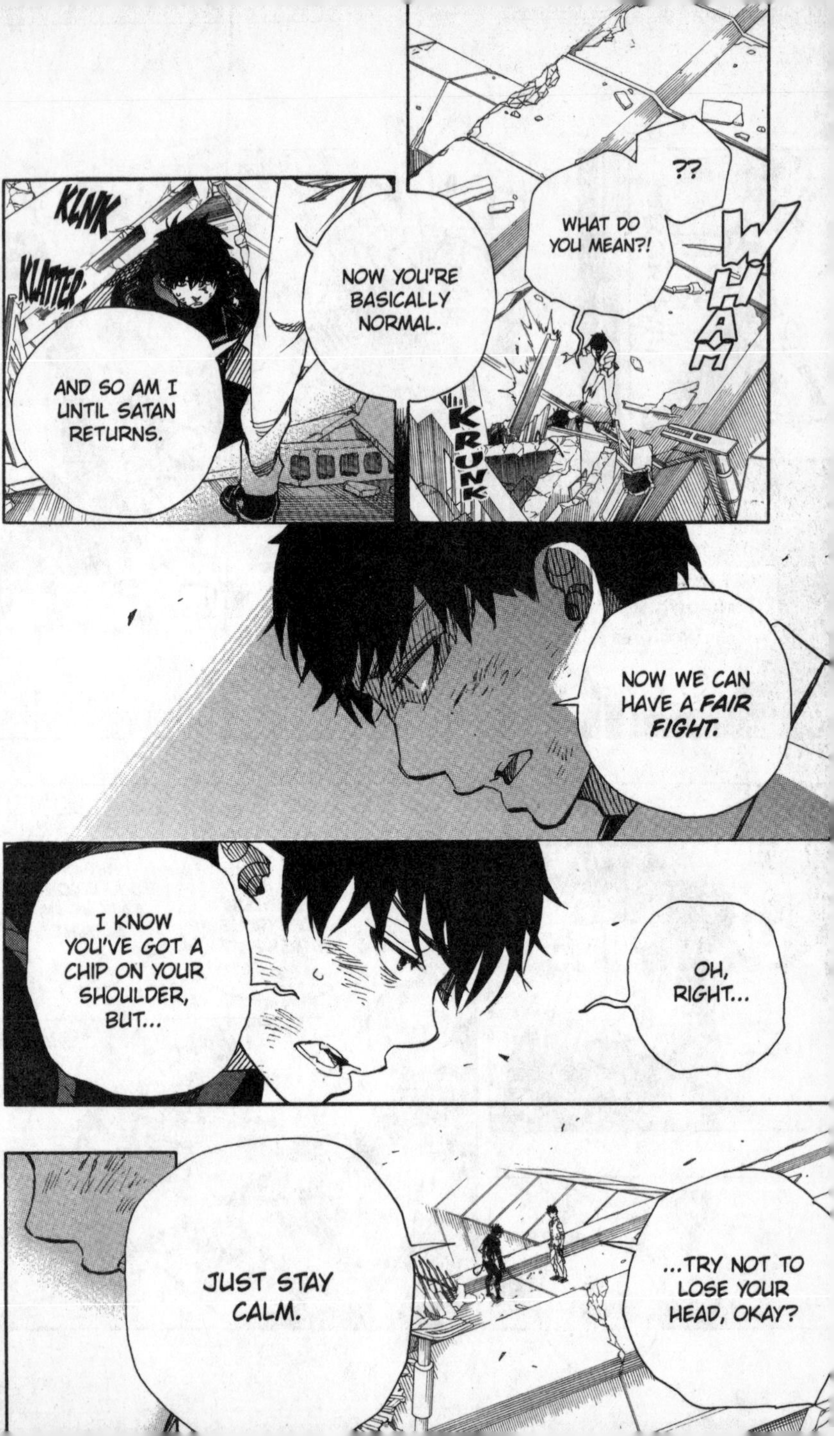
??
WHAT DO YOU MEAN?!
WHAM
KRUNK
KLNK
KLATTER
NOW YOU'RE BASICALLY NORMAL.
AND SO AM I UNTIL SATAN RETURNS.
NOW WE CAN HAVE A *FAIR FIGHT.*
OH, RIGHT...
I KNOW YOU'VE GOT A CHIP ON YOUR SHOULDER, BUT...
...TRY NOT TO LOSE YOUR HEAD, OKAY?
JUST STAY CALM.

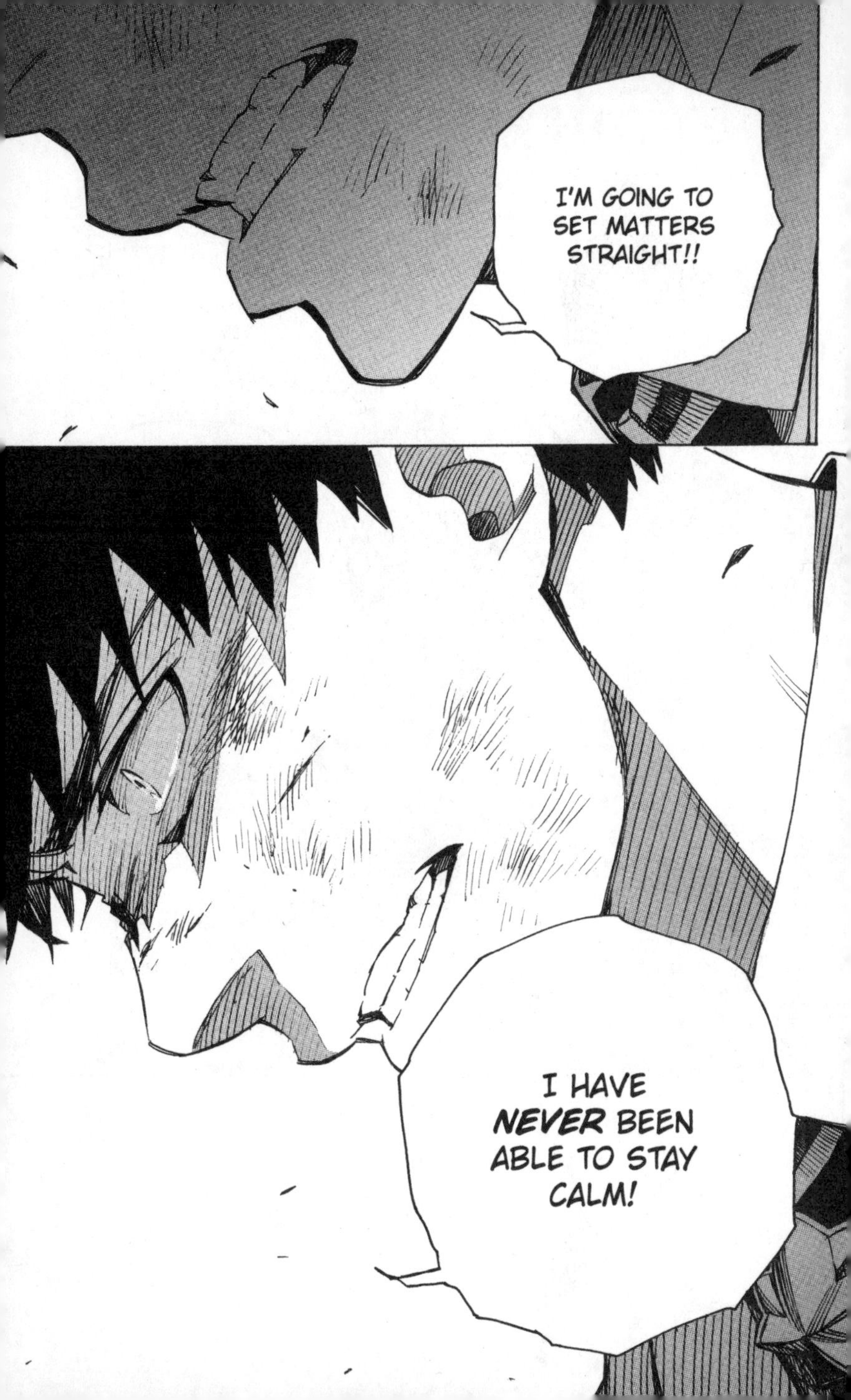
I'M GOING TO SET MATTERS STRAIGHT!!
I HAVE **NEVER** BEEN ABLE TO STAY CALM!

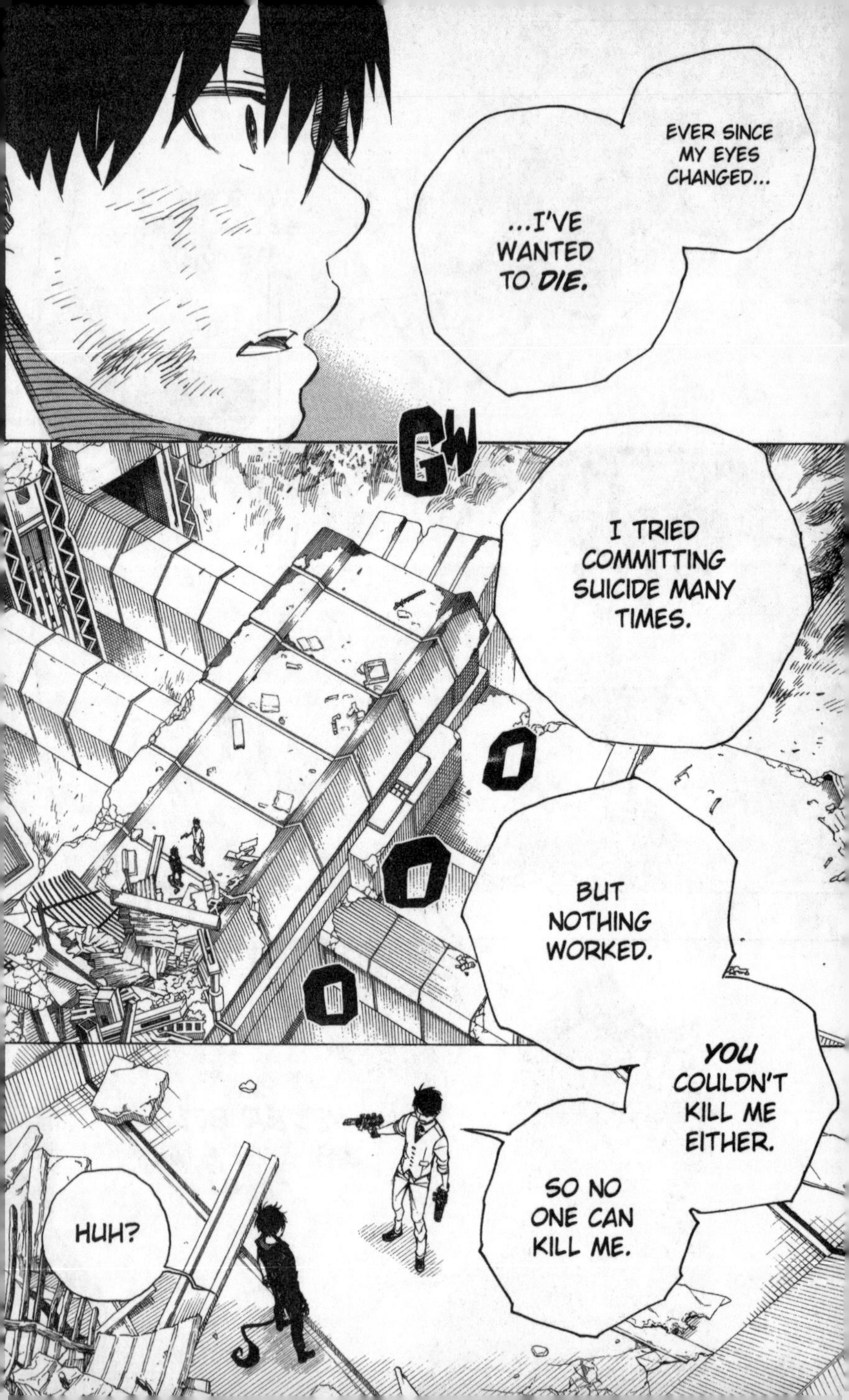
EVER SINCE MY EYES CHANGED...
...I'VE WANTED TO *DIE.*
GW
I TRIED COMMITTING SUICIDE MANY TIMES.
OOO
BUT NOTHING WORKED.
YOU COULDN'T KILL ME EITHER.
SO NO ONE CAN KILL ME.
HUH?

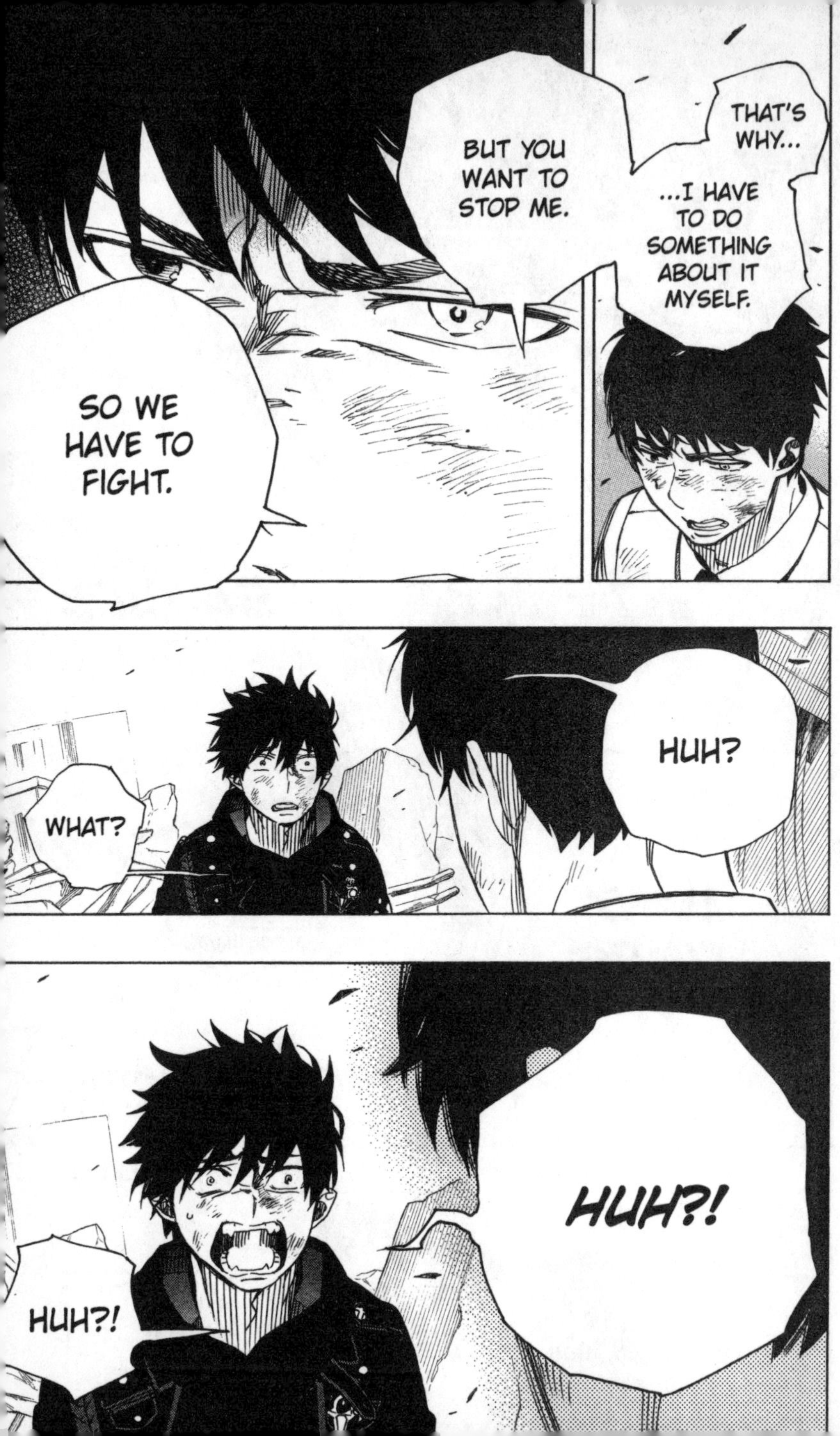
THAT'S WHY...
...I HAVE TO DO SOMETHING ABOUT IT MYSELF.
BUT YOU WANT TO STOP ME.
SO WE HAVE TO FIGHT.
HUH?
WHAT?
HUH?!
HUH?!

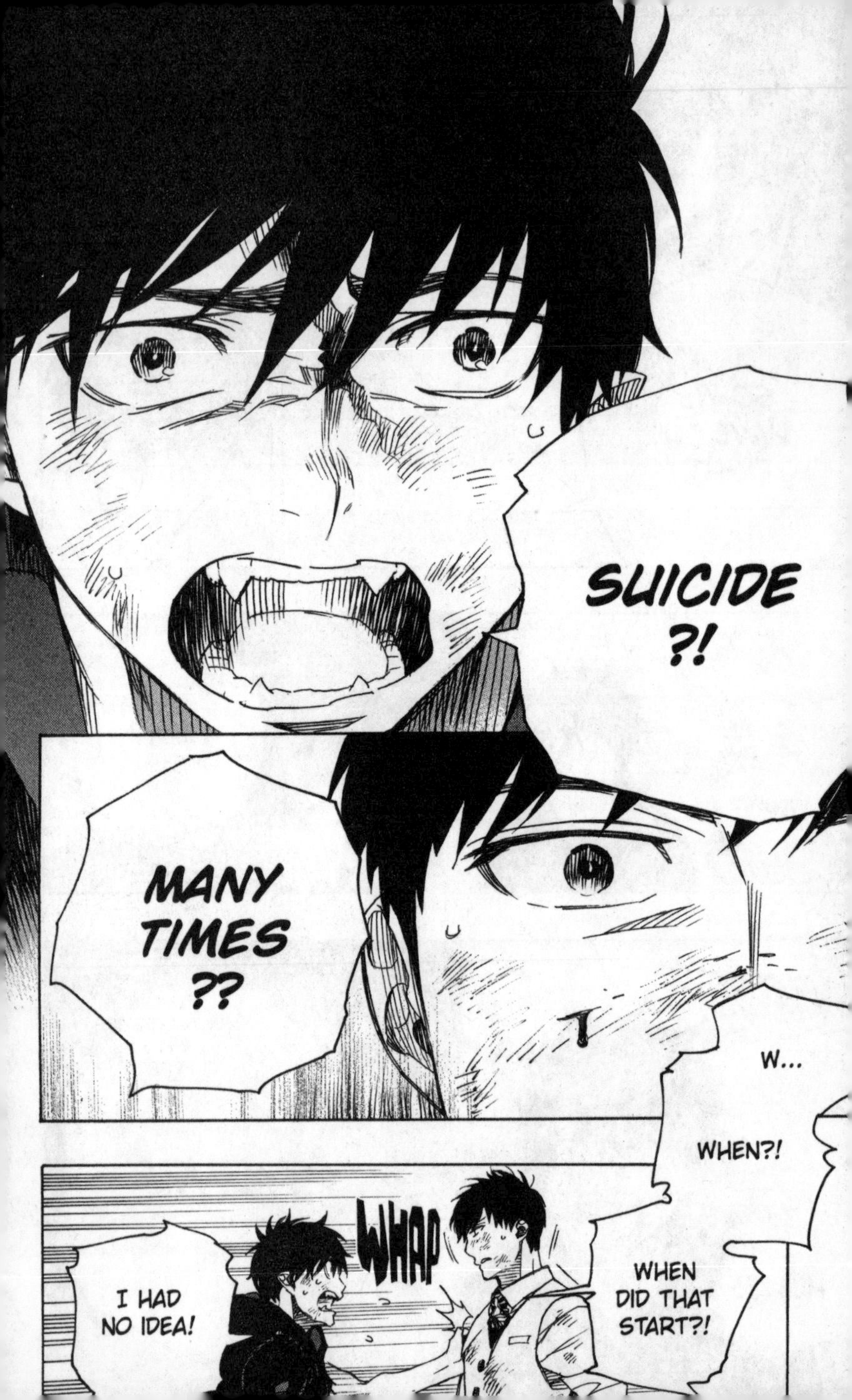
SUICIDE ?!
MANY TIMES ??
W... WHEN?!
WHEN DID THAT START?!
WHAP
I HAD NO IDEA!

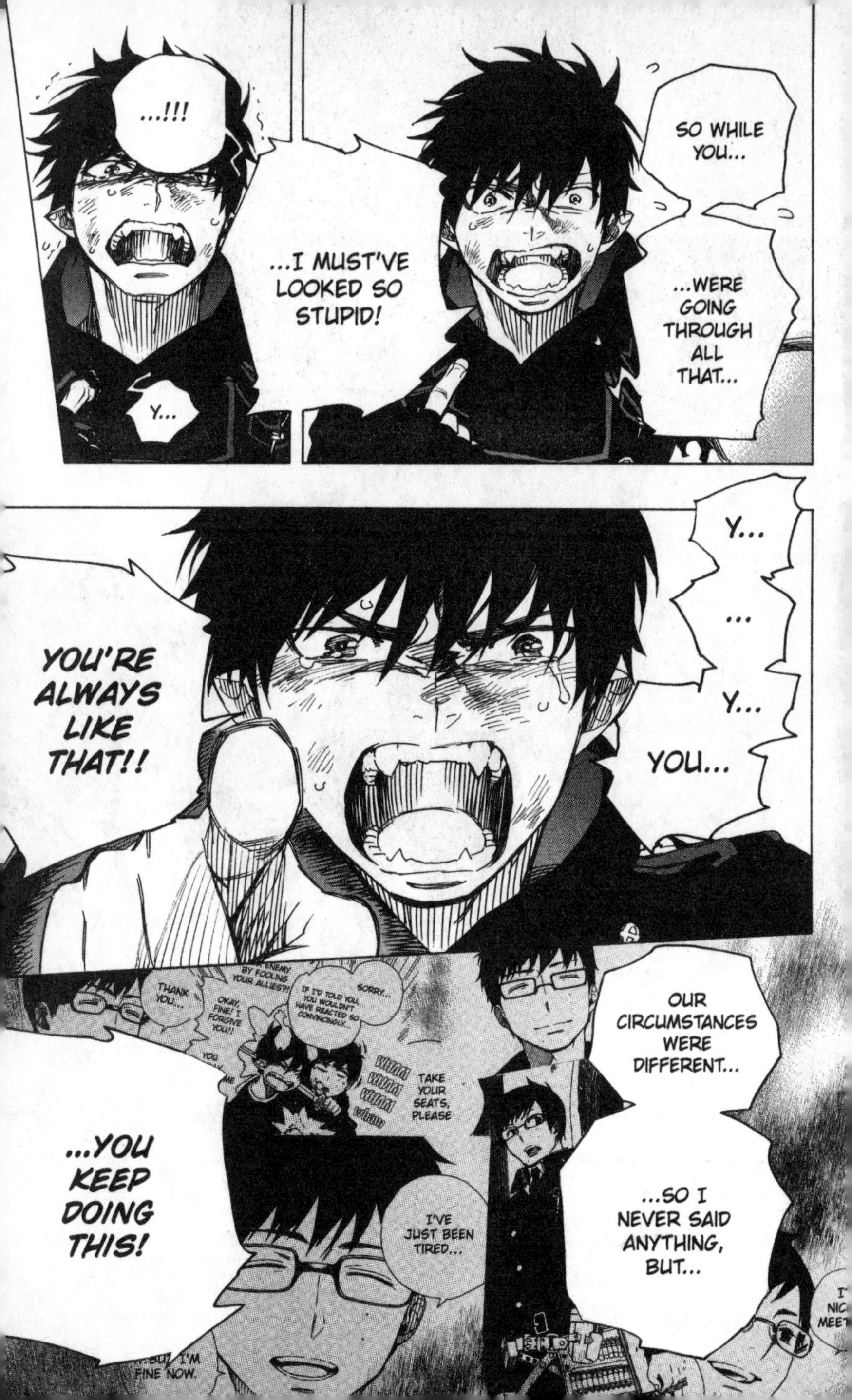
SO WHILE YOU...
...WERE GOING THROUGH ALL THAT...
...I MUST'VE LOOKED SO STUPID!
...!!!
Y...
Y...
...
Y...
YOU...
YOU'RE ALWAYS LIKE THAT!!
OUR CIRCUMSTANCES WERE DIFFERENT...
...SO I NEVER SAID ANYTHING, BUT...
TAKE YOUR SEATS, PLEASE
SORRY...
IF I'D TOLD YOU, YOU WOULDN'T HAVE REACTED SO CONVINCINGLY...
OKAY, FINE! I FORGIVE YOU!!
THANK YOU...
I'VE JUST BEEN TIRED...
...BUT I'M FINE NOW.
...YOU KEEP DOING THIS!

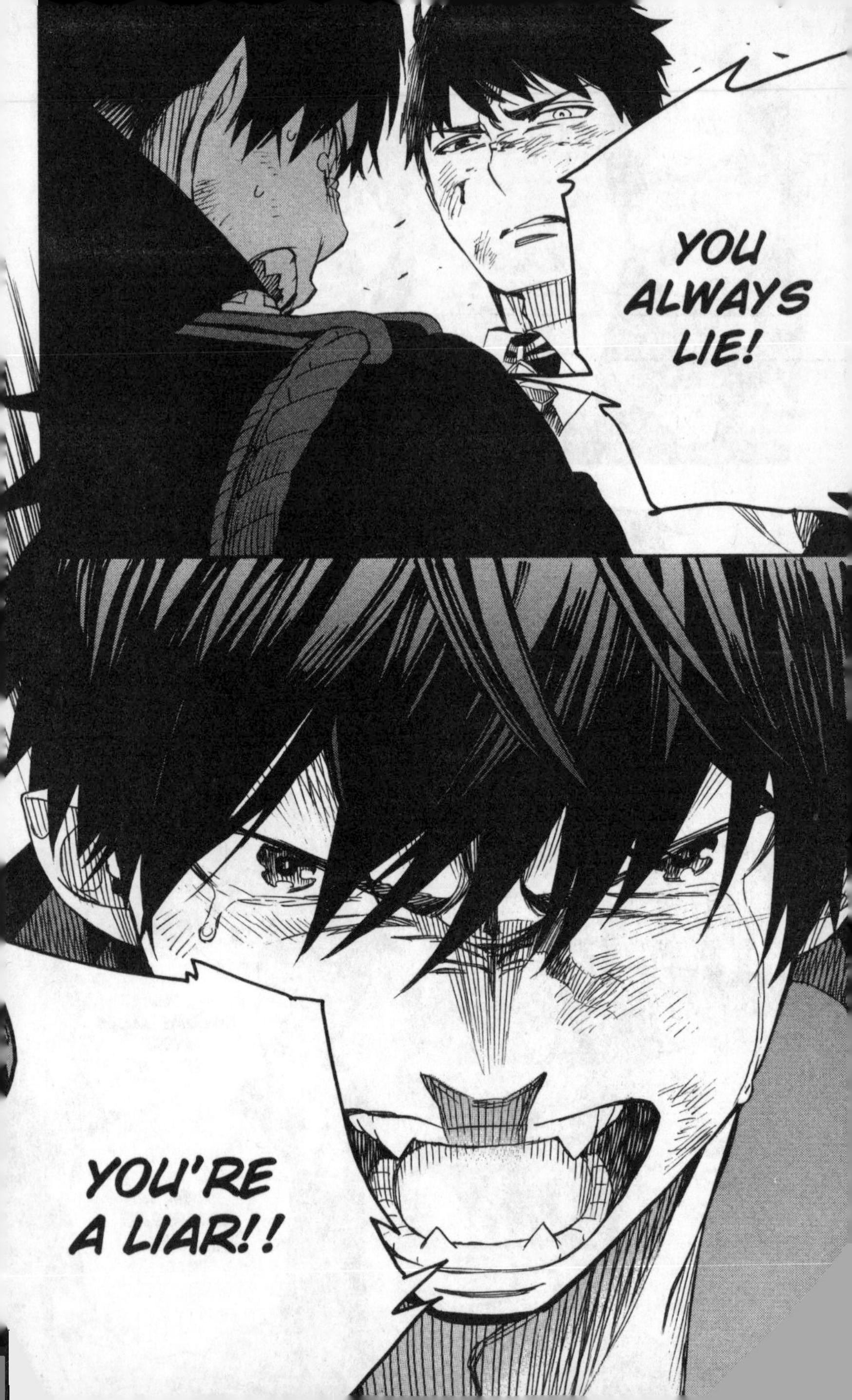
YOU ALWAYS LIE!
YOU'RE A LIAR!!

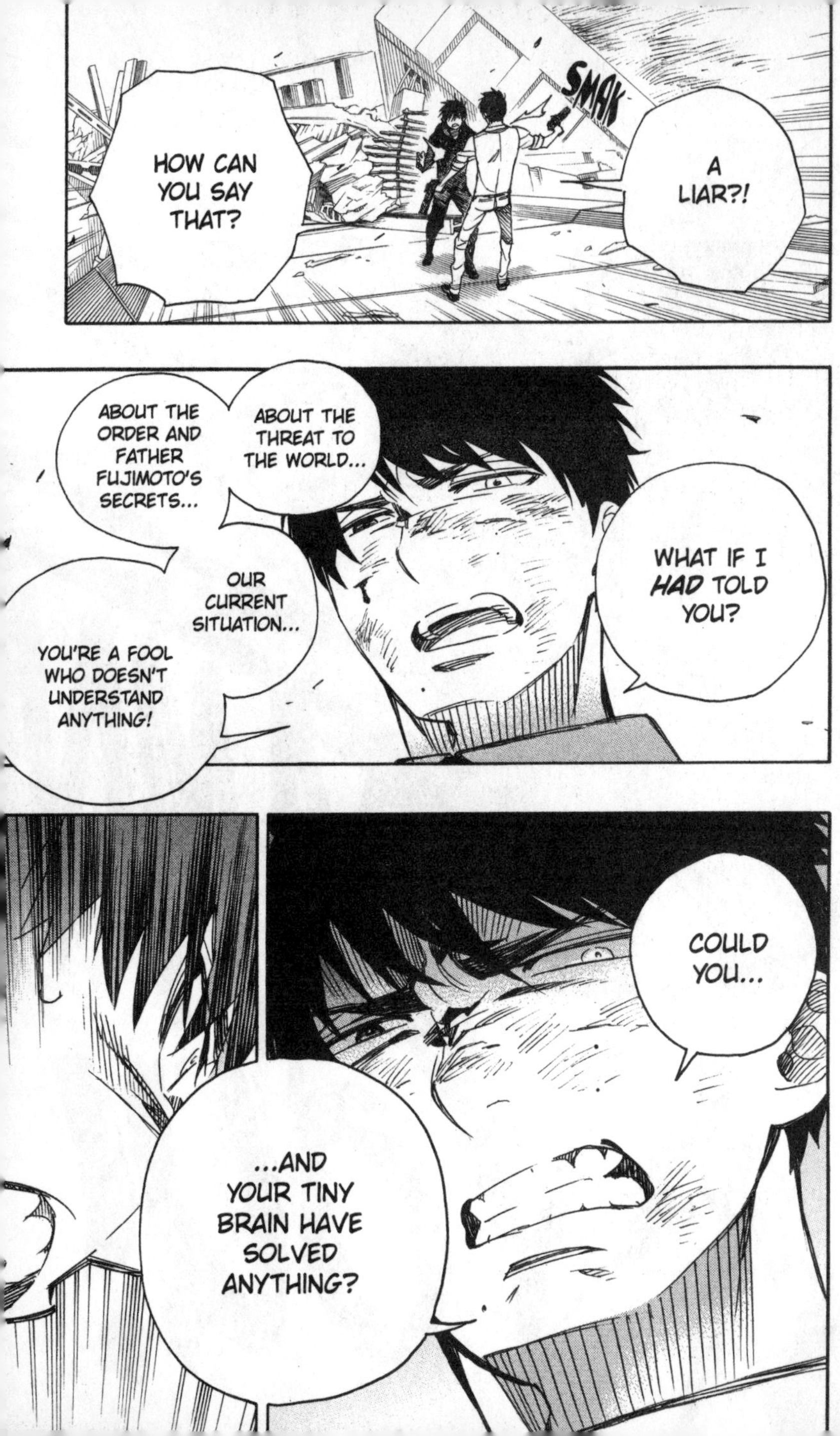
SMAK
A LIAR?!
HOW CAN YOU SAY THAT?
WHAT IF I *HAD* TOLD YOU?
ABOUT THE THREAT TO THE WORLD...
ABOUT THE ORDER AND FATHER FUJIMOTO'S SECRETS...
OUR CURRENT SITUATION...
YOU'RE A FOOL WHO DOESN'T UNDERSTAND ANYTHING!
COULD YOU...
...AND YOUR TINY BRAIN HAVE SOLVED ANYTHING?

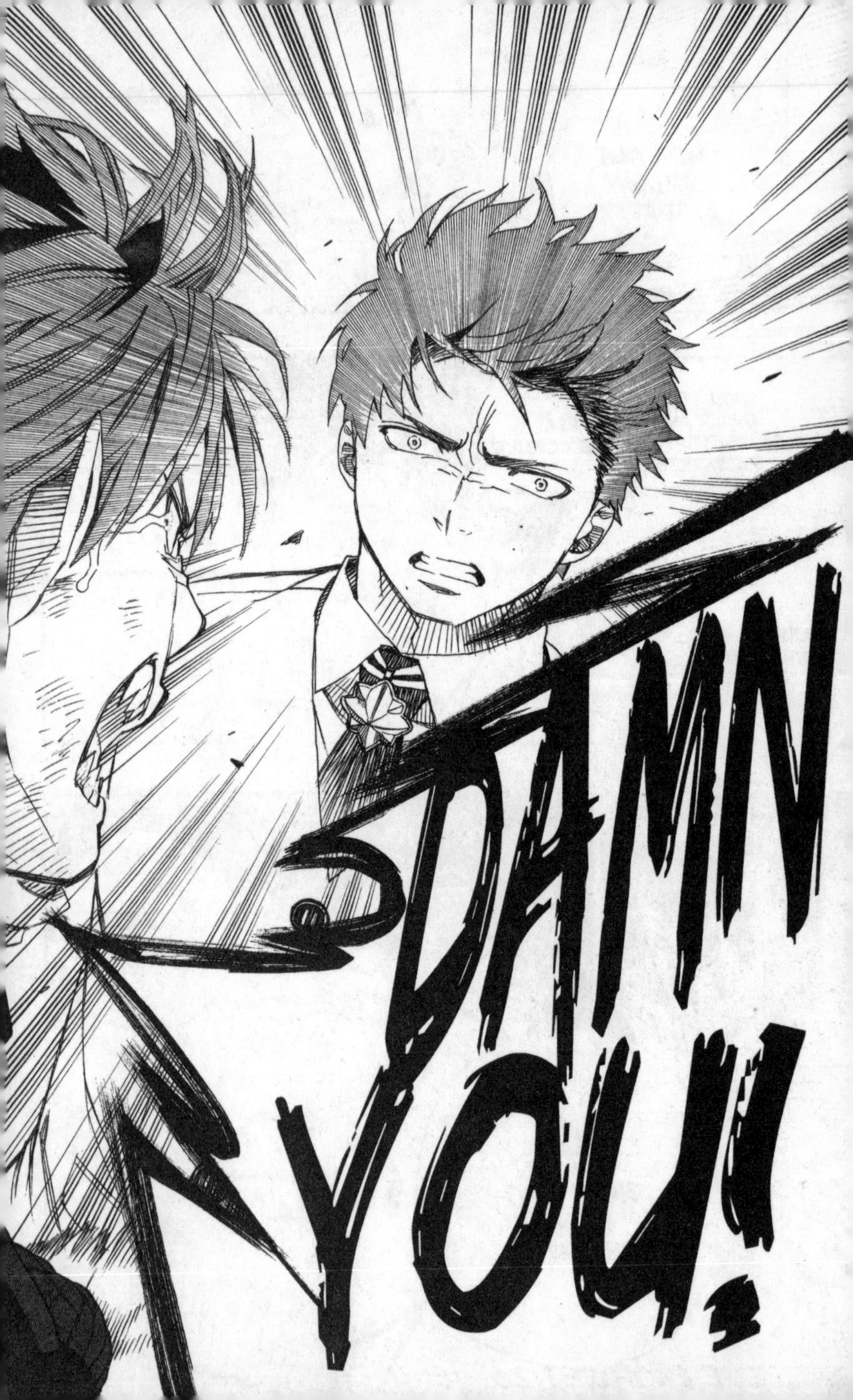
DAMN YOU!

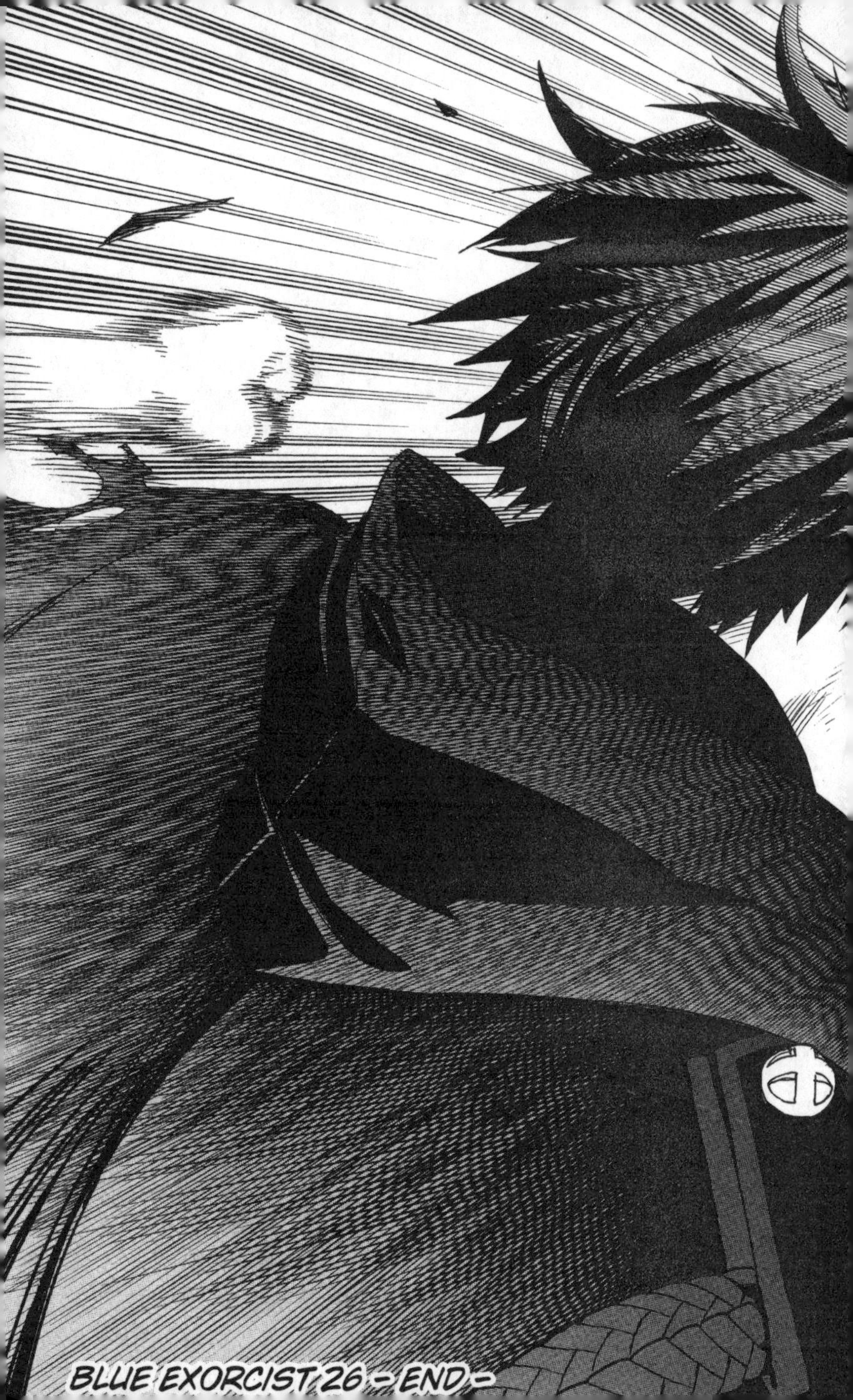
BLUE EXORCIST 26 - END -

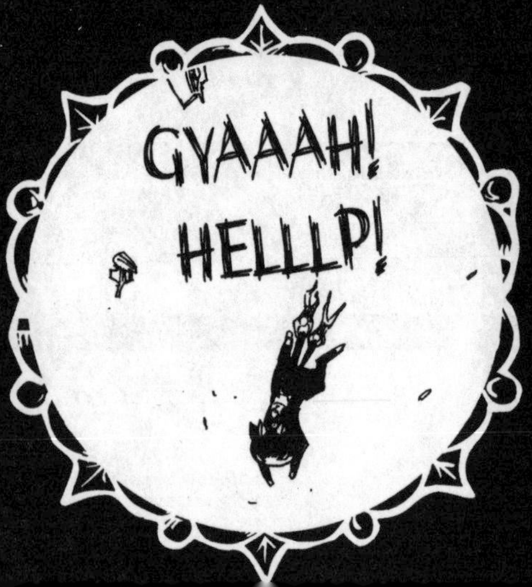
GYAAAH!
HELLLP!

THE BLUE EXORCIST

Art Staff

  THE LEGEND OF ME!! — Erika Uemura

IT'S COLD, SO I'LL GROW MY HAIR LONG! — Ryoji Hayashi

MEEKNESS IS THE BEST POLICY! — Mari Oda

I TOTALLY FALL FOR CHARACTERS BUFFETED BY LOVE! — Aki Shiina

Art Assistants

I'M SO EMBARRASSED! — Yamanaka-san

ALL THE LYING MAKES IT FUN! — Obata-san

 IT'S BETTER THAN ANY TV DRAMA I'VE SEEN! — Ito-kun

 NO THANKS! BECAUSE, UM, YOU KNOW! — Seo-san

Composition Assistant

IT'S SUPER HOT! — Minoru Sasaki

Editors

  I'LL WEAR THIS! — Ippei Sawada

I MADE MY HAIR BLUE! — Yujiro Hattori   THANKS TO EVERYONE IN MEDIA RELATIONS!!

Graphic Novel Editor

  I HOPE I'M ON TIME... — Ryusuke Kuroki

Graphic Novel Design

THANKS FOR THE AWESOME DESIGN WORK! — Shimada Hideaki

Rie Akutsu (L.S.D.)

Manga

HFF HFF  THIS YEAR HAS A LOT OF GREAT TV DRAMAS!! — Kazue Kato

(In no particular order)
(Note: The caricatures and statements are from memory!)

Take care of your health and see you in volume 27!!!

Finally it begins! A mere sibling quarrel!!!!
Weakness
→ Blue Flame (suppressed)
→ Incredible strength (weakened)
→ Accelerated healing (weakened)
Strength
→ Incredible strength (healing)
→ Accelerated healing (healing)
→ Mostly uninjured
→ Emotional stability
Weakness
→ No protection from Satan
→ Cuts and bruises all over
→ No glasses (unequipped)
→ Emotional instability
Strength
→ Armumahel Guns (prototypes, battery: 0)
→ Martial arts
→ Intelligence

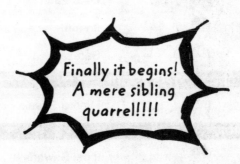

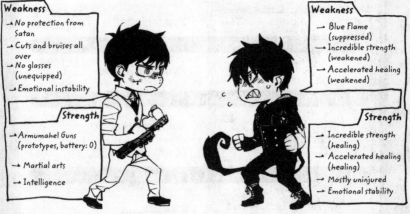

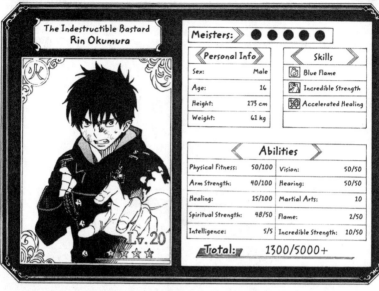

The Indestructible Bastard
Rin Okumura

Meisters: ● ● ● ● ●

《Personal Info》

Sex:	Male
Age:	16
Height:	173 cm
Weight:	61 kg

《Skills》

- Blue Flame
- Incredible Strength
- Accelerated Healing

《Abilities》

Physical Fitness:	50/100	Vision:	50/50
Arm Strength:	40/100	Hearing:	50/50
Healing:	15/100	Martial Arts:	10
Spiritual Strength:	48/50	Flame:	2/50
Intelligence:	5/5	Incredible Strength:	10/50

Lv.20

Total: 1300/5000+

The Sad Rebel
Yukio Okumura

Meisters: Dragoon Doctor ● ● ●

《Personal Info》

Sex:	Male
Age:	16
Height:	181 cm
Weight:	75 kg

《Skills》

- Marksmanship
- Flame Negation
- Close-Range Attack
- Satan's Protection

《Abilities》

Physical Fitness:	10/50	Vision:	6/7
Arm Strength:	18/50	Hearing:	10/10
Healing:	10/10	Martial Arts:	50
Spiritual Strength:	3/15	Marksmanship:	25/50
Intelligence:	50/50	Satan's protection:	0/100

Lv.36

Total: 1000/1500

※The average boy their age: Total: 500
Physical Fitness: 10 Arm strength: 10 Healing: 10 Spiritual Strength: 10
Intelligence: 10 Vision: 10 Hearing: 10 Martial Arts: 10

They've just piled up unintentionally.

HUFF HUFF

Recently I've bought a lot of stylish masks.

KAZUE KATO

I WANT TO GO TO ATAGAWA TROPICAL & ALLIGATOR GARDEN. AND I WANT TO EAT GREEN TEA ICE CREAM, SOME DELICIOUS BARBECUE, FUKUOKA UDON AND YAKITORI. THAT'S HOW I'M FEELING.

PLEASE ENJOY READING VOLUME 26.

BLUE EXORCIST

BLUE EXORCIST VOL. 26
SHONEN JUMP Manga Edition

STORY & ART BY KAZUE KATO

Translation & English Adaptation/John Werry
Touch-up Art & Lettering/John Hunt, Primary Graphix
Cover & Interior Design/Mindy Walters
Editor/Mike Montesa

Printed in Canada

Published by VIZ Media, LLC
P.O. Box 77010
San Francisco, CA 94107

10 9 8 7 6 5 4 3 2 1
First printing, October 2021

VIZ MEDIA
viz.com

SHONEN JUMP

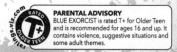

In the next volume...

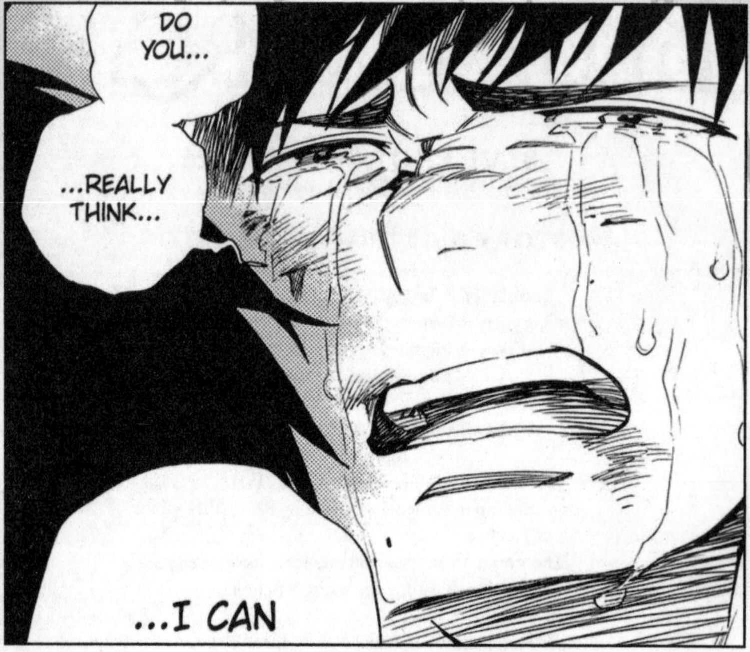
DO YOU...
...REALLY THINK...
...I CAN

Rin and Yukio fight it out on top of the flaming wreckage of the Illuminati airship. All his life, Yukio has felt he was living in his brother's shadow, thinking himself weak and full of self-doubt. What he never understood was just how much Rin relied on Yukio for his own strength. If the brothers can reconcile their feelings they just might be even stronger together. After all the action, the Exwires reunite and take a breather from the ordeal they've just been through. But the battle is not over yet...

Coming soon!